Christian Stier

Adaptation-Aware Architecture Modeling and Analysis of Energy Efficiency for Software Systems

The Karlsruhe Series on Software Design and Quality
Volume 27

Chair Software Design and Quality
Faculty of Computer Science
Karlsruhe Institute of Technology

and

Software Engineering Division
Research Center for Information Technology (FZI), Karlsruhe

Editor: Prof. Dr. Ralf Reussner

Adaptation-Aware Architecture Modeling and Analysis of Energy Efficiency for Software Systems

by
Christian Stier

KIT Scientific Publishing

Dissertation, Karlsruher Institut für Technologie
KIT-Fakultät für Informatik

Tag der mündlichen Prüfung: 09. Mai 2018
Gutachter: Prof. Dr. Ralf H. Reussner, Prof. Dr. Colin Atkinson

Impressum

KIT Scientific Publishing

Karlsruher Institut für Technologie (KIT)
KIT Scientific Publishing
Straße am Forum 2
D-76131 Karlsruhe

KIT Scientific Publishing is a registered trademark
of Karlsruhe Institute of Technology.
Reprint using the book cover is not allowed.

www.ksp.kit.edu

Print on Demand 2019 – Gedruckt auf FSC-zertifiziertem Papier

ISSN 1867-0067
ISBN 978-3-7315-0851-9
DOI: 10.5445/KSP/1000086089

Abstract

This thesis presents an approach for the design time analysis of energy efficiency for static and self-adaptive software systems.

The quality characteristics of a software system, such as performance and operating costs, strongly depend upon its architecture. Software architecture is a high-level view on software artifacts that reflects essential quality characteristics of a system under design. Design decisions made on an architectural level have a decisive impact on the quality of a system. Revising architectural design decisions late into development requires significant effort. Architectural analyses allow software architects to reason about the impact of design decisions on quality, based on an architectural description of the system. An essential quality goal is the reduction of cost while maintaining other quality goals. Power consumption accounts for a significant part of the Total Cost of Ownership (TCO) of data centers. In 2010, data centers contributed 1.3% of the world-wide power consumption. However, reasoning on the energy efficiency of software systems is excluded from the systematic analysis of software architectures at design time. Energy efficiency can only be evaluated once the system is deployed and operational. One approach to reduce power consumption or cost is the introduction of self-adaptivity to a software system. Self-adaptive software systems execute adaptations to provision costly resources dependent on user load. The execution of reconfigurations can increase energy efficiency and reduce cost. If performed improperly, however, the additional resources required to execute a reconfiguration may exceed their positive effect.

Existing architecture-level energy analysis approaches offer limited accuracy or only consider a limited set of system features, e.g., the used communication style. Predictive approaches from the embedded systems and Cloud Computing domain operate on an abstraction that is not suited for architectural analysis. The execution of adaptations can consume additional resources.

The additional consumption can reduce performance and energy efficiency. Design time quality analyses for self-adaptive software systems ignore this transient effect of adaptations.

This thesis makes the following contributions to enable the systematic consideration of energy efficiency in the architectural design of self-adaptive software systems: First, it presents a modeling language that captures power consumption characteristics on an architectural abstraction level. Second, it introduces an energy efficiency analysis approach that uses instances of our power consumption modeling language in combination with existing performance analyses for architecture models. The developed analysis supports reasoning on energy efficiency for static and self-adaptive software systems. Third, to ease the specification of power consumption characteristics, we provide a method for extracting power models for server environments. The method encompasses an automated profiling of servers based on a set of restrictions defined by the user. A model training framework extracts a set of power models specified in our modeling language from the resulting profile. The method ranks the trained power models based on their predicted accuracy. Lastly, this thesis introduces a systematic modeling and analysis approach for considering transient effects in design time quality analyses. The approach explicitly models inter-dependencies between reconfigurations, performance and power consumption. We provide a formalization of the execution semantics of the model. Additionally, we discuss how our approach can be integrated with existing quality analyses of self-adaptive software systems.

We validated the accuracy, applicability, and appropriateness of our approach in a variety of case studies. The first two case studies investigated the accuracy and appropriateness of our modeling and analysis approach. The first study evaluated the impact of design decisions on the energy efficiency of a media hosting application. The energy consumption predictions achieved an absolute error lower than 5.5% across different user loads. Our approach predicted the relative impact of the design decision on energy efficiency with an error of less than 18.94%. The second case study used two variants of the Spring-based community case study system PetClinic. The case study complements the accuracy and appropriateness evaluation of our modeling and analysis approach. We were able to predict the energy consumption of both variants with an absolute error of no more than 2.38%. In contrast to the first case study, we derived all models automatically, using our power model extraction framework, as well as an extraction framework for performance models. The third case study applied our model-based prediction to evaluate the effect of different self-adaptation algorithms on energy efficiency. It involved scientific workloads executed in a virtualized environment. Our approach predicted the energy consumption with an error below 7.1%, even though we used coarse grained measurement data of low accuracy to train the input models. The fourth case study evaluated the appropriateness and accuracy of the automated model extraction method using a set of Big Data and enterprise workloads. Our method produced power models with prediction errors below 5.9%. A secondary study evaluated the accuracy of extracted power models for different Virtual Machine (VM) migration scenarios. The results of the fifth case study showed that our approach for modeling transient effects improved the prediction accuracy for a horizontally scaling application. Leveraging the improved accuracy, we were able to identify design deficiencies of the application that otherwise would have remained unnoticed.

Zusammenfassung

Diese Arbeit präsentiert einen Ansatz zur Entwurfszeit-Bewertung der Energieeffizienz von statischen und selbst-adaptiven Software-Systemen.

Software-Architektur hat einen wesentlichen Einfluss auf nichtfunktionale Qualitätseigenschaften von Software-Systemen wie Performanz und Betriebskosten. Architekturmodelle bilden die für architekturelle Entscheidungen relevanten Qualitätseigenschaften mit angemessener Abstraktion ab. Mithilfe von analytischen Modellen können auf Basis dieser Modelle Architekturentscheidungen bezüglich ihrer Auswirkungen auf Qualität bewertet werden. Durch eine frühzeitige Bewertung können Architekturentscheidungen zielorientiert getroffen werden. Energieeffizienz ist ein wichtiges Qualitätsziel für Software-Systeme, da sich die Effizienz maßgeblich auf die Betriebskosten von Software-Systemen auswirkt. 2010 betrug der Anteil von Rechenzentren am weltweiten Energieverbrauch 1.3%. Ein möglicher Ansatz zur Erhöhung der Energieeffizienz von Systemen ist die Einführung von Selbst-Adaptivität. Selbst-adaptive Systeme können Rekonfigurationen ausführen, um die verwendeten Ressourcen an schwankende Nutzerlast anzupassen. Allerdings können Rekonfigurationen auch die Energieeffizienz verschlechtern. Dies ist insbesondere dann der Fall, wenn der Mehraufwand durch das Ausführen einer Rekonfiguration mögliche Verbesserungen überwiegt.

Bereits vor der Implementierung hat der Architekturentwurf wesentlichen Einfluss auf die Energieeffizienz von Software-Systemen. Architekturentscheidungen sollten deshalb schon frühzeitig bezüglich ihrer Auswirkungen auf Energieeffizienz bewertet werden. Für Performanz und Zuverlässigkeit gibt es etablierte Analysemodelle, die zur Entwurfszeit eingesetzt werden können. Bestehende Techniken zur Bewertung der Energieeffizienz auf Architekturebene konzentrieren sich auf den Vergleich von spezifischen Entwurfsmustern, oder bestimmen die Effizienz anhand von Messungen erst nach Inbetriebnahme. Analysemodelle für die Qualitätsbewertung selbst-adaptiver

Systeme aus bisherigen Arbeiten berücksichtigen die Mehraufwände durch Rekonfigurationen nicht.

Ziel meiner Arbeit ist es, den systematischen Entwurf von energieeffizienten Software-Systemen zu ermöglichen. Dazu entwickle ich einen Ansatz zur Modellierung und Analyse der Energieeffizienz von Software-Architekturen. Der Ansatz ist neben klassischen statischen auch für selbst-adaptive Software-Systeme anwendbar. Neben der Beurteilung der Energieeffizienz von Gesamtsystemen kann er zur Beurteilung der Auswirkung einzelner Entwurfsentscheidungen genutzt werden. Um die systematische Berücksichtigung von Energieeffizienz beim Architekturentwurf von Software-Systemen zu unterstützen, liefert meine Dissertation die folgenden Beiträge:

1. **Konzeption einer Modellierungssprache zur Beschreibung der Energieverbrauchseigenschaften von Software-Systemen.** Das entwickelte Metamodell unterstützt die Modellierung der Verbrauchseigenschaften von Software-Systemen. Das Metamodell komplementiert etablierte Architekturmodellierungssprachen wie das Palladio Component Model (PCM).

2. **Entwicklung einer Energieeffizienz-Analyse zum Einsatz auf Architekturebene.** Die Analyse nutzt Instanzen des entwickelten Metamodells in Kombination mit etablierten Methoden zur Performanzvorhersage, um den Energieverbrauch eines Systems zu schätzen. Auf Grundlage der Verbrauchs- und Performanzvorhersagen kann dann die Auswirkung von Entwurfsentscheidungen auf die Energieeffizienz bewertet werden. Der Ansatz unterstützt sowohl die Analyse von statischen Software-Systemen als auch die Analyse selbst-adaptiver Systeme.

3. **Methode zur Extraktion von Energieverbrauchsmodellen.** Voraussetzung für die Analyse der Verbrauchseigenschaften sind genaue Verbrauchsmodelle. Um diese Modelle bestimmen zu können, werden aussagekräftige Messdaten von Servern benötigt, die für den Betrieb des Systems in Frage kommen. Die entwickelte Methode umfasst ein automatisiertes Verfahren zum Ausmessen des Verbrauchsprofils eines Servers. Das Verfahren trainiert mit dem Profil eine Menge in Frage kommender Verbrauchsmodell-Typen, und bewertet deren geschätzte Vorhersagegenauigkeit.

4. **Entwicklung eines systematischen Modellierungs- und Analyseansatzes zur Berücksichtigung des Mehraufwandes von Rekonfigurationen.** Das Metamodell dient der Beschreibung der Mehraufwände, die beim Ausführen von Rekonfigurationen entstehen. Mit dem Metamodell können explizit Beziehungen zwischen Rekonfigurationen, Performanz und Energieverbrauch beschrieben werden. Die von mir entwickelte Analyse kann mit bestehenden simulativen Analysen für selbst-adaptive Systeme gekoppelt werden. Dadurch kann die Genauigkeit dieser Analyseverfahren gesteigert werden.

Die Beiträge wurden in mehreren Fallstudien validiert. Genauigkeit und Anwendbarkeit der Modellierungssprache und Energieeffizienz-Analyse sind Gegenstand der ersten zwei Fallstudien. Die erste Fallstudie untersuchte die Auswirkung einer Entwurfsentscheidung für eine Medienvertriebs-Anwendung. Dabei konnte die relative Auswirkung der Entscheidung auf die Energieeffizienz mit einem Fehler niedriger als 18.94% vorhergesagt werden. Für absolute Verbrauchsvorhersagen lag der Fehler unter 5.5%. In der zweiten Fallstudie habe ich den Analyseansatz auf zwei Varianten des Spring Fallstudiensystems PetClinic angewendet. Im Gegensatz zur ersten Fallstudie wurden die verwendeten Modelle mit meinem Ansatz zur Modellextraktion in Kombination mit einem Werkzeug zur automatischen Architekturmodell-extraktion erstellt. Dabei konnte ein absoluter Vorhersagefehler von weniger als 2.38% erreicht werden. Die dritte Fallstudie hat meinen Vorhersageansatz auf die Bewertung unterschiedlicher Ressourcenverwaltungs-Algorithmen für Rechenzentren angewendet. Obwohl als Eingabedaten nur grob aufgelöste Daten mit großer Messungenauigkeit verfügbar waren, erzielte mein Ansatz absolute Vorhersagefehler von höchstens 7.08%. In der vierten Fallstudie habe ich untersucht, ob die Methode zur Extraktion von Energieverbrauchsmodellen zu genauen Modellen führt. Dazu habe ich die Genauigkeit der resultierenden Modelle für unterschiedliche Big Data-Anwendungen und das SPECjbb2015-Fallstudiensystem ausgewertet. Die mittels der Methode ausgewählten und trainierten Modelle erreichten für die betrachteten Systeme einen Fehler von unter 5.9%. In einer weiterführenden Fallstudie habe ich den Vorhersagefehler der Modelle für unterschiedliche Migrationsszenarien von Virtuellen Maschinen (VMs) untersucht. Die Ergebnisse der fünften Fallstudie zeigen, dass mein Ansatz zur Modellierung von Rekonfigurations-Mehraufwänden die Vorhersagegenauigkeit bei der Bewertung selbst-adaptiver Systeme erhöht. Für das untersuchte horizontal skalierende System konnte aufgrund der erhöhten Genauigkeit ein Mangel im Entwurf identifiziert und gelöst werden.

Danksagungen

Im Laufe meines Dissertationsvorhaben haben mich viele Personen unterstützt. Zuallererst möchte ich mich bei meinem Doktorvater Prof. Dr. Ralf H. Reussner bedanken, der mir die Möglichkeit zur Mitarbeit und Promotion in seiner Gruppe gegeben hat. Neben fachlichen und methodischen Ratschläge bin ich ihm insbesondere für die exzellente Arbeitsatmosphäre in seiner Gruppe dankbar, die er durch seine faire und aufgeschlossene Haltung und einen vertrauensvollen Umgang prägt. Herrn Prof. Dr. Colin Atkinson danke ich für die Übernahme des Korreferats meiner Arbeit. Seine hilfreichen Rückfragen und konstruktiven Hinweise ermöglichten es mir, meine Arbeit zu verbessern.

Frau Jun.-Prof. Dr.-Ing. Anne Koziolek danke ich herzlich für Ihr Engagement in der Mitbetreuung meiner Arbeit. Insbesondere von unserer Zusammenarbeit bei wissenschaftlichen Publikationen habe ich methodisch sehr profitiert. Zusätzlich vermochte sie es, mir bei Schwierigkeiten in meiner wissenschaftlichen Arbeit stets mit passenden Ratschlägen mögliche Wege aufzuzeigen. Philipp Merkle möchte ich für die hervorragende Betreuung meiner Masterarbeit danken, mit der er mir den Weg in die Gruppe von Herrn Prof. Dr. Reussner eröffnet hat. Danken möchte ich außerdem meinem früheren Abteilungsleiter Dr.-Ing. Henning Groenda. Er hat sich stets dafür eingesetzt, dass meine Forschungsinteressen in Projekten Raum fanden und war auch in wissenschaftlichen Fragen eine wichtige Ansprechperson für mich.

Meinen Kollegen Dominik Werle und Sebastian Krach möchte ich für die Unterstützung bei der Implementierung und der Zusammenarbeit bei Publikationen danken. Diesen beiden und Max Scheerer danke ich für ihre hilfreichen Anmerkungen zu dieser Arbeit. Ich danke den von mir betreuten Studenten Florian Rosenthal und Daniel Hassler für ihre Unterstützung bei Implementierungsarbeiten.

Weiterhin möchte ich meinem Kollegenkreis am FZI Forschungszentrum Informatik und Lehrstuhl Software Design and Quality (SDQ) für die Zusammenarbeit in Projekten, Unterstützung und Rückmeldung innerhalb und außerhalb von Doktorandenrunden und Forschungstreffen danken. Neben meinen Kollegen am FZI und SDQ gilt mein Dank auch den mit uns befreundeten Forschungsgruppen von Herrn Prof. Dr. Samuel Kounev und Herrn Prof. Dr. Steffen Becker. Jóakim von Kistowski, Sebastian Lehrig und Jürgen Walter danke ich für die Zusammenarbeit bei Publikationen und die Unterstützung in Infrastrukturbelangen.

Meiner Schwester Carolin danke ich für Ihre Hilfestellung bei sprachlichen Fragen, Ihrer Unterstützung in Promotionsfragen und allen weiteren Bereichen des Lebens.

Mein besonderer Dank gilt meinen Eltern, die mir seit Beginn meines Lebens Rückhalt geben, und von früh auf meine Interessen und Ausbildung gefördert haben.

Contents

List of Figures

List of Tables

Listings

1. Introduction

The present thesis introduces an approach for the systematic consideration of energy efficiency in the architecture level design of software systems. The approach enables software architects to evaluate the power consumption of static and self-adaptive software systems from a software architecture description. This chapter illustrates why energy efficiency is an important software quality concern that should be considered from early design stages. We identify a gap in state of the art that concerns the design time support of energy efficiency. From this gap analysis, we derive a set of challenges and research questions. We further give an overview of our contributions, use cases and design decisions supported by our approach. The final section concludes with an outline of the thesis.

1.1. Motivation

Energy consumption is a major cost factor in the operation of enterprise software systems. While the interfaces of user-facing services have largely moved to mobile devices, back-end services still run in traditional data center server environments. Koomey [110] estimated the share of data center power consumption from the total consumption at 1.3% worldwide, and 2% in the US. More recent study results estimate US data center energy consumption in 2014 at 73 TW h [190]. This accounts for 1.8% of the total US energy consumption. Shehabi et al. [190] predicted an 8.2% increase of total US data center energy consumption from 2010 to 2020. For data centers based on commodity hardware, energy costs can account for up to 26% of the Total Cost of Ownership (TCO) depending on their load [13]. The industry adoption of the Cloud Computing paradigm has increased the importance of data center energy consumption: Cloud-enabled enterprise applications almost exclusively run in data centers.

The energy consumption of a software system depends on four factors:

- The energy consumption characteristics of its execution environment, e.g., server hardware [14],
- the types and intensity of user interactions with the systems [10, 173, 194]
- the architectural design [101] and implementation [87] of the software, and
- the use of power management mechanisms [14].

In order to meet its purpose, a software system has to fulfill functional and non-functional requirements. The promotion of energy-awareness can entice users and developers to choose functional alternatives which result in a lower energy consumption. However, it does not fundamentally change the energy consumption characteristics of the hard- and software.

The increase of *energy efficiency* is an alternative strategy that can help reduce energy consumption of software systems, while ensuring efficient operation of the system. Energy efficiency of software systems quantifies how much energy is required to offer their services. Energy efficiency is commonly defined as a ratio of the amount of useful work done, and the energy consumption required to complete the work [210]. If one system manages to process the same workload with a smaller energy consumption than an alternative system, it is more efficient. By definition, energy efficiency thus encompasses both performance and energy consumption.

The use of more efficient server hardware is a straightforward measure for increasing energy efficiency of a software system. Another approach is to increase the efficiency of the software design, and its implementation. Example improvements can be, e.g., the use of more efficient algorithms, or the reduction of avoidable computations.

Whether a software system meets its Quality of Service (QoS) requirements "is largely determined by the time the architecture is chosen" [54]. Software architecture can be defined as a set of design decisions [102], or the result of these decisions [170]. Aside from the composition of components, software architecture also includes the mapping of components to their execution environment [170].

Each architectural design decision affects development and operational cost, in addition to its impact on multiple QoS dimensions. Architectural design decisions decisively influence energy efficiency, as is illustrated in [101, 200]. Alternative decisions may require different amounts of development resources. At runtime, design decisions affect performance and energy consumption. Software architects have to make trade off decisions to meet contradictory QoS goals. This also applies to energy efficiency. A deployment of software components on slow but energy efficient servers might improve energy efficiency. However, the resulting performance degradation might lead to unacceptable response times.

In order to make informed trade off decisions, the software architect needs to be aware of the effect of design decisions on energy efficiency and other QoS dimensions. Systematic architecture design and analysis methods enable the evaluation of software systems in early design stages. Established methods support the analysis of performance [22], reliability [33], and further QoS characteristics [176]. Existing methods for the analysis of energy efficiency at design time make simplifying assumptions regarding the power consumption characteristics of software systems. These assumptions affect the accuracy [35] and applicability [182, 184] of the approaches. This makes it difficult for software architects to reason on the effect of design decisions on energy efficiency.

Ideally, servers would have constant energy efficiency at all load levels. This is, however, not the case. When modern servers are idle, they consume just below 30% of their power consumption under full load [155].

Traditional software architecture design produces a one-size-fits-all architecture, which remains static over time. In order to meet performance goals under peak user load, the software architect has to overprovision software components on a large number of servers. This leaves the servers underutilized under average load. Since servers typically offer higher energy efficiency at higher load levels, static software systems showcase poor energy efficiency at low to average load. This can be addressed by collocating workloads with heterogeneous characteristics on the same server [61]. In cases where multiple collocated workloads concurrently encounter a burst in user demand, their performance can deteriorate. Performance measures are commonly part of Service Level Agreements (SLAs) between system operators and service customers. A performance deterioration thus can lead to SLA violations.

In recent years, the concept of *self-adaptivity* has gained traction. Self-adaptive software systems can adapt their structure and deployment, as well as functionality to changing environmental conditions. A frequent use case of self-adaptivity is the autonomic provisioning of resources for the application depending on its current and expected workload [84].

Self-adaptivity can also be used to increase the energy efficiency of software systems. A notable example of an energy-conscious adaptation tactic is the consolidation of software components on fewer servers. This frees up hosts, which in turn may be turned off to save energy. A realization of this tactic is VM consolidation [165]. Hereby, a self-adaptation mechanism consolidates a set of VMs on a smaller number of servers. The emptied servers then may be shut down to save energy. VM consolidation uses VM migration, which moves a VM from a source to a target server. The execution of adaptations, such as VM consolidation, does not necessarily increase energy efficiency. If the number of servers on which components are consolidated is too small, the servers may become overloaded. This in turn worsens performance. If the performance degradation is too large, performance-related SLAs might be violated. In order to reason on energy efficiency, the interplay between performance and energy consumption needs to be considered in the design of energy-conscious self-adaptive software systems.

The goal of this thesis is to enable the energy efficiency evaluation of software systems in early design phases. The presented approach enables a systematic analysis of energy efficiency for traditional static software architectures as well as self-adaptive system architectures.

1.2. Problem Statement

We identified the following problem areas which are addressed as part of this thesis. The areas concern the needed level of abstraction, applicability, and accuracy of an adaptation-aware architecture modeling and analysis approach of energy efficiency.

Representation of Power Consumption Characteristics. Existing power modeling approaches [28, 58] for system or server level power modeling offer a level of detail which is not suited as input for quantitative design time power consumption predictions. Runtime power modeling and prediction approaches often rely on low-level system metrics and hardware performance counters. It is not feasible to obtain predictions of these low-level metrics at design time. Design time approaches [35, 184] model power consumption characteristics with a low level of detail. This restricts the accuracy of derived predictions.

Reasoning on power consumption characteristics of large software systems requires a model that captures the power distribution infrastructure. The infrastructure in data centers follows a hierarchical power distribution topology [69]. The only existing architectural abstraction [35] fails to represent this information. Data center level modeling and simulation approaches represent the hierarchical power distribution infrastructure. They use a simple additive model [45], or a fixed factor abstraction [166] to evaluate power consumption on different levels. The existing approaches, however, fail to provide means to define power models of distribution infrastructure and individual servers in a flexible manner. A modeling language for specifying power consumption characteristics for design time analysis needs be expressive enough to describe heterogeneous server and data center environments.

Power Consumption Prediction Accuracy. The frequency and type of user requests impact both performance and power consumption of a software system. Existing approaches for evaluating power consumption at design time [35, 182, 184] assume an additive effect of requests on power consumption, i.e., each additional request increases power consumption by the same amount. The effect of an additional user request is not additive. This means that its effect can not be approximated accurately as a fixed factor. An architectural analysis needs to accurately predict the effect of design decisions on energy efficiency in order to support informed trade-off decisions with other QoS dimensions.

Effort for Power Model Extraction. The manual construction of accurate power models requires significant effort. It is possible to use a large set of system metrics at runtime to predict the power consumption of a software system. Existing power model extraction approaches [58, 65] focus on the construction of power models for runtime power consumption estimation. The approaches assume that their user is able to measure low-level system metrics and performance counters. The design time prediction of low-level metrics and performance counters requires significant effort, or is impossible. Even if it is possible to predict a low-level metric, it can make sense to exclude it from the metrics considered by the power model extraction. This is the case if the modeling effort required to predict the additional metric at design time outweighs a potential increase in power consumption prediction accuracy. A power model extraction approach that aims to construct models as input to design time analyses needs to consider the tradeoff between modeling effort and accuracy.

Consideration of QoS Effects of Adaptations. An accurate evaluation of self-adaptive software systems requires the consideration of *transient effects*. Transient effects refer to the immediate effect of an adaptation on QoS. This includes, e.g., the performance overhead incurred by the adaptation execution. The execution of adaptations should not further deteriorate performance by using already congested resources. Another example is server power management. A server already consumes power while it boots. It may, however, only be used to host services once it has fully booted. A central goal in the design of adaptation mechanisms is that they effectively and efficiently improve QoS under changing environmental conditions. Existing design time analyses of self-adaptive software systems do not consider transient effects incurred by adaptations [20, 133], or require an explicit modeling of the full adaptation space [77]. Due to the complexity of distributed, service-based applications it is not realistic to model all user interactions and system configurations in advance [208]. The use of resource provisioning mechanisms such as horizontal scaling of VMs compounds this problem. Transient effects need to be considered in design time QoS analyses of self-adaptive systems so that the efficiency and effectiveness of adaptation mechanisms can be evaluated.

1.3. State of the Art

Green Software Engineering and the architectural design of energy efficient software systems has recently become an area of interest to many researchers [88]. In this field, research has emerged that targets the evaluation and improvement of energy consumption or energy efficiency of software systems. This section discusses central work in this field. Chapter 8 discusses the approaches in greater detail and compares them to our approach.

Procaccianti et al. [164, 165] have identified architectural best practices which can increase energy efficiency. The collection of these best practices provides a software architect with a starting point for architectural improvements. However, it remains unclear how their application quantitatively affects energy efficiency.

Schulze [182] presents an approach for the estimation of ecological cost (eco-cost) in early software design phases. In addition to the prediction of high level metrics like greenhouse gas emissions, the approach can also be applied to predict energy consumption. The prediction model of Schulze relies on energy consumption annotations to Unified Modeling Language (UML) objects, their operations and attributes. An example annotation is the energy consumption that results from storing a specific object in a database. The author notes that it is difficult to obtain accurate annotations in early design phases. Schulze [182] hence proposes the continuous refinement of eco-cost annotations throughout software development.

Existing architectural modeling and analysis methods estimate energy efficiency of specific architectural communication patterns [184], or compare the efficiency of different software releases [101]. Palladio [22] is an established method that supports the analysis of QoS properties, e.g., performance and reliability, in early design stages. It predicts performance and reliability on the basis of composable specifications. Brunnert et al. [35] sketch an approach for energy consumption evaluation based on aggregated Palladio performance predictions. The authors rely on linear power models for all servers and their resources. This makes their prediction inaccurate for most modern server environments. Their approach only supports aggregate energy consumption predictions. It fails to offer an analysis of power consumption over time.

System level power models [58, 65, 172] enable the estimation of server power consumption based on measured system metrics. Several approaches support the automated or semi-automated construction of power models from measurements [58, 172]. The approaches focus on the extraction of models to estimate power consumption at runtime. They aim at the prediction of power consumption for servers that lack permanent means to measure power consumption, i.e., via an integrated power meter. Runtime power model extraction approaches can leverage all system metrics as their measurement results with little to no overhead. Runtime approaches lack support for identifying central system metrics that need to be considered to accurately predict power consumption. The identification or selection of central system metrics is needed when extracting power models for use in design time analyses. The reason for this is that the accurate prediction of any additional system metric at design time results in additional modeling effort. This effort should be avoided if it fails to result in an increased prediction accuracy.

SimuLizar [17] extends Palladio to the domain of self-adaptive systems. It supports software architects in designing *scalable*, and *elastic* software systems. SimuLizar focuses on the analysis of performance. Software architects further can use SimuLizar to derive scalability and elasticity metrics from the results of a performance analysis run. SimuLizar lacked support for predicting the power consumption of self-adaptive systems prior to this thesis. It further assumed that adaptations require a negligible amount of time and resources to execute. This clashes with the observation that the execution of some adaptations requires significant time, and causes computational overhead.

1.4. Challenges and Research Questions

A set of challenges have to be addressed to support the systematic analysis of energy efficiency for static and self-adaptive software systems at design time. This section outlines three central areas in which we identified challenges. For each challenge area we derive a set of research questions.

1.4.1. Modeling and Analysis of Software System Power Consumption Characteristics

The power consumption of a software system depends not only upon the hardware components of its servers. The software stack executes hardware instructions on the server it is deployed on. The power consumption of the server varies depending on these instructions. The software stack induces the execution of hardware instructions dependent on user requests. In order to assess the power consumption of a software system, the design and usage of deployed software components hence need to be considered.

Designing a software system, decisions that impact the power consumption of a software system are already made on the architecture level. Manotas et al. [130] conducted an empirical study involving 464 practitioners from ABB, Google, IBM and Microsoft. The study revealed that the study participants judged that "high-level designs are impacted by energy usage concerns more frequently than low-level designs". Examples of such high-level decisions given by the authors are the selection of design patterns and components. This suggests the need for an architecture-level consideration of power consumption and energy efficiency.

Existing approaches for evaluating the power consumption of software require that the software has already been fully implemented and can be deployed. While these approaches enable reasoning on power consumption at implementation and deployment time, they can not be used to evaluate the effect of architectural design decisions on power consumption. Architectural quality analyses that consider power consumption focus on subsets of design decisions, or provide insufficient prediction accuracy. This thesis derives the following Research Questions (RQs) from the need to make the effect of architectural design decisions on energy consumption predictable:

Research Question 1. *What is a good abstraction level for modeling power consumption characteristics of software systems? We consider a model abstraction good if it*

- *produces accurate power consumption predictions,*
- *can be constructed from information available at design time,*

- *contains as little redundant information as possible with existing architectural modeling languages and viewpoints.*

Research Question 2. *How can the power consumption of software systems be predicted on an architectural level?*

Research Question 3. *How accurate are power consumption predictions performed on an architectural level?*

Research Question 4. *How can we evaluate the effect of architectural design decisions on energy efficiency?*

1.4.2. Extraction of Power Models

Reasoning on the effect of design decisions on power consumption requires predictive models that correlate software or system activity with power consumption. In the context of this thesis, system metric-based power models are used to predict the consumption of the software system. Since the power consumption of servers varies significantly depending on their hardware, it is not possible to derive power models that are agnostic of their deployment environment. Extracting power models manually based on measurements is cumbersome and requires significant effort for the construction and analysis of measurement experiments. Existing approaches that automate the construction of power models focus on runtime power estimation. These approaches leverage system knowledge that is not yet available at design time. This thesis addresses the following questions towards the extraction of power models for use in design time analyses.

Research Question 5. *How can the effort in deriving power models for architecture-level power consumption analyses be reduced?*

Prior to this thesis, the construction of power models for use in design time analyses was a manual process. It required the collection of measurement data from experiments. Engineers had to rely on expert knowledge or trial and error to construct a power model for use in design time predictions. Research Question 5 regards the reduction of this effort.

Research Question 6. *What is the effect of considering different system level metrics as input in power consumption analyses?*

Research Question 6 concerns the evaluation of different system metrics and their effect on energy efficiency. System metrics should only be considered in architecture level analyses if they improve the prediction accuracy.

Research Question 7. *How can software architects and system deployers be supported in the selection of input metrics for energy efficiency analyses?*

Research Question 7 aims at the interactions of modeling effort and prediction accuracy. The use of additional input metrics, e.g., storage throughput, may marginally increase the prediction accuracy. A software architect or performance engineer will likely opt against its inclusion if the prediction of the input metric

- relies on the sophisticated modeling of storage access patterns,
- fails to increase performance prediction accuracy significantly.

It hence makes little sense to consider a metric in a power model if it does not improve performance or energy consumption prediction accuracy.

1.4.3. Transient Effects of Reconfigurations

Self-adaptive software systems adapt their configuration to maintain QoS goals under changing user load. Design time analyses of self-adaptive software systems enable software architects to perform QoS analyses before the system has been fully implemented. These analyses enable software architects and operators to reason on the efficiency and effectiveness with which a system adapts itself. If reconfiguration decisions are made too late, additional resources might not become available in time. This then leads to resource contention. If the system triggers a reconfiguration too early, resources are wasted. Should the system reconfigure too frequently, the overhead incurred by the reconfigurations might surpass their beneficial effect on QoS. *Transient effects* refer to the impact of reconfigurations on QoS in transient phases. A transient phase is the interval between reconfiguration start, and the maximum point in time at which the reconfiguration finishes or at which the system recovers from the increase in load. Existing analyses neglect these transient effects. Consequently, their predictions are not accurate for transient phases. This thesis aims at enabling software architects to evaluate the energy efficiency not only of static software systems, but also of self-adaptive software systems. Thus, this thesis investigates the following research questions:

Research Question 8. *How do reconfigurations affect power consumption and performance?*

Research Question 9. *What is an architecture-level description of reconfigurations that describes the effect of reconfigurations on system metrics such as performance and power consumption?*

Research Question 10. *How can we consider the effects of runtime reconfigurations in software quality analyses at design time?*

Research Question 11. *Does the consideration of transient effects enable the (a) detection and (b) solution of design problems in self-adaptive software systems?*

1.5. Contributions

The scientific contributions of this thesis are:

C1: Design of a modeling language for the description of power consumption characteristics of software systems. Our meta-model enables the modeling of server and power distribution infrastructure consumption characteristics. It employs power models to describe the consumption characteristics of servers and their resources, e.g., CPU or HDD.

C2: Development of an approach for energy efficiency analysis at design time. The approach uses instances of the developed meta-model in combination with established performance prediction approaches to predict the power consumption of a software system. The predictions can be leveraged to evaluate the effect of design decisions on energy efficiency. We designed the analysis to support evaluations of static as well as self-adaptive software systems. We validate the analysis for two enterprise software systems. Additionally, we apply it to predict power consumption in a set of data center management scenarios. The validation shows that our prediction approach has a high accuracy. The prediction accuracy outperforms the only other existing architecture level prediction approach.

C3: **A method for the extraction of power models for use in design time predictions.** Accurate power models are a prerequisite for the power consumption analysis. To train the power models, representative power consumption and performance measurements of the servers in the target deployment environment are needed. The presented method encompasses the automated profiling of server power consumption and utilization. We train a set of power models on the extracted server profile. The model with highest predicted accuracy is selected from these candidate models. The validation applies our method to a diverse set of Big Data and enterprise workloads. The extracted power models have a high prediction accuracy. The resulting models are significantly more accurate than state of the art approaches if multiple system metrics are considered, e.g., CPU utilization and HDD throughput.

C4: **Development of a systematic modeling and analysis approach for considering transient effects in software quality analyses.** We present a metamodel for the description of transient effects. The metamodel supports the description of inter-dependencies between adaptations, performance and power consumption. We outline a transient effect analysis that extends existing simulative analyses of self-adaptive software systems. Our analysis improves the prediction accuracy of the analyses via the consideration of transient effects. The analysis builds upon a set of formalized execution semantics presented in this thesis. Our validation shows that the consideration of transient effects significantly improves prediction accuracy for the investigated self-adaptive software system. The validation further illustrates that the analysis enabled us to identify a design deficiency of the system. This deficiency would have otherwise remained undetected.

The following Section 1.5.1 names central prerequisites of our approach. Section 1.5.2 provides an overview of application scenarios for our contributions. Section 1.5.3 goes into detail on categories of supported design decisions.

1.5.1. Prerequisites

Our modeling and analysis approach can be applied if the following conditions are met.

Availability of Architecture-Level Performance Models. The power and energy consumption analyses presented in this thesis build upon existing architecture-level performance analyses, such as the Palladio performance simulators SimuCom and SimuLizar. Our analyses rely on performance prediction results from these analyses. The power and energy consumption analyses use performance metrics like CPU utilization and HDD throughput.

To apply performance prediction methods, input architecture-level performance models must be available. Palladio performance simulators use a Palladio Component Model (PCM) instance that includes performance annotations. PCM encompasses a set of viewpoints, which Section 2.5.1 elaborates on. "If architectural models and deployments are already modeled, Palladio creates virtually no additional overheads" [170, p. 195] compared to other architecture modeling methods and languages. The largest modeling effort results from the creation of performance descriptions, the Resource-Demanding Service Effect Specifications (RDSEFFs). An RDSEFF is a "parametrized, behavioral abstraction and quality specification for a single component service" [170, p. 99]. An RDSEFF consists of a set of activities, similar to UML activity diagram. Resource demand specifications annotate the activities with the amount of work they cause on resources, e.g., CPUs or HDDs.

It is challenging to accurately describe the behavior of a service in early design stages. However, software architects may use design documents, prior implementations or the approximated algorithmic complexity to derive an initial RDSEFF. The behavior models can be refined throughout different design stages, as prototypes or initial component implementations become available. During software evolution, static code analysis [116] and dynamic runtime analysis methods [116, 220] can be applied to obtain performance models from existing implementations.

Information on Power Consumption Characteristics of Deployment Environment. Our Power Consumption metamodel describes the power consumption characteristics of software deployment environments. It relies on power models which describe the characteristics of individual servers. Users of the power consumption analysis must be able to obtain server power models of the servers in the targeted deployment environment. The required power models can be obtained using one of the following methods.

First, the power consumption characteristics can be derived via systematic server profiling. This thesis presents an approach that automates the construction of server power models for use in design time via systematic profiling. It employs representative workloads to profile server power consumption at different load levels. Additionally, we describe an approach for the extraction of power models from historical measurements. A server power model from a profiling run can be used for all servers of the same model or type. Both approaches require a power meter to obtain power consumption measurements of the server. Second, power models of similar servers can be used if the target server type is unknown or the required equipment is unavailable. Finally, power consumption data from publicly accessible benchmark results can be leveraged as a fallback solution, as Schmitt et al. [181] discuss. These substitute models can be refined during development, deployment and operation once the deployment infrastructure is finalized.

1.5.2. Application Scenarios

The QoS offered by a system depends on the implementation, assembly, deployment of its components and the behavior of users that interact with the system.

1.5.2.1. Design Time Energy Consumption Analysis of Enterprise Software Systems

Design decisions made in early stages of design, i.e., on the architecture level, decisively impact QoS and development cost of a software system. This thesis presents a modeling and analysis approach that enables the systematic consideration of energy efficiency in the architectural design of software systems. Our approach builds upon information obtained as part a systematic architectural design process like Palladio [22]. It supports energy efficiency analyses in early design phases. It enables software architects to make informed trade-off decisions between performance and power consumption, and other QoS dimensions such as cost.

We leverage an architecture level, model-based analysis to reason on energy efficiency. The analysis employs architectural performance models like PCM combined with our Power Consumption metamodel presented in this thesis as input. The analysis can be used to predict the energy efficiency of a software system before its implementation has been completed.

1.5.2.2. Energy-Conscious Evolution of Enterprise Software Systems

Software systems must evolve over time to address newly identified user requirements, and to continue a satisfactory QoS [122]. Increased energy efficiency is a quality goal that is of growing significance. Existing approaches use measurements to evaluate the effect of design decisions after they have been implemented. The feedback from the measurements provides feedback to the developers. It thereby can help them make better decisions in the future. The evaluation is only possible once a decision has been implemented. This increases the risk of introducing systematic design deficiencies and, ultimately, inadequate energy efficiency or performance.

Our approach enables software architects to evaluate the effect of design decisions on energy efficiency *before they are implemented.* It thereby reduces the risk from uncertain effects of design decisions on QoS.

1.5.2.3. Data Center Planning

Power consumption is used as a primary cost indicator in data center planning. The estimated power consumption of the planned servers informs the sizing requirements in terms of cooling, power distribution equipment and space [13]. According to Barroso et al., "approximately 80% of total construction cost goes towards power and cooling" [13, p. 92]. The authors note that the construction costs of larger data centers scale linearly with Watts. Barroso et al. estimate the total construction cost at roughly $9-13 total per Watt. Power consumption estimation is thus not only essential to the estimation of operational cost, but also a central factor in data center planning.

Our modeling and prediction approach can be used for data center planning and sizing. It has been applied as part of the CACTOS project [152] to support data center operators, planners and algorithm engineers in the evaluation of design decisions. Our approach enables them to evaluate the effect of infrastructure sizing, and runtime management algorithms design and configuration on data center energy efficiency.

1.5.3. Supported Design Decisions

Design decisions which increase energy efficiency also impact other QoS dimensions, e.g., cost or performance. Decisions commonly have adverse effects on multiple dimensions. An example of this is the consolidation of components on fewer servers. The consolidation reduces energy consumption. It can, however, lead to higher response time under peak user load. The assessment of the design decision depends on the amount of saved energy, and the expected response time degradation. In summary, trade-offs between multiple QoS dimensions require quantitative estimations of energy consumption. We thus designed our analysis approach to support quantitative energy consumption estimations.

The following discusses a set of design decisions and scenarios which can be analyzed with our approach.

Effect of User Load and Behavior Variations. Type and intensity of user interactions with software systems varies over time. This variation may follow a random distribution or a trend, i.e., an increased rate of requests during business hours. Our approach supports the consideration of variations in user load and behavior. Software architects can use our approach to explore whether a system meets energy efficiency goals and other QoS requirements during workload spikes, and for expected changes in the mix of user requests.

Component Selection. Component-based software systems are seldom constructed from scratch. Software architects may reuse existing component implementations to save development effort. For common library functionality, software architects can often choose from multiple component implementations with similar functionality but different QoS characteristics. Software architects can apply our analysis approach to evaluate the effect of component selection on energy efficiency. Tradeoffs of the energy efficiency predictions with other QoS attributes require little to no additional effort, as our approach integrates with the established design time prediction method Palladio.

Infrastructure Sizing. Idle servers still consume a significant portion of their power consumption when idle. Power infrastructure sizing is an additional cost factor. The power distribution infrastructure of data centers needs to be capable of handling peak data center load. If "a data center operates at 50% of its peak power capacity, the effective provisioning cost per Watt used is doubled" [13]. It is common practice to size power distribution infrastructure based on the expected load instead of the theoretical power draw of all installed equipment [13, p. 83]. This is done to avoid cost that results from an oversized power distribution and cooling infrastructure. In practice, sizing decisions are typically made based on rough utilization estimates, see [56]. The use of power beyond the peak power capacity can result in power and server outages. Dynamic load management techniques like *power capping* aim to reduce the risk of outages by limiting the peak load.

The modeling and analysis methods presented in this thesis support reasoning on power consumption at different levels of a hierarchical power distribution infrastructure. The peak power consumption predicted by our analysis can be used to assess whether the planned infrastructure and power management algorithms meet peak power demand with acceptable performance.

Comparison of Deployment Strategies. A central aspect in the operation of energy efficient software systems is deployment, or distribution, of components on servers. The power consumption of individual servers depends on the utilization of its resources, e.g., CPU and HDD, by components that are deployed on the server. The power consumption of servers increases with their load. Energy efficiency of servers improves at higher load levels. Simultaneously, the response time of requests can suffer if a server reaches load levels above a certain threshold.

Deployers can leverage our method to evaluate deployment strategies which achieve good energy efficiency while maintaining other QoS goals.

Design and Selection of Adaptation Mechanisms. Self-adaptive software systems continuously optimize their assembly, deployment and functionality to meet changing environmental conditions. The execution of adaptations can incur an overhead, which results in performance deterioration and increased energy consumption [205, 206]. Our metamodel and analysis for the consideration of transient effects provides architects with the means to reason on adaptation overheads. Thereby, software architects can assess if an adaptation mechanism increases efficiency and effectiveness of a software system or if its use deteriorates QoS.

Additionally, we support the evaluation of energy-conscious adaptation mechanisms such as power capping. These are adaptation mechanisms that aim to improve energy efficiency through the use of active power management. Example power management actions include the boot-up and shutdown of servers.

1.6. Outline

This thesis is structured as follows:

Chapter 2 introduces the foundations of our work. It introduces power models, which our modeling approach builds upon. The definition of energy efficiency as used in this thesis is presented. We discuss power management techniques that can be used in servers to adapt the tradeoff between power consumption and performance of servers. We introduce fundamentals of self-adaptive software systems. We outline the Palladio approach for architecture level modeling and analysis of software systems. Palladio serves as the foundation of our energy efficiency modeling and analysis approach. The overview of Palladio provides an overview of SimuLizar, a simulation-based analysis of self-adaptive software systems.

Chapter 3 presents a modeling language for describing power consumption characteristics of software systems. It describes the Power Consumption metamodel, a metamodel used to characterize consumption characteristics of servers, their components, and connected power distribution infrastructure.

In **Chapter 4** we describe our approach for the design time power consumption analysis of software systems. Our approach uses instances of the Power Consumption metamodel combined with performance predictions to reason on the power consumption of software systems. The analysis supports the architecture level analysis of both static and self-adaptive software systems. We show how aggregate energy consumption and energy efficiency predictions can be derived from the power consumption predictions.

Chapter 5 presents a method for the automated extraction of power models for use in design time analyses. The method consists of three steps: server profiling, model training and model selection. Server profiling performs systematic experiments to extract the power consumption profile of a server. Model training uses statistical learning to produce a set of candidate power models. These models describe the consumption characteristics of the server under investigation. The model selection step selects the model with the highest predicted accuracy from the candidates.

Chapter 6 introduces a modeling and analysis approach for considering transient effects in simulation-based software performance and power consumption analyses. First, the section presents the Adaptation Action metamodel. The metamodel enables a coupled specification of adaptation outcome and the performance effect of adaptation execution. In addition to the structural semantics defined by the metamodel, the chapter presents the formalized execution semantics of the model. Finally, we develop a transient effects analysis approach that extends an existing simulation-based analysis.

Chapter 7 presents the results of our validation case studies. Our case studies cover the contributions discussed in Chapters 3 to 6. The case studies cover a range of applications and benchmarking frameworks.

Chapter 8 surveys related work. It contextualizes our contributions with approaches from related fields, e.g., Cloud simulators, Green Software Engineering, and energy efficiency benchmarks.

In **Chapter 9** we discuss how our contributions can be integrated with existing software engineering development approaches.

Chapter 10 concludes with a summary of this thesis and an outlook on potential future work.

2. Foundations

This chapter introduces foundations that the following chapters build upon. Section 2.1 outlines fundamental power modeling and energy estimation concepts. In Section 2.2 we contrast different definitions of energy efficiency (EE), and establish the definition used in this thesis. Section 2.3 gives an overview of different power management techniques. We summarize central concepts of self-adaptive software systems in Section 2.4, which are relevant to our approach. Section 2.5 outlines the Palladio approach. It discusses the Palladio Component Model (PCM), an architectural modeling language that enables performance predictions in early design phases. Furthermore, the section provides details on the software performance simulators that we use and extend. Section 2.6 discusses model selection criteria, which we apply as part of our power model extraction approach. Finally, Section 2.7 introduces foundations of methods we use in our validation.

2.1. Power Models and Energy Consumption Estimation

This section presents methods which model and predict the power and energy consumption of software systems. The methods address the analysis of power consumption at runtime or implementation time. Power and energy models estimate the power consumption based on measurable software system characteristics. These characteristics may be system level metrics, e.g., CPU utilization, or software metrics like the number of bytes occupied by an object. The main reason for using power models at runtime is a lack of permanent power monitoring or measurement equipment.

Over the years, a multitude of functions have been proposed to model the power consumption of different types of hardware components and device types, e.g., server or mobile phones. Dayarathna et al. [59] provide an extensive survey of different power modeling techniques. At the lowest abstraction level three types of power and energy models can be distinguished. Section 2.1.1 introduces bookkeeping models. Section 2.1.2 presents system metric-based power models. Section 2.1.3 outlines Power State Machines (PSMs) for modeling stateful power consumption characteristics.

2.1.1. Bookkeeping Energy and Power Models

Bookkeeping models estimate the energy consumption of hardware [23] or software instructions [185, 186, 207]. They estimate the consumption by assigning each instruction type or operation with its estimated energy demand.

Definition 2.1 (Bookkeeping Energy Model). *A bookkeeping energy model estimates the energy consumption of a set of operations Op executed in an interval $[t_0, t_e]$.*

$$E_{Op} = \sum_{o \in Op} E_{t(o)}(o),$$

where E_{Op} is the estimated energy consumption of the operations and o is an operation. $t(o)$ is the operation type of o and $E_{t(o)}(o)$ is the estimated energy consumption induced by executing o.

Bookkeeping models enable a straightforward mapping of energy consumption estimates to hardware and software components. The total energy consumption estimate of a server can be aggregated from all instructions, which the server executes in the specified interval $[t_0, t_e]$. Similarly, energy consumption estimates $E(C)$ of a software component C may be calculated as the sum over the energy consumption of all operations that result from calls to the interfaces provided by C [186]:

$$E(C) = \sum_{I \in \text{provInterfaces}(C)} \sum_{m \in I} E_{Op(m)},$$

where $m \in I$ is an operation of interface I that is provided by C. The set provInterfaces(C) contains these operations. $Op(m)$ are the operations executed by all calls to m.

Bookkeeping models are reasonably accurate for predicting the power consumption of a software system deployed on a specific server with a known load. Bookkeeping approaches [23, 183] separately account for the idle power consumption of systems. This increases the accuracy of the predictions when the user load changes. A disadvantage of bookkeeping models is their disregard for nonlinear effects in the power consumption of their execution environment. Bookkeeping models calculate the total consumption as the sum over the energy consumption of individual operation calls $E_{t(o)}(o)$. This implies that the bookkeeping models assume a linear relation between the number of operation calls and the total system consumption. Hence, bookkeeping models have a low prediction accuracy when the relation between utilization and power consumption is non-linear. Variations in user load or execution environment changes compound these inaccuracies.

2.1.2. System Metric-Based Power Models

System metric-based *power models* predict the power consumption of servers or individual hardware components from measured metrics [58, 65, 66, 172]. Power models estimate the current power draw at a given point in time. Power models do not isolate the power consumption of individual instructions. Instead, they predict the power consumption of hardware components from a set of measurable system metrics. System metrics quantify the activity of hardware components. Example system metrics are CPU utilization or disk write throughput. The energy consumption of a system can be calculated as the integral over an interval of the sampled power consumption estimates from the power model.

Definition 2.2 (Power Model). *A system metric-based power model is a function*

$$p : U_1 \times \ldots \times U_n \rightarrow P$$

that maps a set of input metric values $(u_1, \ldots, u_n) \in U_1 \times \ldots \times U_n$ *to a predicted power consumption* $p_{value} \in P$.

The linear power model is a widespread baseline power model used to compare more sophisticated power models [35, 65, 69, 82, 104, 135, 172, 231]. Linear power models estimate the power consumption of servers as a sum of linear factors of system metrics:

Definition 2.3 (Linear Power Model). *A linear power model p is a function*

$$p(u) = c_0 + \sum_{i=1}^{n} a_i * u_i,$$

where $u = (u_1, ..., u_n)$ is a system metric tuple. The constant factor c_0 characterizes the static power consumption of the hardware. Commonly, u_i are utilization metrics normalized to $[0, 1]$.

2.1.3. Power State Machine (PSM)

PSMs model the power consumption characteristics of a hardware component as a Finite State Machine (FSM) [26]. PSMs are a well-established concept in the domain of embedded systems design. They can be used to reflect the effect of active power management mechanisms on power consumption. An example mechanism is the shutdown of idle hardware components after they have remained unused for a defined interval.

PSMs characterize the power consumption as a set of finite states. Power consumption in a state is assumed to be constant. The hardware component transitions between the power states depending on the implemented power management. The power management that triggers the transitions may be implemented in software or hardware. The transitions between power states are assumed to take time. Extensions to PSM annotate transitions with further costs. This includes additional power consumption caused by the transition between power states [73].

Figure 2.1 depicts an example PSM of a StrongARM SA-1100 processor [27]. The example PSM has the three states *run, sleep* and *idle*. The PSM models the power consumption in each state as constant. The PSM captures direct transitions from idle to run or sleep, from run to idle or sleep, and from sleep to run. Each transition takes a fixed amount of time.

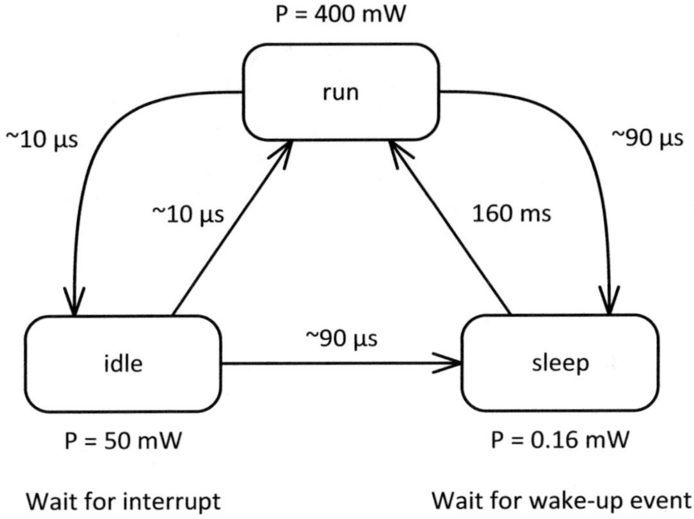

Figure 2.1.: PSM of StrongARM SA-1100 processor, as modelled by Benini and Micheli [27].

2.2. Energy Efficiency

Fundamentally, the energy efficiency of a software system is the ratio of energy consumed to perform a certain amount of work. Tsirogiannis et al. [210] define energy efficiency as "the ratio of useful work done to the energy used":

Definition 2.4 (Efficiency of Software Systems). *The energy efficiency (EE) of a software system is a ratio of the work executed by a software system, and the energy required to perform the work:*

$$EE = \frac{Work\ Done}{Energy} = \frac{Throughput \times Time}{Power \times Time} = \frac{Throughput}{Power}.$$

Definition 2.4 showcases that the EE definition can be expressed as the ratio of throughput (per time period) and power consumption.

Software applications inherently do not consume energy. The hardware required to execute the applications, however, does. When users call the services of an application, the application issues instructions to its execution environment. This leads to an increased level of hardware activity. The increased activity results in additional energy consumption.

Hardware, e.g., servers and their components, consume power even when idle. Some authors [47, 104] only attribute the power consumption to an application which is caused by the additional activity of the software. This definition shows its limitations when distributed deployment scenarios are considered. The focus on active utilization fails to sufficiently reflect the benefits of consolidation strategies. If it is possible to operate a distributed application with a smaller number of servers, this significantly reduces the total energy consumption. The energy efficiency definition of [47, 104] disregards efficiency increases that result from a reduction of static consumption.

Capra et al. [47] note that high energy efficiency is commonly wrongly equated to good performance. This is not the case as the following examples illustrate. The use of less efficient hardware may boost performance in return for an increased energy consumption. Highly parallel executions may offer lower response times. Their energy efficiency, however, can decrease due to parallelization overhead in the shape of additional task distribution and synchronization effort.

Definition 2.4 defines energy efficiency as the amount of useful work done for an amount of energy consumed. In order to compare the energy efficiency of systems, the amount of useful work done is usually kept constant. When comparing the energy efficiency of two systems, it is more intuitive to compare the inverse energy efficiency, i.e., the amount of energy consumed per unit of work:

Definition 2.5 (Difference in Energy Efficiency). *The difference Δ_{EE} in EE of two software systems I and Z is the difference in energy E consumed to complete the same amount of work W:*

$$\Delta_{EE}(I, Z, W) = \frac{E_I - E_Z}{W}.$$

The efficient operation of data center infrastructure is an important cost factor, as Section 1.1 motivated. Barroso et al. [13] present a definition of data center energy efficiency:

Definition 2.6 (Data Center Energy Efficiency). *The energy efficiency of a data center is:*

$$EE = (\frac{1}{PUE}) \times (\frac{1}{SPUE}) \times (\frac{Computation}{Total\ Energy\ on\ Electric\ Components}),\ where$$

- *Power Usage Effectiveness (PUE) measures the facility efficiency,*
- *Server Power Usage Effectiveness (SPUE) quantifies the server power conversion efficiency, and*
- $\frac{Computation}{Total\ Energy\ on\ Electric\ Components}$ *is the energy efficiency of the server.*

The data center energy efficiency definition separates the definition of server energy efficiency, server power conversion efficiency (SPUE), and facility efficiency (PUE). This makes the definition compatible with the previously discussed definition of server energy efficiency.
The factor $\frac{\text{Computation}}{\text{Total Energy on Electric Components}}$ corresponds to the definition of energy efficiency in Definition 2.4.

Definition 2.7 (Power Usage Effectiveness (PUE)). *PUE estimates the facility efficiency as the ratio of total power consumed by the data center facility divided by the power consumed by IT equipment [13]:*

$$PUE = \frac{Facility\ Power}{IT\ Equipment\ Power}.$$

PUE can be modeled as a fixed factor-based on historical measurements or derived from estimation models, e.g., for facility power conversion losses and cooling infrastructure. SPUE is the ratio of "power consumed by the electronic components directly involved in the computation" and the total server consumption [13]. Example components involved in the computation are CPU and HDD. The total consumption subsumes further power consumption from conversion losses, or internal server cooling equipment.

2.3. Power Management

This section provides an overview of the technical foundations of power management on the level of individual servers, and data centers.

Power management mechanisms can be grouped into two categories. *Active power management* [145] mechanisms directly control the power consumption by changing the configuration of hardware components. An example active power management mechanism is Dynamic Voltage and Frequency Scaling (DVFS) and its integration with Advanced Configuration and Power Interface (ACPI), which the next section discusses. *Indirect power management*, or what Nathuji [145] refer to as *Soft Scaling*, aims to reduce power consumption by migrating load away from or reducing load on computing resources.

Indirect power management exploits the energy (dis-)proportionality of servers and their components. For example, modern server have a drastically reduced power consumption when idle [68]. Load consolidation to a smaller number of servers can consequently reduce the power consumption of a software system. The reason for the reduced consumption is that the marginal increase in power consumption on the hosts remaining after the consolidation is much lower than the consumption decrease achieved by clearing up underutilized servers. The underutilized server may then be turned off or switched into lower power states via active power management mechanisms.

On a fully utilized system, the previously discussed power management approaches can not be applied to reduce power consumption without affecting performance. Application *brownout* is an indirect power management technique [229] that can be employed for fully utilized systems. Brownout-compliant applications may "downgrade user experience to avoid saturation" [109]. Xu et al. [229] use brownout-compliant applications to uphold the throughput of applications by reducing the quality of the output.

2.3.1. ACPI

The Advanced Configuration and Power Interface (ACPI) [86] is a standardized interface for motherboard configuration and power management. ACPI was developed as a common standard to enable the implementation of configuration management that is independent of firmware specifics. It is the standard power management interface of PCs and servers. ACPI lets the operating system control the power performance tradeoff for devices and hardware components using a set of predefined states. Within the lower power states, functionality and speed of the devices is limited. There are five types of states in ACPI:

- Global system states (Gx-states) control the power state of the full system. There exist four Gx-states. G0 is the working state, G1 the sleep state. G2 is the soft off, and G3 the mechanical off state.
- Device power states (Dx-states) define the available managed states of hardware components other than the CPU. Example components controlled via Dx-states are network adapters and HDDs. D0 is the on state, while D1-D3 are low power states.
- Processor power states (Cx-states) support power savings by temporarily disabling the execution of instructions. The active processing state C0, and the power state C1 are mandatory. Optional states beyond C1 may be offered to implement lower-power inactive states.
- Target throttling states (Tx-states) optionally support alternative power/performance trade-offs via a reduction of CPU frequency.
- Device and processor performance states (PX-states) offer different power/performance trade-offs within the C0 and D0 states of processors and devices, respectively. In addition to the lower power state P1, up to 14 further performance states can be supported.

Recently, there has been a shift to implement the power management policies in hardware [62]. This allows for a higher responsiveness of power management, but reduces flexibility of the used policies.

2.3.2. Power Capping

As the power draw of hardware components changes with their utilization, a static power provisioning infrastructure on average still ends up being largely underutilized. The reason for this is that the infrastructure not only needs to be able to handle the average consumption load, but also peaks in power usage. *Power capping* is a technique that addresses this problem by dynamically regulating the power draw of hardware components. This is done by switching the components between low and high power states.

Software-level power management controllers commonly use ACPI [86]. There is a multitude of strategies [25] and system architectures [167] for optimizing the power allocation in distributed computer systems. Controlling the power consumption allows for much higher Power Supply Unit (PSU) and Power Distribution Unit (PDU) utilization since the risk of breakdowns is reduced.

Data center power management is often implemented atop the Intelligent Platform Management Interface (IPMI) [99]. IPMI supports the control of server power states as part of its network resource management protocol. On local servers it leverages interfaces such as ACPI to enact power management decisions.

2.4. Self-Adaptive Software Systems

Self-adaptive software systems can adapt their structure and deployment, as well as functionality, to changing environmental conditions. This enables them to maintain SLAs under variable user load, or software and hardware failures.

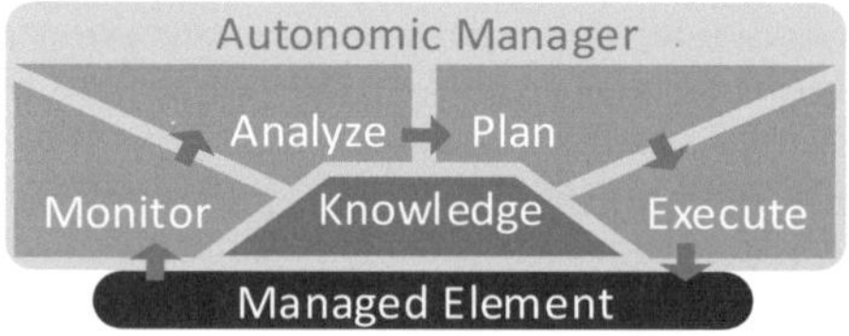

Figure 2.2.: MAPE-K control loop introduced by Kephart et al. [105].

The most prevalent model for structuring self-adaptive systems is the Monitor, Analyze, Plan, Execute, Knowledge (MAPE-K) control loop [105]. In the control loop illustrated in Figure 2.2 an *Autonomic Manager* adapts a *Managed*

Element. The Autonomic Manager follows a continuous iterative process when adapting the system. In a first step, the manager collects data from sensors in the system. These sensors capture system metrics, e.g. the average response times of a specific service over the last minute. The Autonomic Manager then analyzes the measurements to determine if it is necessary to adapt the system. This might be the case if the response times violate QoS agreements. Based on the analysis the Autonomic Manager chooses a set of adaptation actions in the *Plan* step. The planned actions are enacted in the *Execute* step. The adaptation actions can encompass adaptations to both software and hardware of a managed software system. After the autonomic manager has completed a loop iteration, it checks if the adaptations were effective in successive Monitor-Analyze steps. If necessary, the manager triggers further adaptations.

Besides measurements from the system, the Autonomic Manager makes its decisions on the *Knowledge* base that contains information on the system structure and state. Commonly, one part of the Knowledge base of a software system is its representation in an architectural model [97]. An advantage of architecture level adaptation frameworks over low level implementations of MAPE-K is that the current system state and adaptations are easier to comprehend, e.g., for a system operator. Example frameworks that use a an architecture model as the foundation for reasoning of the Autonomic Manager are Descartes [93] and RAINBOW with its Stitch extension [51]. The following section Section 2.4.1 discusses how architecture-based adaptation frameworks describe the space of potential adaptation actions. Section 2.4.2 outlines a method that supports the description of complex adaptation logic from a set of adaptation actions.

2.4.1. Adaptation Point Models

Adaptation decisions made by a an architecture-based self-adaptation frameworks need to be performed automatically as part of the MAPE-K loop. The Autonomic Manager of an architecture-based adaptation framework requires access to an executable description or implementation of potential adaptation operations.

In order to support systematic runtime adaptations, Huber et al. [96] propose to represent the available runtime adaptation operations as part of an

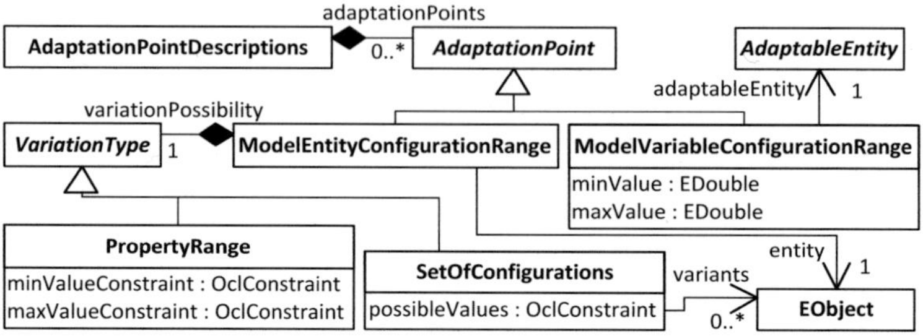

Figure 2.3.: Adaptation points meta-model proposed by Huber et al. [95].

explicit adaptation space model. The model enables automated model-driven reasoning and decision-making on the choice of adaptation actions. The *Adaptation Points* metamodel [95] spans the adaptation space available to the adaptation framework. Figure 2.3 depicts the metamodel. The Adaptation Points metamodel enables the specification of possible variations in the software architecture-based on value or property ranges. It defines the domain of configurations targeted by the execution of adaptation actions. For example, the space of alternative VM deployments compatible to a certain hypervisor would be specified as a `SetOfConfigurations` variation type with values ranging all the servers running the hypervisor, as Huber [94, p. 157] illustrates. A VM deployment action may only deploy new VMs on compatible hypervisors.

2.4.2. Strategies, Tactics, Action (S/T/A)

Strategies, Tactics, Action (S/T/A) is a modeling concept that hierarchically structures adaptation mechanisms into strategies, tactics, and actions.

An *action* is a reconfiguration operation supported by the execution environment of the software system. Example actions are VM migrations or the change of media encoding quality of a media encoder.

A *tactic* composes multiple adaptation actions. Each tactic comes with an estimated expected benefit that results from its execution. This enables a preemptive evaluation of adaptation tactics before they are executed. Each tactic "is guarded by a dynamically evaluated precondition that determines" whether a tactic can be applied [51]. Adaptation tactics are also referred to as adaptation rules. An example of a tactic is the consolidation of VMs in an Infrastructure as a Service (IaaS) data center. First, all VMs deployed to an under-utilized host are migrated to other nodes via the VM migration. Subsequently, the original host is shut down using the corresponding operator.

A *strategy* defines a reactive process for managing a software system using a set of adaptation tactics. It consists of "a tree of condition-action-delay decision nodes with explicitly defined probability for conditions and a delay time-window for observing tactic effects" [51]. The probabilities of executing the tactics can be adapted based on their previous success or failure. The success of a tactic is determined after a predefined delay has passed. It is checked by evaluating whether the tactic has managed to fulfill the previously violated condition.

Examples of S/T/A languages are Stitch and the S/T/A modules of Descartes Modeling Language (DML). Cheng and Garlan [51] propose a self-adaptation language Stitch that structures the adaptation space into *strategies, tactics* and *operators.* Operators correspond to actions.

Huber et al. propose an S/T/A modeling language for designing "run-time system adaptations in component-based system architectures" [96]. Like Cheng and Garlan [51], Huber et al. structure the adaptation process into stragies, tactics and actions (S/T/A). Strategies formulate a high-level QoS objective such as maintaining response times below a certain threshold. Tactics specify how an objective is achieved by successively performing a set of actions. Actions always refer to an adaptation point in the software system [96].

2.5. Palladio

Palladio is a an architecture-level approach for the systematic engineering of component-based software systems in early design phases [170]. It uses the Palladio Component Model (PCM) to describe the architecture of software systems. PCM has similarities to UML component diagrams and UML

Marte [211]. What sets PCM apart from standard UML are its included quality annotations. PCM was designed to be composable. This enables the reuse of, e.g., component specifications in different software architecture models. Palladio supports the analysis of different QoS characteristics based on the quality annotations. Foundation of the Palladio analyses is the PCM. Supported quality dimensions include performance [22], reliability [33], cost [111], maintainability [176], and elasticity [124].

This section provides an overview of the parts of Palladio that this thesis builds upon. It is structured as follows. Section 2.5.1 introduces the PCM. Section 2.5.2 discusses SimuLizar, which extends Palladio to the domain of self-adaptive software systems. In Section 2.5.3, we outline the Palladio software performance simulators. Section 2.5.4 sketches the quality analysis workflow with Palladio.

2.5.1. Palladio Component Model (PCM)

The Palladio Component Model (PCM) is a modeling language for the description of component-based software architectures. Its purpose is the modeling of characteristics that are required for design time analyses of QoS properties. PCM is realized as a Essential Meta-Object Facility (EMOF)-based metamodel. The core PCM couples the structural description of software components with a high level description of their performance and reliability characteristics.

PCM separates different architectural design concerns into distinct modeling viewpoints. The components are modeled in the *Repository* viewpoint. The *System* viewpoint instantiates and composes components from the Repository viewpoint into a software system. PCM models the deployment environment and its hardware characteristics in the *Resource Environment* viewpoint. The hardware characteristics concern performance and reliability properties, which are required to reason on these quality characteristics. *Allocation* maps the component instances in the System to the deployment environment described in the Resource Environment. The *Usage* viewpoint models a set of users and their interactions with the systems. A separate model instantiates each of the viewpoints. This eases the composition of models that represent the viewpoints.

A viewpoint encompasses the modeling concerns that are relevant to a specific role in the Palladio development process [170]. The *component developer* designs component specifications using the Repository viewpoint. In the System viewpoint, the *software architect* assembles the components to a software architecture. The *system deployer* defines the execution environment of the architecture, and deploys the components to the environment. The *domain expert* models users and their interaction patterns with the system.

The following sections provide further details on the viewpoints of Palladio.

2.5.1.1. Repository Viewpoint

The Repository viewpoint addresses the modeling of software components. Component developers use the viewpoint to model components and their provided and required interfaces.

Figure 2.4 illustrates the relationship of a set of key modeling constructs in the Repository viewpoint. It shows an example component definition in the Repository viewpoint. The depicted component *A* has a required and provided interface. Its component specification references the provided interface *MyInterface* via a *Provided Role*. A *Required Role* specifies the required interface *YourInterface* of *A*.

Component developers may specify the behavior of components stored in the Repository. Service Effect Specifications (SEFFs) model the behavior of services provided by a component. A SEFF is an abstract specification of the behavior of a component. It describes the "relationship between provided and required services of a component" [171, p. 53]. SEFFs model the behavior of components similar to UML activity diagrams.

Resource-Demanding Service Effect Specification (RDSEFF) specializes SEFF to model the performance impact of service calls. RDSEFF models the behavior as a sequence of actions. Actions may be control flow abstractions, e.g., branches, loops and forks. *External Actions* model calls to external required services. *Internal Actions* model the performance impact of a set of operations. It describes the impact in terms of execution costs on resources like CPUs. The action models the execution cost as a *Resource Demand*. A Resource Demand can model the cost of a single hardware instruction,

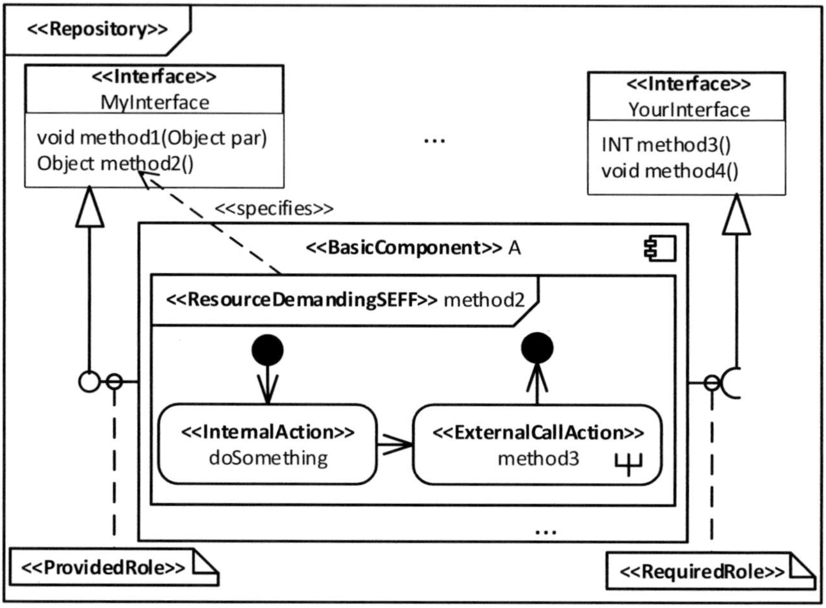

Figure 2.4.: Illustration of modeling construct subset supported by the Repository viewpoint. The figure is based on [171, p. 38].

or subsume the performance impact of a set of calls that are not explicitly modeled. Commonly, Resource Demands are specified as the amount of time it takes to process an instruction relative to the speed of a resource, e.g., CPU.

Component A in Figure 2.4 is annotated with an RDSEFF. It contains two actions that describe the behavior of calls to *method2*. The Internal Action *doSomething* consumes a specified amount of Resource Demand, which the figure omits. The External Call Action links the call sequence to the required service *method3*.

PCM supports the modeling of Resource Demands using stochastic distribution functions. Dependencies to input parameters can be expressed via parametric dependencies. PCM uses the Stochastic Expressions (StoEx) language [21] to specify Resource Demands, including their distribution and parametric dependencies.

2.5.1.2. System Viewpoint

The *System* viewpoint instantiates the components from Repositories. *Assembly Context* is the construct in the System viewpoint that can be used to instantiate a component from a Repository. A component can be instantiated multiple times. Each Assembly Context has a set of component parameters. These parameters can be used to model instantiation specific settings. The system architect composes the Assembly Contexts using *Assembly Connectors*. An Assembly Connector wires a required interface of a component instance to the provided interface of another component instance.

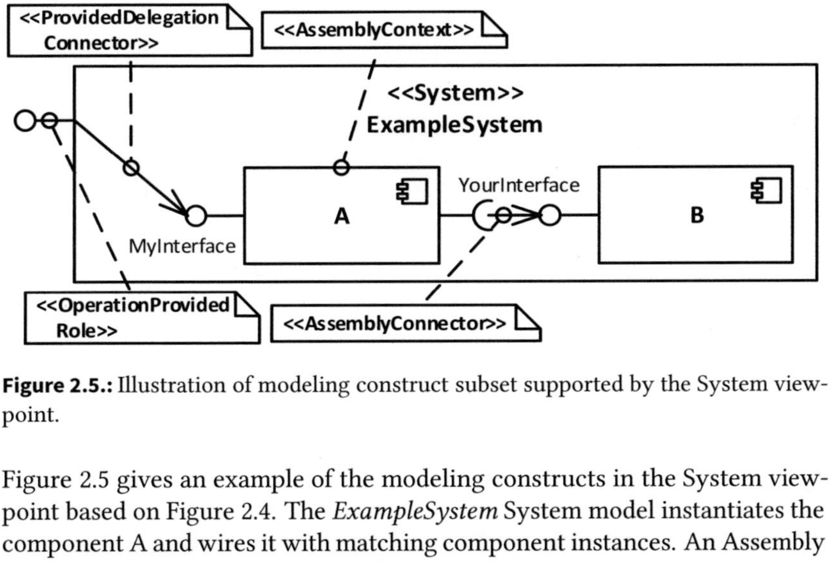

Figure 2.5.: Illustration of modeling construct subset supported by the System viewpoint.

Figure 2.5 gives an example of the modeling constructs in the System viewpoint based on Figure 2.4. The *ExampleSystem* System model instantiates the component A and wires it with matching component instances. An Assembly Context instantiates A. An Assembly Connector links the Required Role of A with the Provided Role of B that offers *YourInterface*. An *Operation Provided Role* exposes the provided interface *MyInterface* to users of *ExampleSystem*. A *Provided Delegation Connector* links the System role to the role of A.

2.5.1.3. Resource Environment and Allocation Viewpoint

The *Resource Environment* viewpoint models the deployment environment of a software system. It focuses on properties that are relevant to performance or reliability. The modeled properties include servers and their resources, e.g., CPUs and HDDs. Additionally, middleware specific properties can be modeled in the Resource Environment.

Figure 2.6 depicts an excerpt of the metamodel classes from the viewpoint, which are relevant in the scope of this thesis. The figure omits reliability characteristics. In addition to the Resource Environment, it includes classes from the supplemental *Resource Type* repository are included. *Resource Environment* contains a set of *Resource Containers* and *Linking Resource.* A Resource Container represents an execution environment, to which components may be deployed. It represents either a physical server, VM, or other deployment environments like enterprise web servers. Resource Containers can contain other Resource Containers. This enables the modeling of hierarchies in the deployment environment.

A Resource Container has a set of *Processing Resource Specifications.* A Processing Resource Specification models processing resources such as a CPU. Its *processing rate* defines the rate at which the resource is able to serve Resource Demands which are scheduled on it. The *number of replicas* is the number of redundant instances of processing units that can be used in parallel. For CPUs it specifies the number of cores.

Resource Type is a supplementary viewpoint. It models *Resource Types,* e.g., CPU and storage resources. Each Processing Resource Specification references its Resource Type. The Resource Type viewpoint includes the definition of *Scheduling Policies.* A Scheduling Policy represents the policy with which the resource serves requests. An example policy is first come, first served (FCFS).

The *Allocation* viewpoint models the deployment of component instances to the execution environment. It contains a set of *Allocation Contexts.* Every Allocation Context maps an Assembly Context to a Resource Container. In combination, Allocation and Resource Environment correspond to the deployment diagram in UML.

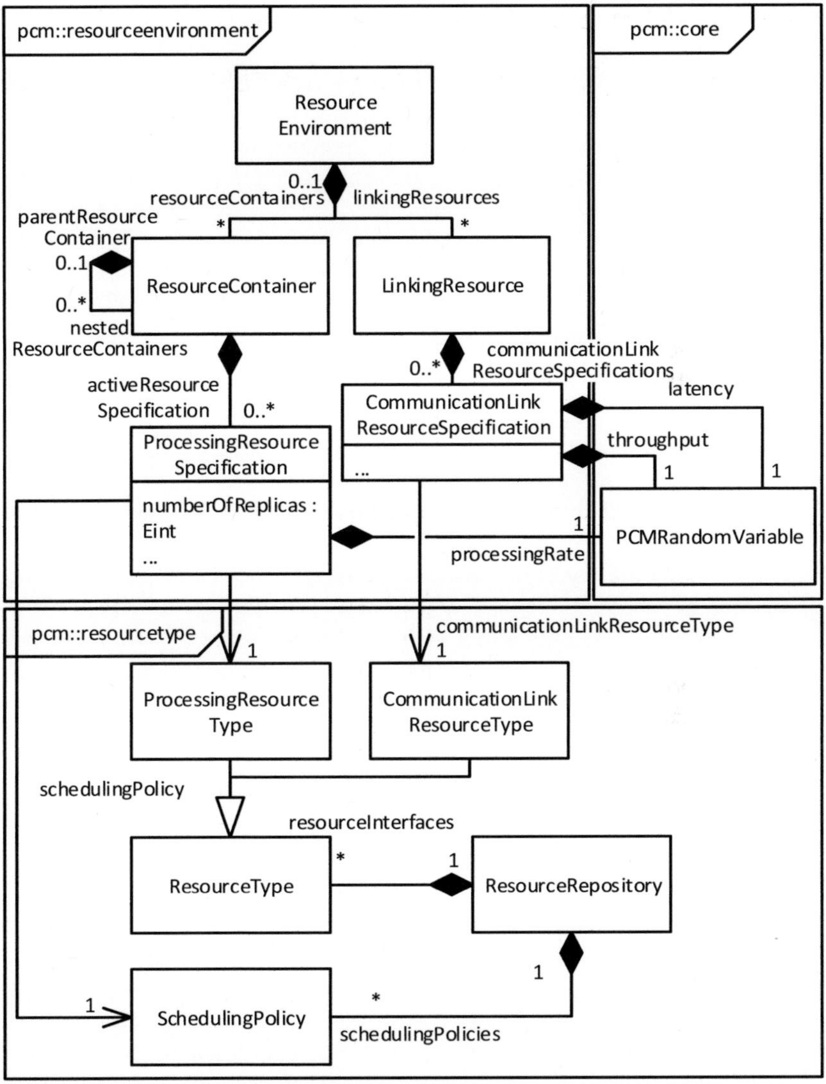

Figure 2.6.: Excerpt of Resource Environment and Resource Type viewpoints. Reliability characteristics are omitted.

2.5.1.4. Usage Viewpoint

The Usage viewpoint models user frequency and behavior of users that interact with the software system. PCM groups users in categories, the *Usage Scenarios*. A Usage Scenario models the behavior of a group of users in a similar way to SEFFs. The domain expert characterizes a Usage Scenario by its number of users, and their behavior. The Usage Scenario models the behavior as a sequence of branches, loops, forks, and calls to the system. Scenarios can issue calls to all services of the *OperationProvidedRoles* of the system. The *Usage* root element stores a set of Usage Scenarios in a Usage model. Palladio analyses consider all contained scenarios to execute concurrently.

PCM distinguishes two types of Usage Scenarios. A *Closed Workload* scenario models a group of users with a fixed population size, e.g., four users. Each user starts a new run every time an iteration of the Usage Scenario completes. User think and wait times can be modeled using *Delay* actions. Each time a user completes an execution of the scenario in a Closed Workload, the next user immediately starts executing. *Open Workload* models assume an open user model, where a new user arrives at the system every t time units. For example, a user could arrive at the system every four seconds. This *interarrival time* can be modeled using stochastic distribution functions. This enables the modeling of fluctuations of user populations according to a distribution.

2.5.2. SimuLizar — Modeling and Analyzing Self-Adaptive Software Systems with Palladio

Palladio initially focused on the systematic design of static component-based software systems. Becker extended the Palladio approach to self-adaptive software systems [17, 18, 20] in order to support the systematic design time engineering of self-adaptive software systems. The name of the extended approach is *SimuLizar*. SimuLizar also refers to the subsumed simulation-based analysis which supports the design time quality analysis of self-adaptive software systems. This section provides an overview of the central extensions of SimuLizar.

Becker [17] introduces the *self-adaptive system architect* role, who is responsible for modeling the dynamic behavior of the system. The self-adaptive system architect is responsible for the same tasks as the software architect in standard Palladio. Additionally, the self-adaptive system architect is responsible for specifying the adaptation behavior of the system. She specifies the behavior in the *self-adaptation viewpoint* [17]. The self-adaptation viewpoint encompasses the specification of reconfiguration mechanisms, and runtime measurements. We refer to [17, p. 68] for a detailed discussion of the integration of self-adaptivity with the modeling process.

This section introduces the modeling and analysis approach by Becker, which this thesis extends. It is structured as follows. Section 2.5.2.1 details how measurement points can be specified in SimuLizar. Section 2.5.2.2 introduces how reconfigurations are specified with SimuLizar. In addition, the section discusses the model for capturing measurements. The reconfigurations may form their adaptation decisions based on the captured measurements. Section 2.5.2.3 outlines an extension to the Usage viewpoint that supports the modeling of load variations and patterns.

2.5.2.1. Monitor Model

The *Monitor* model enables software architects to specify *which* measurements should be collected *where* and *how* in the self-adaptive software system. The collected measurements serve as input to adaptation mechanisms. An example adaptation tactic could trigger adaptation actions when the response time becomes too large.

The Monitor model contains a set of Monitors. Each Monitor references a measuring point in the system under design. The measuring point defines a location in the system at which measurements should be collected. For example, a measuring point may reference a processing resource in a Resource Container.

In addition to the measuring point specification, a Monitor contains a measurement specification. The measurement specification identifies the metric for which measurements should be collected at the measuring point. CPU utilization is an example metric that can be collected at a measuring point installed at a processing resource. Monitors support the specification of an aggregation method and aggregation interval for the metric. For example, CPU utilization might be aggregated over a sliding window interval of a specific length.

2.5.2.2. Adaptation Specification and Runtime Measurement

SimuLizar enables architects to specify the dynamic behavior of a self-adaptive software system. It supports the definition of adaptation mechanisms via in-place model transformations. The model transformations operate on the runtime model of the system. The runtime model represents the runtime state of the simulated software system. If the runtime state meets a set of specified conditions, a transformation reconfigures the system by performing a series of model change operations. For example, an adaptation transformation may add an additional Resource Container to the Resource Environment in order to increase the available computational power. Following this adaptation, reconfigurations can allocate additional component instances on the newly available Resource Container.

SimuLizar uses an instance of PCM as the initial architecture configuration of the self-adaptive system. SimuLizar represents the runtime state of the system, the runtime model, in an instance of PCM. In the scope of this thesis, we added the ability to extend the runtime model by further models. Thereby, additional system aspects like power management can be exposed to adaptation mechanisms.

SimuLizar uses the Palladio Runtime Measurement Model (PRM) to expose measurements to reconfiguration mechanisms. Example measurements are the current CPU utilization and service response times. The measurements represent the state of the simulated software system at the current point in the analysis. Source of the measurements is the simulation-based analysis. The PRM contains the measurements for all measurement points and aggregation methods, which the Monitor model specifies.

Becker [17] presents a metamodel which integrates individual adaptation transformations into an S/T/A framework. The transformations specify conditions for adaptation strategies as well as the execution semantics of adaptation actions. Becker touches upon a potential modeling of resource demands that result from the execution of reconfigurations [17, 98 f.]. The author, however, does not outline the analytical semantics of the sketched modeling.

2.5.2.3. Usage Evolution Model

The *Usage Evolution* [31] model enables domain experts to specify usage patterns and trends in the behavior and number of users that interact with a software system. Interactive software systems seldom serve a fixed number of users with a fixed set of requests. PCM expresses the variability of user requests and interests via stochastic processes. Variations in interarrival rates and requests can be modeled using the StoEx language. Under realistic conditions, the distribution of users and their requests does not remain constant over time. Rather, it follows usage patterns and trends [106].

Brataas et al. [31] introduce the Usage Evolution viewpoint as an extension to the Usage viewpoint of PCM. The Usage Evolution viewpoint is realized as an annotation model to PCM. Figure 2.7 provides an overview of the Usage Evolution metamodel. Usage Evolution consists of a set of *Usages*. Each Usage instance models the variation in a Usage Scenario as a pattern. If the Usage Scenario contains an open workload, the pattern models the variation in the interarrival rate over time. For closed workloads, Usage describes a variation in the user population.

Usage expresses the *loadEvolution* workload pattern variation as an instance of the Descartes Load Intensity Model (DLIM) [106]. DLIM is a metamodel for defining load variations as functions over time. Figure 2.7 shows the core classes of DLIM. *Sequence* is the central entity in the metamodel. It defines a load pattern as a set of piecewise defined *Functions*. *TimeDependentFunction-Container* embeds a Function into a definition interval of length *duration*. The starting point of the Function is defined relative to an internal clock. The metamodel excerpt omits this clock reference. DLIM supports different primitive function types and patterns, e.g., *Seasonal* or *Burst*. Functions can be folded with other functions by applying a *Combinator* to an existing function.

In addition to user intensity variations, Usage Evolution supports the modeling of parameter variations. Each Usage may contain any number of *WorkParameterEvolutions*. A *WorkParameterEvolution* models the variation

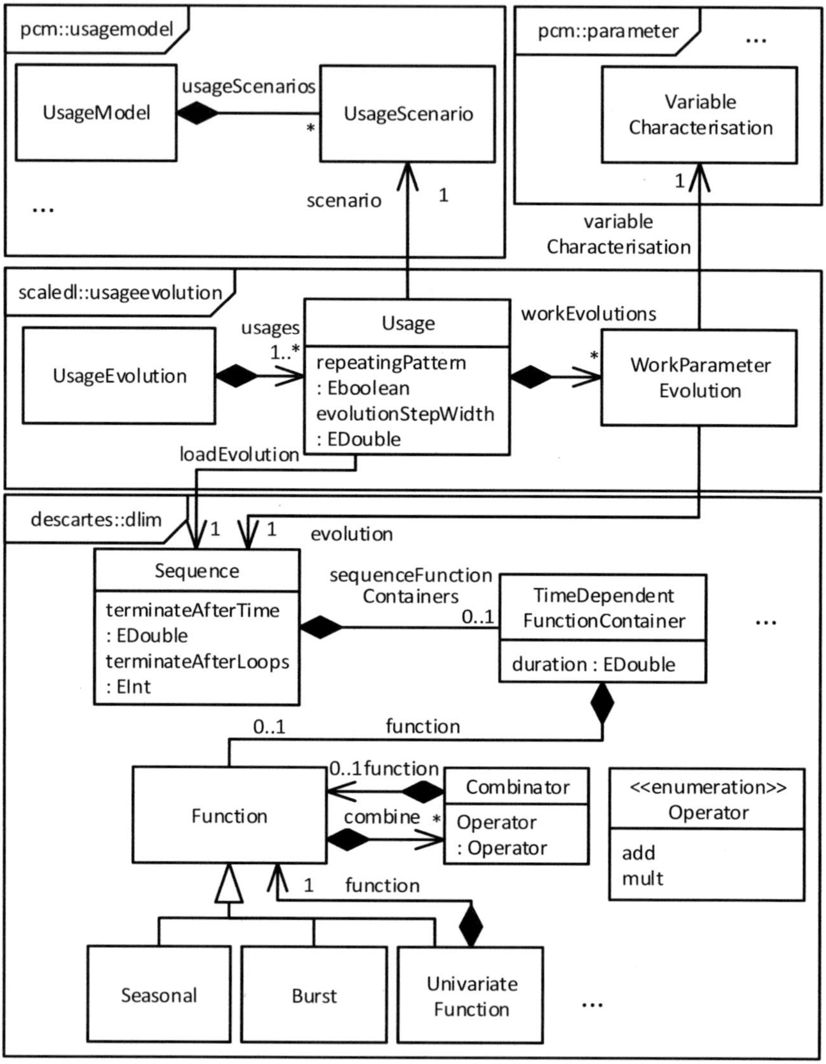

Figure 2.7.: Usage Evolution viewpoint.

of a parameter in any of the PCM viewpoints. The DLIM Sequence referenced by *evolution* models this variation as a function over time.

2.5.3. Software Performance Simulation

There are different analytical [113, 156] and simulation-based quality analysis approaches [18, 22, 138] for PCM. They enable software architects to reason on quality characteristics of software systems that are represented as PCM instances. The following gives an overview of the two performance simulators SimuCom and SimuLizar. This thesis employs the analyses to evaluate the performance of software systems. We use their performance predictions as input to our power consumption analysis. Additionally, this thesis extends SimuLizar to enable reasoning on energy-conscious self-adaptive software systems.

2.5.3.1. SimuCom

SimuCom [21, 22] is a Discrete Event Simulation (DES)-based software simulator for PCM instances. SimuCom supports the analysis of performance and reliability characteristics of software systems. SimuCom uses model transformations to generate a software performance simulator from a PCM instance. The generated simulation code uses SimuCom framework functionality, e.g., to simulate processing resources and their scheduling policies. Example QoS metrics supported by SimuCom are response times of individual user requests, and resource utilization. SimuCom only supports the analysis of static software systems.

2.5.3.2. SimuLizar

SimuLizar [17, 18, 20] is a software performance simulator for self-adaptive software systems. It implements the SimuLizar approach by Becker [17] for modeling and analyzing self-adaptive software systems at design time. Section 2.5.2 introduced the modeling concepts of SimuLizar. The SimuLizar implementation builds upon the SimuCom simulation framework. In contrast to SimuCom, it does not generate simulation code for each PCM instance.

SimuLizar supports the consideration of dynamic aspects in the the behavior and environment of a system under investigation. This includes the variation of user load or behavior over time.

In SimuLizar, Adaptation mechanisms are expressed as in-place model transformations. SimuLizar has been built to support the flexible extension of different model transformation languages and engines. Example model transformation languages supported by SimuLizar are QVTo and Henshin [6]. In addition to the performance metrics of SimuCom, SimuLizar makes it possible for architects to reason on elasticity metrics. Becker et al. [19] provide details on these metrics.

2.5.4. Quality Analysis Workflow with Palladio

Software architects can leverage Palladio to evaluate the effect of design decisions on quality before they are implemented. The central advantage of PCM over general-purpose modeling languages like UML is its focus on quality-aware software architecture specification. PCM models characterize the quality properties of individual hardware and software components in a composable manner. This section sketches how software quality can be performed as part of a quality-aware development process. The steps discussed in the following must not be performed sequentially. They are usually iteratively performed at different stages of the system design development. The PCM model can be refined once additional information becomes available in the development process. The presented workflow description is based on [170, pp. 213–215].

Figure 2.8 represents the quality analysis workflow. It depicts the interactions of the different roles that are involved in a model-based quality analysis using Palladio.

Component developers provide a behavior model of their component. They specify this model using the Repository viewpoint. The model contains a behavior description in the form of the SEFFs, which Section 2.5.1.1 introduced. The SEFFs must be annotated with quality characteristics in order to analyze the quality of the system. The performance analysis of a system, e.g., requires the specialized Resource-Demanding Service Effect Specifications (RDSEFFs). Component developers may estimate the Resource demands in

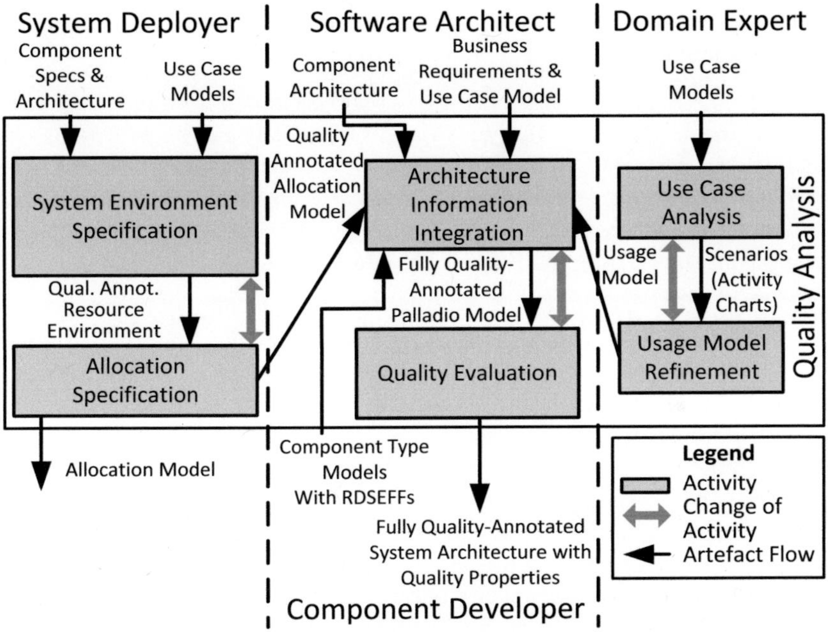

Figure 2.8.: Quality analysis workflow of the Palladio approach for the quality-aware software architecture design. Figure from [170, p. 213].

the RDSEFF via component micro-benchmarks or experience from previous implementations.

In the *System Environment Specification*, system deployers model the deployment environment of the software system using the Resource Environment viewpoint. This model contains quality annotations that, e.g., quantify the processing power of CPUs or throughput of HDDs. The system deployer provides a description of available or projected hardware. She may provide multiple alternative deployment descriptions to reason on QoS trade-offs related to infrastructure sizing. The deployer is furthermore responsible for mapping the components in the system architecture to the deployment environment. This step is part of the *Allocation* activity which produces an allocation models. The activity may produce multiple Allocation models to compare different allocation strategies, or allocations for different Resource Environment models.

The *Domain Expert* derives a set of users and scenarios from input use case models in the *Use Case Analysis.* The input models can be provided, e.g., as UML use case diagrams and accompanying textual descriptions. In later development stages, frontend monitoring data can serve as a source of user interactions. During *Usage Model Refinement*, the domain expert refines or transforms the existing models to PCM Usage Scenarios. For this, the expert enriches activity diagrams with performance related characteristics, e.g., call frequencies, user think times, and probabilistic request distributions.

The software architect drives and coordinates all tasks involved in the quality analysis workflow. The architect assembles individual component specifications from the component developers to a software architecture. She models the architecture as an instance of the PCM System model. The architect validates that the models cover all use cases and design alternatives that shall be explored in the quality analysis. If necessary, she requests the other involved roles to refine their models. The architect can also complete missing specifications in the environment and component models. Figure 2.8 represents this set of activities as the *Architecture Information Integration.* The software architect performs the quality analysis for all investigated quality dimensions. For this, the architect can choose from the available quality analysis approaches presented in the introductory paragraph of Section 2.5. The software architect iteratively checks the predicted quality of different software architecture variants against business requirements. Requirements may include tail response times, e.g., specified as part of SLAs. If the predictions show that the architecture under investigation violates quality requirements, "the software architect either has to modify the specifications or renegotiate the requirements" [170, p. 214].

2.6. Model Selection and AIC

The selection of a prediction model without knowledge of the final input data can be classified as a *model selection* problem. There are a variety of approaches for model selection [7]. In Software Performance Engineering

(SPE), model selection techniques are used to evaluate the quality of a performance model without full knowledge of the target workload. The k-fold cross-validation has been applied to evaluate the quality of performance model predictions [147, 225]. An alternative to k-fold cross-validation is the Akaike's Information Criterion (AIC).

The Akaike's Information Criterion (AIC) is an information-theoretic measure. It estimates the information loss between a model and the "unknown true mechanism" [42] which generated the data. For known distributions, the Kullback-Leibler distance quantifies this loss of information. AIC provides a way to estimate the loss when the underlying distribution is not known. It estimates the distance from the maximum value of the empirical log-likelihood function [42]:

Definition 2.8 (Akaike's Information Criterion (AIC)).
$AIC = -2 \log \mathcal{L}(\hat{\theta}|y + 2k)$, *where*

- $\mathcal{L}$ *is a log-likelihood function of a known distribution with an unknown parameter* θ,
- $\hat{\theta}$ *is the maximum likelihood estimate of the unknown parameter* θ,
- y *are empirical observations, or data,*
- k *is the number of parameters estimated by the model.*

For a set of models, a larger AIC indicates that a model is less likely, or plausible, to accurately describe the true mechanism that has produced y. AIC and k-fold cross-validation are asymptotically equivalent [202]. Compared to k-fold cross-validation, AIC is less complex to compute, as it does not require the partitioning of data. AIC is commonly applied to model selection problems of models which describe empirical data [42].

2.7. Validation Foundations

This section provides an overview of foundations of validation approaches and statistical methods which we use in the validation presented in Chapter 7.

2.7.1. Goal Question Metric Approach

The Goal Question Metric (GQM) approach by Basili et al. [15] systemizes the structuring and planning of experimental validations in the software engineering domain. In essence, the GQM approach enforces the orientation of a validation alongside quantifiable and measurable metrics.

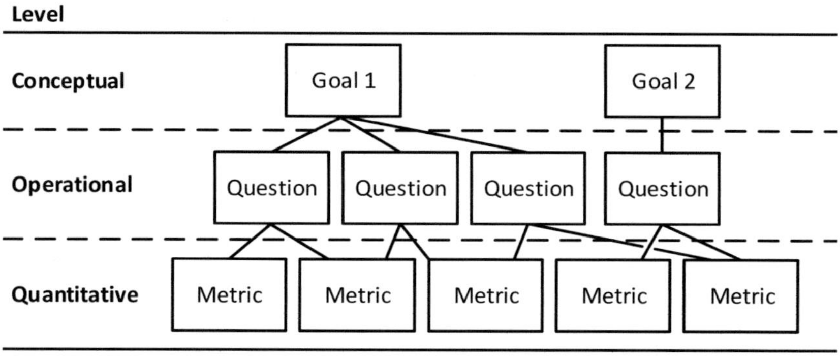

Figure 2.9.: Overview of GQM structure according to Basili et al. [15]

The GQM approach hierarchically structures goals, questions, and metrics. Figure 2.9 illustrates the hierarchical relation between them. Prerequisite of GQM is a definition of goals for the subject under investigation. Each goal has to be formulated so that it can be answered by collecting and analyzing a set of measurement data. Basili et al. name software products, processes, and resources as target candidate categories of goals. According to the authors, each goal should clearly state:

- The *purpose* of the validation,
- the *issue* to be measured,
- the measured *object*,
- the *viewpoint* from which the measurement is conducted.

The purpose hereby refers to the benefit of the approach which the validation is supposed to show. Typically, the viewpoint matches the target user, or beneficiary, of an approach. Table 2.1 lists an example goal statement,

Table 2.1.: Example of a goal formulated using the GQM approach.

Purpose	Improve
Issue	the prediction accuracy
Object	of performance predictions
Viewpoint	from the viewpoint of software architects.

which might be stated as part of the validation of a software performance simulator.

Each goal maps to a set of questions. A question characterizes a way in which the particular goal shall be validated. It refines the goal to a specific quality criterion, evaluated from a viewpoint [15]. For the validation goal listed in Table 2.1, a question could be:

Does the new simulator improve the prediction accuracy of design time architectural performance predictions?

On the lowest level of GQM every question relates to measurable metrics. Each metric serves as input to an answer of one or more higher level questions. Basili et al. [15] state that metrics may be objective or subjective. A metric is subjective if its value depends on the viewpoint from which it is collected. Conversely, it is objective if it does not depend upon the viewpoint. Subjective metrics may quantify, e.g., the user-perceived usability of a simulator on a scale from one to ten. An example objective metric, which answers the prior example question, is the mean response time prediction error of the new simulator compared to the simulation baseline.

2.7.2. Validation Levels

Böhme and Reussner [30] distinguish three levels in the validation of prediction models. The levels categorize validations by their validation purpose. The classification facilitates the estimation of validation effort and necessary measures to show certain properties of the validation object. It suffices to measure and compare the accuracy of the new and baseline approach to evaluate, e.g., if a new performance simulator has a higher prediction accuracy than a baseline approach. The validation levels are level I, II and III.

Level I is called *metric validation.* Validations categorized as level I conduct a validation as a comparison of predictions and measurements. A prerequisite to conduct a level I validation is that an implementation of the analytical metric required "to perform the predictions" is available [30]. Böhme and Reussner [30] note that this requires the metric to be computable. The authors note that the availability of an implementation could be classified as a level 0 validation. The authors, however, explicitly refrain from an introduction of a distinct level 0. Other authors establish a feasibility validation at level 0 [64, 83]. Heger [83] refers to this as a validation "through theoretical assessments".

Level II is the *applicability validation.* It evaluates whether "the input data can be acquired reliably and whether the results of the metric can be interpreted meaningfully" [30]. Böhme and Reussner state that if the input data is not collected automatically, the Level II validation "can be conducted as an experiment or a case study with human participants". Frequently, the definition of level II validation is reduced to its realization as an empirical user study. We also consider a validation a level II validation if the input data of the validated approach is collected automatically.

Level III is called *benefit validation.* Böhme and Reussner [30] prescribe this validation for analytical metrics that are part of a method that covers a software development approach. If this is the case, the validation needs to show the benefit of using the software development approach in comparison to established or competing approaches. A level III validation is difficult to conduct, as it relies on the availability of comparable approaches. Furthermore, it is resource intensive to realize the same software product using multiple development approaches.

2.7.3. Kernel Density Estimation (KDE)

When collecting measurement data, its underlying distribution is usually not known. Kernel Density Estimation (KDE) allows to approximate the distribution of the collected data [227]. The Kernel Density Estimation (KDE) estimates the *underlying true probability distribution* $p(x)$ *of data* $x_1, x_2, \ldots, x_n$ with the estimator $\hat{p}$ [227]:

Definition 2.9 (Kernel Density Estimation (KDE)). *Given a data set $x_1, x_2, \ldots, x_n$.*

$$\hat{p} = \frac{1}{n} \sum_{i=1}^{n} K_\sigma(x, x_i) = \frac{1}{n\sigma} \sum_{i=1}^{n} K[\frac{x - x_i}{\sigma}]$$

is an estimator of the probability distribution function of the data set. K_σ is a non-negative kernel function. with an integral value of 1.

Kernel functions are also known as window functions. This thesis uses the Gaussian kernel function. $\hat{p}$ converges towards the true probability distribution p with increasing size of the input data used to train the estimator.

KDE may be applied to estimate and visualize data distribution over the domain of $x_1, x_2, \ldots x_n$. Compared to histogram-based techniques, KDE is not affected by the choice of bin size and bin size distribution. Additionally, KDE is less prone to the curse of dimensionality.

2.7.4. Correlation Coefficients

Correlation coefficients quantify the relationship between variables. Correlation coefficients assume values between -1 and 1. Depending on the absolute value size, variables are estimated to have a strong or weak correlation. Positive correlation cofficients signal a positive correlation: If one variable increases, the other one increases as well. A negative correlation coefficient signifies an inverse relationship: If one variable increases, the other one decreases. Corder and Foreman [55] illustrate the significance of different coefficient values. Absolute correlation values closer to 0 indicate a weak (negative) correlation. Values closer to 1 signal a strong correlation. There are different statistical approaches for the calculation of correlation coefficient. The two subsequent sections present two well established correlation coefficiencts, which we use in the validation of this thesis.

2.7.4.1. Pearson's Correlation Coefficient

The sample correlation coefficient, or Pearson correlation coefficient, measures how well the relationship between two variables x and y may be described by a linear model $y = a + bx$. It is is defined as follows [175]:

Definition 2.10 (Pearson's Correlation Coefficient). *Let s_x, s_y be the sample standard deviations of x and y. The Pearson's correlation coefficient r of x and y is defined as:*

$$r = \frac{\sum_{i=1}^{n}(x_i - \bar{x})(y_i - \bar{y})}{(n-1)s_x s_y} = \frac{\sum_{i=1}^{n}(x_i - \bar{x})(y_i - \bar{y})}{\sqrt{\sum_{i=1}^{n}(x_i - \bar{x})^2}\sqrt{\sum_{i=1}^{n}(y_i - \bar{y})^2}}.$$

2.7.4.2. Spearman's Correlation Coefficient

The Spearman correlation coefficient, or Spearman rank-order correlation quantifies the relationship of two variables x and y. It is the Pearson correlation coefficient between the ranks of the two variables [55].

Definition 2.11 (Spearman's Correlation Coefficient). *The Spearman's correlation coeffient of two variables x and y is defined as:*

$$r_s = 1 - \frac{6\sum D_i^2}{n(n^2-1)},$$

if there are no ties in D_i. D_i is the difference in ranking of a variable pair in $X \times Y$, when ranked according to the relative position in X and Y. When there are ties, the Spearman's correlation coeffient is defined as:

$$r_s = \frac{(n^3-n) - 6\sum D_i^2 - (T_x+T_y)/2}{\sqrt{(n^3-n)^2 - (T_x+T_y)(n^3-n) + T_x T_y}}, \text{ where}$$

$$T_x = \sum_{i=1}^{g} t_i^3 - t_i, \text{ and } T_y = \sum_{i=1}^{g} t_i^3 - t_i.$$

Hereby, g is the number of ties between the ranks of x and y. t_i is the number of ties in a tie group [55].

Spearman's correlation coefficient expresses to which extent a monotonic function explains the relation between x and y. Compared to the Pearson's correlation coefficient, Spearman's correlation coefficient thus identifies a wider range of correlations.

3. Describing Power Consumption Characteristics of Software Systems

This chapter presents our modeling approach for the description of the power consumption characteristics of a software system. The contributions presented in this chapter build upon the publications [198, 200] and a supervised thesis [114].

This chapter consists of the following sections. Section 3.1 motivates challenges that the metamodel needs to consider. Section 3.2 outlines our metamodel for describing the power consumptions characteristics of a software system. Section 3.3 discusses assumptions and limitations of our modeling approach. Section 3.4 concludes with a summary of the presented modeling approach.

3.1. Challenges

This thesis aims to provide an approach that allows software architects to reason on power consumption characteristics of a software system. Research Question 1 formulates the problem that this chapter addresses:

Research Question 1. *What is a good abstraction level for modeling power consumption characteristics of software systems? We consider a model abstraction good if it*

- *produces accurate power consumption predictions,*
- *can be constructed from information available at design time,*

- *contains as little redundant information as possible with existing architectural modeling languages and viewpoints.*

In order to assess the power consumption characteristics of a software system, one needs a model that links the behavior of the system to its power consumption. Research Question 1 can be broken down into **Ch**allenges.

Ch_1 Suitable Level of Abstraction. The designed model needs to capture the power consumption characteristics on abstraction level that supports power consumption analyses with reasonable accuracy. Simultaneously, it should abstract from details of the execution environment and the software system that can not be predicted at design time.

Ch_2 Portability of model instances. Instances defined using the designed metamodel should capture power consumption characteristics so that they are applicable to multiple software systems and different user workloads. An important part of architectural analysis approaches like Palladio is the comparison of design alternatives before they are implemented. This allows architects to reason on the effect of design decisions without having to implement and benchmark them against each other. The approach presented in this thesis aims to support energy efficiency tradeoff decisions. The metamodel hence has to support analyses that estimate the effect of design decisions. For this, it must be possible to compare different power distribution infrastructure design alternatives with limited modification effort.

Ch_3 Limited semantic overlap with jointly used Architecture Description Language (ADL). The approach presented in this thesis is designed to be applied in conjunction with existing architectural modeling and analysis approaches. Architectural models like PCM capture system characteristics that are relevant to a set of design concerns. PCM focuses on the modeling and analysis of QoS goals related to performance and reliability. Energy efficiency is defined as the ratio of energy consumption and another QoS metric. For performance and reliability there is a strong link between energy consumption and the QoS of the system. The utilization of CPUs strongly correlates with their power consumption. The number of redundant components increases reliability as well as power consumption. The designed metamodel shall have limited semantic overlap with the architectural model used in conjunction with our model. The metamodel must not specify characteristics of a system that can already be derived from the architecture model.

Ch_4 **Non-invasive specification of power consumption characteristics and other quality characteristics.** The developed metamodel should not require changes to the core of an existing ADL. Users of quality aware ADLs usually do not want to consider all quality characteristics at once. The use of the model developed in this thesis should not be mandatory. Rather, it should be usable as an optional module that complements existing quality characteristic specifications.

Ch_5 **Compatibility of modeling constructs with different quality aware ADLs.** There are multiple quality aware ADLs with constructs that are specific to their problem domain, e.g., runtime management or design time analysis. The developed modeling shall be compatible with different ADLs. It should not be tailored to depend on language specifics of a single ADL.

3.2. A Metamodel for Specifying Power Consumption Characteristics

This section presents our metamodel for specifying the power consumption characteristics of software systems. We designed the model to address the challenges identified in the previous section. Our metamodel focuses on the description of power consumption characteristics of the hardware environment. The following refers to the metamodel as the *Power Consumption metamodel*.

Figure 3.1 provides a high-level overview of the package structure in the metamodel. Each of the packages in the metamodel corresponds to one of a set of layered viewpoints on the system under design. The Resource Environment package (*pcm::resourceenvironment*) refers to the deployment environment description in PCM. The Resource Environment viewpoint

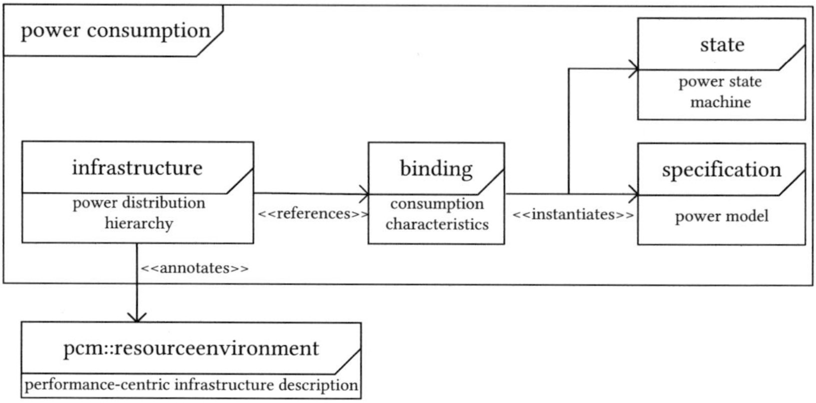

Figure 3.1.: Overview of the designed Power Consumption model.

contains the description of performance and reliability characteristics of the deployment environment as Section 2.5.1.3 explains. The *Infrastructure* viewpoint of the Power Consumption metamodel annotates the processing resources and representations of servers in the Resource Environment with their consumption characteristics. All other parts of the Power Consumption model are agnostic of the PCM or other ADL specific constructs. This strict separation of ADL specific annotation classes and independently reusable modeling constructs addresses Challenge Ch_4.

The Power Consumption metamodel has four viewpoints. Each of the viewpoints corresponds with a metamodel package.

The *Specification* viewpoint supports the definition of power model *types*. Power model types can be reused to describe the power consumption of different types of servers, devices, and processing resources. An example of a power model type is the linear power model based on a set of system utilization metrics:

$$P_{\text{lin}}(u_{\text{cpu}}, u_{\text{read}}, u_{\text{write}}) = c_0 + c_1 u_{\text{cpu}} + c_2 u_{\text{read}} + c_3 u_{\text{write}} \tag{3.1}$$

This linear power model predicts the power consumption of a server based on its CPU utilization u_{cpu}, disk read throughput u_{read} and write throughput u_{write}. P_{lin} is defined independently of the concrete power consumption profile of a server type. In order for P_{lin} to reflect the consumption of a specific server type, its parameters c_0 and c_m have to be instantiated. The resulting instance, the power model, reflects the static and dynamic power consumption of the server components.

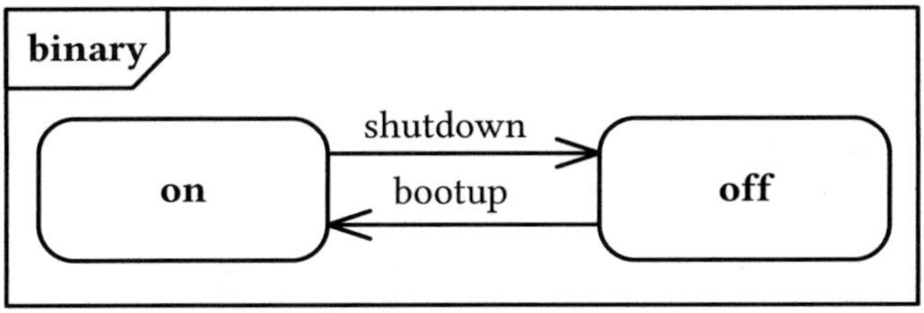

Figure 3.2.: Power State Model example of a server with two power states.

The *State* viewpoint supports the specification of stateful power models as state machines. Figure 3.2 shows an example PSM. The depicted example showcases a simple example of a PSM for a server that can be put in *on* and *off* states. There exist two transitions *bootup* and *shutdown* between the two states. Both transitions represent the transition of the server between its *on* and *off* state. The *State* viewpoint captures the definition of distinct power states. The state definition is independent of the power consumption characteristics of a specific device.

The *Binding* viewpoint encompasses elements for describing the consumption characteristics of specific server types and distribution infrastructure. It supports the modeling of power model instances using the definition of abstract power model types in the *Specification* viewpoint. Binding instantiates a power model type from the *Specification* viewpoint for a specific server type. An example instantiation of the power model type listed in 3.1 for a specific server type is:

$$\begin{aligned} P_{\text{lin, R815}}(u_{\text{cpu}}, u_{\text{read}}, u_{\text{write}}) &= 367.30\text{W} + 300.40\text{W} \cdot u_{\text{cpu}} \\ &+ 13.52\text{W} \cdot u_{\text{read}} + 10.06\text{W} \cdot u_{\text{write}} \end{aligned} \tag{3.2}$$

$P_{\text{lin, R815}}$ models the power consumption of an R815 PowerEdge server. It estimates the power consumption of the server based on its idle consumption, and the estimated correlation of CPU and HDD metrics with power consumption. The power model is specific to servers of the R815 type, but can be applied to any other servers of the same type.

The *Infrastructure* viewpoint describes the power distribution infrastructure of the deployment environment on a structural level. It annotates the Resource Environment with the description that specifies the relation of power consumers and power distribution equipment in the deployment environment. Furthermore, it defines consumption constraints specific to the deployment environment, i.e. upper consumption limits for power capping. The Infrastructure viewpoint defines the power consumption characteristics of servers and PDUs by referencing power model instances defined in the *Binding* viewpoint.

The following sections discuss the individual viewpoints of the model in greater detail. Section 3.2.1 introduces the Specification viewpoint. Section 3.2.2 presents the State viewpoint. In Section 3.2.3 we describe the Binding viewpoints. Section 3.2.4 discusses the Infrastructure viewpoint. Section 3.2.5 concludes with a discussion of the applicability of our Power Consumption metamodel to ADLs other than PCM.

3.2.1. Specification Viewpoint

Figure 3.3 provides an overview of the key entities in the Specification viewpoint. We omit utility attributes of model entities, e.g., Universally Unique Identifier (UUID), from this and all following figures. The viewpoint groups a set of power model types in the *PowerModelRepository*. *PowerModelSpecification* models the power model types. Instances of *PowerModelSpecification* model a relationship between a set of input variables, or factors, and the power consumption of an entity. *PowerModelSpecification* has a set of *ConsumptionFactors* that correlate with or contribute to the power consumption of the modeled entity.

PowerModelSpecifications can be characterized along two orthogonal dimensions. Figure 3.4 shows the relation between the two orthogonal modeling dimensions. The first dimension is the *distribution type*. It is concerned with the type of entity whose power consumption characteristics the model

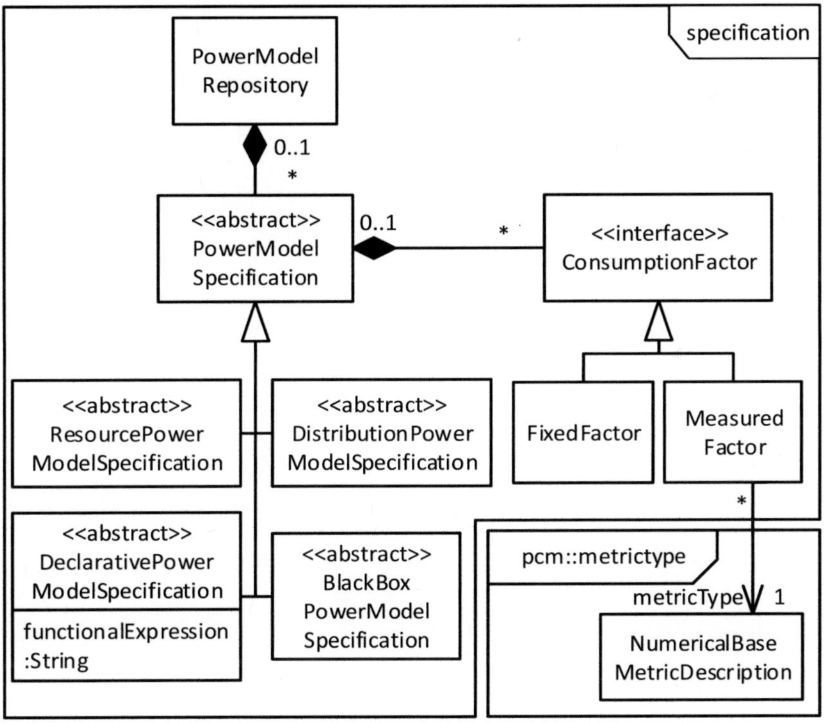

Figure 3.3.: Overview of Specification viewpoint used for defining power model types

explains. The *ResourcePowerModelSpecification* and *DistributionPowerModelSpecification* are two types along this dimension. The *ResourcePowerModelSpecification* models the power model of a resource, or device. *DistributionPowerModelSpecification* describes the consumption characteristics of distribution infrastructure, such as PDUs. The second dimension is the *implementation type* of a power model type. *BlackBoxPowerModelSpecification* refers to a power model type implemented by a black-box library, e.g., written in Java. Its design rationale is to support the specification of power models in code, as Section 4.4 outlines. The implementation of power model types in code is particularly helpful for functions that can not be represented by a closed-form expression, or when a closed form expression is difficult to formulate. Examples for such functions are Multivariate Adaptive

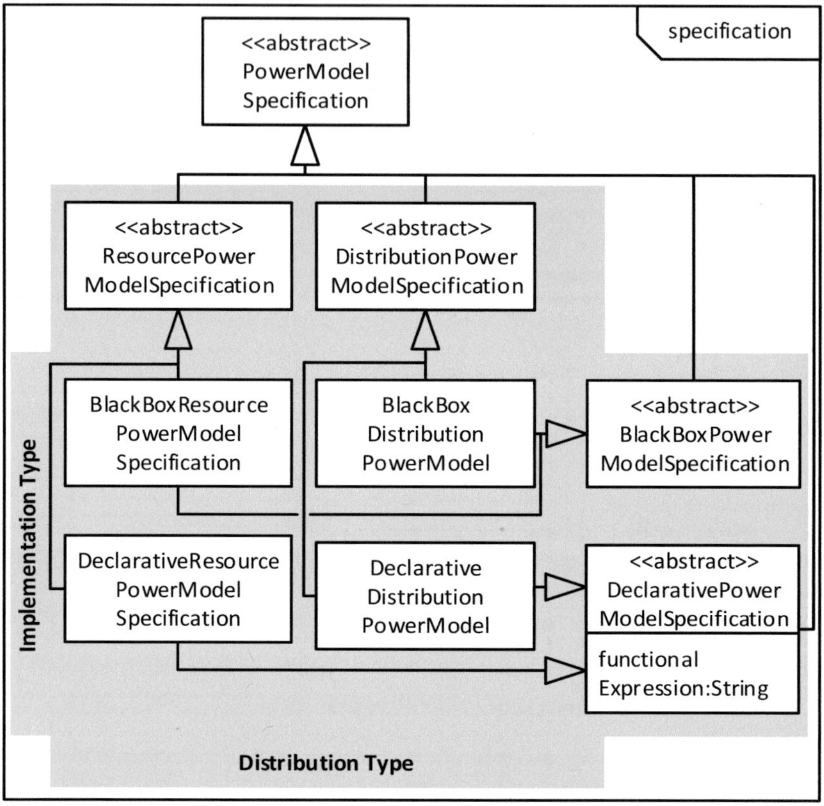

Figure 3.4.: Subtypes of orthogonal power model types for specifying power model types

Regression Splines (MARS) model as investigated by Davis et al. [57, 58] and Lewis et al. [127]. *DeclarativePowerModelSpecifications* define power models as mathematical expressions. The expressions conform to a grammar. Section 3.2.1.4 provides more details on the expressions.

The implementing classes in both dimensions are combined with all other implementing classes of the other dimensions. Figure 3.4 depicts the resulting subtypes. While the combination of two orthogonal classifications can also be solved by composition, as Strittmatter and Heinrich [203] outlined, we opted for an explicit modeling of all potential subtypes.

The following sections further elaborate on the elements in the Specification viewpoint.

3.2.1.1. Consumption Factors

A *ConsumptionFactor* models a factor in a software system which correlates with the power consumption of the software system. The Specification viewpoint differentiates between two factor types, *MeasuredFactors* and *FixedFactors*. A *FixedFactor* models a static factor impacting the power consumption of a device or distribution infrastructure component. In the case of regression models, a *FixedFactor* corresponds with an independent variable. Recalling the prior linear power model example from Equation 3.1, c_0 through c_3 are *FixedFactors*.

MeasuredFactors are measured metrics that influence or correlate with the power consumption of the entity. In contrast to *FixedFactors*, *MeasuredFactors* model dynamic power consumption factors. When *PowerModelSpecification* is a regression model, its *MeasuredFactors* specify the dependent variables of the regression function. In the linear power model example from Equation 3.1, CPU utilization u_{cpu}, disk read throughput u_{read}, and write throughput u_{write} are the *MeasuredFactors*. The factors of power models described in the Specification viewpoint are strictly typed by their units of measurement. The unit of a *MeasuredFactor* must be compatible with the unit of measurement of its *metricType*. The *metricType* characterizes the metric of the *MeasuredFactor* using the *NumericalBaseMetricDescription* entity from the Metric Specification metamodel [123]. Each instance of *NumericalBaseMetricDescription* uniquely identifies a metric type like CPU utilization. While the Metric Specification metamodel finds use in the context of Palladio, its definition of metrics is not specific to the PCM ADL. An alternative to the *Metric Specification* metamodel is the Structured Metric Metamodel (SMM) [204].

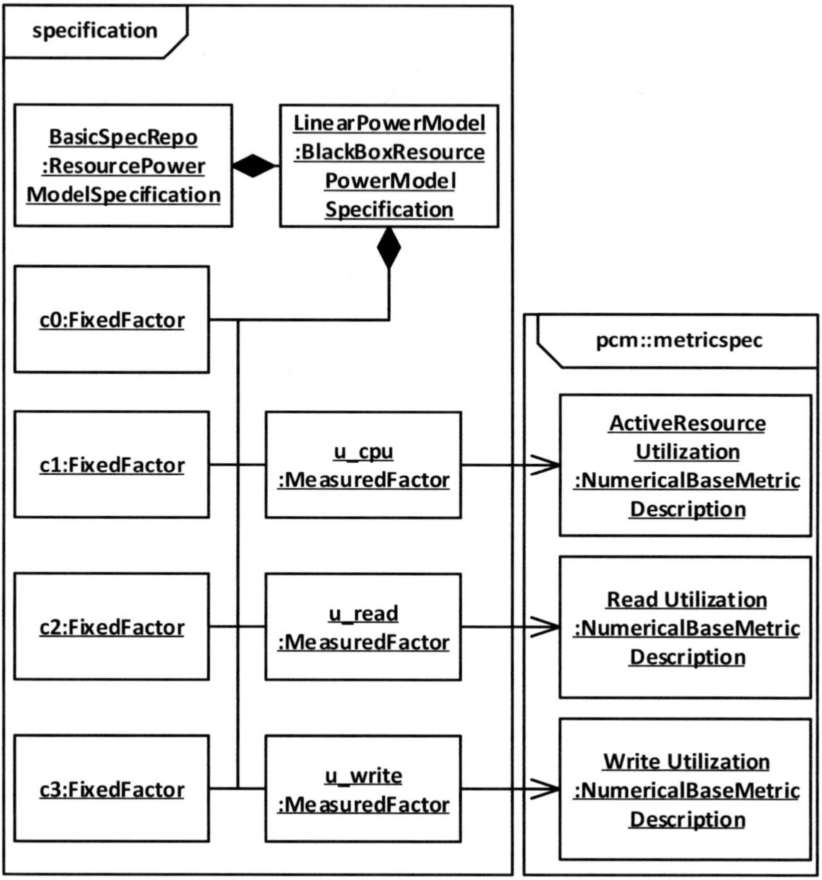

Figure 3.5.: Linear power type P_{lin} defined in the Specification viewpoint

3.2.1.2. Resource Power Models

ResourcePowerModelSpecification defines a power model type for an individual or a set of system resources. Thereby, it supports the specification of power models for individual system components, or groups of system components. *ResourcePowerModelSpecification* has two subtypes, as can be seen in Figure 3.4. A *BlackBoxResourcePowerModelSpecification* describes a black-box power model of a resource. *DeclarativeResourcePowerModelSpecification* expresses the power model of a resource via an associated functional expression.

Figure 3.5 shows an example instance of its *BlackBoxResourcePowerModelSpecification* subtype. The illustrated model realizes the power model type specification of P_{lin} from Equation 3.1. The *LinearPowerModel* reflects the fixed parameters c_0 through c_3 as *FixedFactors*. The independent variables of P_{lin} are modeled as *MeasuredFactors*. Every *MeasuredFactor* references its metric type modeled in a Metric Specification metamodel instance.

3.2.1.3. Distribution Infrastructure Power Models

A *DistributionPowerModelSpecification* models the power model type of an entity type that distributes power to other connected components. Examples for entities that distribute power to connected components are server or rack level Power Supply Units (PSUs).

DistributionPowerModelSpecification specializes *PowerModelSpecification* to model the power consumption characteristics of the distribution infrastructure. This implies that the distribution model is also characterized by *ConsumptionFactors*. For *ResourcePowerModelSpecifications*, each factor models an individual metric measurement source. Applying this modeling abstraction to distribution models would induce significant modeling effort. The distribution model of a PDU with $n = 1, 2, \ldots$ connected servers would have to be modeled separately, since the consumption of each server contributes to the total consumption on the PDU level. Thus, we extended the semantics of *MeasuredFactor* for *DistributionPowerModelSpecification* in comparison to *ResourcePowerModelSpecification*. In addition to the semantics introduced in Section 3.2.1.1, *MeasuredFactors* may refer to sets of measured metric values.

An example application of *DistributionPowerModelSpecification* is the description of consumption overheads in the context of data center power distribution infrastructure. The data center-wide power efficiency estimation equation noted by Barroso et al. [13, p. 67] defines the relation between data center efficiency, power consumption of servers and power consumption caused by other equipment, e.g., cooling. Definition 2.6 introduced this equation. The relation between total consumption and overheads can be expressed as a function:

$$P_{\text{DC}} = \frac{1}{\text{PUE}} \cdot \frac{1}{\text{SPUE}} \cdot \sum_{s \in S} P_s \tag{3.3}$$

Hereby, S is the set of servers where every server consumes P_s power. PUE is the Power Usage Effectiveness factor on the full data center level. SPUE is the PUE of servers.

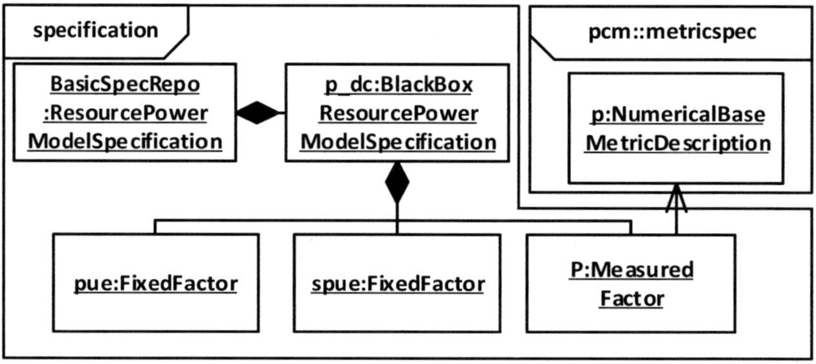

Figure 3.6.: Distribution power model type P_{DC} defined in the Specification viewpoint

Figure 3.6 depicts the distribution power model specification for P_{DC}. It uses the black box subtype of the *DistributionPowerModel*. The distribution power model contains two *FixedFactors* for *PUE* and *SPUE*. Like *ResourcePowerModelSpecification*, the predicted consumption of a *DistributionPowerModel* may depend upon measurable metrics. Each input metric can be modeled as a *MeasuredFactor*. In the example shown in Figure 3.6, P_{DC} depends upon the *MeasuredFactor* P. Hereby, P is the set of power consumption measurements on the server level, with $P_s \in P$ for all servers $s \in S$.

3.2.1.4. Declarative Power Models

We use system metric-based power models to predict the power consumption of servers and their resources. Recalling Definition 2.2, this thesis defines a power model as a function $p : U_1 \times \ldots \times U_n \rightarrow P$ that maps a set of input metric values $(u_1, \ldots, u_n)$ to a predicted power consumption $p \in P$. In many cases, power models can be expressed as closed-form functions of limited complexity [35, 65, 69, 82, 104, 135, 172, 231]. The linear power model example P_{lin} shown in Equation 3.1 is an example of such a model. In order to ease the definition of power models types, the Specification viewpoint allows for the definition of power model types using mathematical expressions.

The *DeclarativePowerModelSpecification* supports the declarative specification of power model expressions for power model types. Its *functionalExpression* attribute contains a mathematical expression specified in conformity with an extensible formal grammar. We use an extended variant G of the mathematical expression grammar defined by the *ExpressionOasis* framework [214]. An expression e hereby is valid if

- it is a sentence derived from the grammar G,
- each identifier in e corresponds to exactly one *ConsumptionFactor* of the *PowerModelSpecification*,
- e parametrized by *ConsumptionFactors* C is a function $p : U_1 \times \ldots \times U_n \rightarrow P$, where $\{U_1, \ldots, U_n\} \subseteq C$.

Applying the example from Figure 3.5 to the declarative specification of the power model, all attributes of the *LinearPowerModel* remain unchanged. Instead of *BlackBoxResourcePowerModelSpecification*, *LinearPowerModel* now has the type *DeclarativeResourcePowerModelSpecification*. The *functionalExpression* of the *DeclarativeResourcePowerModelSpecification* is set to the following expression:

c0+c1*u_cpu+c2*u_read+c3*u_write.

The expression represents the power model type P_{lin} from Equation 3.1. Each variable identifier in the expressions matches to one of the *ConsumptionFactors* by name.

Aside from the specification of power model types for system resources, *DeclarativePowerModelSpecification* can also be used to model power model types for distribution infrastructure. *DeclarativeDistributionPowerModelSpecification* adds a *functionalExpression* to the attributes inherited from its super type *DistributionPowerModel*.

To enable modeling of distribution infrastructure, we introduced folding operations to the *ExpressionOasis* grammar G for sets of measured metric values specified in a *MeasuredFactor*. The distribution power model type from Equation 3.3 can be formulated as a *functionalExpression*:

$$1/(\text{pue}*\text{spue})*\text{SUM(P)}. \tag{3.4}$$

SUM(P) represents the sum expression $\sum_{s \in S} P_s$. The index $s \in S$ is not explicitly specified by the expression, but derived from the input *MeasuredFactor* with the name P. P models all devices that contribute to the power consumption of the distribution unit.

In addition to the sum operator, the grammar supports a multiplication folding operator. MUL(P) represents the multiplication operator $\prod_{s \in S}$, where P and S are defined as in the prior example.

3.2.2. State Viewpoint

The *State* viewpoint encompasses the definition of Power State Machines (PSMs). PSMs model the power consumption of resources as distinct states. Section 2.1.3 outlines foundations of PSMs. Our Power Consumption metamodel uses PSMs to specify the state space of the power consumption behavior for a device. The State viewpoint is independent of the Specification viewpoint.

Figure 3.7 depicts the Power Consumption metamodel package which specifies the PSM metamodel. A *PowerStateRepository* contains a set of *PowerStateMachines*. Unlike some FSM definitions, our PSMs do not define a distinct starting state.

A *PowerStateMachine* consists of states and transitions. Its core semantics match a FSM. States correspond with *PowerStates*, state transitions correspond with *TransitionStates*. *PowerState* and *TransitionState* share a common abstract super class *AbstractPowerState*. *TransitionState* serves as a transitional state that a stateful resource temporarily takes when it transitions between two *PowerStates*.

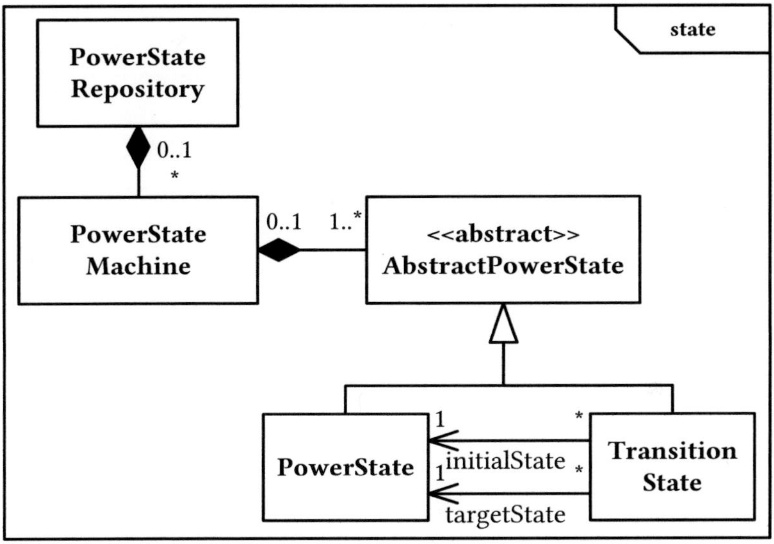

Figure 3.7.: Power State Model viewpoint of the Power Consumption model

Figure 3.8 shows the abstract and concrete syntax for the example PSM introduced in Figure 3.2. The depicted *binary* PSM models the power consumption characteristics of a server that can be put in an on and off state. The model consists of one *PowerState* instance per state. Two *TransitionStates shutdown* and *bootup* model the transition between *on* and *off PowerStates*. The concrete syntax represents the transition states as edges.

The PSM viewpoint does not model the power consumption in each state. Section 3.2.3.2 explains how PSMs can be instantiated to describe the consumption characteristics of specific devices. This separation of PSM state and consumption characteristics definition enables the reuse of the same PSM specification for different devices.

Further, the separation facilitates the definition and analysis of active power management mechanisms. The power management mechanisms can define transition behavior in relation to a general PSM. In the context of the example shown in Figure 3.8, a power management policy may switch off unused servers. The implementation of the power management mechanism may

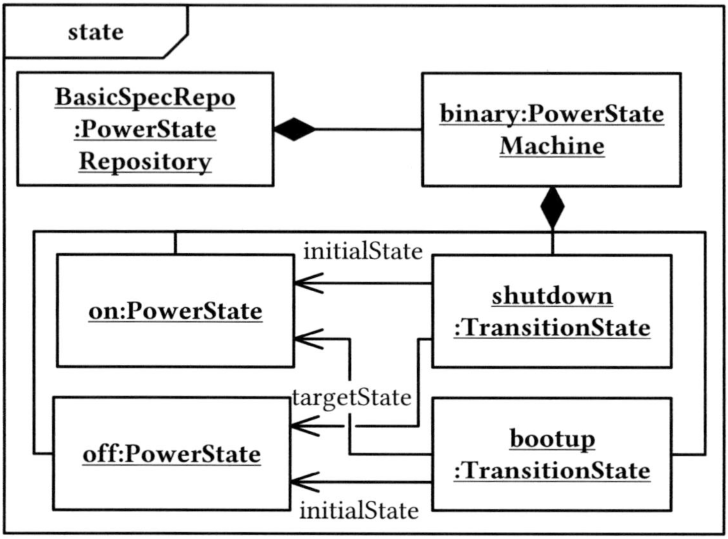

(a) Abstract syntax

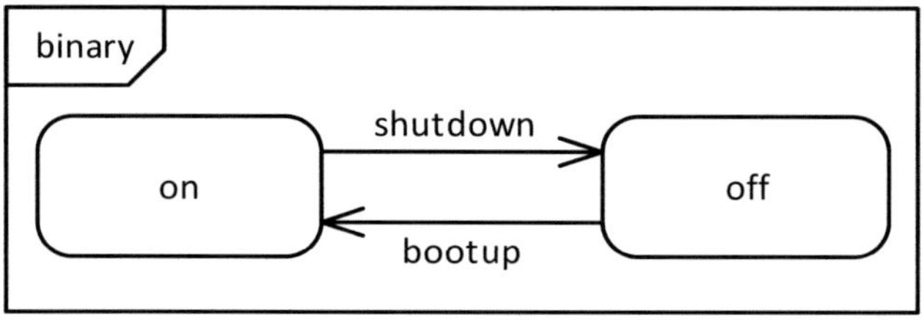

(b) Conrete syntax

Figure 3.8.: Power State Model example of a server with two power states

reference the server independent *on* and *off* states. The implementation can be reused for all server specifications, which reference the PSM from Figure 3.8. Section 6.2.7.3 elaborates on the benefit of the separation of state definition and device consumption specification.

3.2.3. Binding Viewpoint

The *Binding* viewpoint instantiates the power model types defined in the *Specification* viewpoint. It links the power consumption characteristics of a server type with the model used to predict the server power consumption. The bindings defined in the viewpoint instantiate the power model types from the *Specification* viewpoint to specific device types. A binding that represents the consumption characteristics of a server may then be reused across all identical servers.

Figure 3.9 depicts the key model entities in the Binding viewpoint. The *PowerBindingRepository* groups a set of *PowerBindings* to ease their reuse. A binding specified in the repository can be reused across identical hardware components. The abstract *PowerBinding* type models the power consumption characteristics of a specific device type, e.g., a certain server model. *PowerBinding* can be differentiated into two types, the *StatefulResource-PowerBinding* and *PowerFactorBinding*.

3.2.3.1. Power Factor Bindings

A *PowerFactorBinding* is an instance of a power model type defined by a *PowerModelSpecification*. It contains a set of *AbstractFixedFactorValues*. An *AbstractFixedFactorValue* instantiates a *FixedFactor* of a *PowerModel-Specification*. *AbstractFixedFactorValue* is a generic type. Its parameter *Q* defines the metric type of the quantified *FixedFactor*. The *value* attribute serves to specify the metric value. It conforms to the metric type of class parameter *Q*. As of now, there are two subtypes of *AbstractFixedFactorValue*. *FixedFactorValuePower* instantiates a factor with a value of a power unit, e.g., Watt. *FixedFactorValueDimensionless* instantiates a factor with a unit-less value. In the future, further typed values may be introduced. The *MeasuredFactors* of a power model do not get instantiated in the *Binding* viewpoint. The metrics required by a power model type do not depend on the server for which it is instantiated. Thus, the binding only instantiates the server-specific fixed factors.

There are two implementing subtypes of this binding that distinguish between power models for resources, *ResourcePowerBindings*, and power models for distribution infrastructure, *DistributionPowerBinding*. Both subtypes

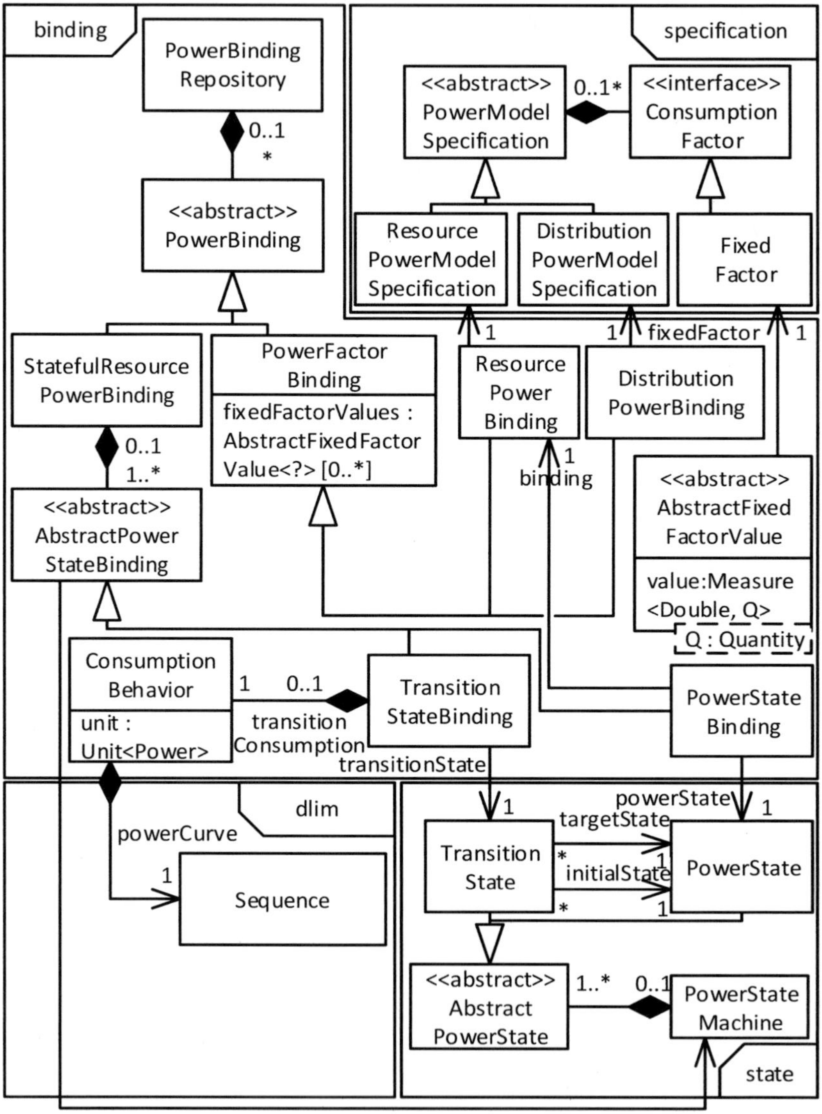

Figure 3.9.: Binding viewpoint of the Power Consumption metamodel

reference the respective distribution or resource power model type they instantiate. *ResourcePowerBinding* and *DistributionPowerBinding* are independent of the implementation type of their referenced power model type.

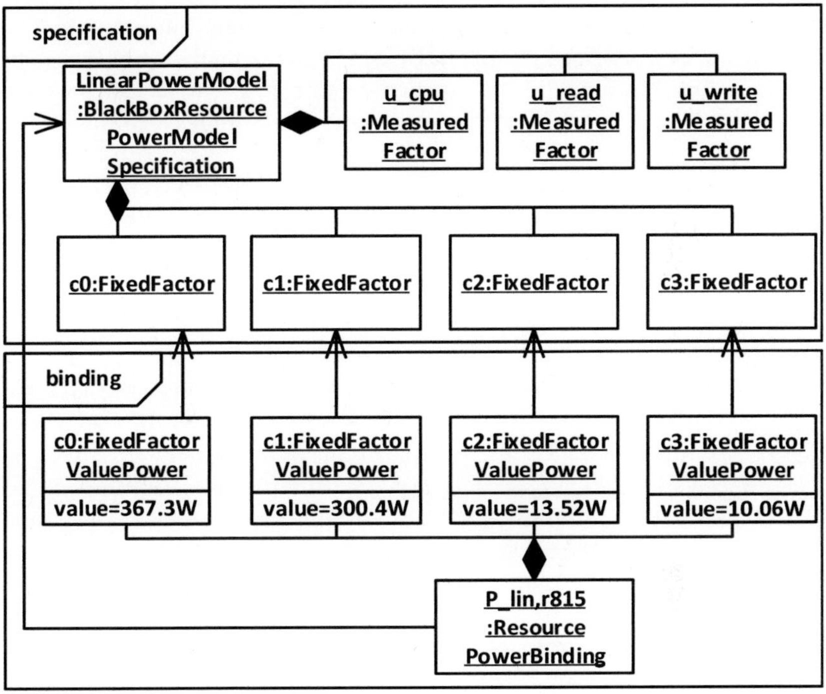

Figure 3.10.: Resource Binding of example linear power model for R815 server

Figure 3.10 shows the specification of the example power model P_{lin} defined in Equation 3.2. The *ResourcePowerBinding* of $P_{\text{lin, R815}}$ instantiates the linear power model type P_{lin}, which *LinearPowerModel* represents. The binding contains the four fixed factors *c*0 to *c*3. Each of the factors has the unit Watt. Hence, the fixed factors are of type *FixedFactorValuePower*.

3.2.3.2. Stateful Resource Power Binding

Section 3.2.2 had introduced the modeling of stateful resources via PSMs. The explicit modeling of power states enables the consideration of power saving policies and reconfigurations in power consumption analyses. The PSM metamodel outlined in this thesis separates the modeling of the states and transitions in the PSM from device specific power consumption characteristics. The *StatefulResourcePowerBindings* instantiates a PSM with the consumption characteristics of a specific resource or device. This addresses Challenge Ch_2 for the reusability of PSM specifications. PSM specifications can be reused for different resource, server and device types. Besides reducing the specification effort when modeling consumption characteristics, the reuse of common PSMs definitions also enables the generic implementation of power management policies as part of the power consumption analysis. Section 6.2.7.3 elaborates on this.

A *StatefulResourcePowerBinding* models the power consumption characteristics of a stateful resource type, where the referenced *PowerStateMachine* describes the power state space and transitions of the stateful resource type. The referenced *AbstractPowerBindings* describe the consumption characteristics each state and transition. A *PowerStateBinding* models the power consumption in a power state. We employ power models to describe the consumption in each state. This extends the modeling capabilities of traditional PSMs, which assume a constant consumption in each state. The power consumption in the state follows the power consumption model of a referenced *ResourcePowerBinding* as described in Section 3.2.3.1.

The separation of power model and state-specific consumption characteristics enables a step-wise refinement of power models of resources. Initially it may suffice to model the power consumption of a running server using a *ResourcePowerModel.* Once power management is considered for the server, the model might be refined to distinguish between consumption in different power states.

The *TransitionStateBinding* models the power consumption of the server when transitioning between two power states. The *ConsumptionBehavior* models the power consumption in the transition as a function $p : [0, t_{\max}] \rightarrow P$. The *ConsumptionBehavior* describes the power consumption $p(t)$ based on the time $t \in [0, t_{\max}]$ that has passed since the start of the transition. The upper limit of the domain, t_{max}, defines the duration of the transition. The transition consumption function $p(t)$ is modeled using a *Sequence* from the DLIM [106]. A *Sequence* models a piecewise defined mathematical function. Since the values *Sequence* are not typed, *ConsumptionBehavior* has a *unit* attribute. The *unit* attribute captures the type of the function, e.g., Watt. *ConsumptionBehavior* abstracts from the potential correlation of system metric values and the consumption in the transition state. The models builds upon the assumption that system metrics can not be predicted or measured during the transition. In the example bootup transition modeled in Figure 3.8, system metrics are not available when the system has not fully booted yet. If there is a distinct transition phase in a system whose consumption can be characterized by system metrics, the consumption behavior should be modeled as a distinct *PowerState*, instead of a *TransitionStateBinding*. Pathak et al. [153] use this modeling technique to describe the transition states they identify for components of mobile devices.

Figure 3.11 depicts an example *StatefulResourcePowerBinding*. It instantiates a PSM-based power model for the R815 server that adheres to the PSM shown in Figure 3.8. The *on* binding uses the linear power model $P_{\text{lin, R815}}$ depicted in Figure 3.10. Power consumption in the idle state is modeled via a separate *ResourcePowerBinding*, which estimates the standby consumption using a flat power consumption value. The figure does not depict the *Sequence* representation of the power consumption during the transitions.

3.2.4. Infrastructure Viewpoint

The *Infrastructure* viewpoint models the power distribution infrastructure of a software system. The chosen abstraction builds upon the power distribution infrastructure entities found in data centers and the operation of enterprise server systems.

The power distribution infrastructure in data centers follows a hierarchical topology [69]. On the top level, a main power supply provisions power to the facility, which then distributes power among subcompartments of the data center, such as server rooms. Power Distribution Units (PDUs) distribute power among further subunits such as server racks. Server racks host the individual servers. Within a server, a PDU or the mainboard, or both, distribute power. Depending on the type of policy used for ensuring

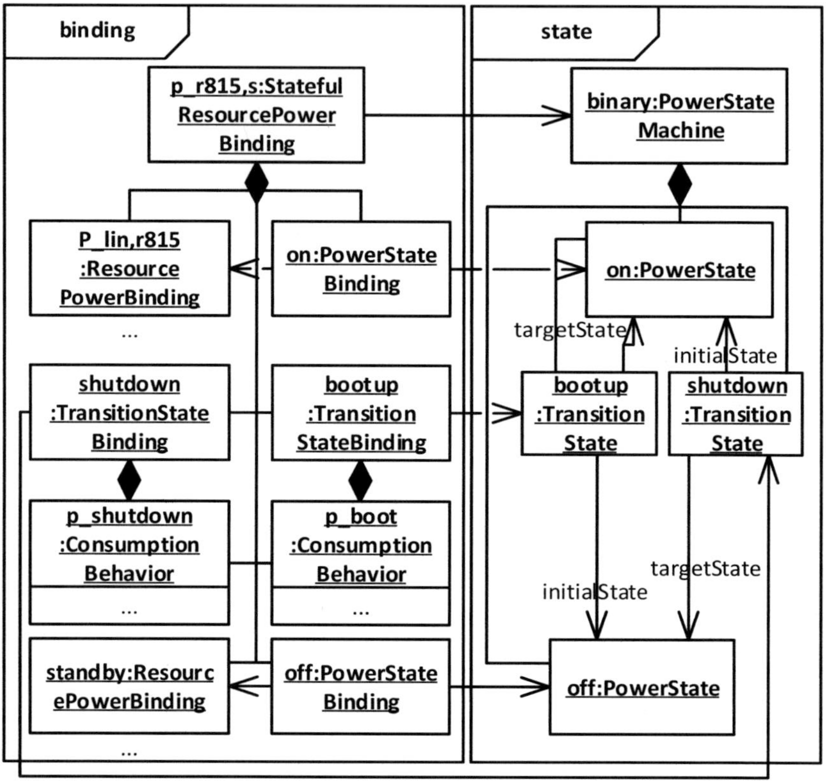

Figure 3.11.: Stateful Resource Binding example of an R815 server with on and off states

continuous operation via an Uninterruptible Power Systems (UPS), multiple conversions between Direct Current (DC) and Alternating Current (AC) may take place [13, p. 48 ff.]. The *Infrastructure* viewpoint supports modeling of power consumers and power distribution infrastructure components. Aside from the power consumption of resources, it allows to model consumption characteristics of the power distribution infrastructure.

Figure 3.12 provides an overview of the central entities in the Infrastructure viewpoint. The Infrastructure viewpoint extends the *Resource Environment*

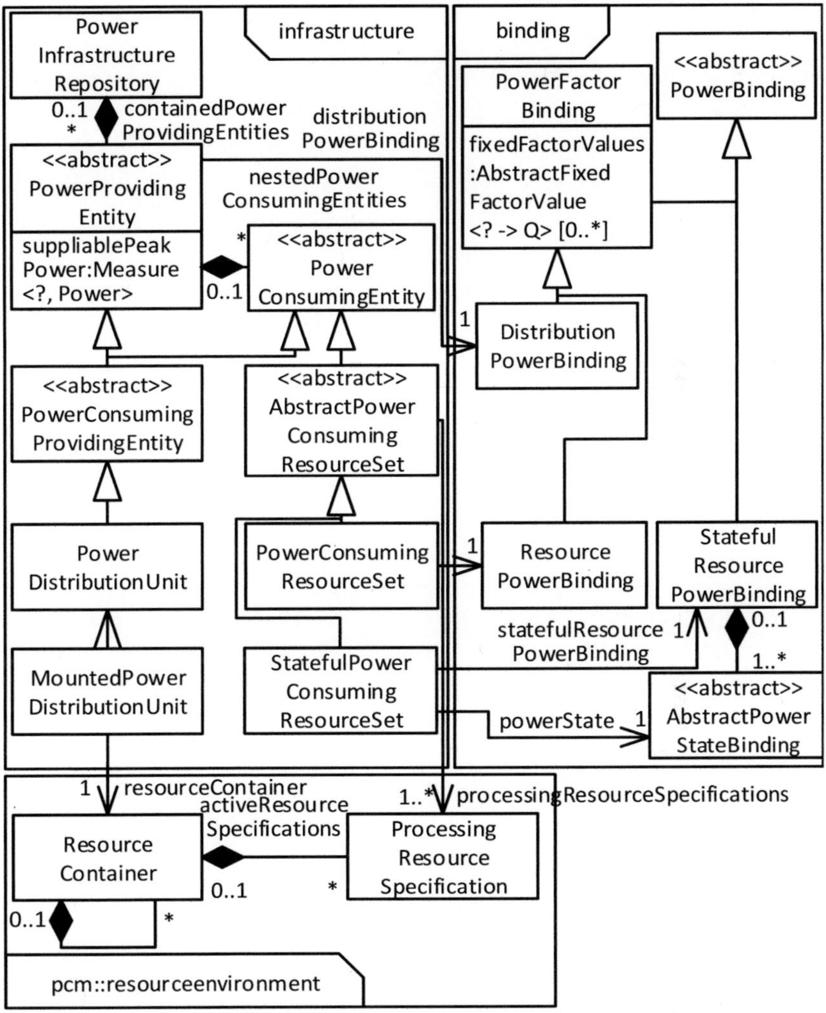

Figure 3.12.: Overview of the classes in the Power Infrastructure metamodel package.

viewpoint of PCM. The viewpoint allows users to add power consumption characteristics to an existing *Resource Environment* view as captured by instances of the PCM ADL. The metamodel extends the PCM by means of annotation. Thereby, the PCM did not need to be modified. The realization of our metamodel as an annotation metamodel addresses Challenge Ch_4, as it separates the specification of power consumption, and other quality characteristics.

The *PowerInfrastructureRepository* stores the devices of a software system that contribute to its power consumption. It defines the system boundaries of the modeled software system with regards to its power consumption characteristics. The *containedPowerProvidingEntities* containment includes all top level entities that affect the power consumption. When modeling a data center, the top level entity is the main supply connecting the data center to the power grid. In smaller-scale server environments the PSU of a server or the PDU of a rack are appropriate top level entities.

The abstract *PowerProvidingEntity* represents an entity that provides or distributes power to other entities or system components. The *suppliable-PeakPower* restricts the maximum peak power that can be supplied by a *PowerProvidingEntity*. An upper bound for the suppliable peak power is the power that it physically can provision at any given time. PSUs are commonly rated for a maximum suppliable peak power. If the peak power threshold is surpassed, safe and continuous operation of the powered components is not guaranteed. Aside from physical contraints, the suppliable peak power can be used to constrain the consumption for subsystems of the power distribution infrastructure. Restrictions on the suppliable peak power can be motivated by limited cooling resources [121], available power [76], or power and cost saving policies [49, 167]. The *PowerProvidingEntity* provides its power to a set of consumers. The *nestedPowerConsumingEntities* containment reference links the consumers to the provider. Power consumption at the *PowerProvidingEntity* comprises of the consumption of contained consumers. The *distributionPowerBinding* links the entity to the *DistributionPowerBinding* instance that models its consumption characteristics. The distribution binding may include an estimation of the consumption caused by distributing power to the connected components. By setting the *distributionPowerBinding* reference to a binding, one defines the distribution model that shall be used to predict the power consumption of the entity.

A *PowerConsumingEntity* is a power consumer in the modeled software system. It draws its power from the parent *PowerProvidingEntity* in which it is contained. We distinguish two types of power consumers, *PowerConsumingProvidingEntity* and its subtypes, and *AbstractPowerConsumingResourceSet.*

3.2.4.1. Types of Power Consuming Resources

PowerConsumingResourceSet represents a set of active hardware components that draw power from the distribution infrastructure. It annotates a set of *ProcessingResourceSpecifications* in the Resource Environment viewpoint with their power consumption characteristics. The *processingResourceSpecifications* reference links it to the annotated processing resources. Each *PowerConsumingResourceSet* references the *ResourcePowerBinding* that can be used to model its power consumption. A *ResourcePowerBinding* instantiates a *ResourcePowerModelSpecification*, as Section 3.2.3.1 outlined. Instances of *ResourcePowerBinding* and its subtypes instantiate a *ResourcePowerModelSpecification.*

In order to perform predictions using the *ResourcePowerModelSpecification*, the annotated hardware environment must model all factors that are needed to predict the system metrics represented by the *MeasuredFactors* of the *ResourcePowerModelSpecification.* This requires that all the metrics specified in the factors must be measurable or predictable for the set of annotated active resources.

PowerConsumingResourceSet realizes *AbstractPowerConsumingResourceSet* for processing resources. It links the set *processingResourceSpecifications* to the *ResourcePowerBinding* that describes the power consumption characteristics of the processing resources. The reference between the set and the referenced *processingResourceSpecifications* is realized as a unidirectional reference from the Power Consumption metamodel to PCM. The reference hence requires no modification of the PCM.

StatefulPowerConsumingResourceSet defines the power consumption of a set of processing resources dependent upon their consumption state. Its *powerState* reference defines the current state that the processing resources are in. The state must be set to one of the *AbstractPowerStateBindings* from the referenced *statefulResourcePowerBinding*. A resource set can be transitioned into a different power state by setting its *powerState* to the target state.

The Infrastructure viewpoint groups multiple active hardware components in a *AbstractPowerConsumingResourceSet* instead of annotating every component with its power consumption characteristics. The rationale for this is as follows. First, it eases modeling in the underlying Binding and Specification viewpoint. The running example power model type P_{lin} shown in Figure 3.5 illustrates this. P_{lin} depends upon the system metrics u_{cpu}, u_{read} and u_{write}. It would be possible to separate P_{lin} into three power model type functions $P_{\text{lin}} = P_{\text{dist}} \circ (P_{\text{lin,cpu}} \circ P_{\text{lin,hdd}})$, where $P_{\text{lin,cpu}}$ is the power consumption of the CPU, $P_{\text{lin,hdd}}$ the storage power consumption, and the distribution power model P_{dist}. By separating the power models, the power consumption has to be broken down per component, even if only the aggregate consumption is relevant. This increases measurement or analysis effort. In cases where two or more *MeasuredFactors* of the power model interact, this separation is not possible. Practical power model examples where two or more variables interact are MARS models as investigated by Davis et al. [57, 58] and Lewis et al. [127].

3.2.4.2. Types of Power Distributing Entities

The *PowerConsumingProvidingEntity* represents entities that simultaneously consume and provide power. This applies to all PDUs in the distribution infrastructure. A PDU draws its power from a source. In relation to the source, it has the role of the power consumer. Additionally, a PDU may convert the electric current before redistribution. Since the conversion incurs a loss, the PDU adds to the total power consumption [168].

PowerDistributionUnit realizes the *PowerConsumingProvidingEntity*. It represents a PDU in a data center. *MountedPowerDistributionUnit* extends *PowerDistributionUnit*. It models a PDU that is physically connected to a specific subunit of the computing infrastructure. Rack mounted PDUs or PSUs of individual servers are example subunits. The *resourceContainer* reference links the modeled *PDU* to the rack or server specification in PCM. Since the referenced PCM models servers and their enclosures as nested *ResourceContainers*, it does not further differentiate *MountedPowerDistributionUnits*. The link between a *ResourceContainer* and its *MountedPowerDistribution* is realized as a unidirectional reference from the Power Consumption model to PCM.

In summary, the Power Consumption metamodel meets Challenge Ch_4 as it only has unidirectional references to PCM in *PowerDistributionUnit* and *PowerConsumingResourceSet*.

3.2.5. Application of Power Consumption Model to Different ADLs

The previous sections introduced our Power Consumption model for describing the power consumption characteristics on an architectural abstraction level. The presented metamodel complements the architectural performance description of PCM. The following steps need to be taken by a language developer in order to apply the metamodel to describe the power consumption characteristics of another quality-aware ADL. First, the developer has to identify the language constructs used to model servers and their processing resources. Second, she has to specialize the abstract class *AbstractPowerConsumingEntity* for each of the ADL processing resource modeling constructs. Optionally, the language designer can specialize *PowerDistributionUnit* to annotate constructs that represent servers with integrated PDUs. We conclude that Item Ch_5 is met by our Power Consumption metamodel, as the core constructs of the metamodel are ADL independent.

This section is structured as follows. Section 3.2.5.1 outlines the application of our modeling language to specific ADLs. Section 3.2.5.2 discusses the integration of the Power Consumption metamodel with the CACTOS Infrastructure Model. The CACTOS Infrastructure Model is a modeling language for the runtime management, and design time analysis of IaaS data centers. The metamodel was developed as part of the CACTOS project [152]. The integration with the model showcases the practical applicability of our modeling language to describe the consumption characteristics of data center-scale server infrastructure.

3.2.5.1. Application to specific ADLs

We designed the Power Consumption metamodel so that its integration with ADLs other than PCM requires little effort.

Descartes Modeling Language (DML) [93] is an architecture-level modeling language used for autonomic resource management of software systems. In DML, a specialized *MountedPowerDistributionUnit* could be defined to *HardwareInfrastructure* entities. The subtypes of *HardwareInfrastructure* correspond to different device groups in data centers. This includes servers, network devices, and dedicated storage servers. *ActiveResourceSpecification* of DML corresponds to the *ProcessingResourceSpecification* from PCM. Hence, a DML specific realization of *AbstractPowerConsumingEntity* as a *PowerConsumingResourceSet* would have to reference the *ActiveResourceSpecification.*

For UML-based ADLs, like *KLAPER* [78] and *UML MARTE* [211], *AbstractPowerConsumingEntity* could be specialized to reference the processing resource specifications in the respective metamodel. For UML MARTE, the specification is found in the Hardware Resource Modeling (HRM) profile. In plain UML, *Device* represents both servers and their processing resources [212]. Thus, both *AbstractPowerConsumingEntity* and *PowerConsumingResourceSet* may be specialized to annotate *Device* in UML.

3.2.5.2. Integration with CACTOS Infrastructure Model

The CACTOS Infrastructure Model [44, 79] is an Ecore-based metamodel for describing IaaS data centers. The metamodel has two central purposes. First, it can be used as input to runtime optimization mechanisms. Instances of the metamodel represent the data center state. This includes the current and planned assignment of VMs and software components to physical resources, i.e., servers. Second, instances of the CACTOS Infrastructure Model can be used for what-if analyses at design time. This enables data center operators to reason on data center sizing. The integration with the CACTOS Infrastructure Model does not include explicit power models for the distribution infrastructure. The modeling assumes a fixed loss factor across all power distribution infrastructure in a data center.

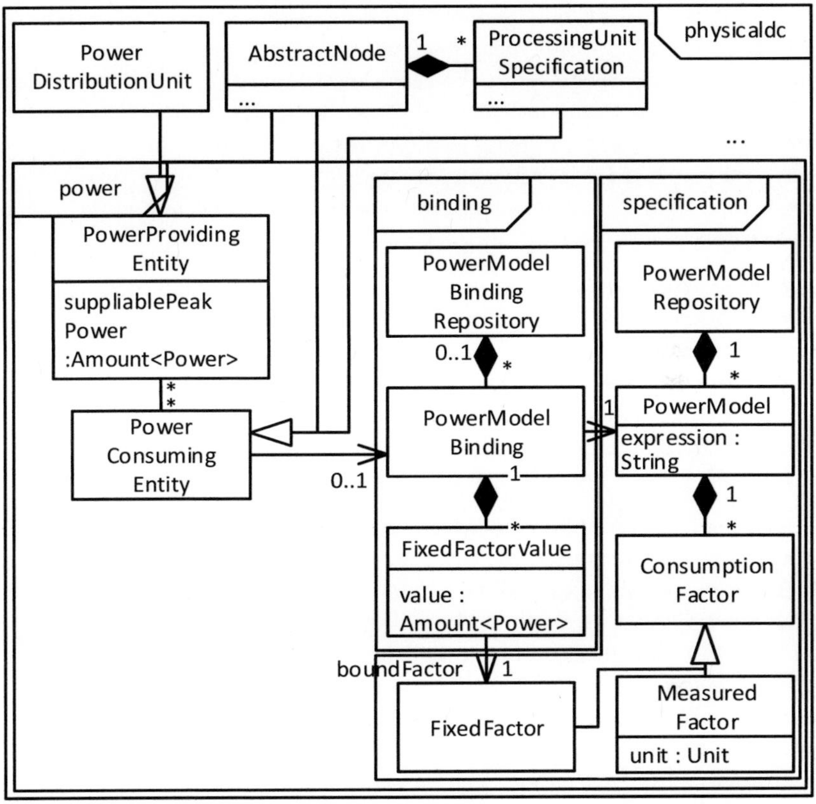

Figure 3.13.: Excerpt of the Power Consumption metamodel integration with CACTOS Infrastructure Model.

In order to support reasoning on power consumption of data centers at design time, we integrated the Power Consumption metamodel with the CACTOS Infrastructure Model. We integrated the core classes and packages into the CACTOS metamodel. Figure 3.13 depicts the integration of Power Consumption metamodel with the CACTOS Infrastructure model. The *physicaldc* package contains the representation of physical devices and hardware in the data center. *AbstractNode* and its subclasses describe servers. The nodes are contained in representations of data center infrastructure, such as racks. Power management, monitoring and analysis is an integral part of CACTOS. For this reason, we opted to integrate the Infrastructure viewpoint of our model with the server specifications. *AbstractNode* extends both *PowerProvidingEntity* and *PowerConsumingEntity.* This replaces the annotation-based modeling in the Infrastructure viewpoint, which Section 3.2.1 presented. All processing resource representations in the CACTOS metamodel extend *PowerConsumingResource. ProcessingUnitSpecification* is an example of a processing resource.

The Binding and Infrastructure viewpoint in the CACTOS Infrastructure Model adhere to the Power Consumption metamodel in its central characteristics. We omitted the State viewpoint from the CACTOS Infrastructure Model, as it already represents the operational state of servers as explicit server characteristics. The CACTOS resource management assumes power distribution to operate at a fixed loss. Thus, we simplified the modeling so that power models are only specified for *PowerConsumingEntities.*

Compared to the general Power Consumption metamodel, the power modeling integrated with the CACTOS metamodel generalizes the relationship between power consumers and providers. The general metamodel assumes each *PowerConsumingEntity* to draw its power from exactly one *PowerProvidingEntity.* The integrated metamodel generalizes this to a many-to-many relation between consumers and providers. This enables a modeling of redundant power distribution infrastructure. In CACTOS, the distribution of power draw among multiple power providers is defined by convention. The next section discusses a more flexible extension of our Power Consumption metamodel, which supports redundancy modeling.

The CACTOS Infrastructure metamodel only supports declarative consumption power model types. *PowerModel* in its Specification viewpoint represents these power model types. We implemented this simplification as the CACTOS tooling solely uses parametric regression techniques to construct power models.

3.3. Assumptions and Limitations

This section discusses the assumptions and limitations of the presented Power Consumption metamodel.

Hierarchical power distribution structure. The Power Consumption metamodel assumes that there exists exactly one power source, a *PowerProvidingEntity*, for each power consumer, a *PowerConsumingEntity*. Power distribution infrastructure of data centers uses redundant distribution to improve the reliability of the infrastructure. As Barroso et al. [13, p. 48 ff.] discuss, data centers leverage Uninterruptible Power Systems (UPS) to supply power in case of temporary power outages. Multiple UPSs are commonly connected in parallel [13, p. 51 f.]. This allows that a subset of the UPSs can fail. The power consumption of individual servers may also be balanced between multiple PDUs. The purpose of this redundancy is to increase reliability by connecting servers to different circuits. The presented model abstracts from redundancy to reduce model complexity. The impact of redundancy can be accurately modeled as fixed overheads [13, p. 67].

Additionally, our modeling abstraction can be extended to model redundancy in the distribution infrastructure. Figure 3.14 sketches a model extension that adds support for modeling redundancy and load distribution. A *RedundantConsumer* connects the contained *connectedEntity* to a set of redundant providers. It links the consumer to the providers via the *redundantProviders* reference. Similar to *PowerProvidingEntity*, a *RedundantConsumer* defines how it consumes power from its providers. The *ConsumerBinding* defines how power consumption is distributed among the providers. It instantiates a power consumption model that the figure omits. Distributed provisioning models found in practice are an even distribution among available connected providers [85, 98], or a failover protected consumption from a single provider [85]. Hereby, the consumer switches to another power provider once the primary provider fails.

The sketched extension illustrates that our power consumption modeling approach is compatible with and can easily be extended to support an explicit modeling of redundancy. We hence consider the limitation minimal.

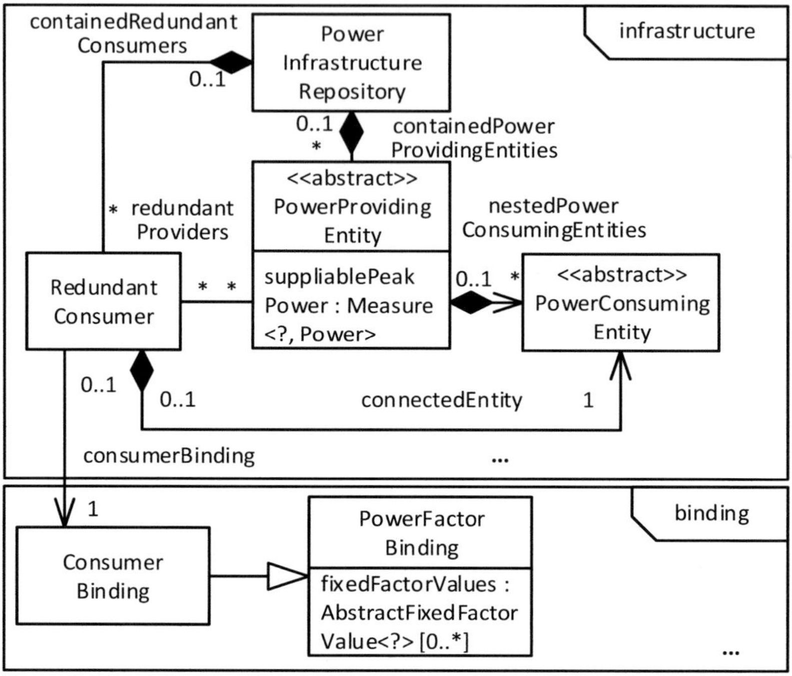

Figure 3.14.: Power Infrastructure extension to model redundancy

No explicit modeling of cooling infrastructure. The Power Consumption metamodel does not explicitly model the cooling infrastructure of servers or data centers. However, the metamodel supports the modeling of the impact of cooling on power consumption. The power consumption of cooling equipment can be specified dependent on server activity. Fan et al. state that the power consumption of cooling equipment "can be approximately modeled as a fixed tax over the critical power" [69]. Since the presented Power Consumption model supports the extension of *PowerConsumingEntity*, sophisticated power consumption models for cooling can be added. Thus, this is a weak limitation.

Knowledge of target deployment environment. The model describes power consumption of software systems in relation to the power consumption of active resources, servers and distribution equipment in its deployment environment. Hence, the modeling approach requires the deployment environment of an analyzed software system to be known. In early design phases, the deployment environment might not be fixed yet. Nevertheless, architecture performance models used in early design phases like PCM assume knowledge of the performance characteristics of the deployment environment. If the deployment environment is not known, the performance characteristics are projected from the current and planned infrastructure. Similarly, the power consumption of the targeted deployment environment can be projected using power models of comparable environments.

Knowledge of power consumption characteristics of deployment environment. The outlined Power Consumption model builds upon system metric-based power models of servers. These power models correlate system metrics with power consumption. In order to correlate power consumption and performance metrics, the used server types need to be derived. One way to derive the models is the use of systematic server profiling to collect system load and power measurements at different load levels. Since a power model only needs to be derived once per server type, the measurement effort that results from the profiling can be justified. Once a power model of a server type is available, it can be reused to evaluate the power consumption of all servers of that type. The models of each server type could be shared online via a central repository, similar to the Server Efficiency Rating Tool (SERT) energy efficiency benchmark results [68]. Software architects could then use the provided models to explore the energy consumption of their projected system.

Availability of metric predictions or measurements. Power and energy consumption analysis approaches that use the presented Power Consumption metamodel require a source of metric predictions or measurements to evaluate the energy consumption of software systems. Most commonly, power models correlate power consumption with performance. At design time, performance predictions like the ones supported by Palladio are viable sources of such measurements. We showed this in our previous work [200]. We consider the assumption that performance models are available at design time to be feasible as the analysis of power and performance is strongly intertwined. Energy efficiency, the operational efficiency of a software system, is defined as a ratio of power and performance.

Abstraction from low-level hardware characteristics. Our modeling language abstracts from low-level hardware characteristics that impact the power consumption of servers. Example characteristics are the influence of supported and used CPU instruction sets [107]. Another example concerns hardware internal power management [135], which is not exposed via monitorable metrics. Our language models the power consumption of hardware resources via power models. The power models predict the power consumption from a set of fixed factors and measured metrics. Consequently, our modeling approach can not capture all hardware characteristics that influence their power consumption. To the best of our knowledge, no modeling approach addresses these shortcomings. Our validation investigates whether power consumption predictions made using instances of our model are accurate enough to inform architecture-level design decisions. Section 7.2 presents the validation results.

3.4. Summary

This chapter discussed the Power Consumption metamodel for describing the power consumption characteristics of a software system. The goal of the metamodel is to capture power consumption characteristics for the use in architecture-level energy efficiency (EE) analyses. The metamodel is realized as an Ecore metamodel.

The instances of the metamodel describe the power consumption of deployment environments. The metamodel separates the definition and instantiation of power models for different server types from the specification of the distribution infrastructure. Three layered viewpoints separate the three concerns power model definition, instantiation and infrastructure modeling. The infrastructure modeling viewpoint annotates the deployment environment description with its power consumption characteristics.

In the design of the Power Consumption model, the challenges presented in Section 3.1 had to be addressed. The following summarizes to which extent the chosen modeling addresses each of the challenges.

Challenge Ch_1 states that instances of the designed metamodel should support analyses to make power consumption predictions with reasonable accuracy. This chapter focused on the rationale and general semantics of the presented Power Consumption model. Chapter 4 outlines how its model semantics can be leveraged to predict the power consumption of software systems at design time. Section 7.2 evaluates the prediction accuracy of the analyses. Aside from enabling accurate predictions, Ch_1 also requires that the level of abstraction should be suitable for architectural design time analyses. Chapter 5 presents an automated approach that allows to automate the extraction of Power Consumption model instances. The extracted model instances can be used to compare different software architectures and design decisions, as Section 7.3 illustrates.

The outlined model does not require annotation of consumption characteristics to service specifications, such as the Service Effect Specification (SEFF) in PCM. This fulfills Challenge Ch_2.

The semantic overlap of PCM and the Power Consumption metamodel is limited to the specification of server and device characteristics. The overlap is constrained to the definition of server enclosures and processing units, and their corresponding representation as power consumers or providers in our model. The Power Consumption metamodel does not replicate any information beyond the name and UUID of the referenced PCM element. Conclusively, our metamodel meets Challenge Ch_3 due to its limited overlap with existing ADLs.

Since we realized the metamodel as an annotation-based model, it is noninvasive by design. Hence, the metamodel fulfills Challenge Ch_4. The presented model only depends on ADL specific constructs to link it with the deployment environment description of the ADL. Section 3.2.4 further elaborated on this. The core packages and entities of the presented Power Consumption model are compatible with a large number of ADLs, as Section 3.2.4 discussed. Thus, the model fulfills Challenge Ch_5.

The next Chapter 4 presents an approach for analyzing the energy efficiency of software systems on an architectural level. The approach uses the Power

Consumption model in combination with the annotated PCM to predict power and energy consumption.

4. Architecture-Level Energy Efficiency Analysis

This chapter discusses the energy efficiency analysis for software systems. The presented analysis approach addresses Research Question 2:

Research Question 2. *How can the power consumption of software systems be predicted on an architectural level?*

The analysis outlined in this section builds upon the Power Consumption metamodel presented in the previous chapter. The energy efficiency analysis predicts the energy efficiency of a software system as the ratio of performance and power consumption. The presented approach leverages existing architectural performance prediction methods. It complements the performance prediction methods with an approach for power and energy consumption prediction. This enables us to combine performance and power consumption predictions. We can then derive energy efficiency (EE) predictions from the power and performance predictions.

The *Power Consumption Analyzer (PCA)* evaluates the power consumption of a software system using instances of the Power Consumption metamodel presented in Chapter 3. The initial design of the prediction approach was proposed in [198]. The analysis approach for static software systems was also outlined and employed in [200]. Its implementation was refined as part of a supervised Master's thesis [114].

This thesis distinguishes between two use cases for design time analyses of power and energy consumption: *post-* and *intra-simulation* analysis. The post-simulation analysis evaluates the power consumption of a software system under investigation *after* a performance analysis has been conducted. The post-simulation analysis provides consumption estimates based on the performance metric measurements collected from simulation. This loose coupling enables a clear separation of our power consumption analysis and the upstream performance analysis. Keeping the power consumption analysis separate from performance analyses offers the following advantages:

- **No modification of existing performance analysis.** Performance and power consumption analysis can be developed and maintained separately.
- **Exchange of used performance analysis.** As the power consumption analysis does not require any modifications of the performance analysis, the performance analysis can be exchanged independent of the power consumption analysis.
- **Decoupling of power and performance analysis steps.** Different power models and power distribution topologies can be compared using the same performance simulation results. A rerun of the performance simulation only becomes necessary once the performance characteristics of the system under investigation are modified, e.g., if an additional server is introduced.

The selection and design of self-adaptation mechanisms is a degree of freedom at design time [20]. This degree of freedom extends the degrees considered in the design of static software systems. An energy-conscious self-adaptive software system performs adaptations based on power consumption measurements or estimations. Examples of power-conscious self-adaptations are discussed in [63, 103, 167, 215]. These energy-conscious adaptation mechanisms require a measurement or estimation source for power consumption. In order to evaluate the mechanisms, they must be provided with a source for power consumption estimations. Our intra-simulation power consumption analysis addresses this by propagating power consumption predictions to a design time analysis of a self-adaptive software system.

Our intra-simulation consumption analysis supports the analysis of an energy-conscious self-adaptive software system. It can be performed *as part of* a simulative performance analysis of a self-adaptive software system. We extended the design time performance analysis SimuLizar with the intra-simulation analysis. The combined analysis supports the consideration of tradeoffs between power and performance at design time.

This chapter is structured as follows. Section 4.1 presents the general approach of Power Consumption Analyzer (PCA) and its application to static software systems. Section 4.2 extends the PCA concept to self-adaptive software systems. Section 4.3 outlines a method for combining energy consumption predictions from PCA and PCM performance predictions to reason on the effect of design decisions on energy efficiency. Section 4.4 provides an overview of the PCA tooling architecture. Section 4.5 discusses assumptions and limitations. Section 4.6 concludes.

4.1. Power Consumption Evaluation Based on Software Performance Predictions

This section presents the approach for evaluating the power consumption of static software systems. We realized the analysis as a post-simulation analysis. The analysis evaluates the power consumption subsequent to a performance analysis.

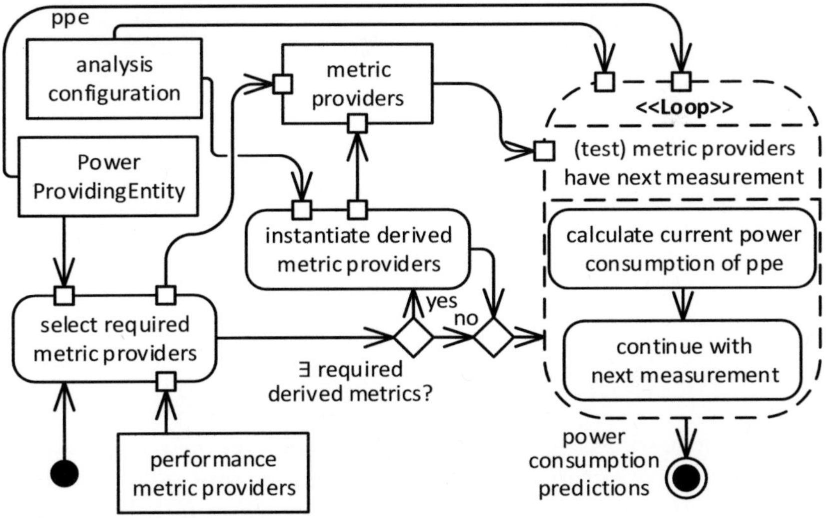

Figure 4.1.: Activity diagram of the power consumption analysis for static software systems

Figure 4.1 provides an overview of the automatic power consumption analysis for static software system as an UML activity diagram. The analysis receives the following inputs:

- the *PowerProvidingEntity ppe* for which the consumption analysis should be performed,
- a set of performance metric providers from the analysis environment,
- the power consumption analysis configuration.

The analysis calculates the predicted power consumption for the *PowerProvidingEntity ppe* which is passed as an input. The analysis aggregates over the power consumption of all consumers connected to the *PowerProvidingEntity*. The *select required metric providers* activity identifies all relevant metric providers from the input metric providers. A metric provider supplies prediction values for a metric. If necessary, *instantiate derived metric providers* calculates derived metrics from the input metrics. An example application of derived metric providers is the aggregation of multiple metrics to a single metric. The activity loop calculates the power consumption for the input metric measurements. It returns the set of power consumption predictions for the passed *PowerProvidingEntity*.

The Power Consumption Analyzer (PCA) evaluates the power consumption of a software system. It implements the activities depicted by Figure 4.1. PCA supports consumption analyses of both static and self-adaptive software systems. This section presents the fundamental design of PCA and its application to static software systems. The following Sections 4.1.1 to 4.1.5 describe the activities shown in Figure 4.1 in greater detail. Section 4.2 discusses the extension of PCA to the design time analysis of power consumption for self-adaptive software systems.

4.1.1. Select Required Metric Providers

The *select required metric providers* activity matches the metrics specified in the *MeasuredFactor* of each *PowerModelSpecification* with metrics available in the input Experiment Data Persistency & Presentation (EDP2) repository. As setup of the analysis, the *select required metric providers* activity selects a subset of all available performance metric providers from the available metrics. The metrics are read from any analysis measurement framework. For Palladio analyses, this framework is EDP2 from the Quality Analysis Lab (QuAL) [123]. QuAL enables analyses to query and process analysis data via unified interfaces. For static analyses, this activity gathers metric providers from the EDP2 components of QuAL. EDP2 persists the results of software quality analyses. In the case of architectural performance predictions, this includes the performance metric measurements needed as input for PCA. The activity selects the performance metric providers based on the metric specifications of *PowerConsumingEntities*. It performs the selection for all consumers contained in the *PowerProvidingEntitiy*, and recursively for its contained consumers.

4.1.2. Instantiate Derived Metric Providers

The source of metrics for the analysis are performance metric values from a previous performance analysis. The scope of available metrics is limited to the metrics available in a specific analysis run. The power models may specify further *MeasuredFactors* that are not contained in the measurements persisted by EDP2. If the missing required metrics can be derived from available performance metrics, the *instantiate derived metric providers* activity instantiates these metrics. An example of such a metric is CPU utilization. Prior to this thesis, all existing Palladio analyses did not support the calculation of resource utilization metrics over time. In order to support power models that rely on input utilization metrics, the activity instantiates a derived metric provider that calculates resource utilization metrics from the available metrics.

The instantiation of derived metric providers may depend upon parameters. In the case of CPU utilization, such parameters are the length of the interval over which utilization should be aggregated, and the step width in which the metric shall be calculated. These additional parameters either need to be specified by the user of the analysis, or set to default values.

Figure 4.2 depicts the abstract class that must be realized and registered to the PCA extension point of the same name. The extension point allows to register additional metric providers to PCA. PCA uses these metric providers as part of the *instantiate derived metric providers* activity. An *ExtendedMeasureProvider* defines a mapping of a set of source (*getSourceMetrics*) to a set

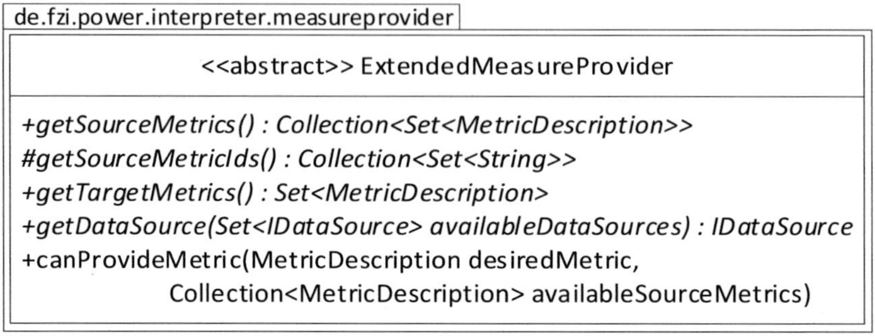

Figure 4.2.: Class diagram view of extension point definition for registering additional metric providers

of target metrics (*getTargetMetrics*). The *getSourceMetrics* method returns sets of *MetricDescriptions*. Each set contains a description of the metrics supplied by an individual input metric provider. A class that extends *ExtendedMeasureProvider* defines a mapping between source and target metrics in its implementation of *availableDataSources*. The returned *IDataSource* is an iterable measurement collection as defined by EDP2. Metric providers may work on different metrics that can be used interchangeably. The method *getSourceMetrics* hence returns a collection of metric combinations that can be used interchangeably. The function *canProvideMetric* checks whether the metric provider can provide a desired target metric for a a set of available source metrics.

An example of a derived metric provider is *UtilizationFilterMeasureProvider*. This utilization measure provider calculates the utilization of a processing resource over time from its queue length.

4.1.3. Power Model Calculators

PCA uses *power model calculators* to determine the power consumption of individual consumers in the software system. Our Power Consumption metamodel classifies all consumers via the *PowerConsumingEntity* type. A calculator implements the power consumption function $p : U_1 \times \ldots \times U_n \rightarrow P$

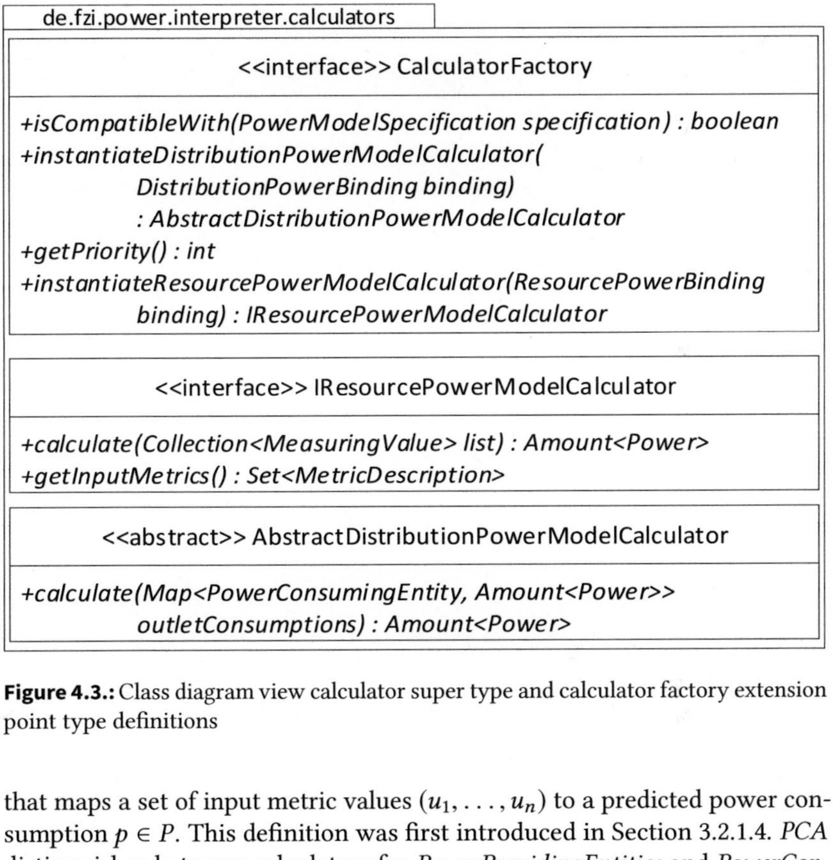

Figure 4.3.: Class diagram view calculator super type and calculator factory extension point type definitions

that maps a set of input metric values $(u_1, \ldots, u_n)$ to a predicted power consumption $p \in P$. This definition was first introduced in Section 3.2.1.4. *PCA* distinguishes between calculators for *PowerProvidingEntities* and *PowerConsumingResourceSets*. Figure 4.3 depicts the respective supertype and interface definitions, *AbstractDistributionPowerModelCalculator* and *IResourcePowerModelCalculator*. Both calculator types define a *calculate* method that returns a power consumption estimate. The calculators estimate the power consumption from values that comply with the parameter types defined by the *MeasuredFactors* of a *PowerModelSpecification*, as Section 3.2.1.1 outlined.

AbstractDistributionPowerModelCalculator calculates the power consumption of a *PowerProvidingEntity*. *AbstractDistributionPowerModelCalculator* calculates the power consumption based on the outlet consumption of all connected consumers. Hence, the metric supplied by all of its input metric providers is *power consumption*. PCA instantiates one calculator per *PowerBinding*. PCA reuses the calculator for all *PowerProvidingEntities*, which reference the same binding.

PCA supports the introduction of additional calculator types and implementations via the Eclipse extension point mechanism. Clayberg and Rubel [53] elaborate on the design of the Eclipse extension point mechanism. In order to introduce a new calculator, an extension needs to supply an implementation of *CalculatorFactory* shown in Figure 4.3. *CalculatorFactory* instantiates the power model calculators supplied by the extension. An example factory is the *CalculatorFactoryImpl* from the *de.fzi.interpreter.calculator.expressionoasis* extension. The factory instantiates the calculators for declarative power models. *PCA* determines the matching calculator factory for each *PowerModelSpecification* by calling its *isCompatibleWith* method. If the method of a factory returns true, PCA uses that factory to instantiate the calculator for a *PowerModelSpecification*. In the case of the factory for declarative power models, the *isCompatibleWith* method checks whether the passed specification is an instance of *DeclarativePowerModelSpecification*. For *BlackBoxPowerModelSpecification*, a factory typically only supports the instantiation of a set of specifications supported by its calculator implementations. The *EssentialCalculatorsFactory* from the *de.fzi.power.interpreter.calculators.essential* extension is an example of a calculator factory implementation that only supports specific power model specifications. As multiple factories could provide a calculator for the same specification, the factories are called in order of their priority (*getPriority*). On matching priority, any factory may be used.

4.1.4. Power Consumption Analysis Algorithm

Once all needed parameters have been selected and instantiated, the core power consumption analysis starts. In the activity diagram shown in Figure 4.1, the power consumption analysis corresponds to the loop and its nested activities. Algorithm 1 shows the algorithm used to analyze the power consumption of a *PowerProvidingEntity ppe*. The algorithm specifies the steps executed as part of the loop activity. It calculates the power consumption of

state : Metric measurements over time $\mathcal{M} \leftarrow \emptyset$
Current point in time $t_{\text{cur}} \leftarrow 0$
input : Metric providers M, PowerProvidingEntity *ppe*, analyzed time interval $[0, t_{\text{max}})$
output : Power consumption measures over time P_t

1 **foreach** $m \in M$ **do**
2 $\quad t \leftarrow$`getCurrentPointInTime`(m);
3 $\quad \mathcal{M}(t) \leftarrow \mathcal{M}(t) \cup \{m\}$;
4 $\quad t_{\text{cur}} \leftarrow \max\{t_{\text{cur}}, t\}$;
5 **end**
6 **while** $\exists t \in [0, t_{max}) : \exists m \in M_t :$ `hasNextMeasurement`(m) **do**
7 $\quad M_{\text{min}} \leftarrow \{m | m \in M,$ `getNextPointInTime` $(m) \leq t_{\text{cur}}\}$;
8 $\quad$ **foreach** $m \in M_{min}$ **do**
9 $\quad\quad \mathcal{M}($`getCurrentPointInTime`$(m)) \leftarrow \mathcal{M}($`getCurrentPointInTime`$(m)) \setminus m$;
10 $\quad\quad$ `moveForward` (m);
11 $\quad\quad \mathcal{M}($`getCurrentPointInTime`$(m)) \leftarrow \mathcal{M}($`getCurrentPointInTime`$(m))) \cup m$;
12 $\quad$ **end**
13 $\quad P_t \leftarrow P_t \cup \{(t_{\text{cur}},$`evaluatePowerConsumption`$(\text{ppe}, M))\}$;
14 $\quad t_{\text{cur}} \leftarrow \min_{\forall m' \in \mathcal{M}_{\text{min}}}$ `getNextPointInTime`(m');
15 $\quad M_{\text{next}} \leftarrow \{m | m \in \mathcal{M}_{\text{min}},$ `getNextPointInTime`$(m)) = t_{\text{cur}}\}$;
16 **end**

Algorithm 1: Power consumption analysis over a defined analysis interval

the *PowerProvidingEntity ppe* over time. The metric providers M from the *instantiate derived metric providers* serve as input to the algorithm.

The power consumption calculation of *ppe* proceeds as follows. First, the algorithm fetches the time of the first measurement for all *metric providers* M (line 2). Then, it associates each metric provider with the initial time and stores them in the map $\mathcal{M}$ (line 3).

Each iteration of the algorithm estimates the power consumption at the current point in time t_{cur}. The algorithm determines the starting point of the power consumption analysis as the first point in time t_{cur}, for which a measurement is available for all required metric providers M. Since M only contains the required metric providers, this matches the maximum over all initial points in time (line 4).

Line 7 identifies all metric providers whose next measurement has a current point in time smaller or equal t_{cur}. For these metric providers, it moves on to the most recent measurement that is smaller or equal t_{cur} (lines 8–12).

Next, the algorithm calculates the consumption of *ppe* at t_{cur} (line 13). The called function `evaluatePowerConsumption` recursively visits the consumers of *ppe* and its contained *PowerProvidingEntities*. The function aggregates the consumption along the composition tree spanned by the providers and consumers.

The input metric providers M are not necessarily synchronized. This implies that they do not provide measurements for all $t \in [0, t_{max})$. In order to get the current metric measurement for any t_{cur}, the function uses the most recent measurement of m.

After calculating the consumption using `evaluatePowerConsumption`, Algorithm 1 moves on to the next relevant point in time (line 15). Hereby, we assume that the metric values remain constant between two sampling times t_{cur} and $t_{cur'} > t_{cur}$. The power consumption between the old t_{cur}, and new $t_{cur'}$ does not need to be evaluated, as the values of all metric providers between these power consumption measurements remain unchanged. If the calculation of measurement values for $t \in [0, t_{max})$ is generalized to other interpolation functions, this does not hold true. In this case, the calculation of power consumption needs to be changed to a sampling-based calculation. Section 4.2 discusses the realization of such a sampling-based power consumption analysis as an extension to PCA.

Power consumption of multiple connected *PowerProvidingEntities* and *PowerConsumingEntities* can be predicted in two ways. A straightforward approach is the execution of the algorithm for each entity. Alternatively, the value of each nested consumer can be persisted within the execution of `evaluatePowerConsumption`.

PCA realizes `evaluatePowerConsumption` by means of the visitor pattern. *PCA* recursively aggregates the power consumption over the nested elements, which draw their power from *PowerProvidingEntity* instances. If a

PowerConsumingEntity also classifies as a *PowerProvidingEntity*, PCA repeats this recursively. PCA determines the power consumption of each entity by calling the referenced power consumption calculator.

state : $\mathcal{M}$, t_{cur}
input : metric providers M, PowerProvidingEntity *ppe*,
switch *Type of* ppe **do**
    case *PowerConsumingProvidingEntity* **do**
        $C \leftarrow \emptyset$ **foreach** consumer *in* ppe.*nestedPowerConsumingEntities* **do**
            `evaluatePowerConsumption` (*consumer*, M);
            $C \leftarrow C \cup (consumer, p_{consumer})$;
        end
        return `calculate` (C) with calculator of *ppe*;
    case *PowerConsumingResource* **do**
        return `calculate` (M) with calculator of *ppe*;
end
output : Power consumption P_{ppe} at time t_{cur}

Algorithm 2: Power consumption analysis `evaluatePowerConsumption` at the point in time t_{cur}

Algorithm 2 lists the calculation logic of `evaluatePowerConsumption` used to calculate the power consumption of *ppe*. If the type of *ppe* extends *PowerConsumingProvidingEntity*, the algorithm calculates the current power consumption of all connected consumers. Then, it uses the calculator of *ppe* to aggregate the consumption. If *ppe* extends *PowerConsumingResource*, the algorithm calculates the power consumption using the resource calculator of *ppe*.

4.1.5. Calculating Energy Consumption

In order to calculate the energy consumption E of a system in an interval $[t_0, t_{end})$, PCA integrates over the power consumption samples by means of numerical integration. PCA uses the power consumption analysis presented in Section 4.1.4 to estimate the power consumption of a software system over time. The estimated power consumption samples serve as input for the energy consumption estimation.

PCA employs Simpson's rule for estimating the energy consumption. Prerequisite for the use of Simpson's rule is that the time intervals between all successive power samples power consumption samples are of equal width. The samples from both post- and intra-simulation power consumption analysis meet this requirement. In case of the post-simulation analysis, all utilization metrics are sampled at the same rate via derived metric providers. PCA calculates power consumption predictions of a selected power provider using the metric measurement values. As the metric measurement values are of equal width, the calculated power consumption samples are as well. Intra-simulation power consumption analysis samples the power consumption using explicitly defined sampling rates. All sampling rates are defined with uniform interval width across all sampled metric values. Consequently, the power consumption estimation samples are of equal width.

When no equi-width power samples are available, the PCA can easily be modified to use the trapezoidal rule to estimate the energy consumption based on power consumption estimates.

4.2. Consideration of Power Consumption in Design Time Analyses of Self-Adaptive Systems

This section discusses the extension of PCA to the analysis of energy-conscious self-adaptive software systems. The previous section outlined the PCA method for calculating power consumption of a static software system. Analyzing the power consumption of self-adaptive software systems introduces the following additional challenges:

- **Ch_1 Availability of power consumption predictions to adaptation mechanism.** Self-adaptive software systems adapt their structure, deployment and composition as a reaction to monitored changes to the environment of the system. Energy-conscious adaptation mechanisms adapt the system to provision its services to achieve energy efficiency goals. Energy-conscious adaptation mechanisms may take adaptation decisions based on the current or past power consumption. They thus require continuous access to power consumption predictions. In order to evaluate the effect of energy-conscious adaptation mechanisms on QoS and energy efficiency of the system at design time, our analysis must support the evaluation of these adaptation mechanisms. This requires us to expose power predictions to the mechanism during the design time analysis.

Ch_2 Effects of reconfigurations on power consumption. Energy-conscious adaptations reconfigure the system with the goal of reducing power consumption of the system. In order to reason on the efficiency and effectiveness of energy-conscious adaptations, the analysis needs to consider the effect of reconfigurations on power consumption. An example reconfiguration that affects power consumption is the startup of an additional server.

Challenges Ch_1 and Ch_2 induce a coupling of design time power consumption analysis, and the performance analysis for self-adaptive software systems. The coupling must be realized specific to a design time analysis of self-adaptive software system. For self-adaptive systems, the power consumption analysis predicts the power consumption as part of the analysis. Hence, it is an intra-simulation analysis. Challenge Ch_2 necessitates that power consumption predictions need to be exposed to the adaptation mechanisms, which execute as part of a design time performance analysis. Consequently, the power consumption measurements need to be exposed to a suitable interface of the design time self-adaptive systems analysis. Challenge Ch_2 requires that the Power Consumption model is part of the runtime models on which the adaptation mechanisms reason. Thus, the Power Consumption model needs to be registered with analysis-specific interfaces.

We opted to realize the coupling between PCA and the design time performance analysis SimuLizar. The following discusses the intra-simulation coupling of power consumption and design time performance analysis by the example of PCA and SimuLizar.

4.2.1. Extending the Runtime Model by the Power Consumption Model

Energy-conscious adaptation mechanisms reconfigure the system to meet energy consumption and other quality goals. For this, the adaptation mechanisms may leverage adaptation actions that actively or indirectly affect the tradeoff between these goals. Section 2.3 introduced different power management actions. Active power management, e.g., DVFS, controls the tradeoff between power consumption and performance. It achieves this by switching between different power states, where each state represents a different tradeoff. Energy-conscious adaptation mechanisms switch between these states depending on past and expected energy consumption. The mechanisms use the power states as adaptation points.

In order to evaluate energy-conscious adaptation mechanisms at design time, a definition of available adaptation points needs to be exposed to the mechanisms. In self-adaptive software systems, adaptation points can be defined as an explicit [96] or implicit [217] part of the runtime model. If the adaptation points are implicit, adaptations are enacted by transforming the runtime model from the current configuration to an intended target configuration. SimuLizar uses PCM as the runtime model. The adaptation points definition is an implicit part of PCM. This means that adaptation mechanisms transform the runtime PCM model to enact adaptations.

This thesis extends the runtime model of SimuLizar with optional instances of the Power Consumption metamodel. The PSM viewpoint of our Power Consumption metamodel can be used to represent the power states and transitions of a power management mechanism. This is a prerequisite for addressing Challenge Ch_2. The model must be accessible to reconfiguration rules. This is a prerequisite to support the evaluation of the rules which use active power management techniques to improve the energy efficiency of the system.

Adaptation mechanisms can affect the configuration of the system by transforming the runtime Power Consumption metamodel instances. The mechanisms may enact changes in the power state of resources, i.e., *StatefulPowerConsumingResourceSet* instances, by changing their power state. To enact the transition to a new power state, an adaptation mechanism simply has to set the *powerState* reference of a resource to the desired target power state.

4.2.2. Consideration of Power State Changes in the Power Consumption Analysis

Active power management mechanisms as subsumed by ACPI allow to adapt the state of resources in the deployment environment of a software system. Active power management can be used to reduce the power consumption of the system. Conversely, it can be used to increase performance in exchange for higher power consumption. Section 3.2.2 presented a model for characterizing the consumption states of resources as Power State Machines (PSMs). Section 3.2.3.2 outlined how power consumption characteristics when transitioning between states can be modeled.

PCA evaluates the power consumption in transition states via a specialized power model calculator. *StatefulPowerConsumingResourceCalculator* implements the *IResourcePowerModelCalculator* interface depicted in Figure 4.3. *StatefulPowerConsumingResourceCalculator* consists of a *TransitionStatePowerModelCalculator* for each state transition, and a *IResourcePowerModelCalculator* for each consumption state of the Power State Machine (PSM).

The *StatefulPowerConsumingResourceCalculator* evaluates the power consumption of a set of resources on the basis of their current state. It delegates the consumption calculation to the calculator of the current state. *StatefulPowerConsumingResourceCalculator* holds an internal state, which represents the current power state. The calculator needs to maintain the state for its associated resource. This is needed as the prediction of the calculator depends not only on metric input values, but also on the current resource state.

The *TransitionStatePowerModelCalculator* evaluates the power consumption in the transition from the source to the target state of the PSM. The calculator evaluates the function $p : [0, t_{\text{max}}] \rightarrow P$ specified in the *ConsumptionBehaviour* of the *TransitionStateBinding*. The calculator parametrizes p with the time that has passed since the transition was triggered.

4.2.3. Integration of Power Consumption Analysis and SimuLizar

This section provides an overview of the integration of PCA and SimuLizar. The integration enables the design time analysis of energy conscious self-adaptive software systems modeled with PCM and the Power Consumption metamodel.

Definition of monitored power consumption infrastructure. This thesis leverages the Monitor specification model of SimuLizar to specify for which parts of the infrastructure the PCA should expose power consumption predictions to adaptation mechanisms. The self-adaptive systems architect creates a monitor for each of the entities in the power consumption infrastructure that she wants to expose to the self-adaptation mechanisms. As part of the monitor specification, the software architect defines the sampling frequency and method by which power consumption predictions should be calculated.

Analyzing power consumption within the performance analysis of SimuLizar. The intra-simulation analysis uses the same power consumption prediction algorithm as the post-simulation anaylsis. Algorithm 1 lists this algorithm. The intra-simulation analysis calculates the power consumption for each *PowerProvidingEntity* specified in the monitor specification model.

Figure 4.4 depicts the power consumption process of the intra-simulation analysis. The analysis triggers a new power consumption evaluation for the interval i specified in a monitor. It calculates the power consumption of the *PowerProvidingEntity* using the consumption prediction algorithm. Subsequently, the analysis exposes the new power consumption measurement to the adaptation mechanism. Reconfiguration rules then may act upon the new power consumption measurement.

Unlike the inter-simulation analysis presented in Section 4.1, the coupled analysis applies a sampling-based strategy for evaluating power consumption. At each sampled point in time, the power consumption algorithm estimates the power consumption of processing resources using the most recently collected metric measurements.

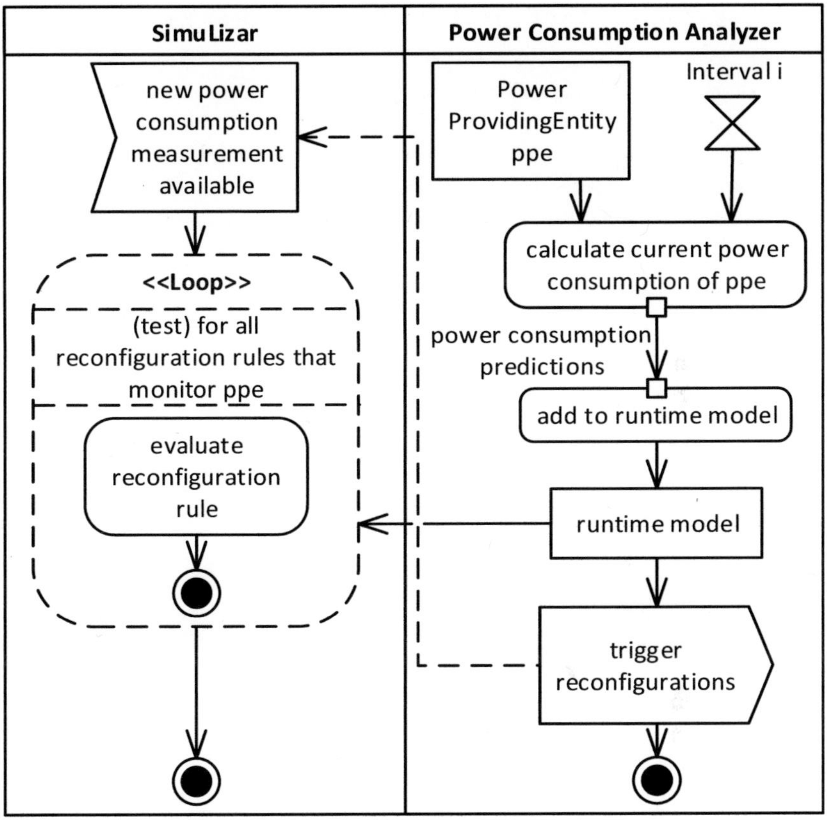

Figure 4.4.: Activity diagram of the power consumption analysis coupling with SimuLizar

For power distribution infrastructure, i.e., *PowerConsumingProvidingEntity*, there are two possible alternative sampling strategies. First, the power consumption of all connected consumers may be sampled every time we evaluate the power consumption of the distribution infrastructure. Second, power consumption at the distribution infrastructure entity may be interpolated from previous predictions for the connected consumers. By default, we employ the first strategy, as it offers the highest prediction accuracy with a minor difference in performance.

4.3. Effect of Design Decisions on Energy Efficiency

In the scope of this thesis, energy efficiency (EE) is defined as the ratio of performance and power consumption (see Section 2.2). Design decisions made on an architectural level impact both performance and power consumption [184, 200]. Consequently, both performance and power consumption of the system have to be analyzed to reason on the effect of design decisions on EE.

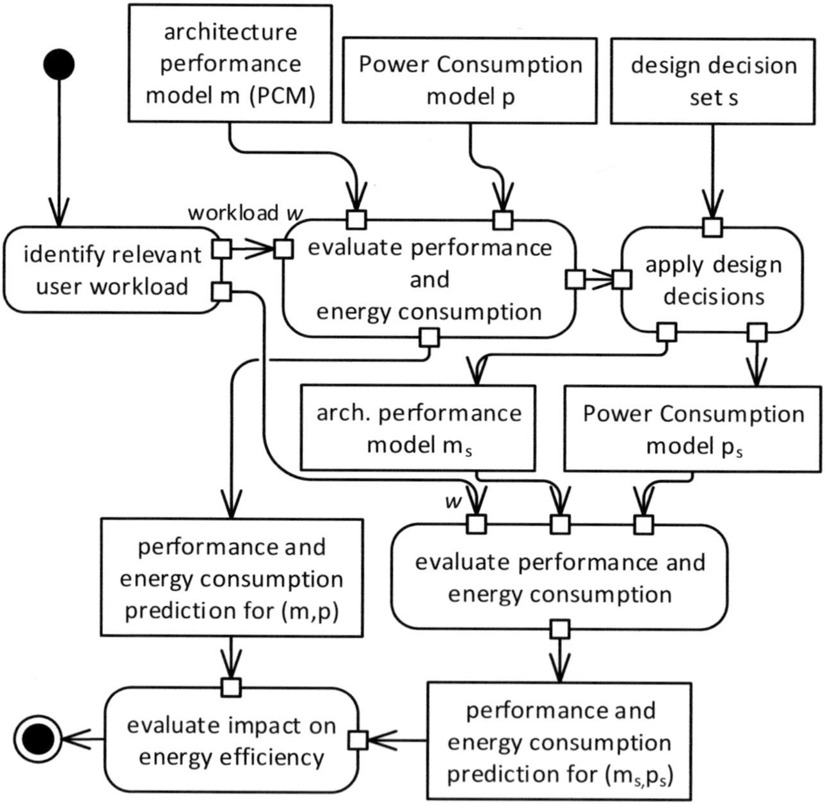

Figure 4.5.: UML Activity diagram of process for evaluating the impact of design decisions on energy efficiency

Figure 4.5 depicts the process this thesis proposes for evaluating the impact of design decisions on EE. The following discusses the involved activities.

In the first step, the software architect has to *identify relevant user workload* definitions. Both performance and power consumption strongly depend upon the load intensity and workload mix. For low load intensities, it might make sense to consolidate multiple components on the same server to reduce power consumption. However, it might not be possible to perform said consolidation for higher load intensities without violating performance SLAs.

The set of workloads w serves as input to the *evaluate performance and energy consumption* activity. The architect triggers a performance and power consumption analysis for every workload definition in w. For the performance analysis, the architect can use the PCM simulators SimuLizar or SimuCom. The architect can either specify the performance model based on early estimates, or extract it via automated tooling [220]. PCA realizes the power consumption analysis, as we discussed in Chapter 4. If a user performs the post-simulation consumption analysis, PCA executes on the results of the performance analysis. For the intra-simulation analysis, the power consumption analysis runs coupled with the performance analysis.

After performing the power and performance analysis on w, the architect applies a set of design decisions s to the architecture performance model m and the Power Consumption model p. The *apply design decisions* activity produces the architecture model m_s and the Power Consumption models p_s. The architect applies the decisions on both models. The architect uses the performance and energy consumption analysis to evaluate the resulting system (m_s, p_s) in the respective quality dimensions.

In the final activity *evaluate impact on energy efficiency*, the architect reasons on the effect of the design decision set s on EE. The architect determines the effect of design decisions on EE as a comparison of EE prior to and after the design decisions set s has been applied. If the architect is indifferent regarding the performance effect of a design decision, its effect on EE can be quantified as the relative change in energy consumption between (m, p) and (m_s, p_s). A scenario where the architect may be indifferent is if both alternatives meet the performance requirements. In this scenario, the scenario with the lower power consumption would meet the requirements in a more efficient manner.

In addition to the comparative EE analysis, the architect may leverage any of the existing EE metrics discussed in Section 2.2 to rank design alternatives. All of the discussed metrics evaluate EE as a ratio of work, and power or energy consumption. In order to reason on EE using the presented metrics, both power and performance metrics are needed.

The EE of a software system depends on the workload issued by its users. If the architect expects different workload intensities and patterns, she has to accumulate the results of multiple EE analyses. Each EE analysis evaluates the efficiency of the system for a specific user workload. The architect may accumulate multiple EE estimates based on the expected workload distribution.

4.4. Toolkit Architecture

This section provides an overview of the PCA architecture and its integration with existing Palladio analysis tooling. The PCA implementation conforms to the component-based design paradigm. It is realized inside the Eclipse framework and integrates with the Palladio Bench [22]. Each component discussed in the following has been realized as an Eclipse plugin. The wiki page [161] gives an overview of update sites via which the PCA tooling can be installed into an Eclipse-based Palladio IDE.

Figure 4.6 shows a simplified view on the architecture of PCA and its integration with Palladio tooling. The core PCA components occupy the *de.fzi.power.** namespace. The diagram groups these components with a frame of the same name. The diagram does not display editor components and interface components that are re-exported by the displayed components. The figure does not depict components and dependencies that are not the focus of the architecture discussion. It only shows essential components from QuAL, and the components of SimuLizar involved in the intra-simulation power analysis.

PCA Core Components The *power* component implements our Power Consumption metamodel on the basis of the Eclipse Modeling Framework (EMF) technology stack. The *power.specification.resources* component offers a base

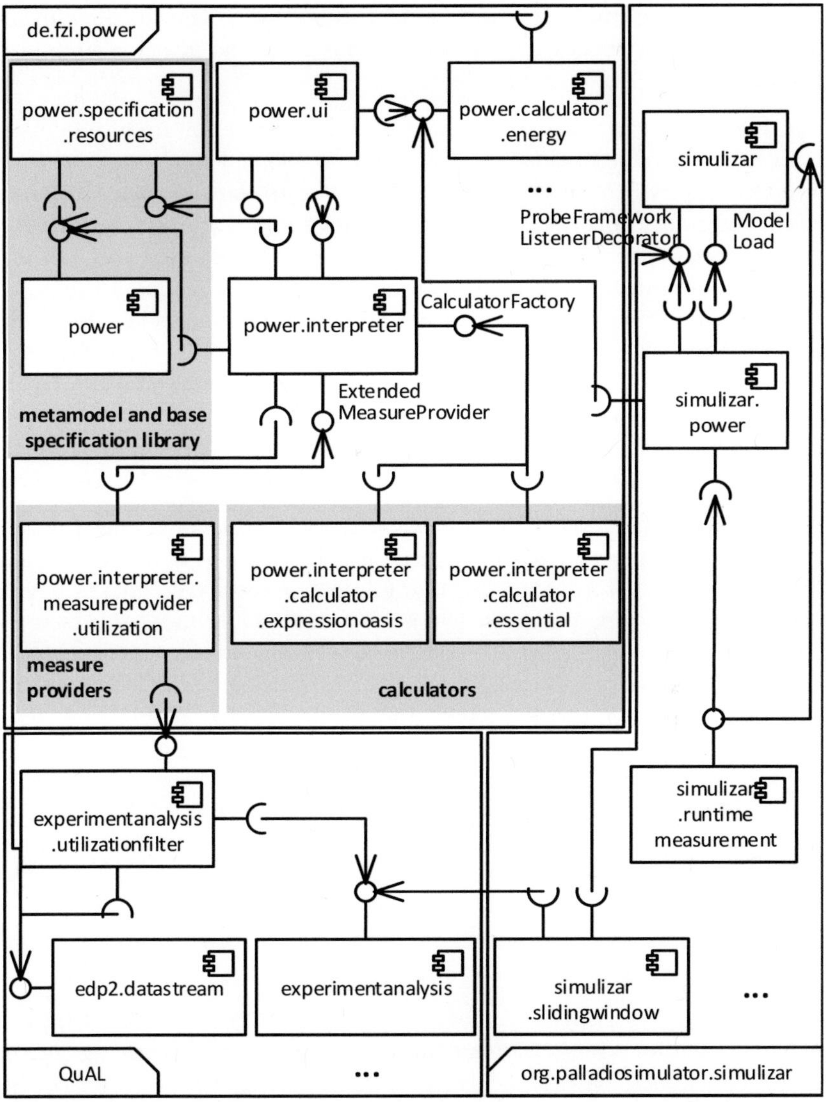

Figure 4.6.: Simplified UML component diagram of *PCA* architecture and integration with Palladio tooling. Component namespace prefixes are omitted for brevity.

library, including common power model specifications. This includes linear power models for processing resources, and distribution models with linear loss factors.

The *power.interpreter* component implements the core power consumption evaluation logic discussed in Section 4.1. The component offers two extension point interfaces *ExtendedMeasureProvider* and *CalculatorFactory*. *ExtendedMeasureProvider* enables the registration of components, which calculate derived metrics from available metrics. *CalculatorFactory* offers support for registering calculators for specific power model types. Section 4.1 provide more information on the purpose and design of the interfaces. The interpreter calculates power consumption of entities in a software system. It uses data streams from EDP2 as the source of input metric measurements. These measurements are then passed to the calculators as Section 4.1 outlined. The EDP2 component *edp2.datastream* defines this shared data stream interface type with *IDataStream*.

The *power.interpreter.calculator.expressionoasis* and *power.interpreter.calculator.essential* components implement the *CalculatorFactory*. Both components offer implementations of the *CalculatorFactory* interface defined in *power .interpreter*. The components lack explicit provided interfaces on a component level. The *power.interpreter* component selects and calls the extensions based on the contract established as part of its *CalculatorFactory* extension point. Vogel and Milinkovich [216] further discuss Eclipse extension point semantics. The *power.interpreter.calculator.expressionoasis* component implements the calculator logic for all instances of the *DeclarativePowerModelSpecification* type from the Power Consumption metamodel. Section 3.2.1 discussed the semantics of this power model type. The component uses the *ExpressionOasis* framework by VedantaTree [214] to evaluate the mathematical expressions specified by the declarative power model type. The expressions instantiate an extensible grammar. The grammar defines the domain of valid declarative power model types.

The *power.interpreter.calculator.essential* component contains calculator implementations for a set of standard black-box power model types, e.g., piecewise defined linear power models for *ResourcePowerModelSpecifications*, and *PowerProvidingEntities* with linear loss factors. The library contains implementations of all black box models specified in *power.specification.resources*.

The *ExtendedMeasureProvider* extension point of the interpreter allows for the registration of additional metric providers that are derived from other input metrics. The previous Section 4.1 had introduced the interface contract of the extension point. The *power.interpreter.measureprovider.utilization* component offers *UtilizationFilterMeasureProvider* that calculates the utilization of resources based on their work queue length. For this, the filter uses the component *experimentanalysis.utilization* component from QuAL. This QuAL component was implemented as part of this thesis to calculate utilization metrics on any EDP2 metric data streams. Krach [114] uses the *ExtendedMeasureProvider* extension point to register additional derived wireless network metric providers for mobile devices. The registered metric providers are added to the power model input metrics, as discussed in Section 4.1.

PCA UI The *power.ui* component serves as the UI entry point to the post-simulation power consumption analysis of PCA. It calculates power consumption via the *power.interpreter*, and the energy consumption with the *power .calculator.energy* component. Unlike the name suggests, *power.calculator .energy* does not implement the calculator interface. Rather, it calculates the energy consumption of a software system based on a set of passed power consumption samples. The calculator estimates the energy consumption by means of numerical integration.

SimuLizar Intra-Simulation Power Analysis The *simulizar.power* component realizes the intra-simulation power analysis. It contributes the Power Consumption metamodel to the runtime model of SimuLizar via the *Model-Load* extension point. The component calculates power consumption using *power.interpreter*, and the energy consumption using *power.calculator.energy*. Instead of EDP2 metric data streams, the intra-simulation integration calculates the power consumption using the measurements in the Palladio Runtime Measurement Model (PRM) [20] of SimuLizar. *simulizar.runtimemeasurement* couples PRM with SimuLizar. It allows for the registration of additional metric providers to SimuLizar. *simulizar.power* contributes the power consumption measurements via this interface. SimuLizar propagates all measurements in PRM and the EDP2 repository of the analysis to all plugins registered via its *ProbeFrameworkListenerDecorator* extension point.

Simulizar uses *simulizar.slidingwindow* to calculate sliding window aggregates on metrics that are recorded in the PRM instance of an analysis. As part of this thesis, a generic metric processing pipeline based on the pipes-and-filters pattern was introduced to SimuLizar. This generic aggregation mechanism is used to calculate the average utilization in the sampling interval. The mechanism is implemented separate from its equivalent for the post simulation analysis, the *UtilizationFilterMeasureProvider*.

4.5. Assumptions and Limitations

The PCA approach bases on a set of assumptions. The following summarizes the assumptions and discusses limitations.

Availability of architecture performance model. The PCA prediction approach requires an architecture performance model as a prerequisite for power and energy consumption predictions. This does not limit the applicability of the approach if an architecture performance model is already used to evaluate the performance of a system at design time. Investigating the impact of design decisions on power or energy consumption in isolation of other quality characteristics offers little insight to a software architect. In disregard of all other quality criteria, power and energy consumption is typically minimal if a minimal number of servers is used. However, the consolidation of software components on a minimal number of servers negatively impacts performance. This illustrates that the evaluation of design decisions regarding their effect on energy efficiency inherently requires both performance and energy consumption predictions. Software architects can use the same architecture performance model as the foundation of performance and energy consumption analyses when they apply our PCA prediction approach. Thus, the assumption does not limit the applicability of our approach due to the interconnectedness of power and performance.

Availability of consumption characteristics description. The presented analysis approach PCA relies on a consumption characteristics description in the form of a Power Consumption model instance. Power Consumption models can be extracted automatically using the method outlined in Chapter 5. Alternatively, they can be defined manually based on power models extracted by different approaches. We designed PCA to be extensible. If the power consumption of a set of power consumers in a software system can not be expressed as a mathematical expression, PCA supports the introduction of complex black-box power models. The implementation of the black-box power models can be added to PCA via custom calculators.

Limited influence of hidden device states. McCullough et al. [135] name "hidden device states" as a source of inaccuracies in power consumption predictions. Hidden device states are power saving states which are not explicitly documented and accessible, e.g., via IPMI. The PCA prediction approach outlined in this thesis assumes that

1. the influence of such hidden states on the power consumption of the system under investigation is limited, or
2. the states can easily be identified via profiling.

Different evaluations [35, 65, 69, 82, 104, 135, 172, 231] show that power models for servers are accurate even when ignoring hidden device states. Thus, assumption 1 holds for servers. For mobile devices, hidden device states can significantly impact power consumption. However, these states can be identified by means of profiling, as illustrated by Yoon et al. [230]. The power consumption of identified states can be analyzed with PCA. Consequently, assumption 2 holds for mobile devices. Other device categories, such as embedded systems, are not investigated in this thesis. Due to their limited influence on power consumption prediction accuracy in the domain of enterprise and mobile computing, the assumption is considered weak.

No explicit modeling of variations in power consumption across identical components. Identical server components can showcase different power consumption characteristics due to variations in the production process [108]. Our metamodel does not explicitly express these variations as part of the Binding or Specification viewpoint. The influence of consumption variations of individual components on the full server is less significant. Hence, we opted to not include an explicit abstraction of consumption variations in the model. In order to apply our model to domains where the variations have a more significant impact, i.e., sensor networks, this limitation can be addressed in one of the following ways:

1. Modeling of variations between components via different *PowerBindings*. The differences in power consumption between individual server components can be expressed by creating a *PowerBinding* for each varying type. A disadvantage of this approach is that it does not model uncertainty, but rather the variations between specific servers.
2. Use of a *FixedFactor* to model the variability across instances of the same device. In this case, the consumption variability can be modeled via a stochastic power model.
3. Introduction of a new type which extends *ConsumptionFactor*. This type could be used to distinguish consumption variations from other factors that describe the power consumption of a component.

Approaches 1 and 2 are supported by the current modeling abstraction. Only 3 would require an explicit model extension regarding the captured consumption factors. As the metamodel has been designed to support the introduction of new *ConsumptionFactors*, we consider the limitation regarding the chosen modeling abstraction minor.

4.6. Summary

This chapter presented the PCA approach for the design time analysis of power and energy consumption of a software system. Our approach complements performance prediction approaches. Thereby, it enables trade-offs between performance and power consumption. PCA predicts the power consumption of individual infrastructure elements based on performance metric predictions. It leverages existing performance analyses such as SimuCom [22] and SimuLizar [18, 20] as the source of its predictions. Furthermore, it supports the integration of derived metrics as input metrics. PCA supports the analysis of power consumption for static as well as self-adaptive software systems. Based on the power consumption prediction approach, the chapter developed a method for evaluating the impact of design decisions on energy efficiency (EE).

We designed PCA to be extensible, e.g., to support the consideration of new power model types. The implementation as of writing this thesis supports a set of black-box power models used in the evaluation of [200]. Additionally, it supports the analysis of power models that are defined as mathematical expressions.

5. Power Model Extraction

This chapter presents an automated approach for power model extraction of servers. We designed the approach to extract power models as input for architecture-level power consumption analyses. The extracted power models predict the power consumption of a server from a set of input system metrics, e.g., CPU utilization. A power model has to be learned once for each server type. Once the power model has been learned, the power model can be used to evaluate the power consumption of different software systems if they were to be deployed on a server of the same server type. We published the method presented in this chapter in [201].

Our approach aims to reduce the effort required to derive power models by automating server profiling, model training, and model selection. The approach uses systematic experiments to obtain a representative power consumption profile of a server. The profile serves as input to model training techniques, such as statistical learning. We leverage these techniques to learn power models. Using an information-theoretic model selection criterion, we support the selection of relevant system metrics, and the power model for design time predictions.

We implemented the systematic server profiling in a server profiling framework. We implemented the framework atop the technical foundation of SERT [29]. The profiling collects power consumption measurements and system level performance metrics, e.g., CPU utilization and HDD throughput. Our framework collects power consumption measurements from a dedicated wall power meter. Our implementation of the model training automates the construction of instances of the Power Consumption metamodel presented in Chapter 3. It automates the parametrization of power model bindings from a *PowerBindingRepository*. Finally, we rank all bindings based on our ranking criterion.

In Section 5.1 we discuss the challenges that have to be addressed by an automated approach for power model extraction. Section 5.2 presents our automated power model extraction method. Section 5.3 outlines an extension of our approach for the extraction based on historical measurements. Assumptions and limitations are discussed in Section 5.5. Lastly, Section 5.6 provides a summary.

5.1. Challenges

Chapter 4 presented the design time power consumption prediction approach PCA. PCA relies on accurate power models to predict the power consumption of a software system. Power models can be derived via manual measurement and model parametrization. However, the manual extraction of power models is cumbersome and error-prone. In this context, extraction refers to the collection of training data, and the training of power models for a server on the data. We derived Research Question 5 from this observation:

Research Question 5. *How can the effort in deriving power models for architecture-level power consumption analyses be reduced?*

Our architecture-level analysis predicts the power consumption of a software system using these power models. Our power consumption analysis uses performance metric predictions as input to the power consumption analysis. This avoids a redundant behavior specification as a prerequisite to analyze power and performance characteristics. The software architect does not need to provide a separate behavior specification, which is tailored towards the prediction of power consumption. Instead, she can use metric predictions from performance model specifications as input to the power consumption analysis.

The Power Consumption metamodel complements the behavior specification with a description of server power consumption. This description can be reused to evaluate the power consumption of different software architectures and workload mixes. Depending on the hardware, the power consumption may correlate with different power consumption metrics. The power consumption of servers has been observed to strongly correlate with CPU utilization. It is not clear whether the consideration of additional metrics, e.g., storage utilization, may improve prediction accuracy. This led us to the following Research Question:

Research Question 7. *How can software architects and system deployers be supported in the selection of input metrics for energy efficiency analyses?*

We derive a set of challenges from the two research questions. Our approach aims at addressing these **Ch**allenges.

Ch_1 Required knowledge of metrics affecting power consumption. The software architect has to identify central metrics that impact the power consumption of a software system. In order to avoid unnecessary effort, only metrics that significantly impact the prediction accuracy of power and performance should be considered. Every additional metric considered by a power model increases the complexity of model learning. The parameter space of a system metric-based power model grows exponentially with the number of input metrics. More importantly, every introduced metric also needs to be predicted by the performance analysis that provides the prediction input for the power model. The prediction of metrics, e.g., storage read and write throughput, requires that the architectural performance model provides the information to predict these metrics. In case of storage metrics, this necessitates a modeling of resource demands caused by storage accesses.

Ch_2 Selection and construction of representative workloads. When extracting power models for use in design time analyses, the implementation of the system is not yet fully available. Consequently, we cannot train power models using the target application and user load. The construction of power models for design time analyses thus relies on workloads that are representative of the target workload. We refer to a set of workloads as representative if it meets the following criteria.

- It produces representative measurements. We consider measurements representative if they cover the system metric load levels expected from the software system under design.
- It allows to correlate the variance of system metrics with power consumption for the considered metric measurement domain.

Ch_3 **Selection of suitable power model.** Over the years, many different power model types have been proposed to model the power consumption of servers using system metrics [59]. The selection of a power model that best describes the power consumption of a server under investigation has not been addressed in previous work.

5.2. Power Model Extraction by Systematic Experimentation

Figure 5.1 depicts an overview of the power model extraction method for extracting power models for architecture-level energy efficiency analyses. The method process is subdivided into three main steps *server profiling*, *model training* and *model selection*. In server profiling, we automatically profile the server under investigation for a set of resource metrics. This produces a server profile used as input for the *model training*. Model training trains a set of power models on the measured system metrics and power consumption. The third step *model selection* ranks power models based on their predicted accuracy. This enables users to select a suitable power models, and reason on the effects of system metrics on prediction accuracy.

The following sections further elaborate on each of the three phases. Section 5.2.1 presents our approach for an experiment-driven server profiling. Section 5.2.2 outlines how the resulting power consumption profiles can be used to learn power models. Section 5.2.3 describes a model selection method that can be used to evaluate the impact of metrics on prediction accuracy.

5.2.1. Server Profiling

This section presents an approach for the automated profiling of server power consumption for predefined metric measurement targets. The following refers to the realization of the approach as profiling framework. Prerequisite to our approach is the availability of a measuring device for collecting power data. This can either be a dedicated power meter connected to the wall socket of the server PSU, or a meter built into the PSU.

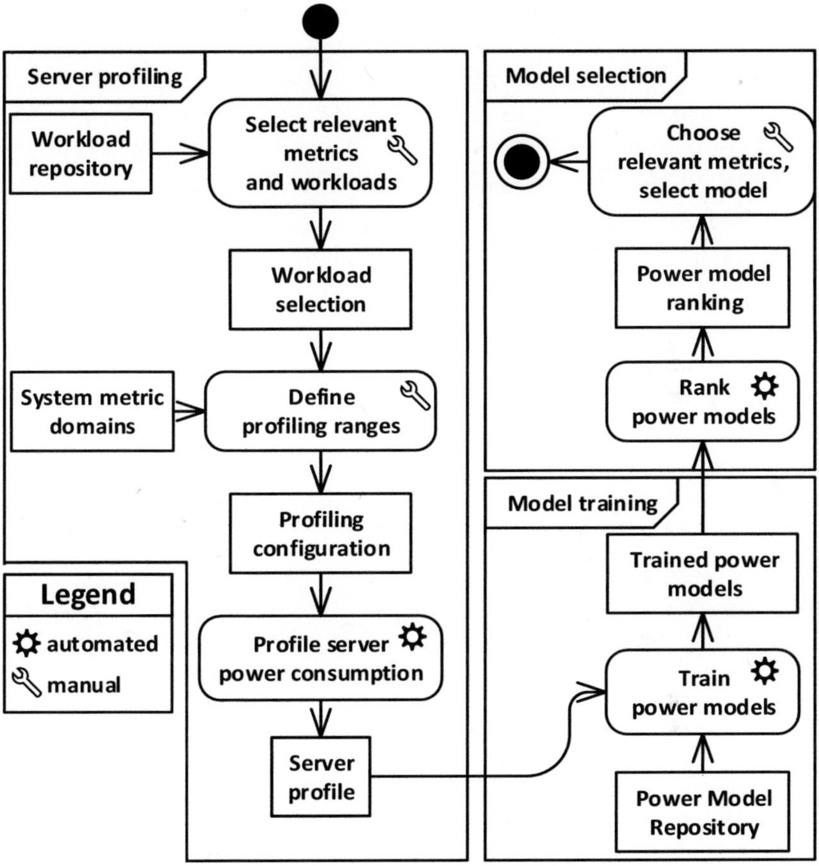

Figure 5.1.: Overview of the power model model extraction process.

5.2.1.1. Running Example

The running example illustrates our profiling method along the analysis of an enterprise server deployment environment. We employ the PowerEdge R815 server as an example of a server in this category.

Design time performance analyses like SimuLizar [20] or SimuCom [22] support the prediction of central system performance metrics. Examples of such metrics are the average CPU utilization u_{cpu}, storage read tp_{read} and write throughput tp_{write}. Our PCA approach uses these system metric predictions as input to its design time power consumption predictions. PCA uses power models to evaluate the power consumption of hardware resources based on the input metric predictions. PCA thus has to rely on metrics supported by the design time performance analysis.

Our running example assumes that the three metrics u_{cpu}, tp_{read}, and tp_{write} can be predicted by the used performance analysis.

5.2.1.2. Selection of Used Resource Metrics and Workloads

The user initially defines the set of metrics that she considers candidates for input parameters of power models. Each metric quantifies the utilization of a system resource such as CPU or storage devices. The metrics selected by the user are the system metrics that the server profiling considers when measuring out the server under investigation.

The metric set is defined as $M_{\text{profile}} = \{m_1, \ldots, m_n\} \subseteq M$. Hereby, M is the set of measurable metrics. The metrics M_{profile} selected by the user are the metrics that she would be able to predict at design time. For our running example, we select the metrics $M_{\text{profile}} = \{u_{\text{cpu}}, tp_{\text{write}}, tp_{\text{read}}\}$

Based on the metrics selected by the user in this step, server profiling can automatically select workloads $W \subset W_{\text{repo}}$ from a set of workloads that are predefined in a repository W_{repo}. Each workload $w \in W_{\text{repo}}$ has a controllable load intensity parameter l. The load intensity parameter $l \in (0, \infty) \cdot 1/\text{s}$ controls the rate with which a load driver executes workload transactions. Every $W \subset W_{\text{repo}}$ is assigned to exactly one metric $m_j \in M$, where steady state measurements of m_j increase monotonically with l. This implies that a workload w stresses the utilization of one of the resources that is quantified by the metrics selected by the user. The increased utilization manifests in higher measurement values of m_j. Information of a relationship of l and m_j is persisted alongside the repository definition W_{repo}. The user does not need to determine the relation between m_j and l. Once a new workload has been added to $W \subset W_{\text{repo}}$, any future user can leverage the persisted relation.

An example workload for u_{cpu} is the AES encryption workload w_{AES} from the SERT framework. For the CPU-intensive workload w_{AES}, u_{cpu} increases monotonically with l. w_{rwrite} is an I/O intensive workload from SERT. It performs storage write operations that follow a randomized access pattern. For w_{rwrite}, tp_{write} increases monotonically in l.

Individual workloads can be combined to workload mixes. A workload mix is a subset $\{w_1, \ldots, w_n\} \subset W$. $\{w_{\mathrm{aes}}, w_{\mathrm{rwrite}}\}$ is a workload mix that combines a CPU- with a storage-intensive workload. As a default, all possible workload mixes may be used. To reduce measuring effort and time, the user can limit the set of considered workloads.

5.2.1.3. Definition of Profiling Ranges

The automated power consumption profiling uses the workloads selected in the previous step to measure out the profiling domain. The profiling domain marks the range of measurements that the user considers relevant. The profiling domain can be derived from benchmarks or stress tests that push the metric to the maximum or minimum measurable value. The range between minimum and maximum values corresponds to the profiling domain of an individual metric. The combined domain of each metric forms a conservative boundary of the multidimensional profiling domain. In conjunction with the workload selection from step 5.2.1.2, the combined domain limits form the profiling configuration.

In order to profile the server for specific metric measurement thresholds, we have to sample its profiling domain. Our profiling framework, by default, employs an equi-width sampling of the profiling domain of each considered metric. Then, it constructs the full profiling domain as the Cartesian product of the individual domains.

For the example PowerEdge R815 server, we determined the maximum write throughput to be around 120 MB/s. Using a sample size of six, equi-width sampling produces the write grid $L_{tp_{\mathrm{write}}} = \{24i\,\mathrm{MB/s} \mid 0 \leq i \leq 5 \land i \in \mathbb{N}\}$ for the R815 server. An equi-width grid for u_{cpu} with sample size 21 results in $L_{u_{\mathrm{cpu}}} = \{\frac{1}{20}i \mid 0 \leq i \leq 20 \land i \in \mathbb{N}\}$. For u_{cpu} and tp_{write}, this results in a combined profiling domain grid of $L_{u_{\mathrm{cpu}}} \times L_{tp_{\mathrm{write}}}$.

5.2.1.4. Profiling Server Power Consumption

The profiling of the server automates the extraction of a representative server for a given profiling configuration. The server profiling executes the predefined workload mixes on the target environment. It conducts a profiling run for each tuple in the profiling grid. An example tuple from the grid $L_{u_{\text{cpu}}} \times L_{tp_{\text{write}}}$ is $(l_{u_{\text{cpu}}}, l_{tp_{\text{write}}}) = (0.55, 24\,\text{MB/s})$.

Figure 5.2 visualizes a profiling run for $(l_{u_{\text{cpu}}}, l_{tp_{\text{write}}})$ of the running example. Figure 5.2b shows the graphs for the storage intensive workload w_{rwrite}. Figure 5.2a displays the results for the CPU intensive workload w_{AES}. The top half graph of Figures 5.2a and 5.2b display metric samples over time as black points. The sliding window average over the measurements is displayed as a gray line. The lower half graph shows the delays between successive transaction executions over time for the given workload. The profiling uses varying delays to target different load intensities.

The framework executes both workloads in parallel. Thereby, it is able to observe and react upon effects of each workload on the metric values of other controlled workloads. In the running example, the storage intensive workload w_{rwrite} also causes some load on the CPU. To consider this load, the framework has to increase the delay of w_{AES} above the delay of an isolated execution of w_{AES}.

A profiling run executes in six phases. The vertical lines in Figure 5.2 highlight these phases. In phase 1, the profiling framework initializes each workload in the workload mix. Phase 2 is the calibration phase. The calibration varies the mean delay value until it reaches a delay value for which the workload stresses the system to the target level. The load intensity calibration is performed to ensure that measurements are collected for the specified target measurements. For this, the profiling framework controls the mean delay of all workloads in a workload mix in parallel.

Algorithm 3 delineates the load intensity calibration algorithm. The profiling framework executes the algorithm in each profiling run. The framework executes the algorithm concurrently for each workload in the workload mix. The framework periodically executes an iteration of the algorithm with the configured calibration interval time. The example profiling run depicted in Figure 5.2 was executed with an interval time of 0.7 seconds.

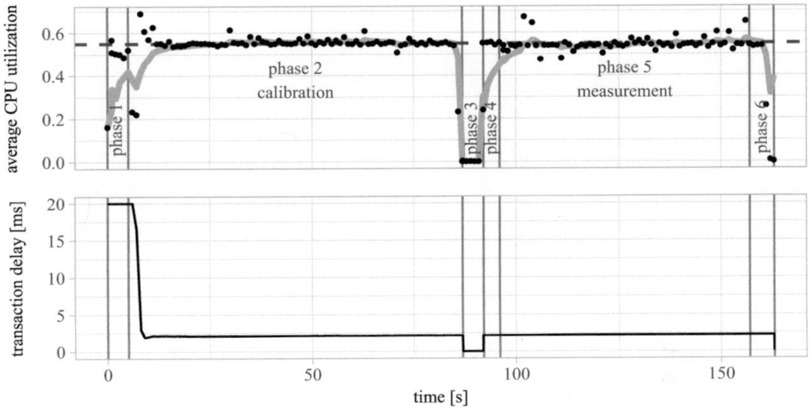

(a) Top: u_{cpu}. In gray: smoothed average of the measurements, and target value 55%. Bottom: Transaction delays for w_{AES}.

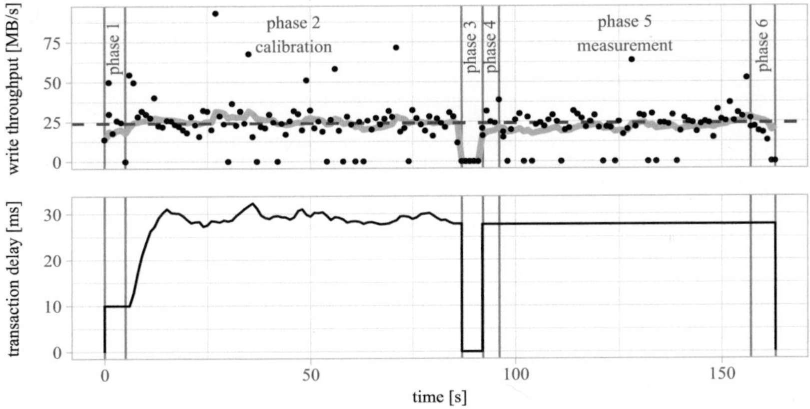

(b) Top: tp_{write}. In gray: smoothed average of the measurements, and target value 24 MB/s. Bottom: Transaction delays for w_{rwrite}

Figure 5.2.: Example run for target level $(l_{u_{cpu}}, l_{tp_{write}}) = (0.55, 24\,\text{MB/s})$ of workload mix (w_{AES}, w_{rwrite}). Both displayed processes 5.2b and 5.2a execute in parallel.

state : *thresholdReached* $\leftarrow$ false
input : Current system metric value u, Target metric value u_t,
Threshold metric value u_{thold}, Metric-specific alpha
α_m,
Initial delay *currentDelay*
output : Delay to throttle workload *currentDelay*

1 **if** $\neg$*thresholdReached* **then**
2   **if** $u < u_{\text{thold}}$ **then** *thresholdReached* $\leftarrow$ *true*;
3   **else** *currentDelay* $\leftarrow 2 \cdot$ *currentDelay*;
4 **else**
5   *targetDelay* $\leftarrow$ *currentDelay* $\cdot \frac{u}{u_t}$;
6   *currentDelay* $\leftarrow$ *currentDelay*$\cdot(1-\alpha_m)+$*targetDelay*$\cdot\alpha_m$;
7   **if** $\alpha_m > 0.1$ **then** $\alpha_m \leftarrow 0.9 \cdot \alpha_m + 0.01$;

Algorithm 3: Adaptive calibration policy for controlling workload intensity.

The calibration algorithm operates on a controlled system metric u. We assume u to be a metric whose measurements grow monotonically with the load intensity l. The load intensity grows proportional to the inverse delay *currentDelay*. u_t is the target metric measurement level. For the example workload mix u_t has the values 0.55 and 24 MB/s, respectively.

The algorithm proceeds in the following way. First, the algorithm tries to reach a practical starting value for *currentDelay* (lines 1–3). The algorithm starts from an initial input value for *currentDelay*. This input value is workload specific, as the size and complexity of transactions varies between workloads. The initial delay is also system specific to a certain extent. Different initial delays should be used if two systems process transactions at rates that are orders of magnitude apart. The algorithm doubles the delay in each iteration, starting from the initial *currentDelay*. The algorithm performs the exponential delay adjustment to prevent contention on the resource of u. Otherwise, if the initial *currentDelay* were set too low, the calibration could overload the resource. Since the initial transaction delay is too high for w_{AES}, it is not visible in Figure 5.2a. For the storage intensive workload w_{rwrite}, the initial exponential delay adaption was not needed. Thus, Figure 5.2b does not display corresponding effects.

After the initial starting value has been found, the algorithm gradually adjusts the delay (lines 5–7). The algorithm estimates the delay required to achieve the target level u_t as the delay value used in the last iteration multiplied with the ratio of the current value u and u_t.

Line 6 applies an exponentially moving weighted average (EWMA) to the controlled delay value *currentDelay*. We employ an exponentially smoothened delay value to lessen the effect of temporary fluctuations of the controlled system metric (line 6). a_m is the metric specific exponential smoothing factor. The EWMA quickly devalues older measurements for larger α_{m}. For smaller α_{m}, older measurements have a higher weight.

The running example illustrates the benefit of the exponential smoothing. As we can see in Figure 5.2b, individual measurements of tp_{write} scatter strongly throughout the calibration phase. One reason for this is the aggregation of write operations in storage drivers and middleware.

The algorithm reduces the exponential smoothing factor α_m throughout the calibration to counteract fluctuations caused by the scattering of measurement values (line 7). This reduces the effect of later target delay estimations. Line 7 causes α_m to approach a smoothing factor of 0.1 from above. For the running example, the reduction causes *currentDelay* to converge towards the delay, which reaches an average utilization close to the intended target metric tuple $(l_{u_{\mathrm{cpu}}}, l_{tp_{\mathrm{write}}}) = (0.55, 24\,\mathrm{MB/s})$.

Figure 5.2b illustrates the functioning of the second part of the load calibration algorithm by the example of w_{rwrite} and tp_{write}. The lower half of the graph shows the value of *currentDelay* at any point throughout the calibration. The starting value of *currentDelay* is 10 ms. Initially, α_m is set to 0.2 for w_{rwrite} and the write throughput metric tp_{write}. Each subsequent run of the algorithm reduces α_m towards 0.1. The algorithm quickly steers $currentDelay$ towards approximately 30 ms.

The load calibration for w_{rwrite} and w_{AES} shown in Figure 5.2a operates with an initial value $\alpha_m = 0.65$. The transaction delay starts at 30 ms and quickly gets reduced below 2.5 ms. Due to the higher stability of the CPU load measurements, the delay remains stable after the initial reduction.

In phase 3, the framework halts all workloads. Phase 4 serves as a warmup phase. In it, the framework restarts the workloads with the final delay values. The purpose of phase 3 and 4 is to increase measurement stability.

In phase 5 (measurement), the framework collects measurements of the considered system level metrics and power. It uses the final value of *currentDelay* from the calibration phase to profile the server under investigation for the target level. The framework keeps the delay value stable. We consider the measurements collected in this phase as representative of the system under the target load level. The framework collects measurements throughout the profiling run using a fixed sampling rate. It smooths the measurements by applying EWMA to the measurements. Figure 5.2 represents raw measurements as points. The EWMA is displayed as a gray line.

The workload continues its execution into phase 6 due to technical reasons. I.e., this gives the framework time to persist the measurements from the measurement phase. The profiling framework assigns the measurements collected in the measurement phase to the corresponding target level. The resulting server profile contains a mapping of each input target level to measurements, and the power consumption measurements collected for the target level.

5.2.2. Model Training

The model training step trains a set of power model types. A power model type is a power model with unbound independent variables, as Section 3.2 explained. It produces a set of power models trained to predict the power consumption of the server under investigation.

The model learning uses the server profile collected in the server profiling phase as training data. The model learning trains the power models types contained in a provided Power Model Repository. Section 3.2.1 introduced the repository specification of our Power Consumption metamodel. Prior to the training, the power model types contained in the repository are filtered to only contain power model types with metrics that were considered in the server profiling. In the running example, we filter the repository to only consider power model types that have a subset of $\{u_{\text{cpu}}, tp_{\text{write}}, tp_{\text{read}}\}$ as unbound input variables.

Model learning techniques that can be used on the profile are nonparametric and parametric regression techniques. An example parametric regression technique is iterated reweighted least squares regression as implemented by Rousseeuw et al. [177]. Instances of nonparametric regression techniques are MARS [71] or symbolic regression [178]. Both MARS [58] and symbolic regression [8] have been applied in related work to model the power consumption of servers.

We employ iterated reweighted least squares regression as the default method to train declarative power model types, i.e., *DeclarativePowerModelSpecifications.* As the regression method requires starting parameters, we apply it to a given *ResourcePowerBinding* of a declarative model. The initial values of the *FixedFactors* of the model serve as starting parameters. From there, our framework uses the implementation by Rousseeuw et al. [177] to train the binding on a given server profile.

5.2.3. Model Selection

The model training step trained a set of power models to predict the power consumption of the server. The power models predict the power consumption with varying degrees of accuracy. In order to get an unequivocal power consumption prediction, we need to select one of the power models.

Selecting a power model for use at runtime is straightforward. The accuracy of runtime power models can be evaluated using the actual workload. Model prediction accuracy of power models can be determined at runtime by comparing the runtime predictions from the power models against measurements. The model that performs best in the direct comparison of measurement and prediction then can be selected.

At design time, the final application architecture, its implementation and user load may not be known yet. Consequently, we can not determine the prediction accuracy of power models by comparing predictions with measurements. The uncertainty regarding the behavior of the final application makes it challenging to determine and select an accurate power model.

We employ AIC to evaluate the prediction accuracy of the power models M in the Power Model Repository that were trained in the previous model training step. Section 2.6 introduced the AIC foundations. We rank all power models in the repository based on their AIC. If all power models with the metric $m \in M$ are dominated by any model in $M \setminus \{m\}$, we deduce that the consideration of m likely does not increase the accuracy for the server under investigation. If the model is not dominated, a trade-off has to be made between the expected gain in accuracy and the effort required to consider m in the design time architecture performance model.

In theory, it would be possible to reason on model quality using the relative likelihood of the models calculated from their AICs [42, p. 75]. This would allow to quantify the difference between the models on a numerical scale. However, we did not observe meaningful differences between the models we considered in our validation. Section 7.3.8 discusses these validation results. The relative likelihood of all but the first place model had very similar relative statistical likelihood scores. Thus, we concluded that the differentation along a numerical scale provided no additional benefit beyond the AIC ranking.

5.3. Deriving Power Models from Historical Measurements

Section 5.2.1 presented a method for deriving power models via systematic experimentation. The outlined method requires the server under investigation to be available in isolation for the profiling period. In this time, no productive workload can be deployed on the server. During operation, it may not be possible to isolate servers that are in use by productive workloads. However, it is possible to use power consumption measurements from production if power consumption measurements can be collected from the server. The training of power models on historical measurements is an alternative to systematic profiling. We can use the historical measurements to learn power models if the server under investigation

- can not be reserved for systematic profiling,
- has historically run workloads that are representative of the target workload.

Prerequisite for the model learning is that historic power and system metric measurements are available for the server over a period of time. In order to avoid an over-weighting of, e.g., idle measurements, the historic measurements should be cleaned up and filtered. One approach towards this is a pre-aggregation of power measurements for measured values of the system metrics. In the case of CPU utilization u_{cpu}, its domain can be subdivided into 100 histogram buckets from 0 to 1. For each of the histogram buckets, the power measurements can be averaged. If the power model of the server is learned using the aggregated profile, this reduces the effect of frequent measurements values such as idle utilization.

Compared to the systematic profiling, the use of historical measurements does not interfere with the productive use of existing infrastructure. However, the accuracy of the resulting power models is limited by the availability of representative measurements. The trained power models have to extrapolate from existing measurements. This leads to inaccurate consumption predictions, if the recorded measurements do not cover the utilization levels and workload types relevant for the target workload. If the historical workload is similar to the expected target workload, the training on historical measurements may produce more accurate power models than the training on the profile from the systematic measurements. Since the profiling workload matches the operational workload, the error introduced by differences, e.g., in memory access patterns, is minimal.

5.4. Implementation

This section provides an overview of the implementation of the profiling framework presented in this chapter. An overview of the tooling implementation is available online [162].

5.4.1. Server Profiling

The implementation of our systematic profiling approach builds upon the technical foundation of SERT 1.1.1 [187]. This enabled us to reuse the existing workload specifications of SERT.

SERT executes a set of representative workloads, also referred to as *Worklets*. SERT issues its load in transactions. Each transaction encompasses a set of calls to the interface of a Worklet. The successive execution of Worklets forms an aggregate workload. The *Director* component of SERT serves as a load driver that runs the individual Worklets on the server under investigation. By default, the load driver performs an initial calibration run for each SERT Worklet. In this run, the controller determines the maximum achievable transaction rate of the Worklet on the system. Then, it derives the load levels lower than 100% by linearly reducing the transaction rate. Section 8.4 elaborates on the differences between SERT and our work.

We replaced the default SERT load driver with a custom one. Our load driver implementation replaces the calibration logic of SERT with the logic discussed in Section 5.2.1.4. During calibration, the load driver changes the delay time to arrive at target metric values. The load driver varies the transaction rate using the calibration method listed in Algorithm 3. Instead of steering the load towards fractions of the maximum measured load, it steers load towards the metric measurement values in the input system metric domains. The input metric domains are passed as input parameters to the tooling. Our implementation collects the input system metrics of the algorithm, e.g., CPU utilization, using Sigar [143]. For power consumption measurements, we leverage PTDaemon [192]. In addition to the steered metrics, further metrics can be captured in the recorded server profile.

The SERT load driver only executes one Worklet at any point in time. Our load driver is able to execute multiple Worklets in parallel. This allows us to simultaneously stress multiple resources, e.g., CPU and HDD. Our implementation instantiates one load driver for each steered metric. Each load driver separately controls the transaction rate of its Worklet. This enables different mixes between the executed Worklets. Additionally, it allows the calibration algorithm running in one load driver to adjust its transaction rate to the resource utilization that other load drivers cause.

The server profiling produces a server profile, which assigns each metric level with the measurements collected for it. This includes the power consumption measurements.

5.4.2. Model Training and Selection

We implemented the model training and model selection steps as an extension to the Power Consumption Analyzer (PCA) tooling environment, which Section 4.4 discussed. We built the model training implementation on the implementation provided by Krach [114]. Compared to the initial implementation, we extended the range of supported power model types, and improved component modularity. The tooling supports the training of declarative power models, i.e., *DeclarativeResourcePowerModelSpecification.*

Figure 5.3 provides an overview of the model training and selection implementation architecture. The *power.profilingimport* components realizes functionality for importing the server profile produced by the profiling into EDP2. The *regression* components train a set of specified power models. The *power.regression.r* component uses regression implementations [67, 177] available for the statistics framework R. Communication with the R backend is realized via the *Rserve* [213] library. We calculate the AIC for the ranking using the log-likelihood values returned by the regression implementations. Thus, this functionality is also offered by the regression components.

In addition to parametric regression methods, our implementation also supports the use of non-parametric regression. Non-parametric regression techniques are particularly useful when none of the known power model types accurately model the relationship between system metrics and power consumption. The two currently supported methods are symbolic regression [70], and Multivariate Adaptive Regression Splines (MARS) [140].

5.4.3. Power Model Extraction from Historical Measurements

We implemented the extraction of power models from historical measurements for the CACTOS variant of our Power Consumption metamodel. Section 3.2.5.2 outlined the core principles of this metamodel implementation. CactoScale realizes the monitoring and data collection infrastructure of CACTOS. It persists system level metrics of servers to an instance of the NoSQL database HBase [4]. Our power model extraction tooling uses the historical data collected in HBase as the source of training data.

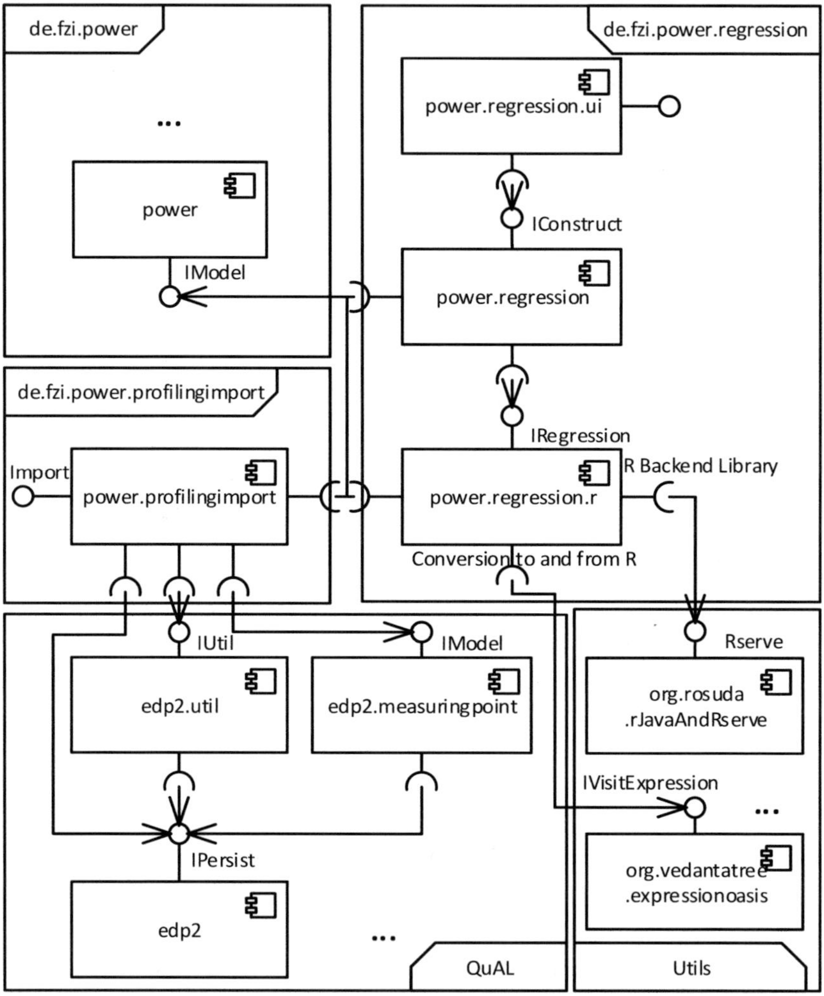

Figure 5.3.: Simplified UML component diagram of model training and selection architecture, and integration with PCA and PCM tooling. Component namespace prefixes are omitted for brevity.

The tooling uses the measurements collected in a specified time window as input to the model training. Prior to training a power model via iterated reweighted least squares regression [177], the input data is cleaned up. Every discrete utilization metric value is assigned the median value over all collected power consumption measurements, which has been collected for this metric value. This reduces the influence of measurement fluctuations and imbalances in the distribution of the input data.

5.5. Assumptions and Limitations

This section discusses assumptions and limitations of the power model extraction method.

Availability of power consumption measurements. The presented profiling approach relies on a source of power consumption measurements. Power consumption measurements can be provided by dedicated external measurement devices, such as power meters. Alternatively, built-in power meters, as found in PSUs of servers, may be used.

Steering of load intensity based on individual system metrics. The presented load calibration algorithm assumes that each workload w is assigned to exactly one system metric m. The load intensity of w is varied with the goal of varying m. The load intensity calibration does not explicitly consider that higher load intensities of w can increase measurement values of multiple system metrics, e.g., u_{cpu} and tp_{write}. If the additional system metrics are simultaneously stressed by separate workloads, the calibration algorithm considers the load caused by w. In summary, this does not restrict the applicability of our approach, as it implicitly accounts for workloads that stress multiple system resources.

Representativeness of the sampling strategy. The presented approach aims to derive power models for use at design time. Thus, its server profiling has to be performed without prior knowledge of the final workload. By default, the systematic profiling approach equally weights all target system metric levels in $L_1 \times \cdots \times L_n$. The equal weighting of target levels results in a distribution of metric measurements that are roughly equally distributed. Individual applications and user workloads, however, seldom stress the full utilization range of a server. The equal weighting does not anticipate the uneven distribution of server utilization levels. This results in a mismatch between the server profile used for power model learning and the utilization distribution. Most model learning techniques such as iterated reweighted least squares regression aim to reduce the error for frequently occurring input parameter values. As a consequence, the prediction accuracy of the learned models is lower than if the distribution was known.

We consider this to be a minor limitation due to the following two reasons. In design time analyses the workload intensity issued to software systems is varied to explore quality characteristics and energy efficiency at different workload levels. A weighting of specific utilization ranges reduces the prediction accuracy of learned power models for values outside of the weighted range. Second, the presented approach supports the consideration of uneven workload distributions. If the user of our approach has prior knowledge of the workload distribution, the distribution can be considered:

- in the selection of input target levels for the profiling,
- by aggregating system metric measurement before the model learning. The importance of different target level runs can then be weighted based on the workload distribution.

Accuracy of AIC-based ranking. In order for AIC to provide any meaningful prediction on model quality requires that the data set is representative of the system's behavior. The power model ranking hence is only accurate under the assumption that the profiling approach produces a representative server profile. Since AIC is an information theoretic criterion, the ranking only reflects the *likelihood* that a model is accurate. It does not imply that the model with the highest AIC has the highest accuracy for any server that the ranking approach is applied to.

No consideration of hidden device states. The presented profiling approach targets specific power system utilization levels. The profiling approach does not consider the influence of "hidden device states" as observed by

McCullough et al. [135]. These states refer to device or resource states that can not be observed, e.g. in different values of system metrics. If the hidden device states are known and can be triggered specifically, the presented approach can be used to profile the power consumption in specific system states. Thus, we consider this limitation not specific to our approach, but a general shortcoming of power models based on system metrics.

5.6. Summary

This chapter presents a power model extraction method. It allows users to obtain power models for use in design time power consumption predictions. The central benefit of the power model extraction method lies in its high degree of automation. Thereby, it reduces the effort for constructing power models compared to a manual or semi-manual power model extraction. The approach focuses on the reduction of effort to obtain the power models, which our design time energy efficiency analysis requires.

The chapter derives a set of challenges from Research Question 5 and Research Question 7. These challenges need to be met to address both questions.

The power model extraction method consists of the three steps server profiling, model training, and model selection. Server profiling leverages systematic experiments to extract representative power consumption profiles of servers. The experiments put varying degrees of load on multiple system resources. By automating the measurement of multiple metrics, this enables the user to reason on the effect of considering different metrics. This addresses Challenge Ch_1. Our server profiling approach builds upon the transactional workload definition of SERT. We added a novel mechanism to derive mixed workloads from the individual workloads. Thereby, our approach supports the integration and reuse of diverse workloads (Ch_2).

In conclusion, the presented approach addresses Research Question 5 by automating the significant parts of server profiling, model training, and model selection.

Using the consumption profiles, we train a set of power model types from a repository. This produces a set of power models that predict the consumption of the server under investigation. A ranking based on AIC supports the selection of an accurate power model for design time predictions (Ch_3).

We provide an implementation of our approach that automates the process from systematic measurement, measurement analysis, model training, to model selection. We validate our approach for a diverse set of workloads. In Section 7.2.2, we apply it as part of an end-to-end case study. The case study evaluates the energy efficiency of a software system on an architectural level. Section 7.3 evaluates our power model extraction approach to a set of Big Data and enterprise workloads.

6. Transient Effects

This chapter presents an approach for the coupled specification and analysis of *transient effects* of reconfigurations in self-adaptive software systems. The approach integrates with existing architectural approaches for the design time analysis of self-adaptive software systems like SimuLizar [18, 20], or SLAstic.SIM [133]. An earlier version of the metamodel, the analysis and formalization is outlined in [199].

After motivating the problem addressed by our approach in Section 6.1, Section 6.2 presents a metamodel for specifying the transient effects of reconfigurations in self-adaptive software systems. Section 6.3 details the formal semantics of the modeling constructs of the metamodel. Section 6.4 explains how the transient effects captured by instances of the metamodel can be considered in an existing quality analysis for self-adaptive software systems. Section 6.5 discusses assumptions and limitations of the presented approach. Section 6.6 concludes this chapter.

6.1. Motivation

Self-adaptive software systems aim to uphold QoS requirements under changing and uncertain environmental conditions. Examples for changes in environmental conditions are bursts in user load or variations of the available power budget of a system. Self-adaptive software systems trigger reconfigurations of their structure, deployment and configuration to deal with these changes.

It is crucial for the QoS offered by a self-adaptive system that its adaptation mechanisms act effectively and efficiently. The mechanisms should adapt the system when changes that violate QoS are expected to occur. For this, the mechanisms have to identify *when*, *where* and *what* to adapt. Ideally, reconfiguration mechanisms prevent QoS violations by preemptively triggering adaptations. The following properties of adaptations contribute to the difficulty of designing efficient and effective self-adaptive software systems.

1. **Adaptations do not complete instantaneously.** While adaptations like the adjustment of the load distribution policy used by a load balancer [20] takes a negligible amount of time, adaptations like VM migrations have execution times well above a couple of seconds [179, 205, 219]. A VM migration moves a running VM from a source host to a target host without requiring the VM to be shut down.
2. **Adaptations require resources to execute.** In the case of VM migration, network bandwidth is needed to migrate the VM, its memory and potentially its storage to the target host. The VM migration algorithm running on the migration host and target causes CPU, memory and storage load. The increased resource utilization increases power consumption.
3. **The impact of adaptations can not be observed immediately.** After an adaptation has been completed, its effect on QoS is delayed. Reconfiguring a load balancer to distribute new requests away from an overloaded server does not cause the response time of user requests to recover immediately. Requests queued up on the server still need to be processed.

This thesis classifies the manifestation of these three adaptation properties as *transient effects*. Transient effects refer to the impact of reconfigurations on quality characteristics that are caused by changes in the system environment and the adaptation made to address the changes. Examples for such changes are an increase or decrease in user load, or the power budget available to a set of servers in a data center.

Design time analyses for self-adaptive software systems like SimuLizar by Becker et al. [18, 20], or SLAstic.SIM by Massow et al. [133] allow software architects to analyze self-adaptive software systems at design time. These existing approaches allow reasoning on the delayed effect of reconfigurations

(3). However, they do not consider the effect of reconfigurations on execution time (1) and consumed resources (2).

It is possible for an analysis to implicitly consider the delay between the completion and the time by which the adaptation effect can be observed. SimuLizar [18, 20] achieves this by separating the analysis of architectural runtime state and the state of pending requests. In order to account for the execution time (1) and consumed resources of adaptations (2) in architecture-level quality analyses, Research Question 9 needs to be addressed:

Research Question 9. *What is an architecture-level description of reconfigurations that describes the effect of reconfigurations on system metrics such as performance and power consumption?*

Section 6.2 addresses Research Question 9 by introducing a metamodel for a coupled specification of adaptation effect on system state and behavior. The proposed metamodel is based on Ecore. As such, it defines the syntax for the adaptation specification. Due to the limited semantic expressiveness of Ecore [134], Section 6.3 provides a formalization of the *behavioral semantics* [37] of the metamodel.

To support reasoning on transient effects at design time, analysis approaches must consider the impact of reconfigurations on quality dimensions like performance and power. Research Question 10 formulates these challenges:

Research Question 10. *How can we consider the effects of runtime reconfigurations in software quality analyses at design time?*

Two approaches can be taken towards the realization of a software quality analysis, which considers transient effects. The first option would be to design a new software quality analysis that considers transient effects. Second, an existing analysis approach can be extended to account for transient effects. The second approach offers the following advantages over the design of a new approach:

- **Reduced validation effort.** The validation of the developed analysis approach can build upon validation results for the existing approach. This reduces the set of analysis characteristics that need to be validated to the newly introduced or altered parts of the analysis.

- **Reuse of existing tooling and models.** The integration with existing analysis approaches allows users to easily evaluate and adopt the approach.

Due to the listed advantages, we opted to develop an approach that is compatible with existing analysis approaches. The following refers to the simulation component which realizes the analysis as Transient Effect Interpreter. We developed the central semantics of the transient effects analysis to be independent of a specific software performance simulation. Section 6.3 outlines the analysis semantics implemented by the Transient Effect Interpreter. As proof of concept, we integrated our analysis with SimuLizar by Becker et al. [20]. Section 6.4 provides more information on the Transient Effect Interpreter, and its integration with SimuLizar.

6.2. A Metamodel for an Architecture-Level Description of Transient Effects

Our Adaptation Action metamodel supports the reusable specification of *self-adaptation actions* for use in design time analyses. A self-adaptation action is an atomic reconfiguration operation. In deployed systems, actions group a set of atomically executed middleware operations. Self-adaptation languages based on the S/T/A paradigm [51, 96] embed actions into higher level reconfiguration abstractions to specify reconfiguration rules and plans.

The presented metamodel links the adaptation effect specification with a behavior specification. The behavior specification defines the overhead of the reconfiguration, i.e., its execution cost. The metamodel links this specification to individual adaptation action definitions. This enables a high level of composability and reuse. The effect of complex reconfigurations on performance and system configuration can be derived from their composed actions. The action specifications can be integrated with S/T/A languages to support design time analyses of reconfiguration mechanisms implemented using these languages.

Figure 6.1 provides an overview of the Adaptation Action metamodel. The model consists of four packages *core*, *parameter*, *instance*, *mapping* and *context*. The *core* package consists of the central entities for describing the

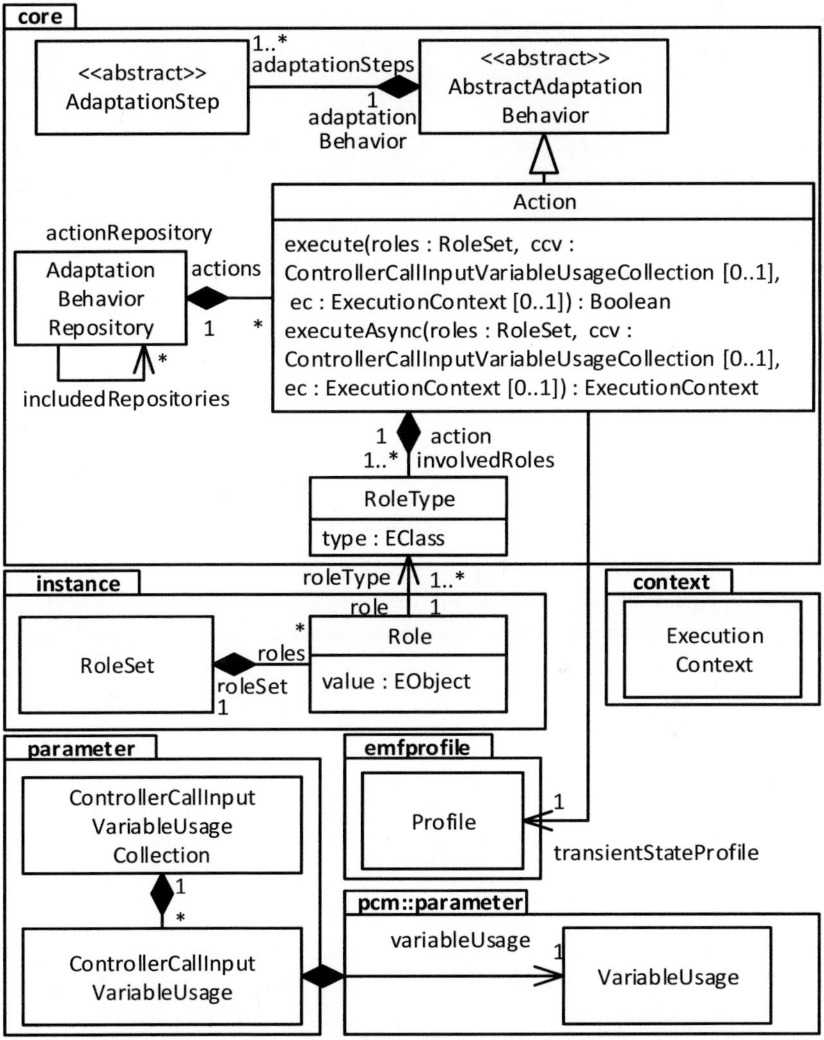

Figure 6.1.: Class diagram overview of Adaptation Action metamodel

structural and behavioral impact of self-adaptation actions. The *instance* and *parameter* packages group entities that parametrize the execution of an adaptation action. The *mapping* package subsumes entities that model a correspondence or mapping relation between entities in the architectural performance model and the input and output variables of an action. The package *context* contains an entity used for identifying the execution context of asynchronously executed actions.

6.2.1. Action Behavior Specification and Instantiation

An *AbstractAdaptationBehavior* couples a structural effect specification of an adaptation action with a specification of its performance effect. An *AbstractAdaptationBehavior* consists of a set of ordered *adaptationSteps* of type *AdaptationStep*. An adaptation step defines a substep of the action. All steps need to be executed before the action completes. Section 6.2.5 elaborates on the different types of steps.

AdaptationBehaviorRepository persists a set of *actions* of the type *Action*. The repository may include and export further referenced repositories via its *includedRepositories* reference. This allows for a composition of a repository from multiple existing repositories.

Action is the central entity of the model. It couples the structural effect specification of an adaptation action with a description of its performance impact. *Action* realizes *AbstractionAdaptationBehavior*. The type corresponds to type specification of an adaptation action in S/T/A frameworks. The steps contained in the action specify its adaptation logic.

An *Action* is instantiated using its *execute* operations. *Action* defines two operations *execute* and *executeAsync*. Each call to an *execute* operation instantiates the *Action* using the passed parameters. The Adaptation Action metamodel implements the operations as *EOperations*. The operations couple the model specification with the Transient Effect Interpreter. Section 6.4 further discusses the Transient Effect Interpreter. An adaptation mechanism triggers the execution of an adaptation action by calling one of the two operations. The Adaptation Action metamodel implementation realizes the two optional parameters of the operations by providing $2^2 = 4$ method implementations. This eases the use of the methods, as they can be called without passing null arguments for the non-used parameters.

6.2.2. Action Parameters

Adaptation actions depend upon parameters. Example parameters are the subjects of an adaptation action. Our metamodel refers to the parameters, which capture the entities involved in executing the adaptation, as roles. Each *Action* is parametrized by a set of roles. The *involvedRoles* containment links the adaptation behavior to the *RoleTypes* involved in the action. A *RoleType* defines the parameters of the action at the type level. It references the *EClass* type of the parameter passed to the action. A *Role* instantiates the *RoleType* it references. The relationship between *Role* and *RoleType* is an ontological instance-of relationship [9]. A *RoleSet* subsumes a set of *Role* instances in its *roles* containment. All operations of *Action* are parametrized by a *RoleSet*.

In addition to the role parameters, the metamodel supports the specification of additional factors that influence the transient effects of adaptation actions. *ControllerCallInputVariableUsageCollection* is the first optional parameter of the *execute* operations of an action. The *ControllerCallInputVariableUsage* parameters contained in the collection parametrize calls to the performance model that describe the transient behavior of the action. *ControllerCall-InputVariableUsage* contains a *VariableUsage* specification from PCM. This matches the instance type of parameters passed to operations as defined in PCM.

The central use of *ControllerCallInputVariableUsage* is the specification of dynamic, performance influencing factors outside of the roles. An example factor is the execution time of an algorithm that formulates a reconfiguration strategy. The algorithm execution time of an *Action* is a factor that influences its execution time. The dependency on algorithm execution time can be expressed as a *ControllerCallInputVariableUsage*. If defined, a reconfiguration mechanism can pass the execution time as an execution parameter of the action via a *ControllerCallInputVariableUsage*.

6.2.3. Synchronous and Asynchronous Execution

Self-adaptive software systems can simultaneously trigger or execute multiple adaptation actions. *Action* offers asynchronous execute operations with *executeAsync*, in order to support the asynchronous execution of actions specified in the presented metamodel. The difference between an asynchronous and synchronous execution of actions is that no simulation time passes before the asynchronous call returns. The optional execution parameter of type *ExecutionContext* identifies the context in which an asynchronous call is executed. The explicit representation of the execution context in the model allows reconfiguration actions to make decisions and progress dependent on asynchronously executed adaptation steps.

The synchronous *execute* returns a Boolean that indicates whether the action has been executed successfully. The *executeAsync* methods return the *ExecutionContext* that identifies the current execution context. If the method caller explicitly passes an *ExecutionContext*, the Transient Effect Interpreter executes the action in the passed context. If the caller does not pass a context, the Transient Effect Interpreter creates a new context. The interpreter emits an event once an asynchronous action completes. Adaptation mechanisms may react upon this event, e.g., to check if it should trigger further adaptations.

6.2.4. Identification of Running Actions

An adaptation action reconfigures the system to reach a target state from its source state. While the adaptation action is executed, the system entities involved in the reconfiguration may be in a transient state. During the transient phase, the subjects of adaptation actions might not be involved in further reconfigurations. An example of this is a VM migration action. While a migration of a VM is in process, it is not possible to migrate the same VM again until the migration completes. Our metamodel represents the subjects of an adaptation that are in transient states by annotating them with their state. We realized this annotation of transient states using a metamodel profile mechanism.

The *Action* references a *Profile* specification. *Profile* is a stereotype annotation that is realized using *EMF Profiles* [120]. The profile annotates the entities reconfigured by the adaptation action. It marks these adaptation subjects as being in a transient state. The explicit marking enables the definition of adaptation preconditions that consider whether an entity is already being reconfigured.

6.2.5. Adaptation Steps

This section outlines the types of steps in the metamodel used to model the effect of adaptation actions on system configuration and performance.

Figure 6.2 depicts the subtypes of *AdaptationStep* that Figure 6.1 omitted. A *BranchingAdaptationStep* contains a set of conditionally executed adaptations. Every execution path is modeled by a *GuardedTransition* and its contained behavior description. The attribute *booleanCondition* models the boolean condition on which the execution of *GuardedTransition* depends. The conditions are specified in QVTo model queries. An alternative solution would have been to allow users to specify the conditions using OCL expressions. While this would have increased the compactness of conditions, it would have limited their expressiveness. The *NestedAdaptationBehavior* contained in a *GuardedTransition* describes the behavior that is executed if the condition evaluates to true. As *NestedAdaptationBehavior* specializes *AbstractAdaptationBehavior*, it consists of a set of contained *adaptationSteps*.

We specify the performance effect of an adaptation action via *ResourceDemandingSteps*. A *ResourceDemandingStep* specifies the performance of an adaptation action as a set of calls to operations offered by the components of an architecture performance model. This thesis leverages the Repository viewpoint of PCM to describe the performance impact of adaptation actions in an *Adaptation Performance Model*. A *ResourceDemandingStep* contains a set of *ControllerCalls*. Each controller call models a call to the Adaptation Performance Model. The execution of the steps that follow the call continues only once the call has been processed.

A *ControllerCall* references the *OperationSignature* in the Adaptation Performance Model that the *ControllerCall* calls. The referenced operation signature definition belongs to a *BasicComponent*. The *BasicComponent* is not part of the initial architectural performance model definition of the analyzed software system. The reason for this is the open world assumption

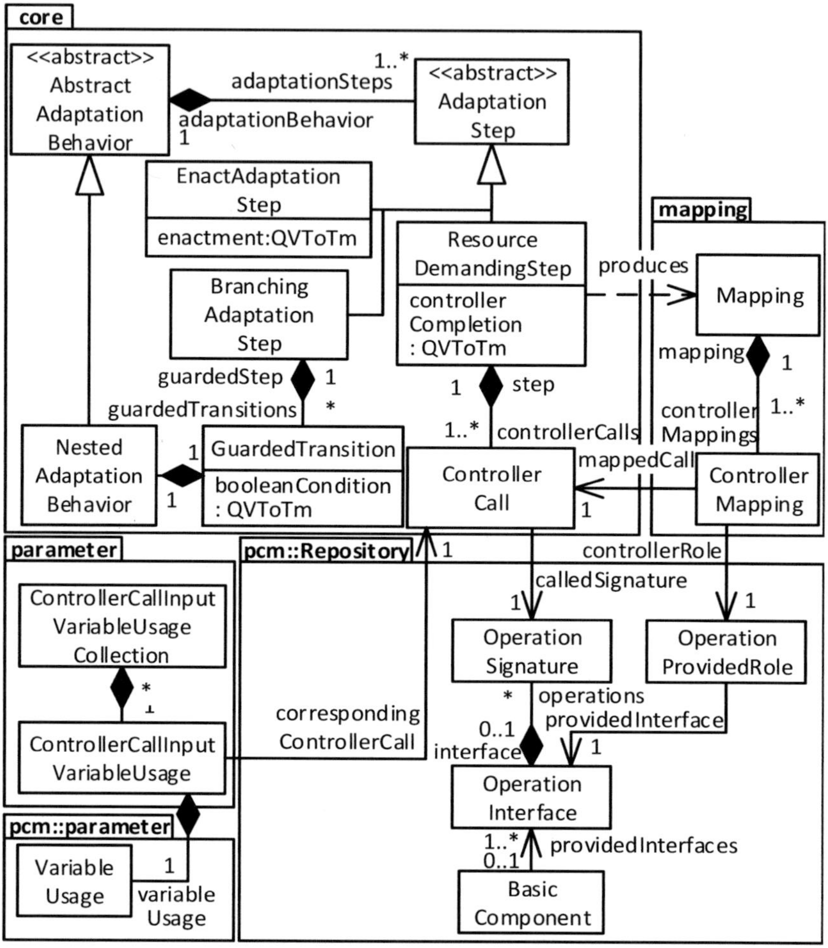

Figure 6.2.: Detailed class diagram view of the coupled behavior specification in the Adaptation Action metamodel.

made in this thesis: We assume that is infeasible to preempt and model all system configurations at design time.

The *controllerCompletion* QVTo model transformation referenced by the *ResourceDemandingStep* ensures that the components involved in processing the *ResourceDemandingStep* are present in the system. The transformation implements a performance model completion. Existing performance completion approaches [80, 228] enhance the analyzed model in a preprocessing step prior to the analysis. Unlike this, the *controllerCompletion* adds the Adaptation Performance Model mid-analysis when the action is executed. The model completion is parametrized by the architectural runtime model of the system under analysis, and the *RoleSet* passed to the action. The model completion produces a *Mapping* of the *Roles* in the *RoleSet* of the action. The *Mapping* contains a set of *ControllerMappings*. A *ControllerMapping* references the *OperationProvidedRole* of the component from the Adaptation Performance Model. Each *ControllerMapping* links the *ControllerCall* to the component, to which the call should be issued. The Transient Effect Interpreter uses the mappings to identify the component instances, and process the *ControllerCalls*.

EnactAdaptationStep expresses the effect of an adaptation on the system configuration. Its *enactment* QVTo model transformation maps the runtime architecture model prior to the execution of the action to the architecture model after the action has completed. Since *EnactAdaptationStep* realizes *AdaptationStep*, the enactment of an action can be executed in multiple steps.

6.2.6. A Process for the Definition of Actions

Our Adaptation Action metamodel provides a modeling language for the reusable specification of reconfiguration effects on system state and behavior. Subject of the modeling abstraction are self-adaptation actions. Self-adaptation actions may be composed to complex self-adaptation rules, e.g., as part of a S/T/A framework.

We identified the following steps as a guideline for the specification of actions in our modeling language:

1. **Establish the intended outcome of the action.** An action reconfigures a set of components or devices. This transitions them from a source to a target state. The action specification needs to model this transition.
2. **Identify actors and subjects involved in the action.** This includes service components, which manage the execution of the action.
3. **Specify preconditions of the action.** An action may only be executed if a set of preconditions are met. A common precondition is that the subject of an action may not already be reconfigured by the ongoing execution of a previous action. The preconditions should be limited to technical constraints, and not conditions of the reconfiguration rule which executes the action.
4. **Model the performance impact of the action.** The performance impact of the action can be derived using standard SPE techniques, e.g., systematic performance experiments. Parametric dependencies between characteristics of the input parameters, or the deployment environment should be explored as part of the performance modeling.

We applied the outlined approach to define coupled specifications of the adaptation effect on system state and behavior using Adaptation Action metamodel. The subsequent section discuss the resulting three example action instances.

6.2.7. Examples

This section illustrates our Adaptation Action metamodel via three example instances. The presented adaptation actions are examples of architecture-level adaptation actions.

6.2.7.1. Horizontal Scaling

This section outlines a specification of a scale-out action used to horizontally scale an application. Horizontal scaling enables applications to adjust the number of service replicas to deal with load variations. In an IaaS context, scale-out is realized by booting additional VMs, on which service replicas are deployed. These replicas are then wired with a load balancer that distributes user requests between all VM instances.

Figure 6.3 depicts a specification of scale-out action using the Adaptation Action metamodel. The QVTo file pictograms represents a QVTo model transformation that the object references. Each model transformation either implements a set of conditions via model queries, or extends the sytem model via model completions. We omit certain details of the action specification, e.g. IDs, from the figure in order to improve understandability.

ScaleOut has three parameter RoleTypes. *InstantiatedComponent* refers to the component which is started up as part of the scale-out. The *Instantiation-Controller* is wired with the component of the passed *LoadBalancer* Assembly Context. *InstantiationController* represents the software component that controls the scale-out execution. The deployment location of the controller does not need to be identical to the target location. This is the case if component instantiation is controlled by a management service. *TargetResourceContainer* is the Resource Container on which the launched component instance is deployed.

The specification root *ScaleOut* references an EMF Profile. The Profile contains a stereotype annotation for the type ResourceContainer. The annotation serves as a marker of Resource Containers, to which the scale-out deploys an additional component instance. Additionally, the root Action composes the adaptation behavior description from a set of Steps. The *preconditionsMet* contains the *checkPreconditions* transition that acts as a guard to the instantiation behavior. A QVTo query realizes the precondition check conditional on which the scale-out executes. In its current implementation, it checks whether any scale-outs that target the same *TargetResourceContainer* are already in execution. An additional conceivable constraint could be, e.g., that only one instance of *instantiatedComponent* can be created by a scale-out at any point in time.

The child element *instantiateComponent* of *checkPreconditions* specifies an ordered sequence of steps which comprise the adaptation behavior.

Its initial step is *instantiationOverhead*. The step triggers the performance overhead induced by the instantiation. The linked QVTo transformation

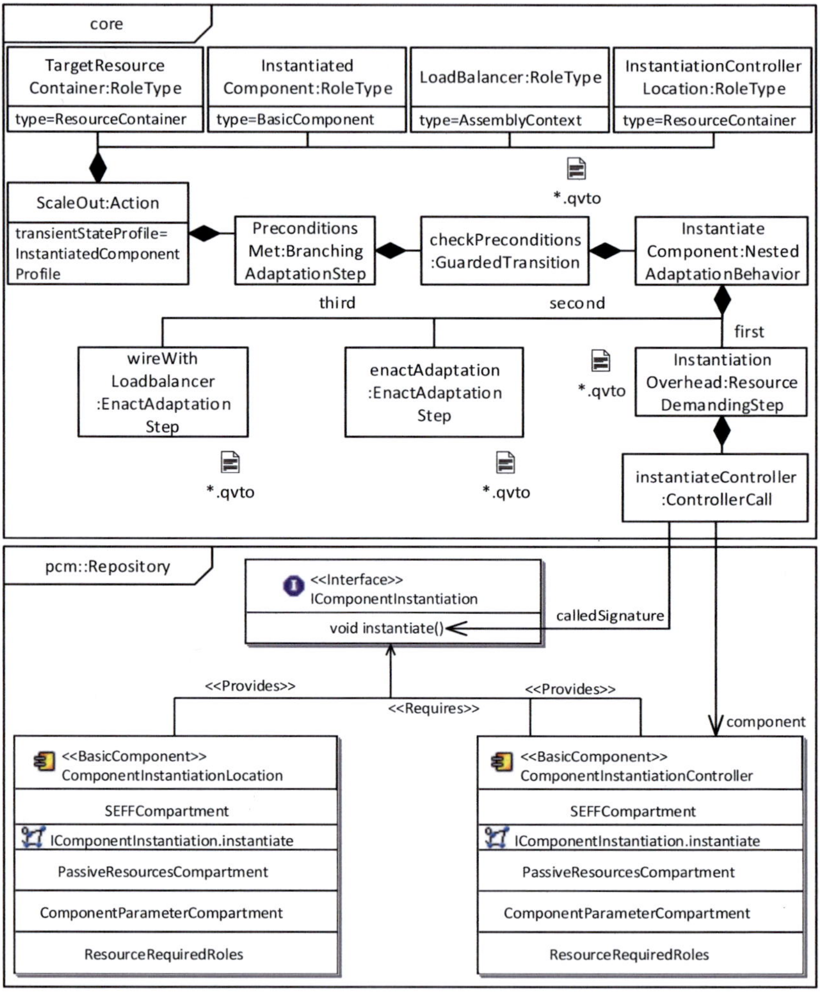

Figure 6.3.: Object diagram view of scale-out expressed as an instance of Adaptation Action metamodel.

implements a performance model completion. The model completion allocates and wires instances of the components that induce the performance overhead. It allocates an instance of *ComponentInstantiationLocation* on the Resource Container passed via the Action parameter *TargetResourceContainer*. In its *ComponentInstantiationController*, the *instantiate* RDSEFF issues a specified resource demand, and calls *instantiate* of the newly allocated *ComponentInstantiationLocation* instance. If a prior execution of the model completion already had allocated the components on *TargetResourceContainer* and *InstantiationController*, the model completion looks up the respective Allocation Contexts. When executed as part of the transient effects analysis, the model completion returns the allocated components in a *Mapping* collection (c.f. Section 6.2). The *instantiateController* ControllerCall defines a call to a *ComponentInstantiationController*. This call needs to be processed as part of the performance analysis, before the scale-out can be enacted.

The second step *enactAdaptation* specifies how the scale-out is enacted in the software system analysis. The linked QVTo transformation links a new Assembly Context of *InstantiatedComponent* with the system architecture, and allocates it to the *TargetResourceContainer*. Finally, the transformation removes the steoreotype annotation from the passed *TargetResourceContainer*. Subsequent scale-outs may then instantiate components on the *TargetResourceContainer* again.

The third step *wireWithLoadBalancer* wires the new component instance with the load balancer component instance that is passed in the *loadBalancer* parameter.

While the resource demands in the scale-out implementation uses fixed resource demands, the parameter can easily be extended, e.g., to resource demands that depend upon Basic Component properties. Example properties could be the memory footprint of components, or specific startup times.

Scale-out allows applications to deal with increases in load. We did not discuss its counterpart, scale-in, which decommissions replicated instances once they are no longer needed. Scale-in follows the same process logic as scale out. However, shutdown replaces startup, and the removal from the load balancer supersedes the addition.

6.2.7.2. Virtual Machine Migration

This section presents a model of VM live migrations that is specified with our Adaptation Action metamodel. The motivation in Section 6.1 introduced VM live migration as an example adaptation action that induces a transient effect. VM live migrations take time to complete. Their completion time depends on the CPU utilization of the migration target and source, network load, and memory activity. The presented example VM migration model abstracts from most performance dependencies. It models the transient effect as fixed resource demand distribution. We opted for this simple modeling as it was sufficient for the investigations we conducted in our validation. More complex performance interactions can be introduced to the linked PCM performance model, if needed.

Figure 6.4 depicts an example model of VM live migration. The outlined model assumes VMs to be represented as composite, or black box software components. The VM migration action has three parameters. *MigratedComponentAssemblyContext* refers to the Assembly Context, which is migrated from one server to another. *TargetResourceContainer* refers to the target server of the VM migration. The third parameter *MigrationController* is the migration service component that orchestrates the migration.

Before the action can be executed, the QVTo model query associated with *checkPreconditions* checks if the component is currently already being migrated. This is achieved by checking if the Assembly Context of the component has been tagged with the *MigratedAssemblyContext* stereotype. If the preconditions hold true, the Assembly Context is tagged with the Assembly Context, and the migration starts.

The migration behavior consists of two steps. The first step *migrateController* specifies the performance effect of the migration. Its *migrateVm* controller call specifies the performance effect of migration as a call to the linked PCM performance model. The performance model completion of *migrateController* defines how the components in the PCM performance model are supposed to be allocated in the system under analysis:

- *MigrationController* should be allocated on the passed *MigrationControllerLocation* Resource Container,
- *MigrationSource* on the migration source Resource Container, and

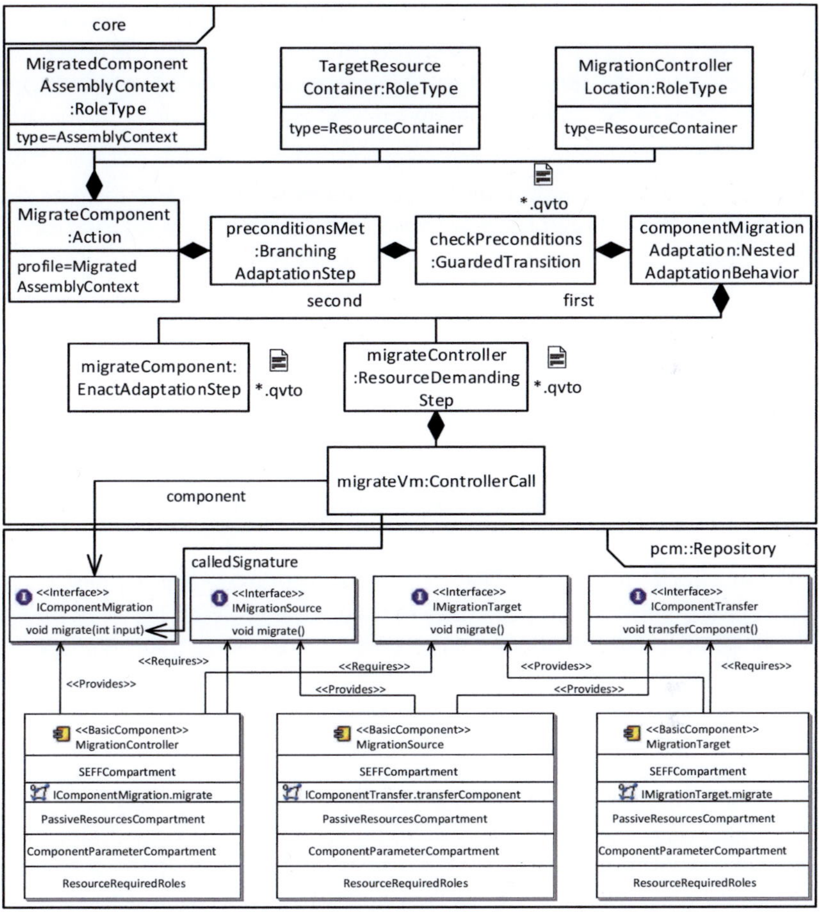

Figure 6.4.: Object diagram view of component migration adaptation expressed as an instance of Adaptation Action metamodel.

- *MigrationTarget* on the migration target Resource Container.

If the PCM system model already contains applicable instances of the migration middleware or controller components, the model transformation returns the existing instances instead. The performance model completion wires the migration controller with the migration source and target, and the migration target with the source. *MigrationController* orchestrates the migration by calling *MigrationTarget*. In turn, *MigrationTarget* starts the VM migration via a call to the *transferComponent* operation of the *MigrationSource* component.

The second step of the migration behavior *EnactAdaptationStep* finalizes the VM migration. Its model transformation moves the allocation location of the migrated component from the source to the target Resource Container. Subsequently, it removes the *MigratedAssemblyContext* from the migrated component instance.

6.2.7.3. Switching of Power States

This section presents a modeling of power state switching, or transitions, in a software system. The proposed modeling accounts for reconfiguration times of adaptation actions, which affect the power state of devices.

Computational and communication devices commonly can operate in different power states. Each state realizes a different trade-off between power consumption and performance. Active power management policies adapt the current power state to reduce power consumption in exchange for reduced performance. The goal of power management policies is to increase the energy efficiency, or battery lifetime of devices. Our Power Consumption metamodel explicitly captures power states, and transitions between power states. Section 3.2.2 introduced the Power State Machine (PSM) viewpoint. This viewpoint can be used to model power states and transitions. The Binding viewpoint instantiates power state machines via device type specific *StatefulResourcePowerBindings*. A *StatefulResourcePowerBinding* models the consumption of a device type in each power state, and during the transition between states. It subsumes a set of *TransitionStateBinding* and *PowerStateBindings*. A *TransitionStateBinding* captures the power consumption during the transition between two power states. It describes the transitional consumption as a function of power consumption over time. *PowerStateBindings* model the consumption in the power states.

We identified a set of constraints which concern the analytical semantics of PSM:

1. It shall only be possible to transition from a source *PowerState* to a target state, if a *TransitionState* links them as *sourceState* and *targetState*.
2. A *StatefulResourcePowerBinding* enters a transition state when its contained *AbstractPowerStateBinding* is set to a *TransitionStateBinding*. Once it is in the transition state, the transition can not be rolled back, or overwritten by the next transition.
3. The transition between two states has to take the amount of time to complete, which is specified in the *powerCurve* of the *ConsumptionBehavior*. The *TransitionStateBinding* references this curve with *transitionConsumption*.

We identified two alternative solutions to enforce the constraints in our power consumption analysis.

1. Enforce the constraints as part of the power consumption analysis. This would have:
    - Required a deep integration of performance simulation and power analysis. Otherwise, it would not be possible to enforce the transition between specific power states dependent on time.
    - Resulted in a loss of flexibility. While it makes sense to enforce the model semantics in general, there are use cases in which it makes sense to make an exception to the constraints. An example exception is an immediate device shutdown. A shutdown stops all current power state transitions and immediately turns off the device. This contradicts constraint 2. Nevertheless, we would still like to be able to express immediate shutdowns without an explicit extension of the PSM metamodel.
2. Define the analytical semantics constraints using our Adaptation Action metamodel. This has the following advantages over the first solution:
    - Non-invasive realization of the time-dependent transition between power states. Our Adaptation Action metamodel supports the specification of dependencies between reconfiguration enactment, and the system performance. Using

ResourceDemandingSteps, we can specify that a certain amount of time must pass before a device transitions from a source to a target state. The corresponding power state transition action may define this time as the duration of the *powerCurve* of a *ConsumptionBehavior* .

- Simplified specification of the performance impact of power state transitions. The transition between two power states usually impacts the performance of the reconfigured device. In case of a server, the transition into a low power mode reduces its processing speed. An Action can couple the effect specification of the state transition on power consumption in the Power Consumption Model, and on performance in the PCM Resource Environment viewpoint.
- Maintained flexibility. Reconfiguration rules can bypass the constraints defined by the state switching action. This allows an implementation of reconfigurations that perform, e.g., immediate device shutdowns.

We opted for the second solution due to its advantages over the first option. The following discusses the realization of the transient effect of power state transitions as an action of the Adaptation Action metamodel.

Figure 6.5 depicts the power state change action. The action has three parameters. The *AffectedResourceSet* specifies the device, or resource, that shall transition from one power state to another. *TargetPowerState* is the power state which the device will be in, once the adaptation action has finished. The third parameter, *CurrentAllocation*, identifies the context in which the action executes. The action executes if the following conditions are met:

- *TargetPowerState* is a valid target state of *AffectedResourceSet*,
- The device modeled by *AffectedResourceSet* is not already in a transition state.

The QVTo model query of *checkPreconditions* implements the conditions. If the conditions hold, the device enters the transition state which connects the source and target power state. The *changeToTransition* step specifies this transition. Its QVTo model query selects the transition based on the assumption

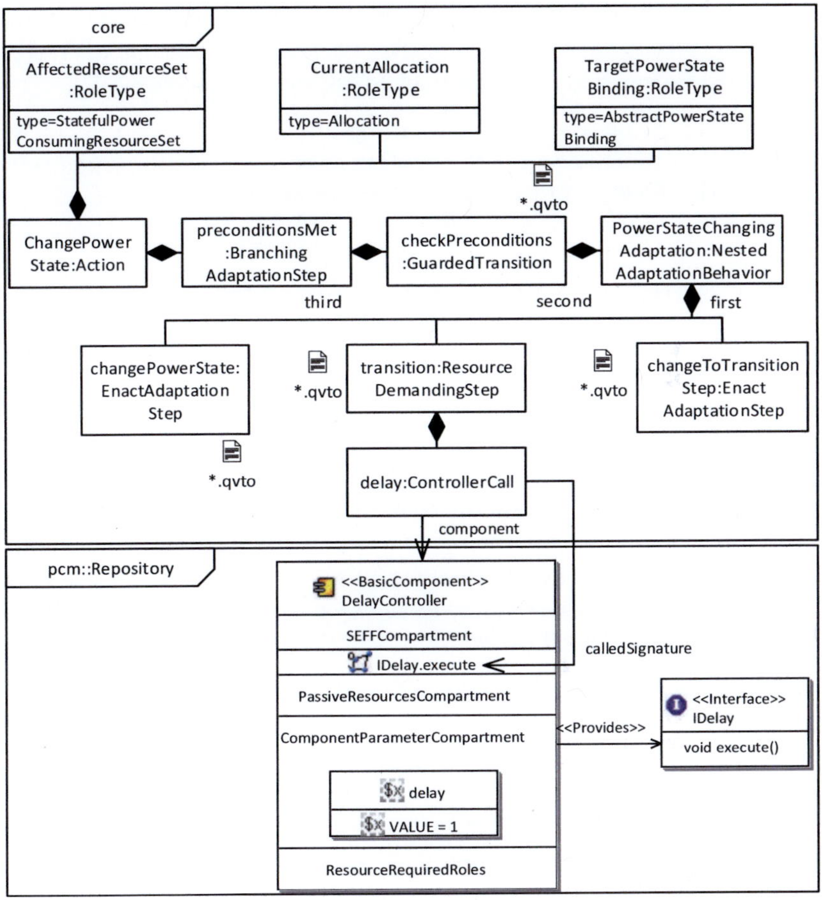

Figure 6.5.: Object diagram view of power state change adaptation expressed as an instance of Adaptation Action metamodel.

that there is exactly one transition from source to target power state. Once the *delay ControllerCall* has been processed, the transition completes. The performance model completion of *transition* adds an instance of the *Delay-Controller* component to the system under analysis. The component models the time that the device remains in the transition state. The performance model completion sets the time to the upper boundary of the definition interval of the power transition function. The *TransitionStateBinding* references this transition function in the contained *ConsumptionBehavior*.

Once the transition time has passed, the *changePowerState* step completes the state transition by setting the binding of the device to the target state binding. This finalizes the power state transition.

6.3. Transient Effect Model Semantics

This section contributes a formalization of the execution semantics for the Adaptation Action metamodel. The formalization complements the syntactical definitions outlined in Section 6.2. It describes the underlying concepts of the model independent of a specific architecture modeling language.

The formalization builds upon the "self-adaptive system model" defined by Becker et al. [20]. An initial version of the formalization was published in [199]. The formalization presented in this section refines the semantics specification and extends it with an execution semantics definition for asynchronously executed *Actions*.

Definition 6.1 (Self-Adaptive System Model based on [20]). *A self-adaptive system model is a tuple* (S, E, σ)*, where*

- S *is the domain of all system states,*
- E *is the domain of monitored environment states,*
- σ *is the set of self-adaptation rules* $\{\sigma_1, \ldots, \sigma_l\}$.

A system state $s \in S$ subsumes all aspects of the state that may be considered by self-adaptation mechanisms. This includes the architectural state, e.g., the deployment of components. Furthermore, the state covers system metrics, such as average response times or power consumption. The state also includes properties that architecture models abstract from. Example details are the state of active user requests and server resources. In the context of design time analyses of self-adaptive software systems, s is not a running software system. Rather, it is the simulation model of the system under analysis.

Refining the formalization by Becker et al. [20], we introduce $M_l \subset S$ as the domain of all architectural runtime models that conform to an ADL l. An instance $m_s \in M_l$ is an abstraction of the system state s. The model m_s represents a runtime architecture model. It only contains system characteristics that can be expressed in l. As an example, PCM instances may only describe system properties that can be expressed according to the PCM metamodel.

The runtime management of a self-adaptive system ensures consistency between an architectural runtime model instance $m_s \in M_l$ and the corresponding system state $s \in S$. The runtime management continuously executes an implementation of the *self-adaptive system runtime management consistency* function.

Definition 6.2 (Self-adaptive System Runtime Management Consistency Function). *The self-adaptive system runtime management consistency function is defined as*

$$\chi : S \times M \rightarrow S \times M.$$

χ is an idempotent mapping that ensures consistency between $m \in M$ and $s \in S$.

The consistency function χ operates on both the domain of runtime states S, and the architectural runtime model domain M. The function definition updates the architectural model $m \in M$ with changes to the system $s \in S$. Secondly, the function enacts any adaptations on s that are realized as model transformations on m.

The Adaptation Action metamodel allows for the decomposition of adaptation mechanisms or tactics into a set of conditionally executed, parametrized adaptation actions. Actions specified in the metamodel consist of a set of adaptation steps.

Becker et al. [20] define a simulation as a function that returns a metric value for an input metric and a given point in time. While this definition is sufficient for the scope of their paper, we complement it with a simulator definition that accounts for simulation state.

Definition 6.3 (Discrete Software System Simulator). *A quality-driven, discrete software system simulator is a function:*

$$\tau : S \times C \rightarrow S \times T,$$

where C is the domain of the set of calls issued on the system. T is the time domain.

The discrete software simulation function defined in 6.3 advances the simulation of a system $s \in S$, until all calls $c \in C_t \in C$ made to s have returned. τ returns the state $s' \in S$ that represents the system state at the time $t' \in T$ at which the last call has completed.

Our definition of a software system simulator focuses on the properties of a simulator which are relevant to the analysis of transient effects. It abstracts from the detailed behavior of the system. An example of this is the relation between user interactions and resource utilization. Koziolek [112] provides a detailed behavioral semantics definition for a specific ADL, namely PCM.

Individual adaptation steps only depend upon a subset of adaptation parameters. Depending on its type, an adaptation step may or may not affect the runtime state and its representation in the runtime model. Definition 6.4 introduces a shorthand notation that we use for composing functions that do not share all inputs and outputs.

Definition 6.4 (Partial Composition Operator). *Let $f_1 : \Gamma_{i_1} \times \ldots \times \Gamma_{i_j} \rightarrow \Gamma_{o_1} \times \ldots \times \Gamma_{o_k}$ $f_2 : \Omega_{i_1} \times \ldots \times \Omega_{i_t} \rightarrow \Omega_{o_1} \times \ldots \times \Omega_{o_u}$. The order of $\Gamma_{i_1}, \ldots, \Gamma_{i_j}$ and $\Gamma_{o_1}, \ldots, \Gamma_{o_k}$ shall be consistent between f_1 and f_2. The partial composition operator $\hat{\circ}$ is defined as:*

$$\begin{aligned}\hat{\circ}(\gamma_i) = &(\Pi_{m_1}((f_2 \bar{\circ} f_1)(\gamma_i)) \cup \Pi_{\Omega_{m_1}}(\Pi_{\Gamma_i - \Omega_o}(\gamma_i)),\\ &\ldots, \Pi_{m_l}((f_2 \bar{\circ} f_1)(\gamma_i)) \cup \Pi_{m_l}(\Pi_{\Gamma_i - \Omega_o}(\gamma_i)), \ldots)\end{aligned}$$

where

- $\gamma_i \in \Gamma_{i_1} \times \ldots \times \Gamma_{i_j}, \Gamma_i = \{\Gamma_{i_1}, \ldots, \Gamma_{i_j}\}$, *and* $\Gamma_o = \{\Gamma_{o_1}, \ldots, \Gamma_{o_k}\}$,
- Π *is the projection operator from relational algebra,*
- $m_1, \ldots, m_l \in \{\Gamma_{i_1}, \ldots, \Gamma_{i_j}\} \cup \{\Omega_{o_1}, \ldots, \Omega_{o_u}\}$.
- $$\begin{aligned}\bar{\circ} : f_2 \bar{\circ} f_1(\gamma_i) = &f_2(\Pi_{\Omega_{i_1}}(f_1(\gamma_i)) \cup \Pi_{\Omega_{i_1}}(\Pi_{\Gamma_i - \Gamma_o}(\gamma_i)), \ldots,\\ &\Pi_{\Omega_{i_j}}(f_1(\gamma_i)) \cup \Pi_{\Omega_{i_j}}(\Pi_{\Gamma_i - \Gamma_o}(\gamma_i))).\end{aligned}$$

The following example illustrates $\hat{\circ}$: Let $f_1 : A{\times}B{\times}C \rightarrow B$, and $f_2 : A{\times}B \rightarrow C$. Then $f_2 \hat{\circ} f_1 : A \times B \times C \rightarrow A \times B \times C$ is a function that passes the fitting attribute values of f_1 to f_2, and otherwise passes the input y_i through.

The partial composition $\hat{\circ}$ enables a definition of an adaptation step as a partially composed set of adaptation step functions and the self-adaptive runtime management consistency function:

Definition 6.5 (Adaptation Action). *Let $\phi = \{\phi_1, \dots, \phi_m\} \in \Phi$ be a set of adaptation parameters, where Φ is the domain of adaptation action parameters. Additionally, let $s \in S$ and $m \in M$. An adaptation action is defined as:*

$$a(s, m, \phi) = \mu_n \hat{\circ} \dots \hat{\circ} \mu_1(s, m, \phi)$$

Here, $\mu_i = p_i \hat{\circ} \chi$ with $1 \leq i \leq n$ is the partial composition of an adaptation step $p_i \in P$, and the management consistency function χ.

The inclusion of χ in the definition of μ_i implies that the execution of a step p_i proceeds only once. It updates the runtime state to include the execution of the step.

Definition 6.6 (Adaptation Step). *An adaptation step $p_i \in P$ is an individual operation executed as part of an adaptation action. $P = P_{br} \cup P_{rd} \cup P_{\sigma}$ combines the domains of the different types of Adaptation Steps to couple the description of conditional branches (P_{br}) and reconfigurations (P_{σ}) with their performance effect (P_{rd}).*

Definition 6.7 (Resource-Demanding Adaptation Step). *A resource-demanding adaptation step $p_{rd} \in P_{rd}$ is a function $p_{rd} : S \times \Phi \rightarrow S$, where*

$$p_{rd}(s, \phi) = \tau(s, C_t(\phi))$$

with $s \in S$, $m \in M$, $\phi \in \Phi$. $C_t(\phi) \in C$ is a set of parametrized concurrent calls issued to components in the simulated self-adaptive software system.

Resource-demanding adaptation steps specify the effect of actions on system performance. They can be used to define both the impact on and dependency to system performance of an adaptation action. The performance impact and dependency result from a set of calls $C_t(\phi)$ to the system. These calls are represented in the system state model s. Once the system has processed a call, other adaptation steps that waited for the completion can be applied to the system.

An example adaptation action that contains a resource-demanding adaptation step is VM migration. VM migration induces a performance overhead on the system $s \in S$ in the shape of network traffic sent from the source to the target host of the migration. The duration and network load caused by a VM migration depends, among other characteristics, on the size of the transferred VM image. This dependency can be expressed as a set of parameters $\phi \in \Phi$.

Definition 6.8 (Enact Adaptation Step). *An enact adaptation step $p_\sigma \in P_\sigma$ is a function $p_\sigma : M \times \Phi \rightarrow M$.*

An *enact adaptation step* applies an adaptation to the runtime architecture model $m \in M$ of the system. Unlike the resource demanding adaptation step, it does not directly modify the system state $s \in S$. It transforms m from the source state prior to the adaptation to the target state.

A *branching adaptation step* groups a set of conditionally executed branches. At most, one of its branches is executed. If none of the conditions of the branches hold, the step leaves the system state unchanged:

Definition 6.9 (Branching Adaptation Step). *A branching adaptation step is a function $p_{br} : S \times M \times \Phi \rightarrow S \times M \times \Phi$*

$$p_{br}(s, m, \phi) = \begin{cases} \mu_m^1 \hat{\circ} ... \hat{\circ} \mu_1^1(s, m, \phi) & \text{if } c_1(m, \phi) = true, \\ \mu_k^2 \hat{\circ} ... \hat{\circ} \mu_1^2(s, m, \phi) & \text{if } \neg c_1(m, \phi) \wedge c_2(m, \phi) = true, \\ \cdots & \\ \mu_l^n \hat{\circ} ... \hat{\circ} \mu_1^n(s, m, \phi) & \text{if } \bigwedge_{1 \leq i < n} \neg c_i(m, \phi) \wedge c_n(m, \phi) = true, \\ (s, m, \phi) & else. \end{cases}$$

c_j is a function $c_j : M_l \times \Phi \rightarrow \{true, false\}$ that evaluates whether the runtime architecture model $m \in M_l$ and a set of passed parameters $\phi \in \Phi$ meet specific adaptation preconditions.

A branching adaptation step groups a set of adaptation step sequences $\{\mu^1, ..., \mu^i, ..., \mu^n\}$, where $\mu^i = \mu_j^i \hat{\circ} ... \hat{\circ} \mu_1^i$.

The formalization sketched thus far assumes that all adaptation actions execute sequentially. The assumption is part of Definition 6.5 of adaptation actions, and Definition 6.7 of resource-demanding steps. First, adaptation actions are defined as a composition of adaptation steps. Second, all resource-demanding adaptation steps apply the simulation function τ. The two definitions imply that all steps are executed in sequence, and that further steps can only be started once a preceding resource-demanding step has completed.

We extend the prior definitions to consider asynchronous executions of adaptation actions. An asynchronously executed adaptation action does not immediately advance the simulation time by applying τ. In order to achieve this, we construct an alternative definition of asynchronous adaptation steps:

Definition 6.10 (Asynchronous Adaptation Action). *Let $\phi = \{\phi_1, \ldots, \phi_m\} \in \Phi$, $s \in S$ and $m \in M$. C is the domain of sets of service calls. An asynchronous adaptation action is defined as $a_{async} : S \times M \to S \times M \times C$ with*

$$a_{async}(s, m, \phi) = \mu_n \hat{\circ} \ldots \hat{\circ} \mu_1(s, m, \phi)$$

Here, $\mu_i = p_i \hat{\circ} \chi$ with $p_i \in P_{async} = P_{br} \cup P_{rd_{async}} \cup P_{rd} \cup P_{\sigma}$.

Definition 6.11 (Asynchronous Resource-Demanding Adaptation Step). *An asynchronous resource-demanding adaptation step $p_{rd_{async}} \in P_{rd_{async}}$ is a function $p_{rd_{async}} : \Phi \to C$, where*

$$p_{rd}(\phi) = C_t(\phi)$$

with $\phi \in \Phi$. $C_t(\phi) \in C$ is a set of parametrized concurrent calls issued to components in the simulated system.

In contrast to synchronous adaptation steps, asynchronous steps do not execute the calls $c \in C_t(\phi)$. The calls are collected and can be executed by later synchronous resource-demanding adaptation steps.

Adaptation actions can be combined to form adaptation mechanisms. Adaptation mechanisms execute adaptation actions dependent on a set of given conditions. The condition combined with the resulting actions are also referred to as *self-adaptation rules*:

Definition 6.12 (Self-Adaptation Rules and Adaptation Actions). *A self-adaptation rule* $\sigma_t : S \times M \times E \longrightarrow S \times M \times \Phi \in \sigma$ *is defined as*

$$\sigma(s, m, e) = \begin{cases} \chi \hat{\circ} k_v \hat{\circ} \ldots \hat{\circ} k_g \hat{\circ} \ldots \hat{\circ} k_1(s, m, e), & \textit{if } c(m, e) = \textit{true} \\ s, & \textit{if } c(m, e) = \textit{false} \end{cases}$$

where

- $c : M_l \times E \longrightarrow \{\textit{true}, \textit{false}\}$ *is the condition of the rule.*
- k_g *is defined as either*
  - *a parametrized call of an adaptation action:* $k_g(s, m, e) = a(s, m, \xi_g(m, e))$*. The function* $\xi_g : M_l \times E \longrightarrow \Phi$ *maps the runtime architecture and environment state to appropriate adaptation action parameters* $\phi \in \Phi$.
  - *an execution of previous asynchronously started calls* $C_{async} \in C$ *of asynchronous adaptation actions on the simulated system* $s \in S$ *via* $\tau(s, C_{async})$,
  - *the execution of an idle action as defined by Pavlović and Abramsky [154] to wait for the completion of the prior* C_{async}.

S/T/A frameworks can formulate self-adaptation rules as part of larger adaptation plans, i.e. adaptation tactics.

6.4. Coupled Evaluation of Transient Effects in Model-Driven Software Quality Analyses

Section 6.3 established the model semantics of the Adaptation Action metamodel. In order to reason on performance effects of self-adaptations, the developed model and its semantics have to be considered in a software quality analysis. This section outlines the approach for the analysis of Adaptation Action metamodel as part of an existing simulative software quality analysis. The approach realizes the simulation of transient effects as a coupled simulation that interacts with an underlying software quality simulation. We refer to the simulation component that implements the analysis as the *Transient Effect Interpreter.* As an example we present the integration with SimuLizar.

6.4.1. Integration Architecture

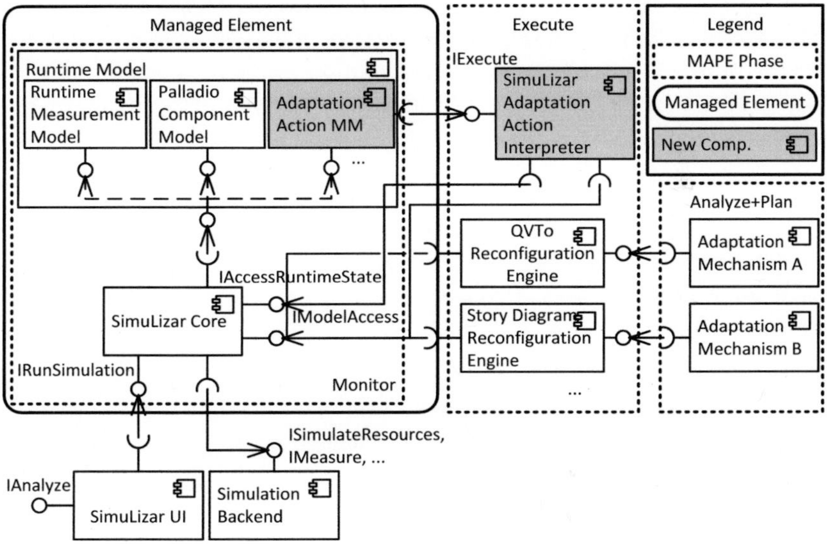

Figure 6.6.: Simplified integration architecture of the Transient Effect Interpreter and SimuLizar.

Figure 6.6 sketches the integration architecture of the Transient Effect Interpreter and SimuLizar. The figure classifies the SimuLizar components by the phase of the MAPE-K feedback loop to which they contribute. Added components are highlighted in gray. The Adaptation Action metamodel discussed in Section 6.2 extends the runtime model of SimuLizar with a set of executable adaptation actions. The actions are available to any reconfiguration mechanism integrated into the simulated self-adaptive system. SimuLizar supports the integration of different reconfiguration engines [17]. Reconfiguration engines enact adaptations by transforming the runtime model of SimuLizar from the current to the desired target state. Self-adaptation mechanisms like the mechanisms A and B shown in Figure 6.6 trigger an adaptation action by calling its *execute* method. The following section details how mechanisms can issue actions, and how the Transient Effect Interpreter processes them.

6.4.2. Use and Execution of Actions

This section discusses the use and execution of actions specified with the Adaptation Action metamodel. An adaptation mechanism instantiates an *Action* by calling its *execute* operation with the relevant instantiation parameters.

Listing 6.1 shows an excerpt from an adaptation rule specified in the QVTo model transformation language. The listed QVTo helper method that starts a scale-out action. Section 6.2.7.1 had introduced the scale-out action executed in the example. Lines 8 to 25 instantiate the roles that parametrize the scale-out. For scale-out, the roles encompass in listed order:

1. The target Resource Container of the scaled component (lines 9-12),
2. the component which is instantiated as part of the scale-out (lines 13-16),
3. the Assembly Context of the load balancer that forwards request to the scaled component (lines 17-20),
4. the allocation location of the management service, which instantiates the component (lines 21-24).

Line 27 calls the *execute* EOperation of the scale-out action. This starts the execution of the action. The call to the helper method *prepareForControllerCall()* initializes a set of input parameters of the type *ControllerCallInputVariableUsageCollection*. These parameters specify factors in addition to the passed roles that impact the performance effect of the action, as Section 6.2 outlined.

When a reconfiguration mechanism calls the *execute* operation, it issues a call to a set of methods implemented in the Transient Effect Interpreter.

Listing 6.1: Example QVTo transformation snippet executing a scale-out action

```
property targetResourceContainerRoleId = . . . ;
property instantiatedComponentRoleId = . . . ;
property loadBalancerRoleId = . . . ;
property controllerContainerRoleId = . . . ;

helper scaleOut(var instantiateVm : Action, instantiatedComponent :
    BasicComponent, targetResourceContainer : ResourceContainer,
    controllerContainer : ResourceContainer) : Boolean {
        // Instantiate parameters for Action
        var roleSet : RoleSet := object RoleSet@roleSets {
            roles += object instance::Role {
                roleType := instantiateVm.getRoleTypeById(
                    targetResourceContainerRoleId);
                value := targetResourceContainer.oclAsType(EObject);
            };
            roles += object instance::Role {
                roleType := instantiateVm.getRoleTypeById(
                    instantiatedComponentRoleId);
                value := instantiatedComponent.oclAsType(EObject);
            };
            roles += object instance::Role {
                roleType := instantiateVm.getRoleTypeById(
                    loadBalancerRoleId);
                value := controllerContainer.oclAsType(EObject);
            };
            roles += object instance::Role {
                roleType := instantiateVm.getRoleTypeById(
                    controllerContainerRoleId);
                value := controllerContainer.oclAsType(EObject);
            };
        };

        return instantiateVm.execute(roleSet,
            prepareInputForControllerCall());
}
```

Listing 6.2: Call to Transient Effect Interpreter by the *execute EOperation*

```
return org.palladiosimulator.simulizar.action.interpreter.
    ActionRuntimeState.getInterpreterBuilder(affectedRoleSet,
    getRepository()).addControllerCallVariableUsages(
    controllerCallsVariableUsages).addExecutionContext(
    executionContext).build().doSwitch(this).
    getExecutionResultAsBoolean();
```

Listing 6.2 shows the method body of the *execute* operation. The operation constructs the execution context of the action using the input parameters. Then, it processes the action and returns.

Figure 6.7 depicts a class diagram excerpt of the classes called by the *execute* method. The *ActionRuntimeState* class offers interfaces to the extension point *IAccessRuntimeState* shown in Figure 6.6. The SimuLizar core component passes an instance of *AbstractSimuLizarRuntimeState* to the Transient Effect Interpreter. This provides the interpreter access to the simulated runtime state of the analyzed software system. The *execute* operation constructs a *TransientEffectInterpreter* via an instance of the *TransientEffectInterpreter-Builder.* The class applies the builder pattern to construct the Transient Effect Interpreter. Once all parameters have been passed, the call to *build* returns the resulting *TransientEffectInterpreter.* This interpreter instance processes the passed *Action.* The interpreter is implemented according to the visitor pattern. It leverages the automatically generated *CoreSwitch* base class for visiting all classes of the Adaptation Action metamodel in the *core* package. Steinberg [195] further explain the functioning of this pattern. The *execute* operation in Listing 6.2 issues the initial visit call to the *Action* by calling its *doSwitch* method. The interpreter realizes the visitor logic in the static nested class *InternalSwitch.* Once the Transient Effect Interpreter has processed the call, it returns a *TransientEffectExecutionResult.* The *execute* operation converts this result to a Boolean by calling *getExecutionResultAsBoolean.*

Listing 6.3 contains the asynchronous variant of Listing 6.2 that is executed when calling *executeAsync.* The asynchronous variant of *execute* differs

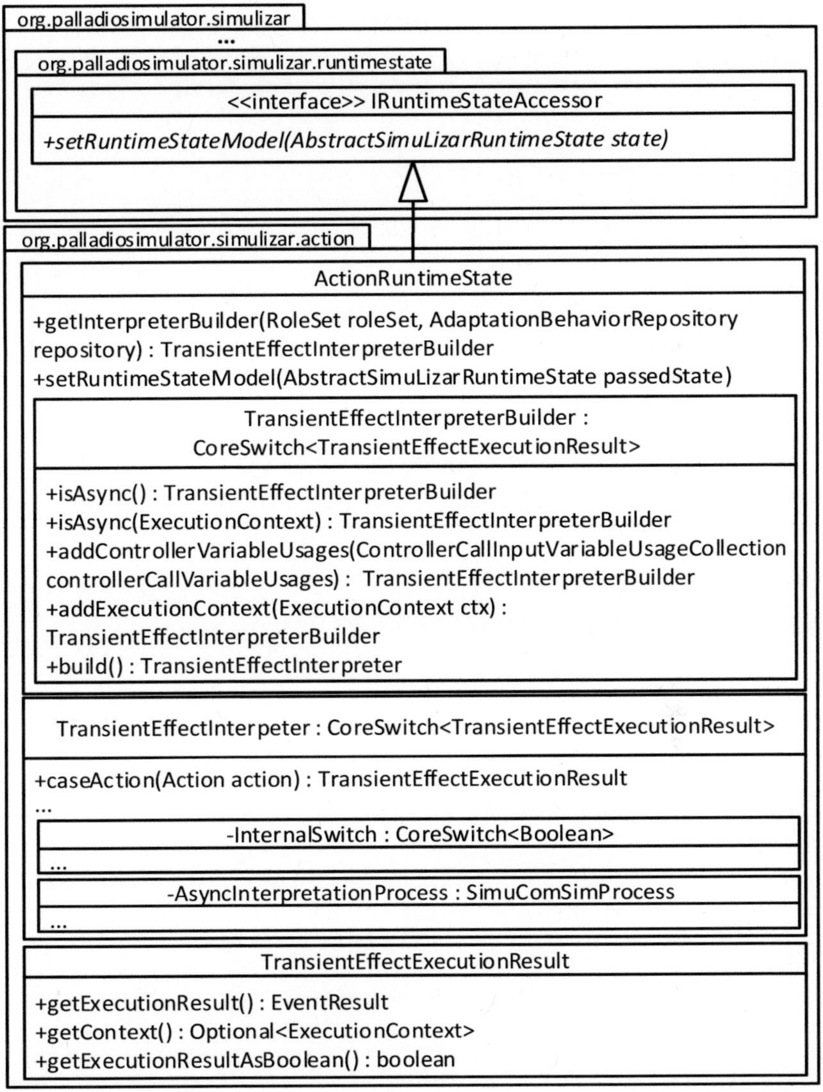

Figure 6.7.: Simplified excerpt of the class diagram overview of Transient Effect Interpreter

Listing 6.3: Call to Transient Effect Interpreter by *executeAsync EOperation*

```
org.palladiosimulator.simulizar.action.interpreter.ActionRuntimeState.
    getInterpreterBuilder(affectedRoleSet, getRepository()).isAsync(
    asyncExecutionContext).addControllerCallVariableUsages(
    controllerCallsVariableUsages).build().doSwitch(this);
return asyncExecutionContext;
```

primarily in two ways. First, the asynchronous execute sets the *ExecutionContext* to the passed context. This signals that the interpreter should process the call asynchronously. Second, *executeAsync* returns the *ExecutionContext* of the call instead of a Boolean. The returned *ExecutionContext* enables adaptation mechanisms to wait for the completion of the asynchronous action. This allows mechanisms to join a set of concurrently executed asynchronous actions. Internally, the Transient Effect Interpreter processes the call in an asynchronously started simulation process. *AsyncInterpretationProcess* implements this process.

6.4.3. Execution of AdaptationSteps

The Transient Effect Interpreter sequentially executes all of its nested *AdaptationSteps* according to their order in its containment collection. It implements the interpreter semantics introduced in Section 6.3. As part of the work conducted in the context of this thesis, we refactored SimuLizar to execute the reconfiguration engines shown in Figure 6.6 in a separate simulation process. This allows reconfigurations to be delayed or interrupted as part of the simulation. The Transient Effect Interpreter makes use of this to consider the performance impact of reconfigurations.

The Transient Effect Interpreter visits the sequence of steps. The following sketches how the interpreter executes the different types of steps.

BranchingAdaptationStep A *BranchingAdaptationStep* defines a set of adaptation behavior transition alternatives. The interpreter sequentially iterates over the contained *GuardedTransitions*. The interpreter executes a behavior alternative if its conditions hold true. It executes the first transition whose Boolean condition evaluates to true. The Boolean condition is implemented as a QVTo query referenced by the *GuardedTransition*. The interpreter continues with the execution of the *NestedAdaptationBehavior* contained in the *GuardedTransition*. This leads the interpreter to execute every step in the *NestedAdaptationBehavior*. Once it has fully processed the behavior, the interpreter moves on to the next step in the *adaptationSteps* set of the parent *AbstractAdaptationBehavior*.

ResourceDemandingStep A *ResourceDemandingStep* defines the overhead incurred by executing a subset of adaptation steps of an *Action*. The step includes calls to a set of operation signatures of component instances. It represents each call to components in the performance model as a *ControllerCall*. Figure 6.8 illustrates how the Transient Effect Interpreter processes the step. The activity diagram uses the component instantiation call *InstantiateController* from Section 6.2.7 as an example. First, the interpreter executes the associated QVTo performance model completion. The completion adds the components to the architectural performance model, which induce the performance effect modeled by the *ResourceDemandingStep*. This results in an extended System and Allocation model. The interpreter produces a *Mapping* as a result of the completion. The mapping consists of *ControllerMappings*. Each contained *ControllerMapping* links a *ControllerCall* to the provided role of a component, which the performance completion has introduced. Second, the interpreter starts a simulated user call for each *ControllerMapping* element. The simulated user executes the call represented by the *ControllerCall*. Finally, the Transient Effect Interpreter continues with the next step in the *adaptationSteps* collection of its parent behavior.

EnactAdaptationStep An *EnactAdaptationStep* transforms the architectural runtime model of the analyzed software system from its current to the target state. To execute this type of step, the Transient Effect Interpreter performs the QVTo model transformation referenced by the step. Subsequently, the interpreter executes the remaining steps in the *adaptationSteps* of the parent behavior.

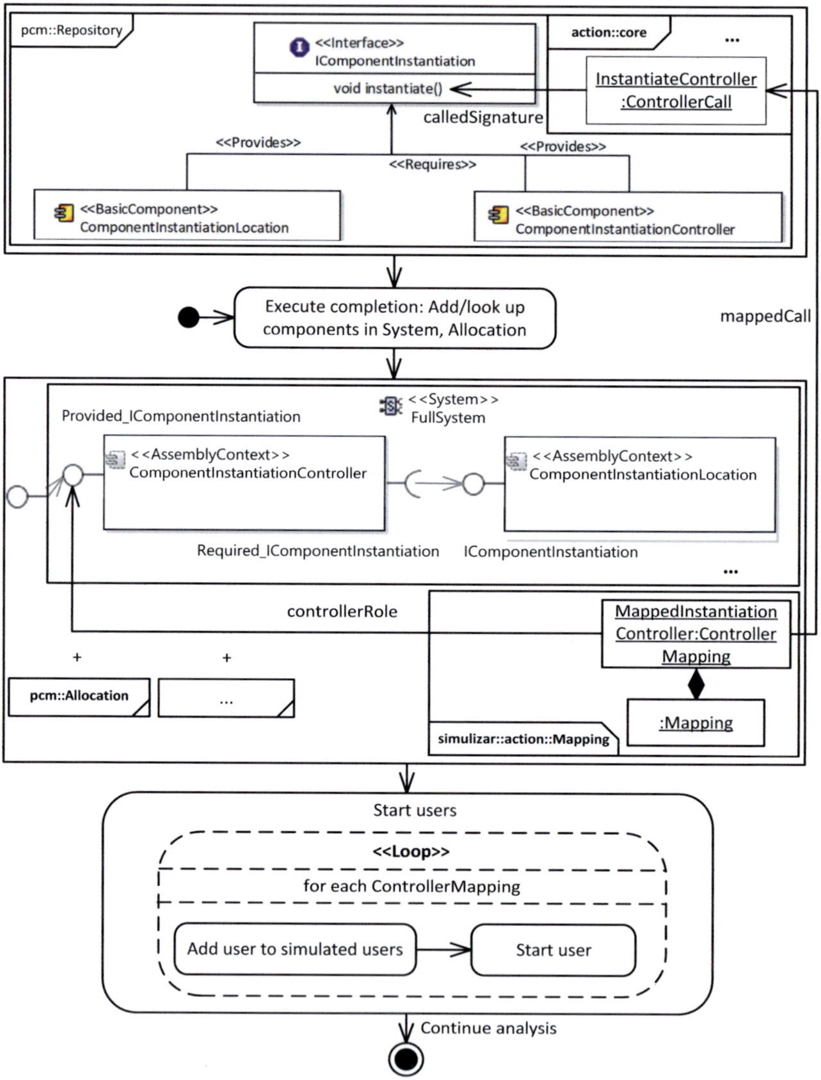

Figure 6.8.: Activity diagram of the Resource Demanding step execution.

6.4.4. Reconfiguration Engine Support

The Adaptation Action metamodel defines the behavior of adaptation actions as a series of steps with well-defined execution semantics. Section 6.3 presented the execution semantics. The Transient Effect Interpreter implements these execution semantics. *Actions* offer a set of executable EOperations that allow adaptation mechanisms to start adaptation actions. When called, an operation constructs an execution context, and defers the execution of the action to the Transient Effect Interpreter. The chosen coupling of Adaptation Action metamodel and Transient Effect Interpreter enables their integration with existing simulation and model transformation logic. SimuLizar defines reconfigurations as model transformations on the runtime model of the simulated system. The model transformations may be implemented in different transformation languages. As of writing this thesis, SimuLizar offers QVTo, Henshin [6] and Story Diagrams (SDs) [60] reconfiguration engines. SimuLizar supports the addition of further reconfiguration engines, e.g., engines that support different model transformation languages. Hence, this section also discusses whether further popular model transformation languages support the execution of EOperations as part of transformations.

In QVTo, EOperations can be called directly as part of any transformation. QVTo thus natively supports the execution of actions as part of reconfiguration rules. We extensively used instances of our Adaptation Action metamodel in reconfigurations, which we implemented in QVTo. An example application of QVTo as the reconfiguration engine is the validation presented in Section 7.4.

QVT Relations (QVTr) allows for calls to black-box methods implemented in Java as part of its *enforce domain* clause. The clause can specify a call to any Java method within its *implementedBy* sub-clause. Using these language constructs, EOperations like *execute* of the Action type can be called.

The SDs implementation outlined by Detten et al. [60] allow for the execution of arbitrary code or statements via *StatementNodes*. Henshin can execute arbitrary Java code within its *AttributeConditions* [6]. Intuitively, this also applies to the execution of the Java method generated for the EOperations of *Action*. There are SimuLizar reconfiguration engines for the SD and Henshin implementations.

Like QVTo, ATL Transformation Language (ATL) allows for direct calls to *EOperations*. ATL code can issue calls to an *EOperation* in both *to* or *do* section of a rule. Thus, a potential ATL reconfiguration engine would also support the execution of actions.

6.5. Assumptions and Limitations

The model and analysis presented in this chapter are based on a set of assumptions. The following discusses these assumptions, alongside a set of limitations of our approach.

Analysis based on DES of self-adaptive software system. The analysis presented in Section 6.3 and 6.4 builds upon the semantics of a DES for self-adaptive systems. The analysis can not be integrated with analytical performance analysis approaches that focus on steady state system analyses. An example of this analysis category is PCM2LQN by Koziolek [112]. Transient effects and the resulting behavior of the system in transient phases are essential to the QoS of the system. The steady state assumption does not hold for scenarios in which transient effects occur. Hence, our extended transient effects analysis is not compatible with these analyses. We do not consider the incompatibility of our approach with analyses based on the steady state assumption a significant limitation, as these analyses do not support reasoning on QoS in transient phases. This makes these analyses inapplicable for scenarios in which the transient behavior of the system is relevant.

Use of EOperations to realize Action instantiation. The Adaptation Action metamodel defines self-adaptation actions on a categorical, or type, level. Instances of the Action type describe the effect of a self-adaptation action independent of a concrete software architecture. Reconfiguration rules may instantiate Actions by calling one of its *execute* EOperations with its instantiation parameters. This eases the use of Actions in reconfiguration engines built upon all prevalent model transformation languages, as discussed in Section 6.4.4. However, it might not be possible to leverage this integration mechanism in every reconfiguration engine. This limitation can be addressed

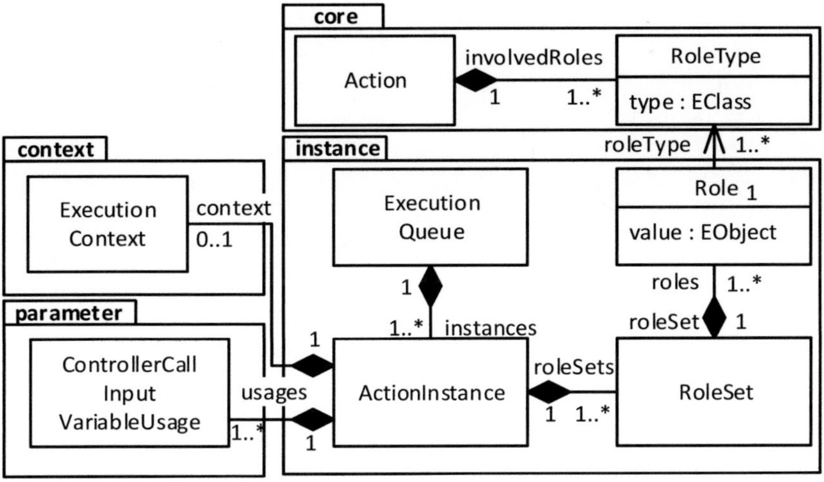

Figure 6.9.: Sketch of model extension with explicit Action instantiation.

with the addition of an instantiation model to the metamodel. Figure 6.9 sketches this solution. Instead of calling the *execute* operation of *Actions*, actions would then be issued via the creation of *ActionInstances*. The Transient Effect Interpreter would be triggered when an action is added to the *ExecutionQueue*. The activation of the interpreter then could be realized via the EMF listener infrastructure. In conclusion, we consider potential technical limitations of the chosen approach for action instantiation marginal. All core concepts of our modeling and analysis approach are compatible with the sketched generalized realization.

6.6. Summary

In this chapter we present our modeling and analysis approach for considering transient effects in the analysis of self-adaptive software systems. The goal of the approach is to improve the prediction accuracy of design time analyses of self-adaptive software systems.

Our Adaptation Action metamodel supports the definition of reusable self-adaptation actions. It couples the specification of performance effect and reconfiguration outcome. This allows a detailed consideration of tradeoffs between the benefits of reconfigurations and their costs. The metamodel supports the modeling of power consumption and performance overheads. This addresses Research Question 9. The metamodel describes an adaptation action as a sequence of adaptation steps. It distinguishes between steps that check conditions, describe the effect of actions on the system state, and which express the performance effect. Action specifications can be reused in different reconfigurations, and for different system analyses.

We formally defined the execution semantics of our Adaptation Action metamodel. Building upon this formal specification, we discussed how the analysis of actions can be incorporated in an existing simulative performance analysis (Research Question 10). We integrated a prototype implementation of our analysis with Simulizar by Becker et al. [20].

The use of our action modeling language does not restrict software architects in their approach towards specifying reconfiguration rules. Becker et al. [20] describe reconfigurations by means of model transformations. We illustrated that our analysis is compatible with a variety of model transformation languages, including the languages supported by SimuLizar.

We applied our Adaptation Action metamodel in the CACTOS project to implement composable adaptation action specifications for use in IaaS data center simulation [115, 196]. The metamodel facilitated the reuse of different data center management actions, i.e., for the instantiation and horizontal scaling of different application types. The application to the simulation of complex IaaS Cloud scenarios illustrated the applicability and appropriateness of our metamodel and analysis.

Section 7.4 evaluates the benefits of our approach by applying it to a horizontally scaling IaaS application.

7. Validation

This chapter presents the validation of our contributions towards a systematic consideration of energy efficiency of software systems at design time. We conducted a set of case studies to evaluate the four central contributions of this thesis:

C1: Design of a modeling language for the description of power consumption characteristics of software systems

C2: Development of an approach for energy efficiency analysis at design time

C3: A method for the extraction of power models for use in design time predictions

C4: Development of a systematic modeling and analysis approach for considering transient effects in software quality analyses

The contributions aim to address the research questions presented in Section 1.4. We aligned the validation to investigate whether our contributions answer the research questions. For this, we applied the GQM [15] method. Section 7.1 derives a GQM plan from the research questions. Furthermore, it classifies the conducted case studies by the questions they address. The case studies cover static and self-adaptive enterprise software systems, data center resource management and a set of Big Data workloads. A subset of the presented case studies have been published as part of our papers [115, 196, 199, 200, 201].

The remainder of the chapter presents the case studies and results, grouped by the main contribution they intend to validate. Section 7.2 presents a set of studies that investigate the accuracy of architecture level energy efficiency predictions. Section 7.3 evaluates the applicability of the power model extraction method. Finally, Section 7.4 investigates whether the consideration of transient effects improves the accuracy of design time predictions of self-adaptive systems. Section 7.5 subsumes the validation findings, and outlines starting points of further potential validations.

7.1. Validation Goals and Overview

This section presents the validation goals. We used the GQM approach proposed by Basili et al. [15] to validate our contributions. Section 2.7.1 outlined the fundamentals of the GQM approach.

This section is structured as follows. Section 7.1.1 presents the GQM plan of our validation. In Section 7.1.3, we classify each of the conducted case studies by the research questions they answer. Additionally, we categorize the case studies by their validation levels according to Böhme and Reussner [30]. Section 2.7.2 explains our view on the different validation levels.

7.1.1. GQM Plan

For each of the contribution we defined a validation goal in accordance with the GQM approach outlined by Basili et al. [15]. The following presents the validation goals. We organize the plan according to the organization of Research Questions (RQs) in Section 1.4. Alongside each validation goal and question, we name the Research Questions (RQs) from Section 1.4, which the goal and its questions aim to address. To improve the readability, we restate the Research Questions (RQs) at the beginning of each section.

7.1.1.1. Modeling and Analysis of Software System Power Consumption Characteristics

Research Question 1. *What is a good abstraction level for modeling power consumption characteristics of software systems? We consider a model abstraction good if it*

- *produces accurate power consumption predictions,*
- *can be constructed from information available at design time,*

- *contains as little redundant information as possible with existing architectural modeling languages and viewpoints.*

Research Question 2. *How can the power consumption of software systems be predicted on an architectural level?*

Research Question 3. *How accurate are power consumption predictions performed on an architectural level?*

Research Question 4. *How can we evaluate the effect of architectural design decisions on energy efficiency?*

Goal 1. Evaluate the prediction accuracy of our energy efficiency predictions for architecture-level design time analyses.

Addressed RQs: 1, 2, 3, 4.

Question 1.1. Can our approach accurately predict the power consumption of software systems on an architectural level?

Metric 1.1.1. Prediction accuracy as (percentage) difference of aggregated measured and predicted power consumption for an observation period.

Addressed RQs: 1, 2, 3.

Question 1.2. Does our approach produce predictions that have a higher accuracy than predictions from state of the art approaches?

Metric 1.2.1. Prediction accuracy as (percentage) difference of aggregated measured and predicted power consumption for an observation period.

Addressed RQs: 1, 2, 3.

Question 1.3. Are the power consumption predictions accurate enough to evaluate the effect of design decisions on energy efficiency?

Metric 1.3.1. Aggregated energy consumption prediction accuracy calculated as percentage difference of the predicted and measured energy consumption.

Metric 1.3.2. Energy efficiency prediction accuracy calculated as percentage difference of the predicted and measured effect of design decision on energy consumption.
Energy efficiency is hereby defined as energy consumed per operation. As the usage profile and throughput remains unchanged, energy efficiency can be compared by directly comparing the aggregated power consumption before and after the decisions have been applied.

Addressed RQs: 1, 4.

Goal 2. Validate the appropriateness of our power consumption model for describing the power consumption characteristics of software systems.

Addressed RQs: 1, 2.

Question 2.1. Are the essential characteristics that determine the power consumption of a software system reflected by our power consumption model?

Metric 2.1.1. Energy consumption prediction accuracy calculated as percentage difference of measured and predicted power consumption.

7.1.1.2. Extraction of Power Models

Research Question 5. *How can the effort in deriving power models for architecture-level power consumption analyses be reduced?*

Research Question 6. *What is the effect of considering different system level metrics as input in power consumption analyses?*

Research Question 7. *How can software architects and system deployers be supported in the selection of input metrics for energy efficiency analyses?*

Goal 3. Validate the applicability of our approach for the automated construction of power models based on automated systematic experiments.

Addressed RQs: 5, 6, 7.

Question 3.1. Does our automated power and system metric profiling approach extract a representative system profile?

Metric 3.1.1. Energy consumption prediction accuracy as (percentage) difference of measured power consumption and power consumption predicted by power models.

Metric 3.1.2. Two-Dimensional Kernel Density Estimation (KDE) over server profile.

Addressed RQs: 5.

Question 3.2. Does the combined profiling of system metrics improve the accuracy of trained power models over their separate profiling?

Metric 3.2.1. Prediction error of power models trained on server profile from full and separate profiling.

Addressed RQs: 5.

Question 3.3. Does our profiling approach produce more accurate power models than state of the art?

Metric 3.3.1. Percentage difference of prediction error of power models trained on data using our approach, and a state of the art approach.

Addressed RQs: 5.

Question 3.4. What is the influence of system metrics considered by power models on their prediction accuracy?

Metric 3.4.1. Difference of prediction accuracy of

- power models that consider CPU and HDD,
- models that only consider CPU.

Metric 3.4.2. Difference of Pearson's/Spearman's correlation coefficient between CPU utilization and HDD throughput metrics.

Metric 3.4.3. Difference of prediction accuracy between aggregated CPU utilization and multi core power models.

Addressed RQs: 6.

Question 3.5. Is it possible to estimate the impact of considered system metrics on the prediction accuracy of power models?

Metric 3.5.1. Rank of power models in AIC-based ranking compared to prediction accuracy ranking from measurements.

Addressed RQs: 7.

7.1.1.3. Transient Effects of Reconfigurations

Research Question 8. *How do reconfigurations affect power consumption and performance?*
Research Question 9. *What is an architecture-level description of reconfigurations that describes the effect of reconfigurations on system metrics such as performance and power consumption?*
Research Question 10. *How can we consider the effects of runtime reconfigurations in software quality analyses at design time?*
Research Question 11. *Does the consideration of transient effects enable the (a) detection and (b) solution of design problems in self-adaptive software systems?*

Goal 4. Validate the influence of transient effects on the accuracy of performance predictions for architecture-level analyses of software systems.

Addressed RQs: 8, 9, 10, 11.

Question 4.1. Does the consideration of transient effects improve the prediction accuracy of architecture-level analyses?

Metric 4.1.1. Percentage difference of prediction accuracy of design time quality predictions with and without our approach.

Addressed RQs: 8, 9, 10.

Question 4.2. Does our approach enable the detection of design deficiencies of self-adaptive software systems that would have otherwise remained undetected?

Metric 4.2.1. Percentage difference of prediction accuracy of design time quality predictions with and without our approach

Metric 4.2.2. A requirement that is predicted

- to be violated by the baseline prediction is not violated at runtime, or
- not to be violated is violated at runtime.

The metric evaluates if the prediction extended by our approach correctly predicts the violation, or fulfillment.

Addressed RQs: 8, 11.

Question 4.3. Does our approach enable the resolution of design deficiencies of self-adaptive software systems?

Metric 4.3.1. Prediction accuracy of design time quality predictions with our approach compared to measurements.

Metric 4.3.2. Our approach correctly predicts whether changes applied to the software system have resolved a design deficiency.

Addressed RQs: 8, 11.

We implicitly validate the suitability and appropriateness of our modeling languages. RQs 1 and 8 express these concerns. We demonstrate the appropriateness and applicability of our Power Consumption metamodel in three ways. First, we demonstrate that power consumption predictions performed using instances of the metamodel are accurate enough to support architectural decisions. Second, our automated power model extraction approach showcases that software architects can obtain these models with reasonable effort. We finally discuss differences in expressiveness and modeling complexity between our model and a state of the art modeling approach. We show the applicability of the Adaptation Action metamodel (Research Question 8) by presenting how it can enable software architects to make sound decisions. The validation does not address the general appropriateness of Adaptation Action metamodel for use in design time modeling and analysis of self-adaptive software systems. However, Section 6.2.7 demonstrates the applicability of the metamodel for a set of adaptation actions. Section 7.5.1 additionally discusses the application of our modeling approach to the analysis of data center resource management scenarios.

Research Question 5 is the only research question that is not implicitly or explicitly addressed by our GQM plan. The RQ concerns a reduction of effort for the application of our power consumption modeling and analysis approach. We did not conduct an empirical study to evaluate whether our approach reduced the effort compared to the manual or semi-manual construction of power models. Our power model extraction approach automates all major steps involved in the construction of power models: profiling, learning or training, and selection of power models. Hence, we consider the implementation of the approach to answer RQ 5.

7.1.2. Case Study Systems

This section provides a brief summary of case study systems we used to validate the contributions of this thesis. A more thorough description of the systems is provided in the respective sections of this chapter.

- **Media Store 2** [22] is a Java EE-based case study system that allows users to upload and download music files. The used variant is the second release version of the system.
- **Spring PetClinic** [159] is a community case study system for different framework technologies from the Spring community. It realizes a simple web system for appointment management in a veterinary clinic via Spring framework technology.
- **VM Placement** subsumes four case studies conducted in an IaaS data center testbed. They have been performed as part of the European research project CACTOS [152]. The case studies employ different VM placement and migration algorithms to distribute VMs on the testbed.
- **SPECjbb2015** is an industry standard Java benchmark "to evaluate the performance and scalability of environments for Java business

applications" [193]. SPECjbb2015 replicates user interactions with a web shop in a typical client server setting.

- **HiBench** [91] is a Big Data benchmark suite. It covers a diverse set of Big Data workloads implemented atop Hadoop and Spark. Individual workload implementations cover the programming languages Java, Python, and Scala.
- **VM Migration Bench** is a VM migration benchmarking framework which we implemented to measure power consumption during VM migration. It re-uses the workload definitions of SERT [187] to stress the servers or the VM involved in the migration.
- **Scaling Media Store** is a variant of the third release version of the Media Store application. Compared to the second release, the third release improves the modularity of components. Reussner et al. [170] use this release as a running example, and in a set of presented performance and reliability prediction case studies. We extended the baseline implementation by the capability to scale out dependent on load.

7.1.3. Validation Coverage

This section discusses the coverage of Validation Goals and their corresponding Questions by the conducted case studies. We classify the case studies with respect to the validation level categories outlined by Böhme and Reussner [30].

This thesis does not focus on establishing a process for developing energy-efficient software. Rather, it establishes a method for evaluating the energy efficiency of software systems as part of existing model-driven development approaches, e.g., the Palladio process [22]. It would be possible to conduct a validation that investigates the benefit of considering energy efficiency as part of these existing approaches. However, the effort needed for conducting a Level III validation is very high. Hence, we did not perform a Level III validation as part of this work.

Table 7.1.: GQM Overview. The dot highlights if a case study covers a Question.

Goal	Question	Media Store 2	PetClinic	VM Placement	SPECjbb	HiBench	VM Migration Bench	Scaling Media Store	Validation Level
1	1.1	•	•	•					I, partially II
	1.2	•	•	•					I
	1.3	•	•						I
2	2.1	•	•	•	•	•			I
3	3.1		•		•	•	•		I, II
	3.2				•	•			I
	3.3				•	•			I
	3.4				•	•	•		I, II
	3.5				•	•			I
4	4.1							•	I
	4.2							•	I
	4.3							•	I

Table 7.1 provides an overview of the case studies systems, with the goals and derived questions they address. Per Question, the table notes the validation type.

Goal 1. The first goal aims at the validation of the prediction accuracy of our design time energy efficiency predictions approach. Question 1.1 inquires the accuracy of design time power consumption predictions. We evaluated the accuracy of the predictions for all three case study systems. Sections 7.2.1 and 7.2.2 apply our design time power consumption analysis to evaluate the energy efficiency of the Media Store software system, and the PetClinic application. The VM placement case study presented in Section 7.2.3 investigated the accuracy of the predictions in data center testbed that optimizes, and adapts, the placement of VMs over time. All input data used for the case studies has been obtained via automated measurements.

We reconstructed the architectural performance model of PetClinic with the Performance Model eXtractor (PMX) [220]. The used power model was automatically trained using our power model extraction approach. The PetClinic and VM placement case studies constitute a level II validation as the significant part of input data was collected automatically. We compared the accuracy of our approach against state of the art for all three case study systems (Question 1.2). The two round-trip case studies Media Store and PetClinic are level I validations of Question 1.3. Both case studies applied our prediction to evaluate the effect of a design decision on energy efficiency. The case studies compared the prediction results with measurements.

Goal 2. Goal 2 states that our modeling approach shall model all essential characteristics that influence the power consumption on an appropriate level of abstraction. All case studies but the Scaling Media Store used our Power Consumption metamodel to describe the power consumption characteristics of the involved software systems. We consider the application of our modeling approach a level I validation: Power consumption predictions that used the models defined in our modeling language produced accurate predictions. Chapter 3 matches our Power Consumption model against challenges regarding the architectural modeling of power consumption, which we had identified. In the section we show that our modeling language tackles these challenges. Thus, Chapter 3 constitutes an appropriateness validation.

Goal 3. In order to apply an analysis approach at design time, it must be feasible to acquire all of its input data. Our power model extraction method addresses this requirement by automating server profiling and power model training. Goal 3 targets the applicability of the power model extraction method. From the goal, we derived four Questions. Question 3.1 addresses the representative character of the extracted system profile. We investigated this question using the SPECjbb2015 and HiBench case studies. We evaluated whether power models trained on the profile accurately predict the power consumption of the case study systems. Question 3.2 concerns the accuracy of the combined profiling of system metrics compared to their separate profiling. We compared the prediction accuracy of the same power model types trained on a profile from combined profiling, and from separate profiling. Question 3.4 targets the impact of additional metrics on prediction accuracy.

We reasoned on the effect of additional metrics by comparing the prediction accuracy of power models that consider only CPU utilization against models that also take storage metrics into account. We evaluated Questions 3.1, 3.2 and 3.4 by comparing predicted and measured power consumption. We compared the measurements and predictions of the power models for the SPECjbb and HiBench case study systems. According to the classification by Böhme and Reussner [30], this qualifies as a level I validation.

The VM Migration Bench case study applied our power model extraction method to a benchmarking environment for VM migration scenarios. Section 7.3.9 presents the results of the case study. The case study investigated whether the power models produced by our approach accurately predict the power consumption of VM migrations. This addresses Question 3.1. The study focused on the accuracy of extracted power models. Additionally, it examined the accuracy of aggregated CPU utilization compared to multi core power models. This concerns Question 3.4.

In Section 7.3.7, we address Question 3.3. We contrast the prediction accuracy of power models, trained on a profile extracted using our approach, against power models trained on a profile from a baseline state of the art approach. We realized the state of the art approach using the same measurement and workload implementations. Böhme and Reussner [30] note that a level III validation investigates the benefit of the evaluated approach "over other competing approaches". However, we did not empirically determine and compare the difference in effort for identifying suitable workload definitions. This would be needed to qualify the validation as a level II validation. A level II validation of the compared approaches is a necessary prerequisite for a level III validation. In conclusion, the comparison of both approaches only qualifies as a level I validation.

We explored Question 3.4 by comparing our AIC-based ranking of power models with the relative prediction accuracy of power models for the SPECjbb2015 and HiBench case studies. We compared the predicted accuracy of power models with their actual accuracy. This covers a type I validation of Question 3.4.

Goal 4. We employed the Scaling Media Store case study in the validation of Goal 4. The case study addresses Questions 4.1 to 4.3 via a comparison of predictions and measurements. Our simulation tooling automatically performed the analysis of transient effects. However, we manually used the prediction tooling, and defined the input instances of the Adaptation Action metamodel. The case study thus constitutes a level I validation. It is not a level II validation as it did not validate the practical applicability of our modeling approach.

7.2. Energy Efficiency Analysis

The case studies presented in this section address Goal 1 of the validation. The case studies investigate Questions 1.1 to 1.3. Subject of our investigation are the two application systems *Media Store* and *PetClinic*, and a set of IaaS scenarios recorded in a data center testbed.

This section is structured as follows. Section 7.2.1 presents the results of the Media Store case study. Section 7.2.2 discusses the PetClinic case study. The results of the IaaS data center case study are outlined in Section 7.2.3.

7.2.1. Media Store

In this case study, we applied the PCA approach to evaluate the effect of a design decision on energy efficiency for the Media Store application. As a basis, we investigated the absolute power consumption prediction accuracy for different workloads. The presented case study has been published in [200].

The Media Store application is a component-based reference application. Media Store is a simple web-based media hosting application. It has been the subject of case studies that investigated the applicability of Palladio [132], and the accuracy of its performance predictions [22]. Various iterations of Media Store have been developed over time. The case study presented in this section used the version 2.0[1] predecessor of the most recent release

[1] `https://svnserver.informatik.kit.edu/i43/svn/code/CaseStudies/MediaStore2/trunk/`, retrieved 05.06.2017 with anonymous credentials.

3.0[1] of the Media Store presented by Reussner et al. [170]. Media Store is implemented atop the Java EE platform.

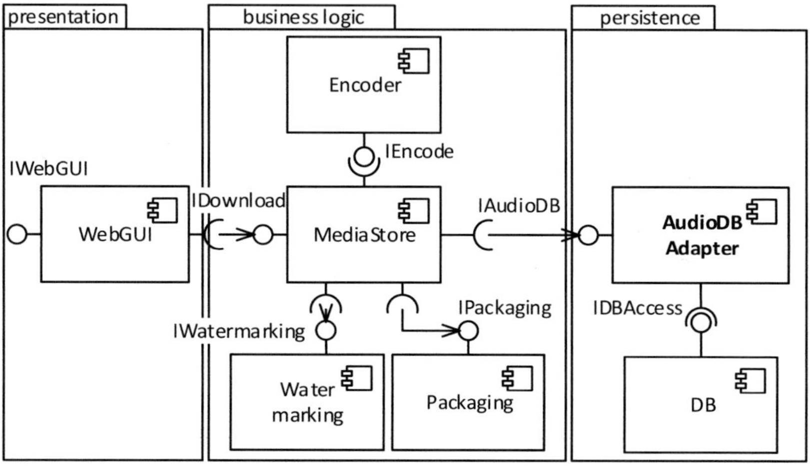

Figure 7.1.: System diagram view of Media Store

Figure 7.1 shows the System diagram view on Media Store. The system adheres to the three-tier architecture style. The *WebGUI* component realizes the web GUI frontend of the application. Via the GUI, users can upload and download music files. In the business logic tier, the *MediaStore* component acts as a facade to the central business and persistence layer components. When a music file is downloaded, it fetches the file from storage, and re-encodes the file to the target audio quality by calling the encoding service of *Encoder*. Afterwards, metadata is added to the music file by the *Watermarking* component. The metadata is stored in a relational database represented by the *DB* component. These steps are repeated for all music files requested by a user. If multiple files are requested, the files are packaged before being sent to the user.

There are a set of alternative design decisions for Media Store. Reussner et al. [170] discuss a set of example design decisions for Media Store. One such design decision is the choice of the *Encoder* component. The re-encoding of music files performed by the *Encoder* component is the service with the

[1] `https://sdqweb.ipd.kit.edu/wiki/Media_Store`, retrieved 05.06.2017.

highest resource intensity. We thus investigated re-encoding as the part of the software architecture where energy efficiency could potentially be improved. In its baseline implementation, Media Store re-encodes music files in the mp3 format via the LAME library. We identified the use of the Vorbis encoder implementation libvorbis as a design alternative to the mp3 encoding of LAME. We selected comparable audio quality settings for both encoders. *LAME* was configured to use a fixed bitrate of 192 kbit/s. We launched *libvorbis* with the `-qscale:a 4` setting.

7.2.1.1. Evaluation Setup

We conducted the measurements on a Dell PowerEdge R815 server with four Opteron 6174 CPUs and 256 GB RAM as the target deployment environment. We deployed Media Store on a Glassfish 3.1 application server running atop an Ubuntu 12.04 VM. The VM was assigned 16 cores of the 48 availablephysical cores. The VM was deployed on the XenServer 6.2 hypervisor running on the server. MySQL 5.5 was used as the realization of the *DB* component. The compared versions of the *LAME* library were 3.99.3, and version 1.32 of *libvorbis* as distributed in the *ffmpeg* framework.

For power measurement, we utilized the IPMI interface of the PowerEdge server. IPMI collects power measurements via a built-in power meter. Frequency, resolution and accuracy of built-in power meters are lower compared to standalone, certified power meters as used in the case studies presented in Sections 7.2.2 and 7.3. However, built-in power meters do not need to be invasively connected to the server, consume less energy, and take up significantly less space. The technical specifications of the server [163] do not state the measurement frequency or accuracy of the server. Our measurements had shown that all power measurements were rounded to multiples of ten. Furthermore, the measurement frequency appeared to be lower than 1 Hz.

As preparation for the case study, we used a manually constructed PCM model of Media Store. We re-calibrated the resource demands in the RDSEFFs of the central components on our deployment environment in semi-automated measurements. We calibrated the performance model with a single user workload, and collected the performance measurements via *perf4j*. Figure 7.2 shows the calibrated RDSEFF of the *LAME* implementation

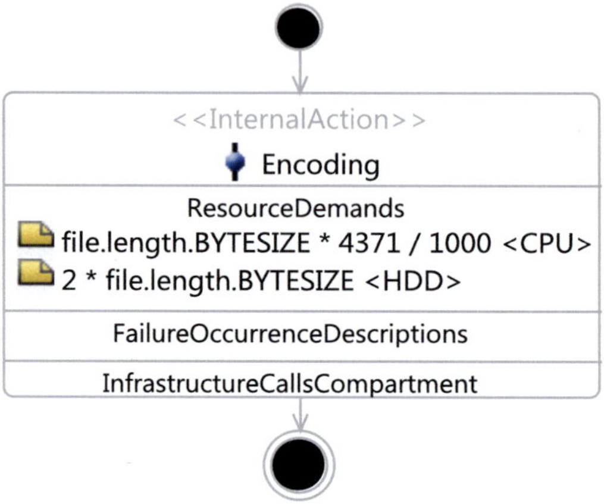

Figure 7.2.: Resource-Demanding Service Effect Specification (RDSEFF) of the *LAME* implementation of the Encoder component calibrated on the deployment environment.

of the Encoder component. We based the RDSEFF estimation on the observation that the encoding time linearly correlated with the file input size of the re-encoded music file. The RDSEFF assigns the encoding a resource demand consumption of 4731 demand units per kB of file size on the CPU of the R815 server with a single core processing rate of 2200. For the calibration workload, the response time prediction error of the model was 0.05%. We used a simple download usage scenario to evaluate power consumption, and energy efficiency of our application. Each usage scenario consists of a user downloading a random song from Media Store.

We manually extracted the power model of the server. For this, we issued different load levels to the server using the Linux microbenchmarks *stress* and *lookbusy*. In an initial step, we profiled the server by varying the utilization of cores from 1 to 16 fully utilized cores. Figure 7.3 depicts the resulting measurements. The power measurements for utilization levels between single and 16 core utilization can be well described by a linear power model. The figure depicts this power model P_{mult}:

$$P_{\text{mult}}(u) = 352.47 + 7.19u$$

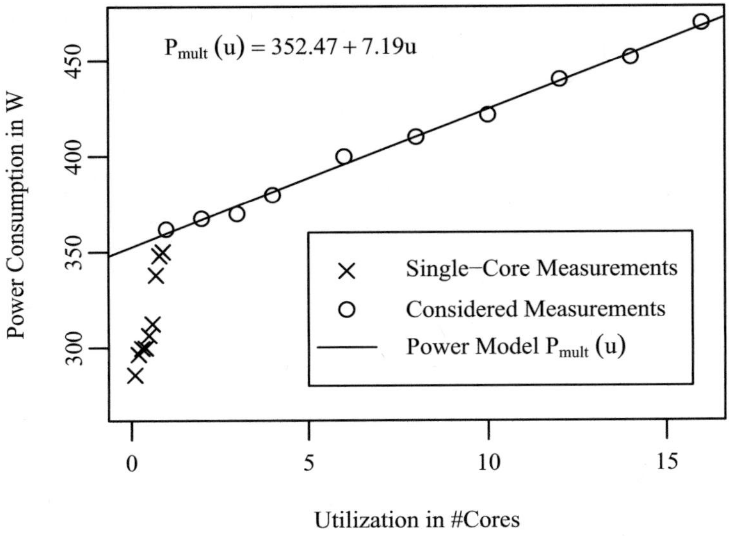

Figure 7.3.: Power consumption and per core power model based on microbenchmarking with *stress* and *lookbusy*. The line represents the power model constructed using the measurements for utilization levels from 1 to 16 cores.

For utilization levels below single core utilization, the power measurements strongly deviate from the other measurements. Hence, we opted to construct a separate power model for utilization levels between idle and full single core utilization. Figure 7.4 shows the power measurements for this range, together with the power model P_{single} that describes consumption in this utilization range:

$$P_{single}(u) = 8212.67x^6 - 23872.19x^5 + 25345x^4 - 11469x^3 + 1934.88x^2 + 39.96x + 270.54.$$

We combined both power models to form a stepwise defined power model:

$$P_{full}(u) = \begin{cases} P_{single}(u) & \text{if } u \leq 1 \\ P_{mult}(u) & \text{if } 1 < u \leq 16 \end{cases}, \quad u \in [0, 16].$$

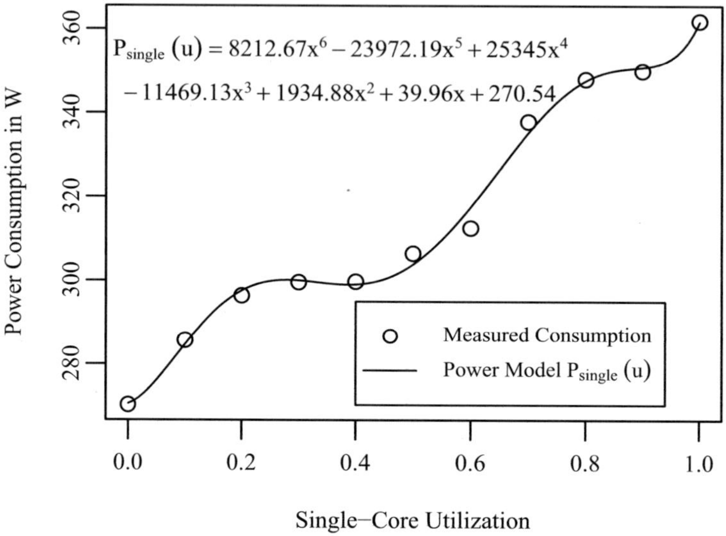

Figure 7.4.: Power consumption for single core utilization levels extracted via *lookbusy*. The line represents the power model constructed for the utilization levels between idle and full single core utilization.

In this case study, we employed the SimuCom simulator [22] and SimuLizar to derive performance predictions for the system under investigation. The performance predictions served as input for PCA. We set the sampling interval for the power samples from PCA to one second. Power consumption samples were collected with an interval around 1.4 to 3 seconds from the R815 server. We calculated the energy consumption in each scenario using the measured and predicted power consumption samples. We derived the energy consumption from the power samples by means of trapezoidal numerical integration. We compared energy consumption between the predictions from simulations and measurements using the following error formula:

$$\text{Error} = |\frac{E_{\text{Meas}} - E_{\text{Pred}}}{E_{\text{Meas}}}|,$$

where E_{Meas} is the measured and E_{Pred} the predicted energy consumption.

7.2.1.2. Power Consumption Model

Figure 7.5 depicts an excerpt of all relevant instances of viewpoints in our Power Consumption metamodel. The *Infrastructure* view of our model only captures PSU and the resource by which we model the power consumption of the server, the CPU. It references the *Resource Environment* view of the PCM model that represents the server environment. The figure only depicts model elements referenced in the *Infrastructure* view. Not depicted is the *DistributionPowerModelSpecification* and the respective binding. The model uses a passthrough distribution power model that models the PSU as lossless. We opted for this modeling as we built the server power model using measurements that we had collected at the power outlet of its PSU. Thus, the power model already implicitly considers any potential PSU loss.

We implemented the piecewise-defined power model P_{full} as a black-box power model. Thus, the specification contains the model as a model of type *BlackBoxPowerModelSpecification*. The fixed factors of the model correspond to the fixed factors of P_{full}. The two segments of the power model P_{single} and P_{mult} can be specified via *DeclarativeResourcePowerModelSpecifications*. However, the Power Consumption model in its presented form does not support the definition of piecewise-defined functions via native metamodel classes. *PieceWiseModel* represents the power model type P_{full}. It has nine parameters in total. The *FixedFactor* instances represent these parameters. *PieceWiseModel* references the *MeasuredFactor* u that quantifies the utilization of a resource like CPU. The *Binding* view contains one *FixedFactorValuePower* instance per *FixedFactor*. The *ResourcePowerBinding* with the name *r815full* instantiates the power model type P_{full} for the specific server.

7.2.1.3. Prediction Accuracy

As a first step, we evaluated the absolute prediction accuracy of our PCA prediction approach for the Media Store application. We analyzed the power consumption for the Power Consumption model of the server. Our consumption analysis used system metrics extracted from the SimuCom design time performance analysis of the Media Store PCM model. For the single user calibration workload W_1 we determined an error of 0.17% for the total energy consumption prediction. We increased the user load to evaluate the

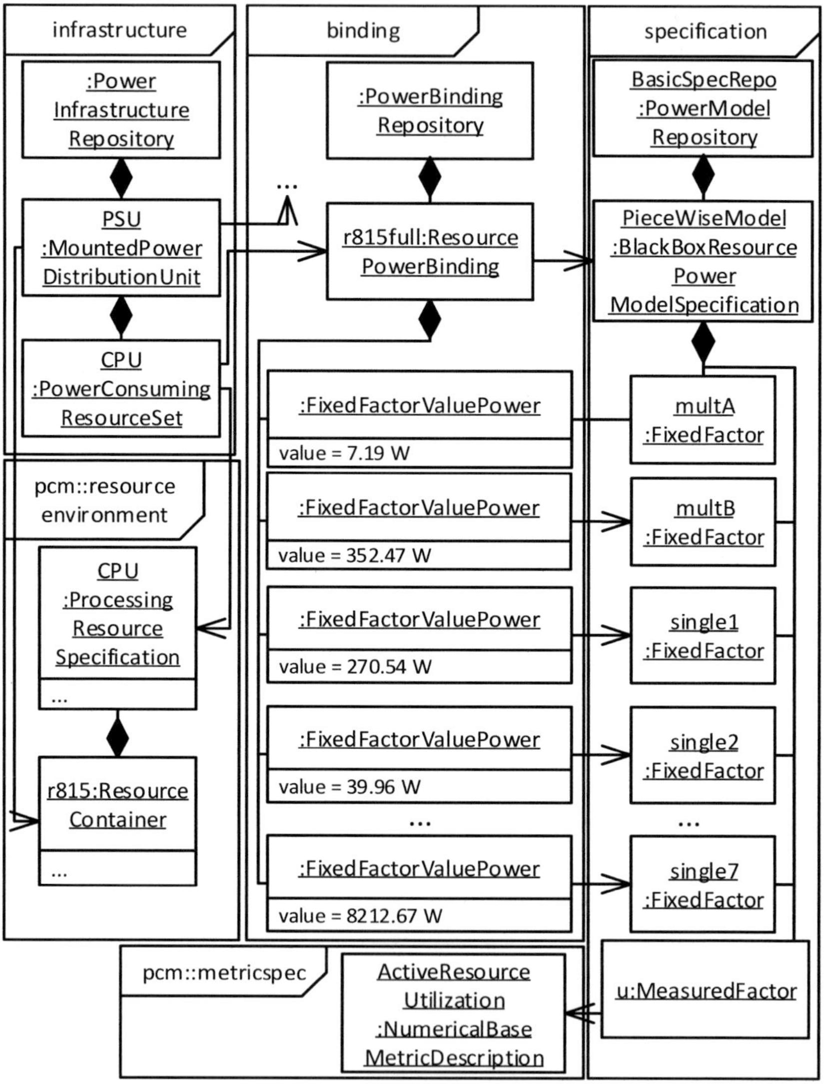

Figure 7.5.: Excerpt of Power Consumption model instance for deployment environment used in Media Store case study.

prediction accuracy under higher load. The workload W_2 consisted of a closed workload with 16 users, where each user repeatedly downloads a random song from the Media Store. In the case of increased workload we established an energy consumption prediction error of 5.47%. The average response time prediction error increased to 2.31%.

In addition to the closed workloads with a single, and 16 concurrent users, we investigated the prediction accuracy of our approach for two open workload variants W_3 and W_4. In the first workload W_3, a new user arrived at the system every 16 seconds. The second workload W_4 decreased the interarrival time to one second. The energy consumption prediction error for W_3 was 1.60%. The prediction error for W_4 was 3.60%.

In order to evaluate whether PCA accurately predicts power consumption for varying workloads, we employed the gradually increasing workload W_5. W_5 starts with no active users. Every 160 seconds the request rate increased by one additional user request per 16 seconds. After reaching a request rate of one request per second, the workload concluded. SimuCom does not support the analysis of workloads patterns and trends. Hence, we employed SimuLizar with its Usage Evolution extension [31] to simulate the increasing workload W_5. The Usage Evolution extension enables the modeling of variable user interarrival times as piecewise defined mathematical functions over time [106]. The absolute energy consumption error for the gradually increasing workload W_5 was 3.68%.

In summary, our approach produced accurate power consumption predictions for the Media Store application. The absolute error of energy consumption predictions for five different load intensities was no higher than 5.5%. Thus, we consider Question 1.3 positively answered by the results of the case study.

7.2.1.4. Comparison with State of the Art

We investigated the accuracy of our prediction approach compared to state of the art. Our prediction approach uses instances of Power Consumption metamodel as input. The Power Consumption metamodel is more expressive than the modeling abstraction proposed by the state of the art approach by Brunnert et al. [35]. The prediction approach of the authors is restricted to linear power models. As the implementation of Brunnert et al. was unavailable to us, we compared the prediction accuracy of the previously introduced piecewise-defined power model P_{full} and a simple linear power model P_{linear} to quantify the benefit of our approach.

We trained the linear power model using linear regression to have an optimal R-squared error on the training data. The training data was the same we used to train our piecewise-defined power model.

The prediction error of P_{linear} reached 1.41% for W_1, and 7.65% for W_2. The error was notably higher than the 0.17% for W_1 and 5.47% for W_2 of P_{full}. This illustrates that the consumption prediction accuracy can be increased by a noticeable margin when non-linear power models are employed. Conclusively, our modeling and analysis approach offers higher prediction accuracy over state of the art for the investigated workload and application scenarios (Question 1.2).

7.2.1.5. Impact of Design Decision on Energy Efficiency

We investigated whether energy efficiency of the Media Store application could be improved by using an alternate encoding. The goal was to validate whether our approach accurately predicted the impact of design decisions on energy efficiency. We identified Vorbis-based music encoding as an alternative to the mp3 encoding performed by the baseline implementation. To reason on the effect of the design decision, we estimated the resource demand of the Vorbis encoder. We estimated the resource demand based on a set of calibration measurements for the *libvorbis* implementations. We performed these measurements separate from the initial model calibration with mp3 encoding. Finally, we modeled the Vorbis implementation of the *Encoder* component in the PCM component Repository model.

We then used SimuCom ($W_1, \ldots, W_4$) and SimuLizar (W_5) and PCA to predict the power consumption for the alternative system. Then, we performed measurements to evaluate the accuracy of the power consumption predictions. We ran measurement experiments on the baseline LAME *Encoder*, and the Vorbis component variant. We deployed and measured the energy consumption over time on the R815 server deployment environment. We leveraged the workloads W_3, W_4, and W_5 to compare the energy efficiency for

Table 7.2.: Predicted and measured power consumption for mp3 and Vorbis encoder. Saved energy quantifies the difference in consumption by using Vorbis instead of mp3 encoding.

(a) Workload W_3 with interarrival time of 16s

	Energy Consumption		
Encoder	Measured	Predicted	Error
LAME	173.77 Wh	171.00 Wh	-1.60%
libvorbis	129.11 Wh	133.10 Wh	+2.78%
Saved Energy	44.67 Wh	37.91 Wh	-15.14%

(b) Workload W_4 with interarrival time of 1s

	Energy Consumption		
Encoder	Measured	Predicted	Error
LAME	215.30 Wh	223.06 Wh	+3.60%
libvorbis	195.05 Wh	198.97 Wh	+2.01%
Saved Energy	20.25 Wh	24.09 Wh	+18.94%

(c) Workload W_5 with increasing request rate

	Energy Consumption		
Encoder	Measured	Predicted	Error
LAME	289.38 Wh	300.02 Wh	+3.68%
libvorbis	267.82 Wh	274.50 Wh	+2.50%
Saved Energy	21.56 Wh	25.52 Wh	+18.34%

different load intensities. Table 7.2 lists the results for each of the workloads. Table 7.3a contains predictions and measurements for W_3, Table 7.3b denotes the results for W_4. In Table 7.3c, measurements for W_5 are listed. The encoder rows contain the energy consumed in Watt hours (Whs) over a 30 minute experiment interval in the case of W_3 and W_4. Measurements and predictions for W_5 cover just above 42 minutes. The *Saved Energy* row contains the predicted and measured energy consumption for the two architecture variants. The saved energy quantifies the effect of the design decision on energy efficiency, since the load intensity has remained the same between both variants. It uses the metric Δ_{EE}, which we introduced in Definition 2.5. We determined the accuracy of energy efficiency predictions as the measured and predicted improvement in energy efficiency. The relative prediction error for all three workloads was below 19%.

The predictions indicated a potential reduction in energy consumption by employing *libvorbis* compared to the *LAME* baseline. The predicted absolute reduction was 22.16% for W_3, 10.85% for W_4, and 8.51% for W_5. This closely matched the energy savings of 25.70%, 9.45%, and 7.45% we measured.

In conclusion, our PCA approach accurately predicted the impact of replacing mp3 with Vorbis encoding on the energy efficiency in the Media Store architecture. Hence, we consider the results to positively answer Question 1.3.

7.2.2. Spring PetClinic

The following outlines the results of the application of the PCA approach to the PetClinic community case study system. It presents the predicted and measured energy consumption and energy efficiency. The case study compared predictions and measurements for the standard Spring Boot and microservices variant of PetClinic [159]. The case study constitutes an end-to-end case study of our power model extraction and PCA approach. It applied our automated power model extraction approach, in combination with a performance model learning framework [220], to evaluate the accuracy of design time energy efficiency predictions for automatically constructed models. The model learning framework [220] extracts a PCM model instance from monitoring data. We combined the PCM model with a power model we obtained using our power model extraction method. This supplied us with all models required to perform energy consumption predictions.

7.2.2.1. Case Study System

Spring PetClinic [159] is a sample open source application developed by the Spring community. Its purpose is the experimentation and testing of

Spring framework technology. PetClinic models a simple Enterprise Resource Planning (ERP) scenario for a veterinary clinic. Users interact with the application via a web frontend. The frontend offers services for browsing and managing appointments, doctors and customers. There are different variants of the PetClinic application for different development and technological variants of Spring. PetClinic is commonly used to illustrate differences between the variants, and showcase the use of new framework developments. Many authors, e.g. [50, 189, 191], have applied PetClinic to validate SPE approaches. The Spring Boot PetClinic variant showcases the use of lightweight deployment and delivery mechanisms introduced by Spring Boot. A microservices variant [158] has been derived from the Spring Boot PetClinic. The microservices variant separates services for managing customers, vets, and appointments. Furthermore, it introduces microservices pattern implementations from Spring Cloud, e.g., circuit breaker and API gateway. We compared the power consumption and energy efficiency of Spring Boot, and the microservices variant of PetClinic across different workloads. This allowed us to evaluate whether the transition from the initial to the microservices architecture affects the energy efficiency of PetClinic.

Spring Boot variant. Figure 7.6 depicts a simplified system diagram view of the Spring Boot PetClinic variant. PetClinic follows the classic Model-View-Controller (MVC) design pattern. The *OwnerRepository* and *VetRepository* components persist and provide access to owner, veterinary and appointment data. Each of the components is configured to store the data in an HSQLDB in-memory database instance. The *ClinicService* component serves as a facade for the persistence layer components. Each of the components in the business layer offers services to manage owner, veterinary and appointment information. The presentation layer provides web access to the services of the components in the business logic layer. The Spring Boot baseline implementation uses the Thymeleaf template engine to realize the web frontend. In PetClinic Boot, all components, or modules, but HSQLDB need to be deployed together.

Spring Cloud microservices variant. Figure 7.7 shows a simplified system diagram view of the Spring PetClinic Cloud/microservices variant. Each

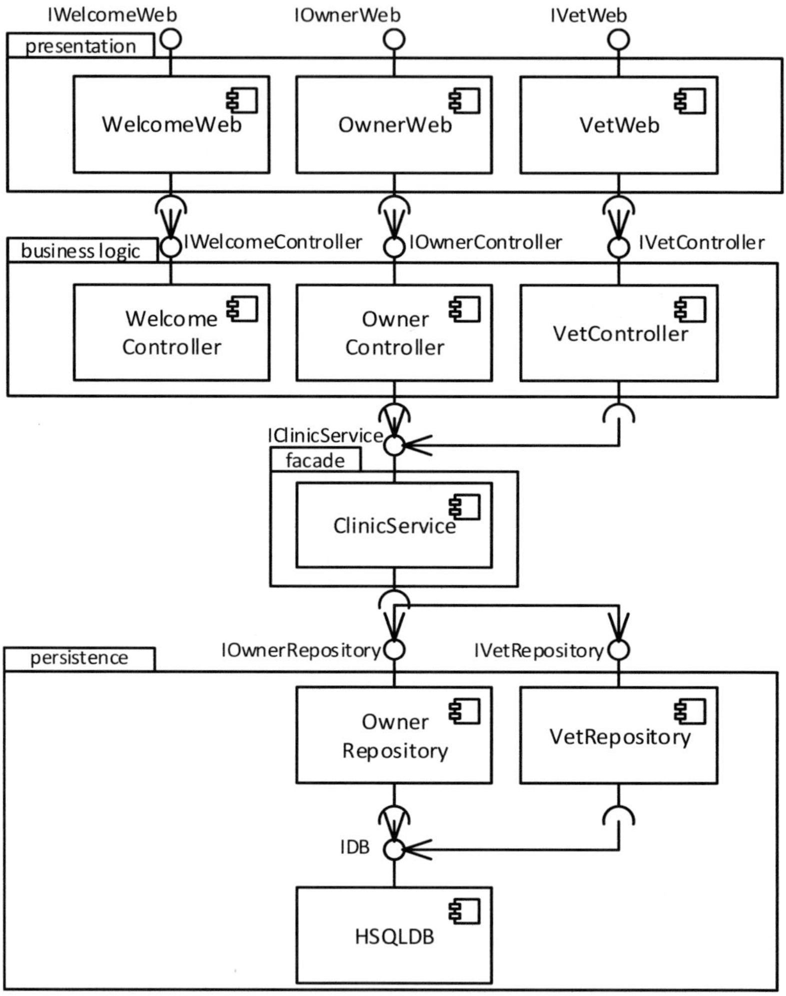

Figure 7.6.: System diagram view of the PetClinic architecture of the Spring Boot variant.

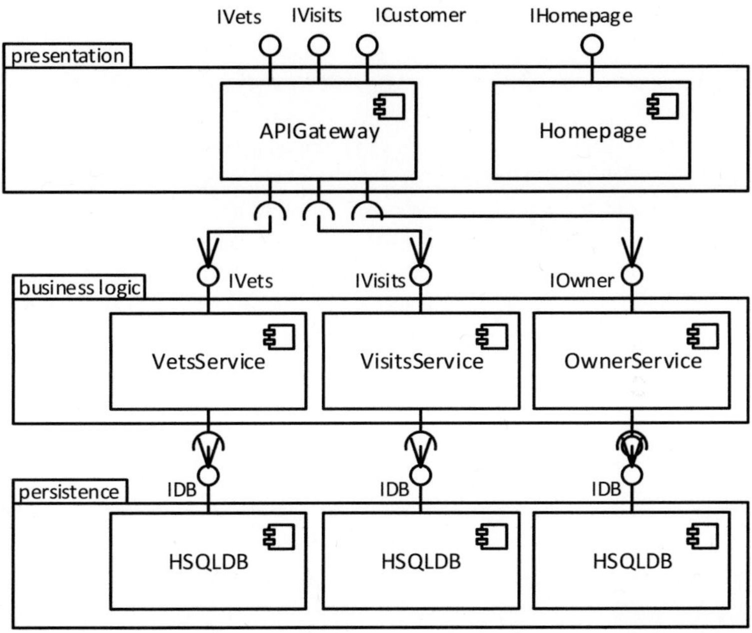

Figure 7.7.: Simplified system diagram view of the PetClinic microservices architecture.

of the depicted components represents an independently deployable composite component. The variant separates the landing page in the dedicated *Homepage* component. Additionally, it separates the appointment planning service *VisitsService* in a dedicated component. The *APIGateway* component acts as a gateway to the back-end services. It uses the Netflix *Zuul*[1] API gateway implementation. The *APIGateway* component also provisions and delivers web content to the users. The microservices-based PetClinic replaces the web content of the baseline, which was built using Thymeleaf, with a NODE.JS front-end. Every service separately organizes its persistence. We instantiated a HSQLDB instance for each service.

[1] `https://github.com/Netflix/zuul`, retrieved 16.11.2017.

7.2.2.2. Evaluation Setup

We deployed both PetClinic variants on a PowerEdge R815 with four Opteron 6174 CPUs and 256 GB RAM. The execution environment of PetClinic was an Ubuntu 14.04.5 LTS VM with 40 virtual cores and 16 GB RAM. The VM ran atop a XenServer 7.0 hypervisor. Power monitoring was conducted using a ZES Zimmer LMG95 power meter connected to a dedicated notebook. We looped the electrical outlet of one of the two redundant PSUs of the servers through our power meter. We disconnected the second PSUs to guarantee that the full power draw of the server was captured by the power meter. An agent installed in the PetClinic VM collected power measurement data and system metric measurements. JMeter 3.0 was used as the load driver issuing user requests. We deployed JMeter on a workstation PC equipped with an i7-7700 CPU and 32 GB RAM. The workstation was connected to the R815 server via 1 Gbit/s Ethernet.

We deployed each of the services of the microservices variant in the same VM. While the microservices variant supports the isolation of services in separate containers, we opted to run them in separate Java VMs in the same user space.

We used PMX [220] to extract the performance models of PetClinic Boot, and PetClinic Cloud. PMX extracts PCM instances from the monitoring traces of an application that has been instrumented by Kieker [90]. To extract the power model for the evaluation, we conducted an automated power model extraction using our systematic profiling approach. Chapter 5 presents this approach. The profiling run was executed within the target Ubuntu VM, in which we deployed the PetClinic instances. As Section 5.2.3 discussed, the extraction approach ranks a set of power models based on their prediction accuracy. From the power models detailed in Section 7.3 we restricted the set of considered power models to power models that consider solely CPU utilization. This restriction is induced by the fact that PMX only learns resource demands for the CPU. Power models that rely on HDD metric predictions hence were ruled out.

In order to obtain a power model of the R815 server, we applied our power model extraction approach. We employed the CPU workloads discussed in Section 7.3.3. As target levels we used $\{0, 0.05, \ldots, 1.0, \infty\}$. We executed the profiling run in the same VM as the PetClinic instances. The PetClinic instances were not running during the profiling. We used a set of power models from literature as input to the model training. Section 7.3.2 provides an overview of the considered models. From the available models, we selected the models which used CPU utilization as their only input metric. We employed the iterated reweighted least squares regression as implemented by Rousseeuw et al. [177] to train the power models. Our tooling calculated the AIC of each trained power model. From the ranking, we selected the power model with the highest ranking. The selected power model was:

$$P_{\text{Exp}}(u) = 254.488\text{W} + 310.121\text{W} \cdot u^{0.395},$$

where $u \in [0, 1]$ is the aggregated CPU utilization measured within the VM. The model instantiates power model type 6 from Table 7.8.

For performance and power consumption predictions, we used SimuLizar coupled with the Power Consumption Analyzer (PCA). We used a sampling rate of 1 Hz, and sampling window size of 1 time unit for the power consumption predictions. The predicted CPU utilization was averaged over an interval of 10 seconds.

7.2.2.3. Evaluation Scenario

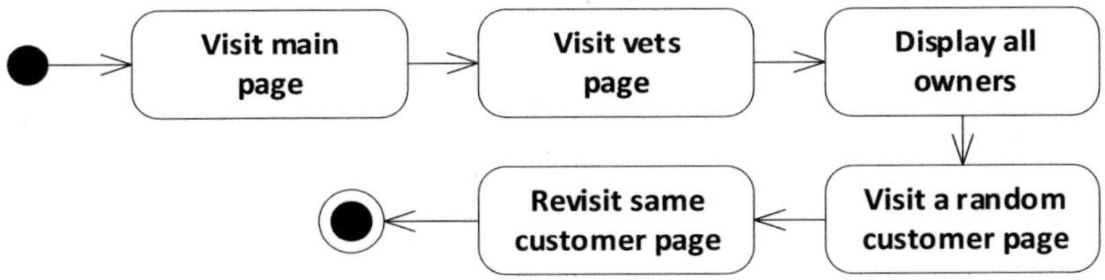

Figure 7.8.: Activity diagram view of the browsing usage scenario behavior for PetClinic

In order to evaluate the energy efficiency of the application of the PetClinic application, we defined a baseline usage scenario. We compared the measured and predicted energy efficiency of both application variants for the same usage scenarios. The usage scenario describes a sequence of interactions of a user with the PetClinic system. Figure 7.8 depicts the used scenario behavior. The scenario is a browsing workload which was derived from the JMeter test plan found within the repository [159]. Interactions that resulted in database write operations were removed. This was done in order to factor out contention effects, which resulted from database locking. Otherwise, much lower maximum throughput rates could have been achieved. This would have limited the range of workload intensities for which we could have explored the energy efficiency.

PetClinic Cloud groups information retrieval for front-end services by the different back-end services. The Representational State Transfer (REST) requests sent by the interactive front-end user web pages do not match those of the Spring Boot baseline. Thus, we implemented a JMeter test plan that conforms to the interfaces of the PetClinic Cloud services. The test plan contains the same user interactions as the baseline plan.

The scenario behavior was executed in an open workload usage scenario. We varied the interarrival rate between users to evaluate the power consumption of the system at different load levels.

7.2.2.4. Power Consumption Model

Figure 7.9 shows the Power Consumption model instance of the evaluation environment of PetClinic. The model represents the used power model $P_{\text{Exp}}(u)$ as a declarative resource power model. The topology structure represented in the Infrastructure view is the same as in the Media Store case study, since the study used the same server.

7.2.2.5. Prediction Accuracy

This section discusses the predicted and measured energy consumption for each of the two PetClinic variants.

Table 7.4 provides an overview of measured and predicted energy consumption at different throughput rates. Our predictions obtained via PCA coupled with SimuLizar achieved an absolute error of at most 2.13% for all considered workloads. Due to the high accuracy of power consumption predictions, energy efficiency predictions are naturally also accurate. Figure 7.10 depicts the predicted and measured energy efficiency of the application as energy

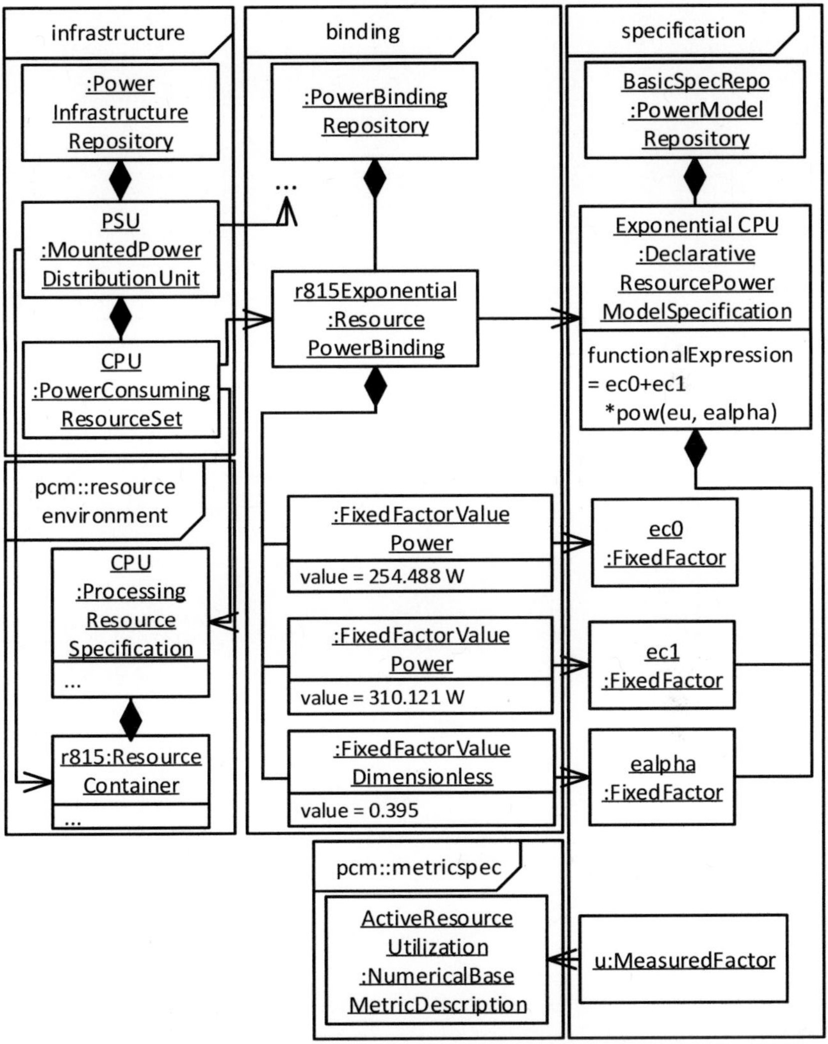

Figure 7.9.: Excerpt of Power Consumption model instance for deployment environment used in PetClinic case study.

Table 7.4.: Total energy consumption for different user scenario behavior rates for PetClinic system. Energy consumption in W h over an interval of 30 minutes.

Workload in User Scenario Behaviors per Second	Measured in W h	Predicted in W h	Error in %
296	193.78	193.13	0.34%
715	217.00	221.37	2.01%
963	228.61	233.18	2.13%
1377	247.14	250.78	1.48%

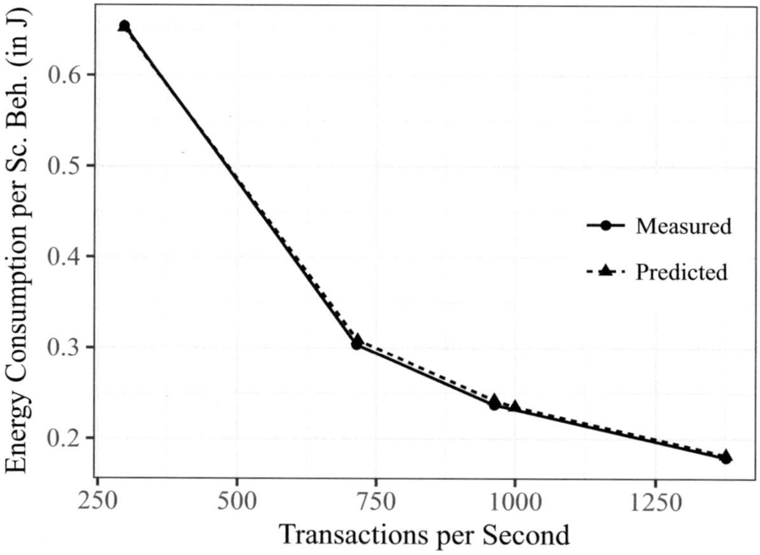

Figure 7.10.: Power consumption per completed User Scenario Behavior for the Spring Boot baseline.

Table 7.5.: Total energy consumption for different user scenario behavior rates for PetClinic Microservice system variant. Energy Consumption in W h over an interval of 30 minutes.

Workload in User Scenario Behaviors per Second	Measured in W h	Predicted in W h	Error in %
294	179.00	188.50	5.31%
710	217.87	214.72	1.45%
960	228.49	226.31	0.96%
1361	247.88	242.11	2.34%

consumed per transaction over the observed interval. The workload was picked to reflect a large range of utilization levels. The noted User Scenario Behaviors per seconds rates were the actual measured throughput rates when executing a specific target user workload. Measurements for the rate 296 were, e.g., performed for an intended target rate of 300. The predicted energy efficiency closely matched the measured energy efficiency.

As one would expect, the energy efficiency increased for higher transaction rates. A major reason is the fact that the static power consumption is spread among more requests. Another reason is the power consumption behavior of the server for higher utilization levels. The extracted power model $P_{\text{Exp}}(u)$ estimates the consumption at different load levels. The power model is strictly concave on $[0, 1]$. This implies that the marginal power consumption of the server decreases at higher utilization levels. Thus, an increase in throughput increases the energy efficiency. This holds as long as an increase in load does not lead to a violation of another quality goal.

Table 7.5 lists the measured and predicted energy consumption for the microservices variant of PetClinic. Over all predictions, the highest error is 5.31%. The predictions closely match the measured results for the microservices variant. The energy consumption per User Behavior Scenario of the microservices variant only marginally deviates from the standard PetClinic variant. This shows that the overhead introduced by the separation of func-

Figure 7.11.: Power consumption per completed User Scenario Behavior for Microservice system variant

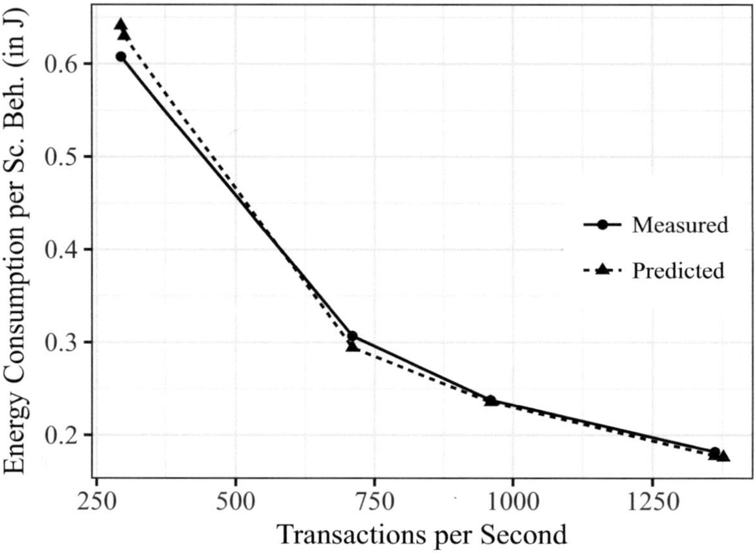

tionality into microservices was limited. The energy consumed per user transaction shown in Figure 7.11 also reflects this.

The energy consumption analysis of PCA accurately predicted the energy consumption of the PetClinic microservices variant. The results from the PetClinic case study indicate that our analysis offers high accuracy (Question 1.1). The high absolute accuracy for both PetClinic variants enabled us to reason on the effect of refactoring PetClinic into a microservices based architecture. We identified no significant impact of the refactorings on energy efficiency. The results thus affirm Question 1.3. Our model extraction approach managed to train and identify an accurate power model. Therefore, the results positively answer Question 3.1.

Table 7.6.: Prediction error of $P_{\text{Exp}}(u)$ compared with linear power model $P_{\text{Linear}}(u)$ for the microservices-based PetClinic. Error in %. Positive errors correspond to an overestimation, negative an underestimation.

Workload in User Scenario Behaviors per Second	$P_{\text{Exp}}(u)$	$P_{\text{Linear}}(u)$
294	+5.31%	+7.89%
710	−1.45%	−4.08%
960	−0.96%	−4.19%
1361	−2.34%	−4.99%

7.2.2.6. Comparison with State of the Art

We investigated Question 1.2 using the microservices-based PetClinic variant. The approach by Brunnert et al. [35] is the only state of the art approach that supports architecture-level reasoning on the energy consumption of software systems. We replicated their prediction method by using a linear power model, as the implementation by Brunnert et al. was not available to us. We leveraged the same training data and regression technique to train $P_{\text{Linear}}(u)$ as for $P_{\text{Exp}}(u)$. The training resulted in:

$$P_{\text{Linear}}(u) = 364.604 + 227.87 \cdot u,$$

where $u \in [0, 1]$ is the aggregated CPU utilization measured within the PetClinic VM.

Table 7.6 lists the prediction error of $P_{\text{Exp}}(u)$ and the linear power model $P_{\text{Linear}}(u)$ for the microservices variant of PetClinic. $P_{\text{Exp}}(u)$ outperformed the linear across all throughput rates. The linear power model overestimated power consumption at low throughput rates, and underestimated consumption at high rates. This is indicated by the plus/minus sign. It was hence not possible to improve the accuracy by adjusting the linear model by a fixed factor: This adjustment would have either increased the accuracy at low utilization levels at the cost of an increased error at high utilization levels, or the other way around. The results show that the use of power models beyond linear models can improve the prediction accuracy. They positively answer Question 1.2 for the Petclinic microservices variant.

7.2.3. Virtual Machine Placement in Data Centers

The central goal of our PCA approach is to enable the design time energy efficiency analysis of software systems on an architectural level. Aside from its use in architectural design, power consumption predictions can aid data center operators in decision making for their infrastructure. Example decisions in the context of IaaS data centers are the choice of resource management algorithms. Resource management algorithms aim to improve, e.g., the mapping of VMs to servers. The algorithms perform this with respect to the algorithm heuristics or optimization criteria. This section discusses the application of PCA in the validation and evaluation of resource management algorithms for data centers. It addresses Question 1.2 and Question 1.1 for a self-adaptive software system.

The CACTOS project [152] developed an integrated approach for monitoring, optimization, and simulation of IaaS data centers. The implementation of the integrated approach consisted of two complementary toolkits. The *CACTOS Runtime Toolkit* integrates monitoring and autonomic resource management of data centers. The framework continuously improves the configuration and resource allocation at runtime. It uses resource management algorithms to identify reconfiguration plans that improve QoS according to the algorithm heuristics. The *CACTOS Prediction Toolkit* enables what-if analyses for data center sizing, and the configuration and selection of resource management algorithms. In Stier et al. [196] we provide an overview of the central features of the Prediction Toolkit.

The CACTOS Prediction Toolkit includes an IaaS data center simulator. The simulator uses PCA to perform power consumption predictions. The simulator builds upon SimuLizar and our Transient Effect Interpreter extension. The toolkit supports an in-the-loop coupling of resource management algorithms with the simulator. Unlike existing Cloud simulators, the toolkit can include these algorithms in its simulation-based evaluation without modification. It does not require optimization algorithms to be re-implemented against simulator specific APIs. The simulator continuously calls the configured resource management algorithms to improve the mapping between VMs and server resources. The integration of simulator and resource management algorithms matches the integration in the Runtime Toolkit. A data center managed by CACTOS constitutes a self-adaptive software system, as it continuously aims to improve QoS by performing adaptation actions such as VM migrations.

The CACTOS tooling uses a specialized metamodel to represent data centers. Instances of the metamodel serve as a runtime model. Compared to PCM, the metamodel contains additional information needed for the management of virtualized data centers, such as further hardware information, and a representation of VMs as first class entities. The Prediction Toolkit continuously synchronizes the CACTOS runtime model with the PCM and SimuLizar models. We presented the integration method applied to couple simulation and optimization in [197]. The power consumption characteristics representation in the CACTOS metamodel was developed based on the Power Consumption model. Section 3.2.5.2 outlines the CACTOS integration of the central modeling concepts. As part of the simulation, CactoSim maps the power consumption characteristics to an instance of the Power Consumption model. SimuLizar then executes PCA on the target Power Consumption metamodel instance.

7.2.3.1. Evaluation Setup

The case studies presented in this section were conducted as part of the CACTOS project. The studies were carried out in a data center testbed built using commodity hardware. The testbed was managed using the OpenStack [151] Cloud platform, enhanced with the CACTOS Runtime Toolkit. The CACTOS Runtime Toolkit determines initial placement locations for VMs. Additionally, it continuously optimizes the mapping of VMs to resources, e.g., by performing VM migrations.

In total, four scenarios were evaluated. The four scenarios and the results were published in [196]. The first three scenarios covered a setup with eight servers. Power measurements were collected using IPMI. Power measurements could be collected from six out of the eight servers. The other two servers lacked power meters. The fourth scenario was conducted using six servers. From the six servers, power measurements could be collected from the four servers. In each scenario, a load driver submitted a set of VMs to the Cloud middleware. The VMs ran scientific computing workloads. Each VM executed a Molpro [221] scientific computing job after it had booted. Molpro is a framework for quantum chemistry computations. Molpro jobs adhere to run-to-completion semantics. The load driver submitted the Molpro VMs over time. Each set of submitted jobs was designed to follow typical daily submission patterns at the High Performance Computing Center at Ulm University. The workload mix covered Molpro jobs with short and long run times. Jobs with short run times lasted up to two hours. Long running jobs covered up to eight hours.

We predicted the power consumption of the testbed using CPU-based power models. In the first scenario, we used linear power models to predict the power consumption of servers. We trained the power models on historic measurements that were collected for all servers, which the scenario covered. In the other three scenarios, we used a mix of linear, cubic polynomial, and exponential power model types. The exponential power model type was:

$$P(u) = a \cdot (1 - e^{-u}) \cdot b.$$

Initially, we had used linear power models to predict the power consumption in all four scenarios. We were able to reduce the prediction error through the use of the previously mentioned non-linear models. This illustrates the increased prediction accuracy of our approach compared to state of the art predictions (Question 1.2).

We queried historic power and load measurements from a monitoring database that recorded measurements from the testbed. As the power measurements strongly varied for each recorded CPU load level, we aggregated the measurements for each load level in $\{0, 0.01, \ldots, 1\}$ using the median function. The aggregated input values served as the training set of the regression. We applied the iterated reweighted least squares regression as implemented by Rousseeuw et al. [177] to train the power models. Section 5.3 provides further details on this power model extraction from historical measurements.

We performed a simulation of a specific workload mix, and optimization configuration based on historical load data. We reconstructed black-box VM models from the load data stored in the monitoring database. The black-box modeling concept we employed to describe VM load is described in

[115]. In order to minimize the effect of variations in VM behavior on the predictions, we compared the simulation results against the historical run from which the load models were constructed. We only considered VMs that were successfully deployed on the testbed. This was done as information on VMs with failed deployments were not recorded.

We determined the total energy consumption of simulation runs and measurements using numerical integration. We employed the Gauss-Kronrod quadrature formula to calculate the total energy consumption from the measured and predicted power samples. In our predictions, we only compared the measured and predicted energy consumption of the servers with power meters.

7.2.3.2. Evaluation Scenarios

This section provides details on the conducted experiments. No VMs were running at the start of each experiment scenario.

Scenario 1 The first scenario encompasses 26 VM submissions to a data center testbed setup which consisted of eight servers. Six of these eight servers had a power meter, from which we could collect measurements. No power measurements were available for the other two servers. The experiment covered just below one and a half hours. We used consolidation algorithms for VM placement and migration. The algorithms consolidated the VMs based on their RAM requirements. The project deliverable [117] describes the RAM-based consolidation algorithms.

Scenario 2 The second scenario contained 15 VM starts. It lasted for approximately eight and a half hours. In this scenario, both VM placement and optimization of the Runtime Toolkit were configured to use load balancing algorithms. The algorithms target an even distribution of used RAM across all servers based on the RAM requirements of VMs. A description of the algorithm is available in [117].

Table 7.7.: Total energy consumption for the three evaluated scenarios. Energy Consumption in W h. Prediction error in %.

Scenario	Duration	Measured	Predicted	Error
1	75 min	1 783 W h	1 661 W h	6.85%
2	514 min	5 443 W h	5 464 W h	0.39%
3	526 min	5 238 W h	5 609 W h	7.08%
4	1561 min	13 558 W h	12 826 W h	5.40%

Scenario 3 The third scenario covered the same basic experiment configuration as Scenario 1, but with an extended experiment time of eight hours and 46 minutes. The number of VM starts was reduced to 19. We used the same VM consolidation algorithms as in Scenario 1.

Scenario 4 The last scenario consisted of 37 VM starts. It covered an interval of approximately 26 hours. The scenario used the same consolidation algorithms for VM placement and optimization as Scenario 2. Unlike the eight servers used in the first two scenarios, the third scenario used six servers.

7.2.3.3. Experiment Results

This section discusses the prediction accuracy we achieved when applying PCA to the power consumption prediction of a self-adaptive IaaS data center.

Table 7.7 lists the measured and predicted energy consumption for each scenario. In the first scenario, the prediction error was 6.85%. The prediction error in scenario 2 reached a low 0.39%.

Scenario 3 had the highest prediction error 7.08%. We attribute the high prediction error to an overestimation of CPU utilization in one of the servers that was equipped with a power meter. The simulation model did not contain one VM that was actually running on the testbed. In the run, this VM was initially placed on a server without a power meter. Later, the VM was consolidated to a server with a power meter. This migration did not happen in simulation. Consequently, the server with a power meter continued to have spare resources in simulation. This led to the placement of a highly active VM on the server, since the resource management algorithm were configured to consolidate VMs on as few servers as possible. . In the measured run, the VM was placed on a server without a power meter due to RAM limits. The VM increased the power consumption of one of the monitored servers in simulation. Byrne et al. [43] provide an extensive discussion of the deviation. Even though the missing measurement data led to a major deviation in simulation, the aggregate energy consumption prediction was accurate.

In the fourth scenario, which covered over 24 hours, the prediction reached 5.40%.

Our PCA approach accurately predicted the power consumption of the data center testbed across all four scenarios. Hence, we conclude that the results positively answer Question 1.1.

7.2.3.4. Limitations

We achieved a high prediction accuracy despite the following limitations regarding the quality of input data, and our test setup:

- **Resolution and accuracy of measurement data.** The monitoring database collected power consumption measurement data with a resolution of ten seconds. CPU utilization measurements were also only available with a resolution of ten seconds. The low measurement resolution hindered the construction of accurate performance and power models. The monitoring tooling collected power consumption measurements from power meters built into the server PSUs. The use of built-in power meters limited the measurement accuracy.

  We observed a large variation of power consumption measurements for the same load level. Our model learning addressed this by averaging over all measurements of each load level. Nevertheless, we consider the fluctuations to have had an impact on prediction accuracy.

- **Missing measurement data.** In the third scenario utilization measurements from one of the VMs were missing due to a monitoring failure. This led to inaccuracies in the reconstructed behavior model for simulation. The resulting prediction inaccuracies of CPU utilization reduced the energy consumption prediction accuracy.
- **Lack of a representative range of measurement data covered by historical data.** Most servers reached at most an overall CPU utilization of 20% for time frame, in which measurement data were available. This made it difficult to train power models that were representative of the power consumption behavior of the servers outside of the observed utilization range.
- **Missing power meters in a subset of servers.** Two of the servers lacked a power meter in all three scenarios. Power consumption resulting from the activity of VMs that were allocated on these servers could not be considered. Consequently, we could only reason on power consumption for the remaining servers. In Scenario 3 this introduced a noticeable error in the simulation predictions.

7.3. Automated Extraction of Power Models

This section investigates the appropriateness of the power model extraction method as stated in Goal 2. The evaluation addresses the validation questions 3.1 through 3.5. Parts of the validation results were initially published in [201].

The main power model extraction case study involved three central steps. First, we executed the profiling approach presented in Section 5.2 for a server. Second, we trained a set of power models on the resulting profile. Finally, we evaluated the accuracy of the power models for a set of workloads. We reasoned on the utility of the AIC-based power model ranking approach via a comparison of measured and predicted accuracy.

This section is structured as follows. Section 7.3.1 introduces the setup of the profiling for the case study. Section 7.3.2 gives an overview of power models used as in input for the profiling and model training. Section 7.3.4

discusses the server profile produced by our profiling approach. Section 7.3.5 introduces the case study systems used to evaluate the accuracy of power models. In Section 7.3.6 we investigate the prediction error of power models for the case study systems. Section 7.3.7 compares our approach with a state of the art approach. Section 7.3.8 discusses the application of the AIC-based ranking of power models to the system under investigation. In Section 7.3.9 we present a complementary case study that evaluates the prediction accuracy of the extracted models for VM migration scenarios.

7.3.1. Profiling Setup

The server under investigation for the evaluation of the profiling approach was a PowerEdge R815 with four Opteron 6174 CPUs, 256 GB RAM, and six 900 GB 10,000 RPM Serial Attached SCSI (SAS) HDDs. The six HDDs were connected to an internal storage RAID. The profiling framework and evaluation workloads were executed in Ubuntu 14.04 VMs. Each VM had 48 virtual cores and was running atop XenServer 6.5. Only one VM was running at any given time during the profiling and measurement. The profiling VM was assigned 64 GB of RAM.

Power measurements were conducted using a ZES Zimmer LMG95 power meter. We connected the power meter to the electrical outlet of one of the two redundant PSUs of the servers. We disconnected the other PSUs to guarantee that the power meter captured the full power draw of the server. Power meter measurement data was collected using a dedicated notebook. The notebook ran SPEC PTDaemon [192], which polled power measurements from the power meter. A monitoring utility collected all system metric and power measurements. We implemented the utility upon the technical foundation of SIGAR [143] and Metrics [139].

Our server profiling uses an input configuration. The configuration determines the set of workloads, and the set and range of system metrics that should be considered by the profiling. We configured the profiling as follows. We included CPU utilization u_{cpu}, storage write throughput tp_{write}, and storage read throughput tp_{read} in the profiling metrics. Our profiling framework only actively steered one of the two storage metrics at any point in time. The framework monitored the other storage metric during that time. We configured the profiling framework to perform the calibration of the workload intensity over 80 or 90 seconds. We set the measurement phase to last 60 seconds. The calibration phase was 90 seconds for all workloads involving *XMLvalidate*, and 80 seconds for all other workloads.

7.3.2. Metric Selection and Considered Power Model Types

We selected u_{cpu}, tp_{write}, and tp_{read} as candidate metrics for the power model training, since they can be predicted with Palladio simulators [18, 22, 92] and available extensions [148]. Modeling storage systems requires additional effort, as the work by Huber et al. [92] and Noorshams et al. [148] demonstrates. If we are able to accurately predict the power consumption and performance of a software system without explicit consideration of storage, this option is the more desirable option. The reason lies in the lower effort required to create PCM models that solely consider CPU.

As outlined in Section 5.2, the power profiling performs the profiling and training of the server under investigation for a set of power model types specified by the user. Each power model type subsumes a set of power models that predict the power consumption of a server using a set of system metrics.

Prior to the evaluation, we had collected power model types that supported system level metrics for CPU and HDD. For these models, we limited the used metrics to u_{cpu}, and optionally tp_{write}, tp_{read}, or all three metrics. Table 7.8 provides an overview of the identified power models. The only model not explicitly stated in literature is model 6. We derived model 6 from model 5 by eliminating its linear component.

7.3.3. Workload Selection and Definition of Profiling Ranges

We selected the workloads *SequentialWrite*, *RandomWrite*, *XMLvalidate*, *CryptoAES*, *Compress* and *SOR* from Server Efficiency Rating Tool (SERT) to profile the server under investigation. *SequentialWrite* performs sets of sequential disk writes, while *RandomWrite* randomly writes to disk. *XML-validate* stresses the CPU by performing XML document validations. *SOR* numerically solves differential equations. *Compress* (de-)compresses data. Further details on the used workloads are available in [187].

Table 7.8.: Overview of considered power models. M is the set of considered metrics. The referenced papers propose or apply the listed power model.

No.	Power Model	Considered Metrics
1	$P = c_0 + \sum_{m \in M} c_m u_m$	OS-level system metrics [35, 65, 82, 104, 135, 172], or only CPU utilization [69, 231]
2	$P = c_0 + \sum_{m \in M} (\sum_{l=1}^{l_{max}} c_l {u_m}^l)$	OS-level system metrics [135], or only CPU utilization [231]
3	$P = c_0 + \sum_{m \in M} \sum_{l=1}^{l_{max}} (e^{u_m} + c_l {u_m}^l)$	OS-level system metrics [135]
4	$P = c_1 \cdot e^{-(\frac{u_{\text{cpu}} - c_2}{\alpha_1})^2}$	CPU utilization [231]
5	$P = c_0 + c_1 u_{\text{cpu}} + c_2 u_{\text{cpu}}^{\alpha}$	CPU utilization [69, 172]
6	$P = c_0 + c_1 u_{\text{cpu}}^{\alpha}$	CPU utilization

We formed workload mixes from the considered individual workloads by forming the cross product of workloads that stress the CPU (u_{cpu}), and workloads which mainly use the HDD (tp_{write}). Table 7.9 lists the combined workloads with the target levels per workload combination. In total, the run of the combined workload took approximately 38 hours. We did not control tp_{read} via a separate workload. We only passively monitored and recorded tp_{read}. We defined the target level ranges of tp_{write} based on simple throughput tests using utilities like the Linux command line tool *hdparm*. By slightly varying tp_{write} target levels across the workload mixes, we were able to cover a larger range of throughput levels. The profiling framework formed the target load levels as the cross product of the u_{cpu} and tp_{write} levels of workloads 1 through 4. The listed load level 850 000 matches ∞, as it is higher than the achievable throughput rates for tp_{write}. It could have been omitted from the workload level definition as it practically resulted in a repeat of the ∞ target level. Since measurements can be filtered prior to power model training, we deemed that the repeat definition did not impair the representativeness of our measurements.

Table 7.9.: Workload mixes with used target level per steered system metric. The cross product of target values form the target measurement tuples. Workload mixes marked with (★) have an additional target level (∞, ∞).

No.	Workload (combination)	Controlled Metrics	Target Level Ranges
(1)	*SequentialWrite*	tp_{write}	{0, 6 000, 25 000, 40 000, 60 000, 100 000, 850 000, ∞}×
	and *XMLvalidate*	u_{cpu}	{0, 0.05, 0.10, 0.15, . . . , 1.0, ∞}
(2)	*RandomWrite*	tp_{write}	{0, 6 000, 25 000, 40 000, 60 000, 100 000, 850 000, ∞}
	and *XMLvalidate*	u_{cpu}	{0, 0.05, 0.10, 0.15, . . . , 1.0}
(3)	*SequentialWrite* and *CryptoAES* (★)	tp_{write} u_{cpu}	{10 000, 20 000, . . . , 120 000} ×{0.05, 0.10, 0.15, . . . , 1.0}
(4)	*RandomWrite* and *CryptoAES* (★)	tp_{write} u_{cpu}	{6 000, 12 000, . . . , 72 000} ×{0.05, 0.10, 0.15, . . . , 1.0}
(5), (6), (7), (8)	*Compress*, *XML-validate*, *SOR*, *CryptoAES*	u_{cpu}	{0, 0.05, 0.10, . . . , 1.00, ∞}

7.3.4. Discussion of the Server Profile

We used the workload mixes discussed in Section 7.3.3 to profile the server under investigation. This produced a server profile for use in the model training step.

Figure 7.12 visualizes the server profile as a scatter plot. The scatter plot shows the combined measurements collected when profiling the system under investigation using the workload mixes listed in Table 7.9. The plot indicates that power consumption strongly correlates with CPU utilization. A relation between consumption and storage throughput is not apparent.

We applied Pearson's and Spearman's correlation coefficients to investigate the degree to which measurements of different system metrics and

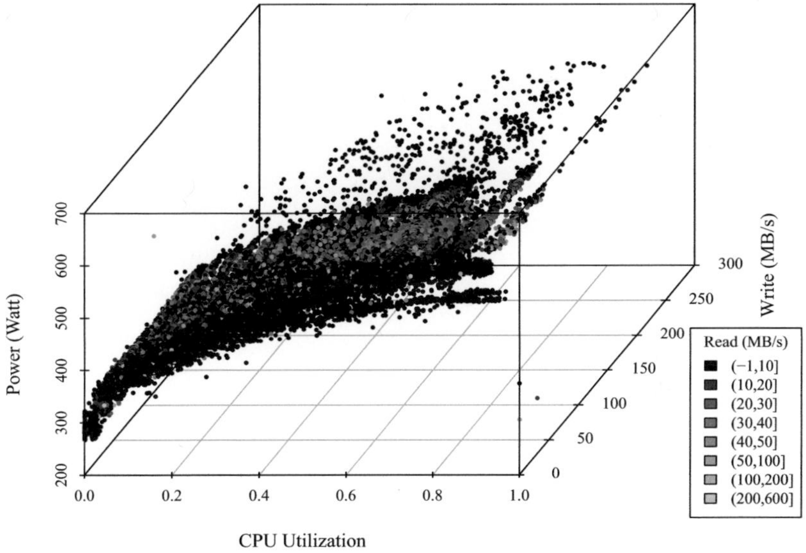

Figure 7.12.: Scatter plot of power measurements (vertical axis) drawn over measurements of considered system metrics. The horizontal axis represents CPU utilization, the diagonal axis write throughput. The color of dots in the plot illustrates the read throughput.

power consumption correlate. Section 2.7.4 introduced the foundations of the correlation coefficients. CPU utilization and power consumption had a Pearson's correlation coefficient value of 0.95, which indicated a strong positive correlation of CPU utilization and power consumption. This confirmed and is consistent with the well-established observation that CPU utilization and power consumption strongly correlate. For write throughput and power consumption, Pearson's correlation coefficient produced a value of 0.06. Read throughput and power consumption had a correlation value of 0.03. The Spearman's correlation coefficient values for CPU utilization, read and write throughput were 0.95, 0.06, and 0.10. Hence, we could infer that CPU utilization by far had the strongest correlation with power consumption. Storage throughput and power consumption appeared to have a weak correlation with power consumption. When we reduced the set of measurements to the measurements with idle CPU load, power consumption and write throughput had a Spearman's correlation value of 0.76. Power consumption and read throughput had a correlation of 0.58. This indicated that storage activity increased the power consumption. However, the effect of CPU activity was much stronger. This can be seen in the weak correlation of power consumption and storage activity for the full profile.

A comparison of power consumption of storage intensive workloads with CPU intensive workloads explained the weak correlation values of storage throughput for the whole data set. More than 99% of the power measurements of runs where u_{cpu} was not explicitly stressed fell in the interval [269.64, 375.21]. Over 99% of the measurements collected for workloads that stressed u_{cpu} fell into the interval [284.88, 607.37]. This indicates that the correlation of total power consumption and I/O is much smaller than power consumption and CPU. Consequently, I/O does not appear to strongly correlate with total power consumption when analyzing the full data set.

7.3.5. Prediction Accuracy Evaluation for the Case Study Systems

We used the HiBench benchmarking suite [91] version 5.0[1] and SPECjbb2015 [193] to evaluate the accuracy of our power model extraction approach. HiBench consists of a set of Hadoop benchmarks. The benchmarks contained in HiBench cover a set of typical Big Data application workloads and microbenchmarks. We categorized the encompassed benchmarks into the three categories I/O-intensive, CPU-intensive and idle. We considered workloads I/O-intensive if they contained phases in which tp_{write} or tp_{read} increased well above idle throughput rates. We identified *K-means*, *TeraSort*, *DFSIOe*, *Page Rank*, and *Nutch Indexing* as I/O intensive workloads. We distinguished *Sleep* from the remaining workloads as it does not perform any actual work. We categorized all other workloads as CPU-intensive. This subsumed *Sort*, *Word Count*, *Join*, *Aggregation*, and *Scan*. SPECjbb2015 is a benchmark application that aims to evaluate the performance of a system environment for business applications implemented in Java. Its application workload is modeled after transactions in a "world-wide supermarket IT infrastructure" [193].

[1] `https://github.com/intel-hadoop/HiBench/tree/175ad8771fdeebfc637bd4ad3c09a23df3c9cc50`, retrieved 16.11.2017.

SPECjbb2015 determines the throughput of the deployment environment by continuously increasing the user load issued to the application.

The evaluation setup matches the profiling setup. The only difference was the RAM sizing of VMs in which we executed the evaluation VMs. The SPECjbb2015 VM operated with 32 GB RAM, while the HiBench VM had 16 GB RAM.

7.3.6. Prediction Error of Trained Models

In order to reason on the actual accuracy of the models, we evaluated the prediction accuracy of the power models listed in Table 7.8 for the case study applications. For this, we ran the case study application benchmarks. We executed each benchmark eight times. During the execution of each benchmark, we collected both power and system metric measurements. We used the system metric measurements collected during the run as input to the power models. This gave us power consumption predictions for all sampled points in time during the run of each application workload. Next, we performed numerical integration on the predicted and measured power consumption samples. This produced energy consumption estimates on the basis of the predicted (E_{Pred}) and measured energy consumption (E_{Meas}). Finally, we compared the predicted with the measured energy consumption, and determined the Mean Absolute Error (MAE) over all eight runs as $|\frac{E_{\text{Meas}}-E_{\text{Pred}}}{E_{\text{Meas}}}|$. The tooling we used in the evaluation is available online via[1].

Initially, we trained the power models using the full server profile discussed in Section 7.3.4. The profiling framework had obtained the full server profile by profiling the server under investigation for all target levels listed in Table 7.9. To assess the benefit of using a server profile obtained via combined profiling of CPU and HDD over a separate profiling, we compared the accuracy of power models from combined with the accuracy from separate profiling. In order to reduce the influence of measurement variations introduced by reruns, we extracted the profile from the existing profile. The server profile from separate profiling only contained measurements from runs that individually stressed either CPU or HDD. This corresponded to the subset of profiling

[1] `https://sdqweb.ipd.kit.edu/wiki/Power_Consumption_Profiler`, retrieved 16.11.2017.

runs from all target levels shown in Table 7.9, where either u_{cpu} or tp_{write} targeted zero.

Surprisingly, the models trained on the profile from separate profiling had a smaller or similar prediction compared to the models trained on the full profile. The error rates of the models trained on the full profile can be found in Appendix A. The prediction error results thus negatively answer Question 3.2 for the system under investigation. One explanation for the lower accuracy of models trained the on the server profile from the combined profiling is the high number of measurements in the profile, where at least one of the observed metrics reached high measurement values. Since the used regression approach minimized the error for the full training set, this could have over-emphasized high model accuracy for high utilization levels. This is hinted at by the large difference in prediction error between combined and separate profiling for workloads with low utilization, e.g. Sleep. The power models from combined profiling had prediction errors of up to 28.6% for Sleep, while the highest error of the models from separate profiling was 15.7%. Another reason for the missing improvement in prediction accuracy is that none of the models listed in Table 7.8 have interactions among system metric variables. Interactions refer to a simultaneous effect of two variables on the result, e.g., $u \cdot tp_{\text{write}}$. The model training could not train the models to consider potential interactions as the models lacked such interactions. The following focuses on the results from separate profiling as the prediction error of the resulting power models was lower than the error from separate profiling.

Tables 7.10 to 7.13 contain the prediction errors from separate profiling for the evaluation workloads. Power models of types 4, 5 and 6 were the most consistently accurate power models. They achieved a median error of less than 2.3%. The power models of type 1 and 3 with $l = 1$ were inaccurate for utilization levels close to idle, e.g. for the Sleep workload. All power models reached prediction errors lower than 5.9% across all workloads except for Sleep.

As noted in Section 7.3.5, the following workloads were particularly I/O-intensive: Word Count, TeraSort, Page Rank, K-means and Nutch Indexing. Model 3 with $l = 3$ and the metrics u_{cpu}, u_{read}, u_{write} was the best performing power model that considered storage metrics. The predictions from model 3 had an error that was up to 1.5% lower than the error of the CPU-only models.

Table 7.10.: Prediction error per power model and workload type, errors in percent. Power models 1 and 2. Microbenchmarks, web search and clustering workloads.

Power Model	Params.	Metrics	Workload Type							
			Microbenchmarks					Web Search		Clustering
			Sort	Word Count	TeraSort	DFSIOe	Sleep	Page Rank	Nutch Indexing	K-means
1		u_{cpu}	1.8	0.0	0.2	0.0	10.7	0.7	2.2	0.5
		$u_{cpu}, u_{read}, u_{write}$	2.9	1.1	1.5	0.7	12.5	0.3	1.5	1.3
2	$l = 3$	u_{cpu}	2.5	1.0	0.2	1.0	1.7	0.5	4.8	1.6
		u_{cpu}, u_{read}	3.4	1.5	0.8	1.5	0.3	0.9	5.6	1.7
		u_{cpu}, u_{write}	3.6	1.8	0.1	1.9	0.4	1.3	5.7	1.2
		$u_{cpu}, u_{read}, u_{write}$	3.7	1.8	0.2	2.0	0.4	1.3	5.9	1.3
	$l = 2$	u_{cpu}	2.6	1.3	0.5	1.1	2.2	0.9	4.8	1.2
		u_{cpu}, u_{read}	3.3	1.7	0.2	1.4	1.1	1.4	5.5	1.2
		u_{cpu}, u_{write}	3.4	1.9	0.9	1.6	1.0	1.5	4.9	0.8
		$u_{cpu}, u_{read}, u_{write}$	3.5	1.9	1.1	1.7	1.0	1.6	5.1	1.0

Table 7.11.: Prediction error per power model and workload type, errors in percent. Power models 1 and 2. Analytical and server workloads.

Power Model	Params.	Metrics	Workload Type: Analytical Queries: Join	Analytical Queries: Aggregation	Analytical Queries: Scan	Server: SPECjbb-2015
1		u_{cpu}	2.1	1.8	1.6	5.5
		$u_{cpu}, u_{read}, u_{write}$	3.3	2.9	2.8	5.7
2	$l = 3$	u_{cpu}	2.9	2.7	3.4	4.5
		u_{cpu}, u_{read}	3.7	3.4	4.4	4.6
		u_{cpu}, u_{write}	3.8	3.8	4.6	4.7
		$u_{cpu}, u_{read}, u_{write}$	3.9	3.8	4.7	4.7
	$l = 2$	u_{cpu}	3.1	2.7	3.4	4.3
		u_{cpu}, u_{read}	3.7	3.3	4.1	4.2
		u_{cpu}, u_{write}	3.9	3.5	4.2	4.2
		$u_{cpu}, u_{read}, u_{write}$	3.9	3.5	4.3	4.3

Workloads that performed little to no I/O did not benefit from considering storage metrics. For most of the other workloads, model 5 outperformed the models that considered storage metrics.

Overall, power models that only considered CPU utilization had a high accuracy. They were outperformed only for Nutch Indexing and TeraSort by power models that explicitly consider tp_{write} or tp_{read}. In summary, we were able to accurately predict the power consumption of the server under investigation without the consideration of storage metrics. Performance models of software systems deployed on the server under investigation only

Table 7.12.: Prediction error per power model and workload type, errors in percent. Power models 4–6. Microbenchmarks, web search and clustering workloads.

Power Model	Params.	Metrics	Workload Type							
			Microbenchmarks					Web Search		Clustering
			Sort	Word Count	TeraSort	DFSIOe	Sleep	Page Rank	Nutch Indexing	K-means
3	$l = 3$	u_{cpu}	2.5	1.0	0.2	1.0	1.7	0.5	4.8	1.6
		u_{cpu}, u_{read}	3.4	1.5	0.8	1.5	0.3	0.9	5.6	1.7
		u_{cpu}, u_{write}	3.6	1.8	0.1	1.9	0.4	1.3	5.7	1.2
		u_{cpu}, u_{read}, u_{write}	3.7	1.8	0.1	2.0	0.4	1.3	5.9	1.3
	$l = 2$	u_{cpu}	2.6	1.2	0.4	1.1	2.1	0.9	4.8	1.2
		u_{cpu}, u_{read}	3.3	1.7	0.3	1.5	1.0	1.3	5.5	1.2
		u_{cpu}, u_{write}	3.4	1.8	1.2	1.6	0.9	1.4	4.7	0.9
		u_{cpu}, u_{read}, u_{write}	3.5	1.9	1.3	1.7	0.9	1.5	5.0	1.1
	$l = 1$	u_{cpu}	3.7	1.1	0.4	0.8	13.8	0.1	0.9	1.0
		u_{cpu}, u_{read}	4.8	2.0	0.9	1.5	15.2	0.9	0.1	1.3
		u_{cpu}, u_{write}	4.7	2.0	1.5	1.5	15.5	1.0	0.9	1.9
		u_{cpu}, u_{read}, u_{write}	5.0	2.2	1.6	1.7	15.7	1.2	0.4	1.8
4		u_{cpu}	2.3	1.7	1.2	1.0	3.8	1.8	4.7	0.3
5		u_{cpu}	1.3	0.7	1.7	0.1	0.3	1.8	3.3	3.6
6		u_{cpu}	0.6	2.4	3.4	1.3	0.1	3.6	1.1	5.2

Table 7.13.: Prediction error per power model and workload type, errors in percent. Power models 3–6. Analytical and server workloads.

Power Model	Params.	Metrics	Workload Type: Analytical Queries: Join	Analytical Queries: Aggregation	Analytical Queries: Scan	Server: SPECjbb-2015
		u_{cpu}	2.9	2.7	3.4	4.5
3	$l = 3$	u_{cpu}, u_{read}	3.7	3.4	4.3	4.6
		u_{cpu}, u_{write}	3.8	3.8	4.6	4.7
		u_{cpu}, u_{read}, u_{write}	3.9	3.8	4.7	4.7
		u_{cpu}	3.1	2.7	3.4	4.3
	$l = 2$	u_{cpu}, u_{read}	3.8	3.3	4.2	4.3
		u_{cpu}, u_{write}	3.8	3.5	4.2	4.3
		u_{cpu}, u_{read}, u_{write}	3.9	3.6	4.4	4.3
		u_{cpu}	4.2	3.7	3.7	5.3
	$l = 1$	u_{cpu}, u_{read}	5.1	4.6	4.8	5.6
		u_{cpu}, u_{write}	5.2	4.8	4.7	5.6
		u_{cpu}, u_{read}, u_{write}	5.4	5.0	5.0	5.6
4		u_{cpu}	3.0	2.3	2.9	3.8
5		u_{cpu}	1.6	1.5	2.3	5.2
6		u_{cpu}	0.5	0.4	0.3	5.9

need to explicitly model storage if it has a decisive impact on performance. We thus concluded regarding Question 3.4 that there is limited benefit in using power models that consider the HDD system metrics tp_{write} or tp_{read} for the server environment under investigation.

7.3.7. Comparison with State of the Art

This section presents a comparison of our approach with the state of the art approach for server profiling. It assessed whether our approach improved the accuracy over state of the art approaches for our server under investigation. This concerns Question 3.3. We identified the approaches by [65] and [58] as representative state of the art profiling approaches. As we did not find an implementation of either approaches [58, 65], we replicated the behavior of the approaches on the basis of our measurement tooling. The implementation of the state of the art approach passively monitors a set of workloads, and collects power measurements and system metrics. We implemented this by monitoring an execution of SERT. We configured SERT to execute the same individual workloads as the run of our profiling. Section 7.3.3 outlined the used workloads.

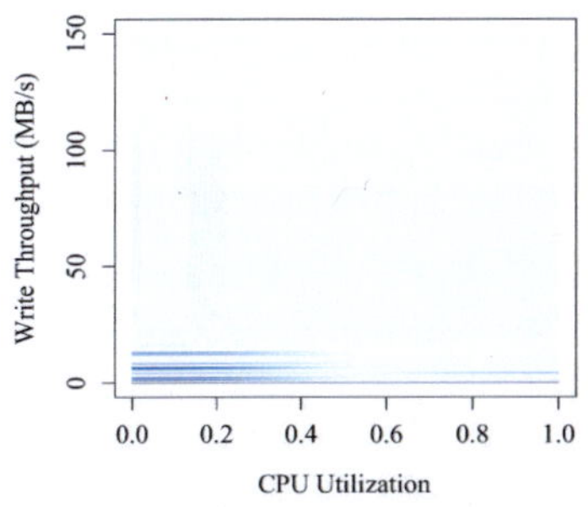

(a) Profile extracted from SERT run

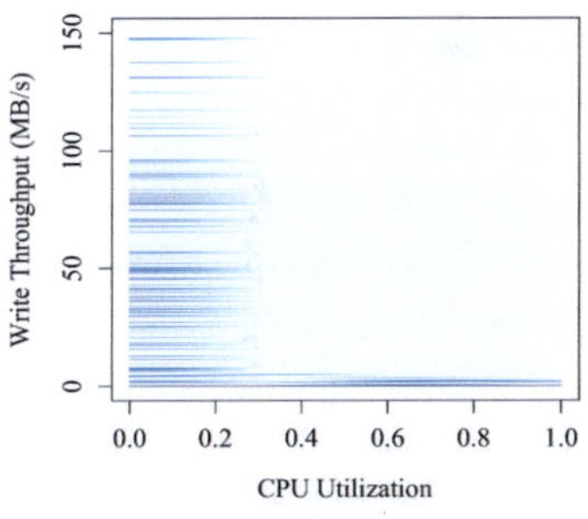

(b) Profile extracted using our approach, separated CPU and storage profiling

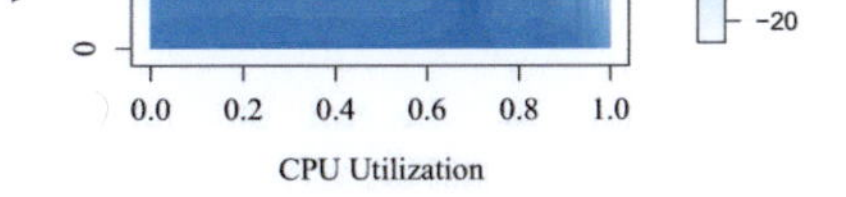

(c) Profile extracted using our approach, simultaneous CPU and storage profiling

Figure 7.13.: Two-Dimensional Kernel Density Estimation (KDE) of CPU utilization and write throughput with 200 grid points per dimension. The scale of the density values is adjusted to a logarithmic scale.

We compared the representativeness of the three samples using their KDE. KDE estimates the density function of a data distribution, as Section 2.7.3 explained. Figure 7.13a shows the two-dimensional KDE over the dimensions CPU utilization and write throughput for the SERT run. The plots contain 200 grid points per dimension. We adjusted the scale of the density values to a logarithmic scale to make the plots easier to compare. Values of 0 on the scale are equivalent to a KDE of 1, -20 to a KDE of 0, and 5 are equivalent to a KDE of 150. Comparing the KDE of the SERT run to the separate profiling variant of our approach shown in Figure 7.13b illustrates that a passive monitoring of SERT does not fully cover the range of measurements for storage. The measurements collected during the state of the art profiling run contained only few measurements for tp_{write} that were higher than 20 MB/s. This contrasts the maximum write rates of up to 150 MB/s we had measured with our systematic profiling approach. In conclusion, we deduce that our profiling approach produced a server profile that better covered the domain of considered system metrics than state of the art profiling.

Figure 7.13c contains the KDE plot from the combined, or simultaneous profiling. The plot illustrates that our method also manages to extract server profiles that covers the combined domain of multiple system metrics. Section 7.3.6 had outlined that the simultaneous profiling did not improve the accuracy of trained power models. However, the simultaneous profiling can potentially improve the accuracy for system metrics whose values interact on the total power consumption.

Question 3.3 brings up the point whether our approach produced more accurate power models than state of the art. We trained the same power models discussed in Section 7.3.2 with the measurements collected during the standard SERT run to investigate this question. We investigated if the passive monitoring of a state of the art profiling approach produced a training set that was sufficient for training power models that consider both CPU and storage metrics. The accuracy of power models that were only trained on measured power consumption and CPU utilization, u_{cpu}, was high when trained on the resulting profile. However, the accuracy of models that considered tp_{write}, or tp_{read} suffered. Power models 2 and 3 with $M = \{u_{\text{cpu}}, u_{\text{read}}, u_{\text{write}}\}$ had a prediction error of over 7000%. We attributed the high prediction error to the sparseness of the profile that resulted from the passive monitoring of SERT. The profile does not cover the full range of measurements that can be monitored for realistic workloads. Consequently, the power models were over-fitted to a non-representative sample. This caused the low prediction accuracy of the models trained on the sample.

The results positively answer Question 3.3. Single metric power models from our approach are at least as accurate as models from state of the art power model extraction approaches. Our profiling approach results in multi-metric power models with notably higher accuracy than from state of the art.

7.3.8. Model Selection

The goal of our method is to automate the construction of power models suited for use in design time predictions. Since the target workload is not fully known at design time, it is not possible to select a power model based on its actual accuracy for the target workload. Aside from the challenge of model selection, it would be beneficial to the user of the approach if she could judge the impact of metric selection on prediction accuracy (Question 3.5). Section 5.2.3 proposed a ranking of power models based on their AIC value to address both challenges. The ranking aims at eliminating system metrics that fail to improve power consumption prediction accuracy for the server under investigation. Furthermore, the ranking is intended to help select a power model that likely has a high accuracy.

We evaluated the accuracy of the AIC ranking as follows. First, we calculated the AIC as part of the initial model training on the basis of the input server profile. Second, we compared the ranking with the prediction error for the validation workloads.

Creating an unequivocal ranking of power models using their measured prediction error over all case study workloads listed in Section 7.3.5 was not possible. 17 of the 25 power models were Pareto optimal, meaning that there was no other power model that performed at least as well across all workloads. We hence evaluated if each model that placed high in the Δ_{AIC} ranking also had a competitive accuracy across the case study systems.

The ranking of power models from their difference in AIC (Δ_{AIC}) placed the power models 6 and 5 first and second, respectively. Both power models only consider the CPU metric u_{cpu}. Power model 3 with $l = 3$ and $M = \{u_{\text{cpu}}, u_{\text{read}}, u_{\text{write}}\}$ placed third. It was the highest placing power model that considered HDD system metrics. Consequently, all power models that had tp_{write} or tp_{read} as input variables were outperformed by CPU-only power models 5. According to our approach, we could conclude that the consideration of the storage metrics likely would not increase the prediction accuracy for the server under investigation. The prediction error results of the power models for the case study systems confirmed this. Power models that consider tp_{write} or tp_{read} had a higher prediction error than models parametrized solely by u_{cpu} for all but two workloads.

Power models 5 and 6 were among the most consistently accurate power models. Power model 5 achieved a median prediction error of 2.3%, and a maximum prediction error of 4.7%, which can be seen in Tables 7.12 and 7.13. Power model 6 reached a median prediction error of 1.7%, and a maximum prediction error of 5.2%. All three models had an error no higher than 5.9% for all workloads.

The comparison of Δ_{AIC} ranking and relative prediction error across the case study systems showed that the ranking approach can give helpful guidance to users of our approach in selecting an accurate power model. The evaluation positively answers Question 3.5 as we were able to reason on the influence of selected metrics on prediction accuracy using the ranking.

7.3.9. Accuracy of Power Models in VM Migration Scenarios

This section presents the results of our VM Migration Bench case study. The study validated whether our approach for power model extraction enables accurate power consumption predictions for VM migrations. We investigate VM migrations as a central adaptation action used in autonomic data center resource management. The case study compares predictions from power models, which were extracted using our approach, with measured energy consumption. The study concerns Questions 3.1 and 3.4.

This section is structured as follows. Section 7.3.9 discusses the scenarios we investigated in the presented case study. Section 7.3.9.2 provides an overview of the evaluation setup. Section 7.3.9.3 applies our power model extraction approach to predict the energy consumption when a collocated workload stresses the hosts during VM migration. Section 7.3.9.4 investigates scenarios where the workload ran inside the migrated VM. Section 7.3.9.5 investigates whether the use of multi-core metrics improved prediction accuracy for the considered scenarios. Section 7.3.9.6 summarizes our findings.

7.3.9.1. Evaluation Scenarios

Our evaluation investigated the power consumption during VM migration. It considered a set of scenario with two hosts S_1 and S_2. Each scenario alternated between live migrations from S_1 to S_2, and S_2 to S_1. Each iteration migrated the same VM. During migration, a load driver ran a workload at a predefined load level. The simultaneous execution of VM migrations and other workloads enabled us to observe interactions between power consumption and system performance. We repeated each migration at least three times per load level. The experiment results cover two variations of the baseline experiment scenario.

Section 7.3.9.3 presents the results for the first scenario variant, in which S_1 ran the load driver. It covers the cases where the VM migrates

- from an idle server to a server which is stressed to a specific load level (S_2 to S_1),
- from a server which is stressed to a specific load level to an idle server (S_1 to S_2).

Sections 7.3.9.4 and 7.3.9.5 discusses the second scenario variant. In the second variant, the migrated VM ran a workload at the predefined load level. We investigated this scenario, as the level of VM activity influences the convergence behavior and execution time of the VM migration algorithm.

7.3.9.2. Evaluation Setup

This section discusses the case study workloads, execution environment and power model extraction setup. We conclude with the accuracy metrics that we applied to evaluate the prediction accuracy of the trained power models.

VM Migration Bench VM Migration Bench is a benchmarking framework we built for evaluating the power consumption of reconfiguration actions in virtualized, IaaS environments. The framework enables the measurement of power consumption and system level metrics during the execution of adaptation actions. The framework consists of an experiment driver, a load driver, and a monitoring utility.

The experiment driver orchestrates the experiment execution. It triggers a set of virtualization actions on the libvirt Java API. An experiment subsumes the execution of one or multiple virtualization actions. The experiment driver coordinates the collection of power and system metric measurements with multiple instances of the monitoring utility, which was presented in Section 7.3.1. We deployed the experiment driver on S_1.

The load driver extends the server profiling load driver described in Section 5.4.1. This enables a reuse of existing SERT [187] worklet definitions to stress the servers, or the VMs involved in a reconfiguration action. The load driver builds on the technical foundation of our profiling framework. Prior to a set of VM migrations at a load level, the workload driver calibrates the workload intensity of a configured workload to reach a target utilization level.

In the scenarios discussed in Section 7.3.9.3, the load driver was deployed on S_1. Sections 7.3.9.4 and 7.3.9.5 outline the results for scenarios where the load driver ran inside the migrated VM. Our migration experiments used *SOR* and *SORT* from the standard set of worklets provided by SERT as workloads. The workload driver ran one of the two workloads in both scenario variants.

Execution Environment We used two ProLiant DL160 Gen9 servers for our experiments. Each server had an Intel Xeon E5-2640 v3 CPU, 32 GB RAM, and a 500 GB 7200 RPM HDD. The following refers to the servers as S_1 and S_2. Both servers were connected via 1 Gbit/s LAN. We collected the measurements using the monitoring utility described in Section 7.3.1. It obtained all measurements, including power consumption measurements, with a sampling rate of 1/s. S_1 was running Debian 8.7, S_2 was running Debian 8.6.

All migrated VMs were constructed from a Debian 8.7 image. Each VM ran atop the KVM 2.1.2 hypervisor. The VMs had 4 GB of RAM, and 16 GB of storage. The storage of a VM was persisted on the server which currently hosted the VM. We employed pre-copy, peer-to-peer live migration, where the storage was copied between the migration source and target.

Power Model Extraction We applied our power model extraction method in order to get models that predict the power consumption of S_1 based on system metrics. We did not repeat the profiling for S_2, as its hardware components were identical to S_1.

We selected the workloads *XMLvalidate*, *SOR*, and *CryptoAES* from SERT to profile S_1. We restricted the target metrics to u_{cpu} in order to reduce the execution time of the profiling run. . We set the target levels of each workload to $\{0, 0.05, \ldots, 1.0\}$.

We used the power model types listed in Table 7.8 as input to the model training and selection. From these models, we considered the two power models with the highest AIC in our accuracy evaluation. Additionally, we evaluated the accuracy of a power model that we trained using non-parametric MARS [71] regression.

Prediction Accuracy Evaluation Per load level L_u, we calculated the prediction accuracy $M(L)$ of every models as:

$$M(L_p) = \frac{\sum_{l \in L_p} E_{\text{predicted}}(l) - E_{\text{measured}}(l)}{E_{\text{predicted}}(l)}, \text{ where } p \in \{0, 0.05, \ldots, 1.0\}.$$

Hereby, $l \in L_u$ are the individual migrations executed at load level L_u. E is the energy consumed during migration. We calculated $E_{\text{measured}}(l)$ by means of numerical integration on the power consumption samples recorded during migration. We determined $E_{\text{predicted}}(l)$ as the numerical integral of the power model samples. We obtained the samples by evaluating a power model for each set of system level performance metric measurements.

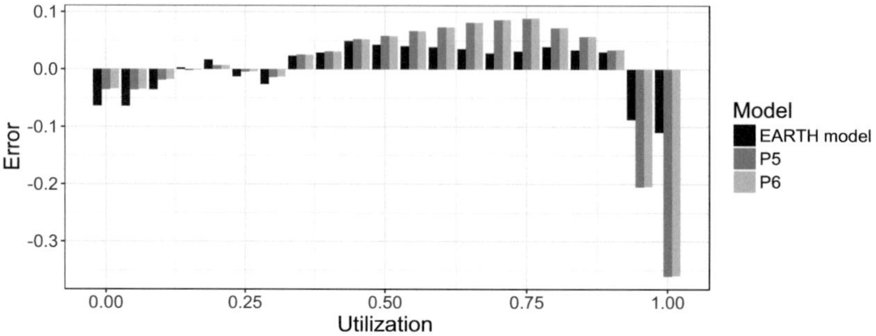

Figure 7.14.: Power consumption prediction error for SOR workload executed on S_1. Measurements collected on S_1. Migration from S_2 to S_1. Each set of three error bars represents the prediction error at a load level $u \in \{0, 0.05, \ldots, 1.0\}$.

7.3.9.3. Workload Collocation on Host

This section discusses the prediction accuracy of the extracted power models when a collocated workload stresses S_1 during VM migration.

Figures 7.14 and 7.15 display the power consumption prediction error we determined for S_1 when it ran the SOR workload outside of the migrated VM. Power models P_5 and P_6 refer to the power models 5 and 6 listed in Table 7.8. Figure 7.14 shows the prediction error for the VM migrations from S_2 to S_1. When VM migration targeted S_1, all three models predicted the power consumption accurately for load levels of up to 0.9. This can be seen in Figure 7.14. For utilization levels higher than 0.95, the MARS model had an average prediction error just above 10%. The predictions from the two highest ranking models $P5$ and $P6$ reach an error of over 20%.

Figure 7.15 shows the error for migrations from S_1 to S_2. Overall, the models performed slightly worse compared to the power consumption predictions for the opposite migration direction. In the load range below 0.35, error rates reached prediction errors of up to 22%. Low prediction accuracies for this utilization range were not limited to only the three discussed models. All power models listed in Table 7.8 underestimated the energy consumption by over 20%. Once the server reached the maximum load level 1, only the

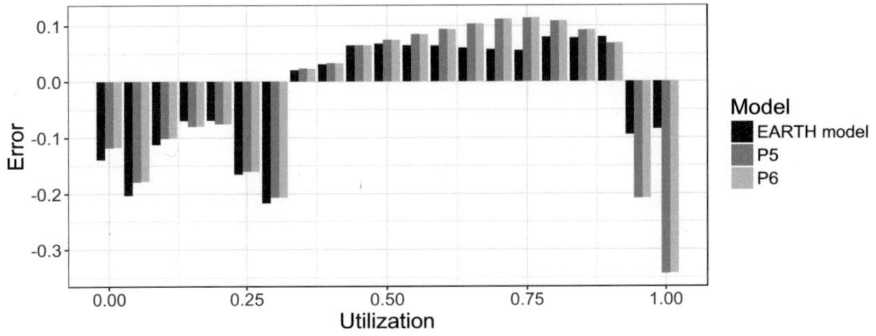

Figure 7.15.: Power consumption prediction error for SOR workload executed on S_1. Measurements collected on S_1. Migration from S_1 to S_2.

MARS model achieved acceptable prediction errors. The other power models underestimated the energy consumption by over 30%.

In conclusion, the MARS model performed the most consistently across different load levels. It predicted the power consumption of systems performing VM migrations with an error of 2.7% to 10.9% when migrating from $S_2$to S_1. When the migration was issued from S_1 to S_2, the error was between 2.0% and 21.6%.

7.3.9.4. Workload Execution in Migrated VM

The experiments outlined in the prior section left the migrated VM idle. The load of the server originated from a workload which ran collocated to the VM. We conducted a set of experiments in order to validate whether our extracted power models were accurate when predicting the power consumption of VMs that actively ran workloads during the live migration. This section discusses experiments in which the VM executed a workload during VM migration. As part of the experiment setup we deployed our workload driver inside the migrated VM.

Prior to each set of VM migrations, the load driver calibrated the workload such that it reached the target load threshold inside of the VM. A VM was designated four virtual cores. The host system had sixteen available logical cores. Our experiment setup varied the VM internal load between 0 and

100% in intervals of 5%. A VM internal utilization of 100% resulted in an approximate system-wide average utilization of $100\% \cdot \frac{4}{16} = 25\%$. Thus, the experiments covered system-wide CPU utilization levels between 0 and 25%.

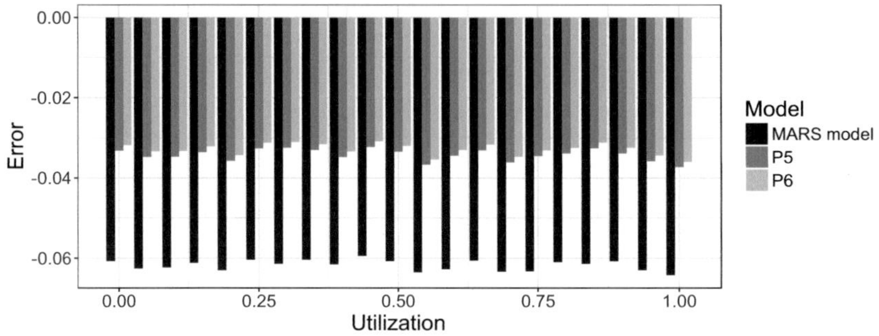

Figure 7.16.: Power consumption prediction error for SOR workload executed in migrated VM. Measurements collected on S_1. Migration from S_2 to S_1.

We reused the server profiling results from Section 7.3.9.3 in order to derive a representative consumption profile. The profiling ran on the hypervisor level outside of the migrated VM. The power models extracted from this profiling predict the energy consumption on S_1 from hypervisor, system level metrics, e.g., aggregate CPU utilization. Our predictions treat the VM like any other system process, which utilizes the CPU. Figure 7.16 shows the prediction error for the SOR workload, and VM migrations from S_2 to S_1. All three depicted models predicted the total energy consumption with an error of 3% to 7%.

When we used the power models to predict the consumption for migrations from S_1 to S_2, the prediction error of all models was lower than 10% for VM internal load levels below 95%. Figure 7.17 shows the corresponding error bar plot. Once the SOR workload fully utilized all available virtual cores, the measured energy consumption was more than 27% higher than predicted by any of the three models. The likely source of this discrepancy was a dynamic frequency increase of the S_1 CPU: Once a set of individual cores reach full utilization, the CPU dynamically increases the frequency of these cores. This results in an increased power consumption. Our profiling did not systematically stress individual CPU cores. Thus, models trained

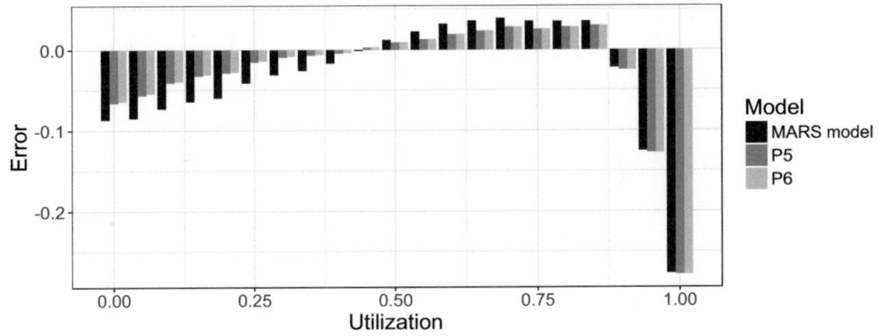

Figure 7.17.: Power consumption prediction error for SOR workload executed in migrated VM. Measurements collected on S_1. Migration from S_1 to S_2.

on the profile can not reflect power consumption increases that result from frequency scaling of individual cores.

We investigated whether accurate power consumption models can be built for S_1 that abstract from the CPU frequency. This required a server profiling run where we stressed individual cores of the server. We achieved this by conducting a profiling run in which the workload driver was deployed inside the VM.

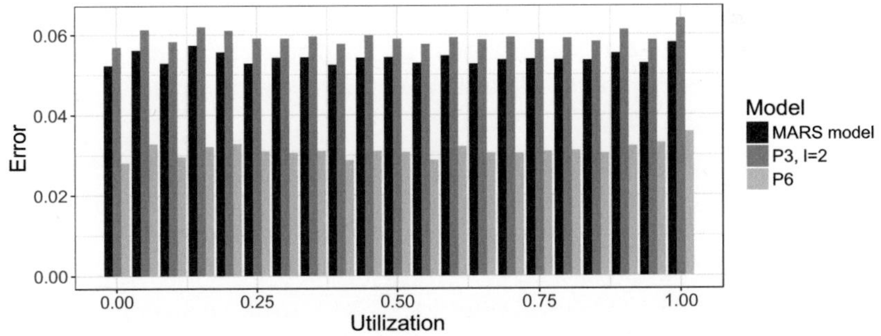

Figure 7.18.: Power consumption prediction error for SOR workload executed in VM. Power models from VM internal profiling. Measurements collected on S_1. Migration from S_2 to S_1.

We trained all considered models on the resulting profile. The AIC ranking predicted that P_3 with $l = 2$, and P_6 had the highest likelihood to be accurate. Additionally, we included a MARS model trained on the profile. Figure 7.18 shows the prediction error of VM migrations from S_2 to S_1. Prediction errors of all models remained below 7%.

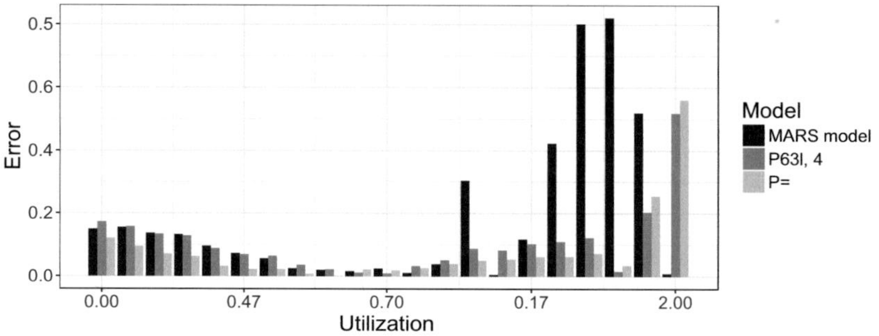

Figure 7.19.: Power consumption prediction error for SOR workload executed in VM. Models from VM internal profiling. Measurements collected on S_1. Migration from S_1 to S_2.

The prediction error was significantly higher at most load levels when the active VM was migrated from S_1 to S_2. Figure 7.19 shows this in contrast to Figure 7.18. None of the power models clearly outperformed the other considered models. The MARS model was highly accurate for utilization levels outside of 0.8 to 0.95. P_3 and P_6 with $l = 2$ were more accurate for most utilization levels but the maximum level 1.

The prediction error for the VM internal run of the SORT workload followed a similar distribution of error rates to the SOR error rates. The range of utilization levels shifted when we moved from VM internal to external profiling. Figure 7.20 depicts the error rates of SORT from internal profiling. Compared to the external profiling, we did not see a clear improvement across the full utilization range. The models extracted from internal profiling underpredicted power consumption. Conversely, the models from external profiling overpredicted the power consumption. We deduced that power models which were trained purely using the aggregate utilization did not accurately predict power consumption for utilization levels at which the processor dynamically scaled its frequency.

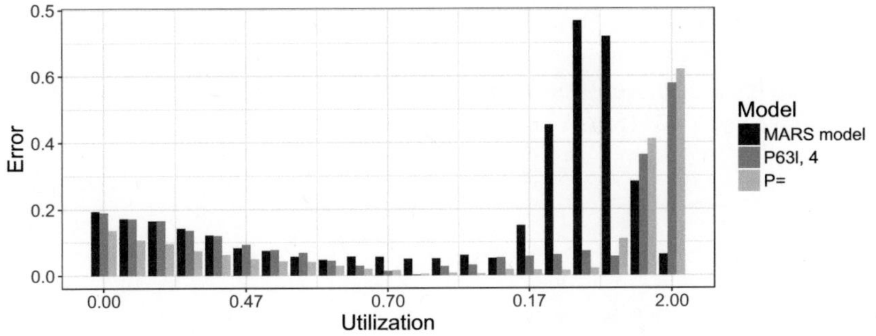

Figure 7.20.: Power consumption prediction error for SOR workload executed in VM. Models from VM internal profiling. Measurements collected on S_1. Migration from S_1 to S_2.

7.3.9.5. Prediction Accuracy of Multi-Core Power Models

The scenario investigated in the previous section ran a workload inside the migrated VM. When the VM approached full utilization of the four virtual VM CPUs, the prediction error of otherwise accurate power models surged to values above 30%. We attributed this increase to the dynamical frequency scaling of the CPU.

Previously, we relied on the aggregate CPU utilization to predict power consumption. We extended the considered set of metrics by per-thread CPU utilization to investigate potential increases in accuracy,

We used the following power models to predict the power consumption:

- P_1 from Table 7.8,
- a modified $P_{1,\text{common}}$ with $c_{m_a} = c_{m_b}$ for all $m_a, m_b \in M$,
- a MARS regression model P_{MARS} trained using the same configuration as previously,
- and $\max\{P_{\text{MARS}}, p_{\text{idle}}\}$, where p_{idle} is the idle power consumption of the server.

The power models used the extended set of metrics $u_{\text{full}}, u_{\text{core}_0}, \ldots, u_{\text{core}_{15}}$. Each u_{core_0} refers to the per-hyperthread utilization of the CPU. We trained the models on the combined profile from workload profiling executions conducted on $S_1$and from VM internal profiling.

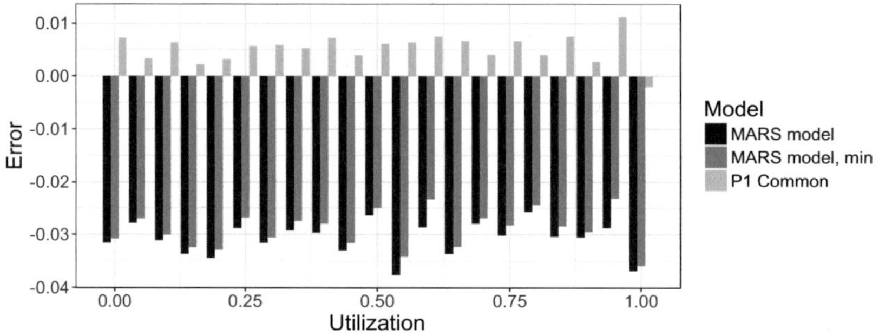

Figure 7.21.: Power consumption prediction error for SOR workload executed in VM. Errors of multi-core models that result from the combination of VM internal and hypervisor level profiling. The measurements were collected on S_1. Migration from S_2 to S_1. *P1 Common* refers to $P_{1,\text{common}}$. *Mars Model, min* is $\max\{P_{\text{MARS}}, p_{\text{idle}}\}$.

Figure 7.21 lists the power consumption prediction error for VM migrations from $S_2$to S_1. The utilization levels note the targeted aggregate VM internal CPU utilization. P_1 is not displayed and discussed further, as it reached errors of up to 80%. The error rates of the per-core power models are similar to the error rates of models solely based on aggregate CPU utilization, c.f., Figure 7.16.

More interesting are the differences, or lack thereof, for migrations from S_1 to S_2. As we used pre-copy live migration, the workload running in the VM stressed S_1 until the migration completed. The prediction error shown in Figure 7.22 is similarly distributed to the prediction error achieved with the external models (Figure 7.17). This indicates that the use of multi-core metrics did not improve the prediction error. It even resulted in an average error increase. The MARS model performed poorly due to overfitting. Individual power consumption predictions from the model fell well below the idle power consumption of S_1. Thus, we introduced the idle power consumption as a lower limit to the MARS model. This is the $\max\{P_{\text{MARS}}, p_{\text{idle}}\}$ model. Figures 7.21 and 7.22 list the model as *MARS model, min.* At peak utilization,

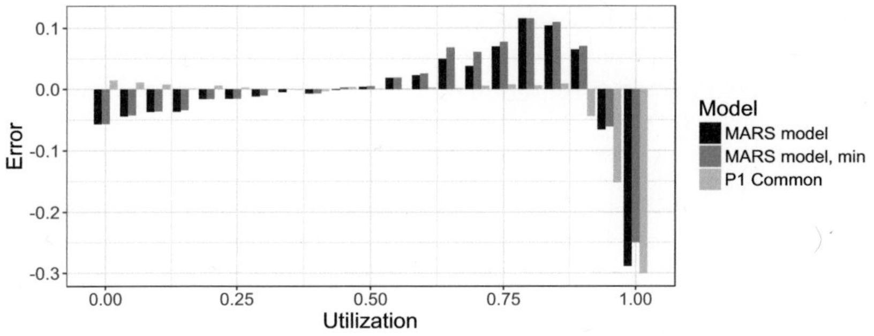

Figure 7.22.: Power consumption prediction error for SOR workload executed in VM. Multi-core power models from combined profiling. Measurements collected on S_1. Migration from S_1 to S_2.

the introduction of a lower bound reduced the prediction error by an absolute value of 5%.

7.3.9.6. Summary

In this section, we applied our profiling approach to extract power models for predicting power consumption in different VM migration scenarios. We used robust non-linear regression and MARS as model learning techniques. We evaluated the prediction accuracy of the models at different load levels. Both collocated workloads, and workloads executed in the migrated VM were considered. Our experiments showed that we could accurately predict the total energy consumption induced during VM migration. At all load levels, the best performing model achieved an average prediction error below 11%.

All multi-core CPU power models performed worse when the workload was executed inside of the VM. At VM internal target load levels below 0.95, the error was comparable to collocated execution. The power consumption prediction accuracy dropped significantly once the VM internal target utilization reached 0.95. We attribute this to an increase in power consumption due to DVFS.

We explored two alternatives to address the high consumption prediction error at high VM internal utilization. First, we performed a targeted profiling of a subset of physical cores. Second, we extended the range of considered system metrics by per-core CPU utilization. Neither approaches fully addressed the drop in prediction accuracy when a workload caused high load on select cores.

Frequency-based power models could increase the prediction accuracy when the CPU scales frequency of a subset of cores. We did not investigate these models due to the following reason. To the best of our knowledge, no performance model has been proposed that accurately predicts the frequency scaling implemented by modern processors. Further work needs to be spent to create models that predict the effect of proprietary performance and power management features like Intel Turbo Boost.

In summary, the case study shows that our model extraction approach produces power models which accurately predict the energy consumption of VM migrations at most load levels. When the virtual CPUs of the migrated VM reach load levels in the region of 100%, the prediction error approaches values in the region of 30%. With this limitation, the results positively answer Question 3.1 for the investigated server environment. Section 7.3.9.5 compared power models built using aggregate CPU utilization models with models that distinguished per-core CPU utilization. The results indicated that the consideration of per-core utilization does not significantly improve prediction accuracy (Question 3.4).

7.4. Transient Effect Analysis

This section investigates to which extent the consideration of transient effects in software performance analyses improves the prediction accuracy of design time analyses for self-adaptive software systems. It presents the results of a case study which we conducted to validate the transient effect modeling approach outlined in Chapter 6. The validation targets Goal 4 of this thesis. The case study results have been published in [199]. As the evaluated case study system we used a Media Store application enhanced with horizontal scaling capabilities. We explored Question 4.1 by comparing the accuracy of predictions of the SimuLizar baseline with SimuLizar extended by our approach. Additionally, we investigated the benefit of considering transient effects for design time decision-making (Questions 4.2 and 4.3).

7.4.1. Case Study System

Media Store is a component-based reference application [170]. Section 7.2.1 introduced a prior Media Store iteration. Media Store allows users to download and upload music files. When downloading, users can choose between different encoding bit rates. Music files are only stored in their original bit rate. Upon download, they are re-encoded to the target bit rate, if the rate differs. Re-encoding is the most computationally intensive service offered by the Media Store system. A high number of concurrent encoding requests can quickly cause contention in the system. In order to address this potential bottleneck, we extended the Media Store architecture by a rule-based *Horizontal Scaler* component. This component leverages horizontal scaling to adjust the resources available for re-encoding.

The Media Store variant used in this case study extends the most recent Media Store release 3.0[1]. Reussner et al. [170] provide further details on the Media Store case study system. Section 7.2.1 had presented a case study that evaluated Question 4.2 for the previous version 2.0 of Media Store.

Figure 7.23 shows a simplified view on the system architecture of the horizontally scaling Media Store. The *Horizontal Scaler* component delegates re-encoding requests to all available *Reencoder* instances. If the conditions for a scale-out are met, the *Horizontal Scaler* triggers the instantiation of another *Reencoder* instance. Once the instance is available, the *Horizontal Scaler* starts distributing requests to it. The *Horizontal Scaler* evenly distributes re-encoding requests among all available instances. We implemented horizontal scaling using VM scaling techniques as found in IaaS platforms. Each *Reencoder* instance deploys onto a separate VM. All other components are deployed on a shared VM.

We formulated the requirement that the average response time of the re-encoding component shall not surpass 120 seconds. In order to achieve this requirement, we designed a set of scale-out conditions. The *Horizontal Scaler* starts a scale-out when the following conditions are met:

[1] `https://sdqweb.ipd.kit.edu/wiki/Media_Store`, retrieved 05.06.2017.

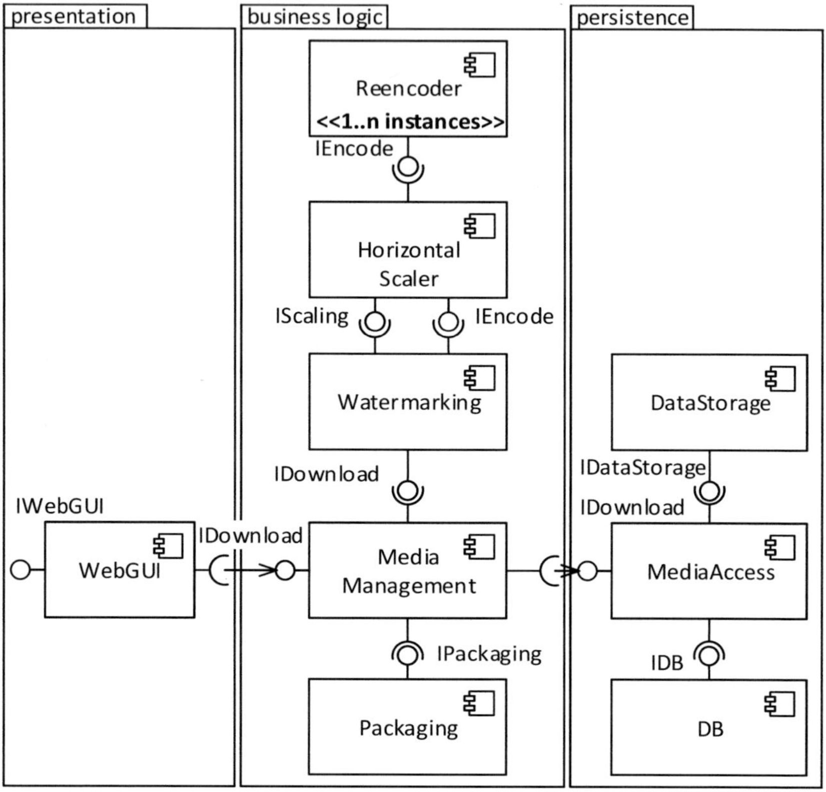

Figure 7.23.: System diagram view of horizontally scaling Media Store variant.

1. The average response time of the re-encoding service over the last five minutes is at least twice as high as the average response time.
2. At least five minutes have passed since the last scale-out action has been started.
3. All previous scale-outs have been completed.
4. There are less than *n* active *Reencoder* instances.

Rule 1 causes a scale-out when the response time increases. Rules 2 and 3 are intended to prevent an overeager scale-out on small increases of load. Further scale-outs may only occur after a time interval has passed, which is long enough to observe the intended effect of the scale-out. Rule 4 limits the number of Reencoder instances.

7.4.2. Experiment Setup

We implemented the horizontal scaling functionality of Media Store on the OpenStack [151] Cloud middleware platform. We refactored the *Reencoder* component to a standalone REST service. We prepared a bootable VM template to host the *Reencoder* instances. Every Reencoding subsystem was deployed on an individual Glassfish 4.1 server instance. All other components shared a common Glassfish 4.1 instance. We realized horizontal scaling of the *Reencoder* realized as the creation and bootup of a VM that instantiated the VM template. The re-encoding service automatically becomes available after the bootup of a new *Reencoder* VM.

We implemented the outlined horizontal scaling mechanism in simulation to validate its effect on QoS prior to its implementation and execution. We used the existing manually created Media Store PCM model as the starting point of the model-based analysis of our system. We refactored the PCM model to the horizontally scalable architecture depicted in Figure 7.23. We defined the horizontal scaling rules in simulation as a QVTo model-to-model transformation. The simulation executes these rules via the *QVTo Reconfiguration Engine* component of SimuLizar. To consider transient effects, we used a definition of a scale-out action which we derived from the action outlined in Section 6.2.7.1. We calibrated the resource demands of the PCM model using a single user workload. Without contention, re-encoding requests took 26 seconds on average. Section 6.2.7.1 introduced the scale-out action modeling we employed in our design time evaluation. The action execution depends upon a parameter that models the VM boot duration. We determined the input scale-out duration model parameter over a set of more than ten Reencoder VM bootups.

A private IaaS OpenStack setup served as the measurement environment of the case study. We set up OpenStack to deploy all VMs on a Dell PowerEdge R815 server with four Opteron 6174 CPUs. The server ran a XenServer hypervisor. All component instances but the *Reencoder* instances shared a two core VM with four GB of RAM. The *Reencoder* VMs were assigned two GB of RAM. All VMs used CentOS 6.6.

We used a PC running JMeter 2.11 as the load driver to issue re-encoding requests. The PC was equipped with an i7-2620M and 8 GB of RAM. 1 GBit LAN connected the PC to the OpenStack setup. Prior to each experiment, we ran a warmup workload over ten minutes with an inter-arrival time of 29 seconds between re-encoding requests.

Per scenario, we ran ten measurement runs and 100 simulations for both simulator variants. We compared measurements and simulation using the moving window average response time over five minutes. We contrasted the results from measurements and simulations via box plots. The end of the box plot whiskers are within 1.5 times the interquartile range (IQR). In addition, we calculated the error distribution of response times of simulation predictions compared to measurements. We calculated the distribution as the errors on the cross product of measurement and simulation runs. This gave us $10 \cdot 100 = 1000$ error samples.

7.4.3. Evaluation Scenarios

In the following we provide an overview of two scenarios we used to investigate the accuracy and efficiency of our approach for considering transient effects in software performance analyses.

Scenario 1 The first scenario investigated the effect of considering transient effects for a simple two-server scale-out. Its intent was to isolate the effect on response time prediction accuracy for a single server scale scale-out. We thus set the maximum number of *Reencoder* instances n to 2. The experiment scenario covered 30 minutes. The inter-arrival time between user requests was 29 seconds for the first interval with a length of 10 minutes. In the last 20 minutes, it decreased to 15 seconds. As the average re-encoding response time was 16 seconds, requests started to overlap in the last two thirds of an experiment run. Scenario 1 focused on Question 4.1.

Table 7.14.: Workload used in scenario 2.

Interval	1	2	3	4	5
Length (in min.)	10	10	10	10	10
Inter-arrival Time (in s)	29	15	10	15	29

Scenario 2 We designed the second scenario to evaluate to which extent the horizontally scaling Media Store with the designed scalability rules was able to fulfill our maximum response time requirement. The scenario decreased the inter-arrival rate in two steps. After this, the inter-arrival iteratively returned to its initial time of of 29 seconds. Table 7.14 lists the inter-arrival time per interval of the workload. In order to handle the increased load, we set the maximum allowed number of active *Reencoder* VMs to $n = 5$. Scenario 2 aims to address Questions 4.1 and 4.2. We had designed the scenario to evaluate to which extent potential inaccuracies of response time predictions affected our ability to identify design deficiencies (Question 4.2).

7.4.4. Experiment Results

This section presents the experiment results for scenarios 1 and 2.

7.4.4.1. Scenario 1: Two-Server Scale-Out

The box plots in Figure 7.24 illustrates the response time distribution from measurement, SimuLizar baseline, and SimuLizar extended by our approach. We opted to investigate the maximum response time, as the maximum response time correlates with the maximum degree of contention observed in the system. The median maximum response time over the ten measurement runs was 137.17 seconds. Our approach predicted the maximum response time with much greater accuracy than the SimuLizar baseline. SimuLizar extended with our approach produced a median response time of 141.53 seconds. The baseline underestimated the maximum response time. It resulted in a median of 122.18 seconds. The mean response time distribution shows a similar improvement in accuracy of our extended approach over the baseline. Median, lower and upper quartile of the extended approach match well with

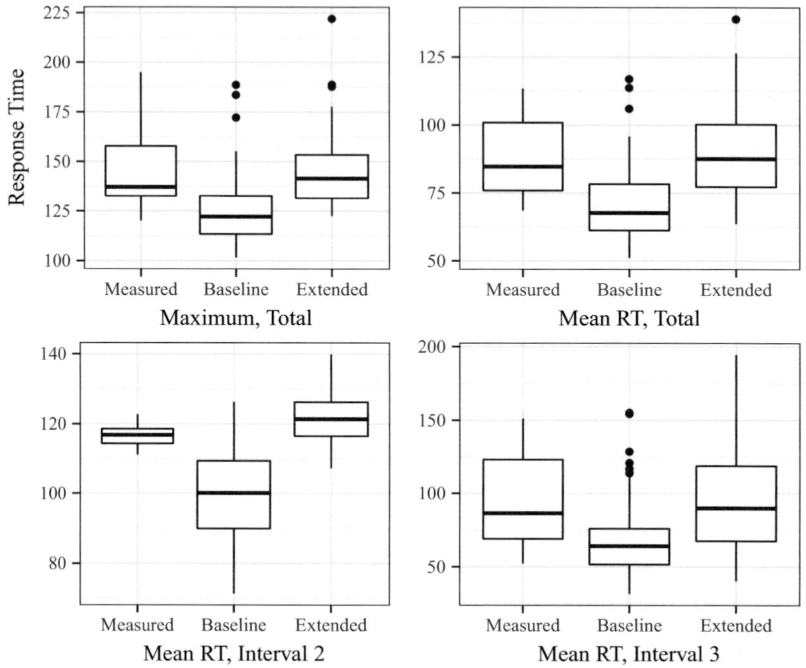

Figure 7.24.: Comparison of RTs from measurements and simulation for scenario 1. The simulation results cover the SimuLizar baseline and our extended approach.

the measurements. The baseline predictions deviate significantly from the predictions.

We partitioned the scenario into three intervals of ten minutes each. This partitioning allowed us to differentiate between stable and transient phases. In the first and second interval, the extended and baseline SimuLizar produced identical predictions. Both were identical because the constant inter-arrival time of 29 seconds in the first interval did not necessitate a scale-out. The lower row of Figure 7.24 contains box plots of the mean response time in the second and third interval. In the second interval, the baseline predictions scatter much more strongly. This is illustrated by the lower box plot whisker extending beyond 80 seconds. The median value of the baseline is also far less accurate than the value of our extended approach.

Table 7.15.: Response time prediction error per interval for scenario 1. Error for the Baseline (Base) and our Extended (Ext) SimuLizar implementations. The error distribution was derived from the cross product comparison of 10 measurement runs and 100 simulation runs.

Interval	Median Error		Mean Error		Estd. Std. Dev.	
	Base	Ext	Base	Ext	Base	Ext
1	2.3%	2.3%	2.7%	2.7%	0.8%	0.8%
2	14.6%	5.4%	15.5%	6.2%	9.8%	4.5%
3	36.1%	33.7%	37.3%	42.8%	24.5%	38.8%
Total	22.5%	16.5%	22.7%	20.1%	14.1%	16.2%

We explored the differences of aggregate metrics in each interval. Table 7.15 lists aggregate prediction error metrics for the first scenario. The table notes median, mean, and the estimated standard deviation over three experiment intervals of ten minutes length. The error distribution results confirm our observation that the extended approach is more accurate for the first scenario. In total, our approach reduced the median prediction error from 22.5% to 16.5%. The only marginally higher error metric value of our approach is the mean error in the third interval. We deem this deviation to be negligible, since related work has indicated that mean value analysis is strongly affected by outliers [34, 125].

Figure 7.25 illustrates the effect the consideration of transient effect had on the response time distribution over time. The figure displays the moving average response time over time of the simulation, baseline, extended, and measured median runs. The median runs are the runs that produced the median response times, which we previously noted. The bars at the bottom show the scale-out time as a bar between start and completion time. Both baseline and extended runs progressed identically up until and during the first scale-out. The moving average window response times of the baseline simulation quickly recovered from the increase in workload after ten minutes. After approximately 18 minutes, the response time started to decrease. The maximum moving window average was 111.9 seconds. This did not match the median measured run, where the maximum response time reached 131.6 seconds after 21.5 minutes. We attributed the difference between measured

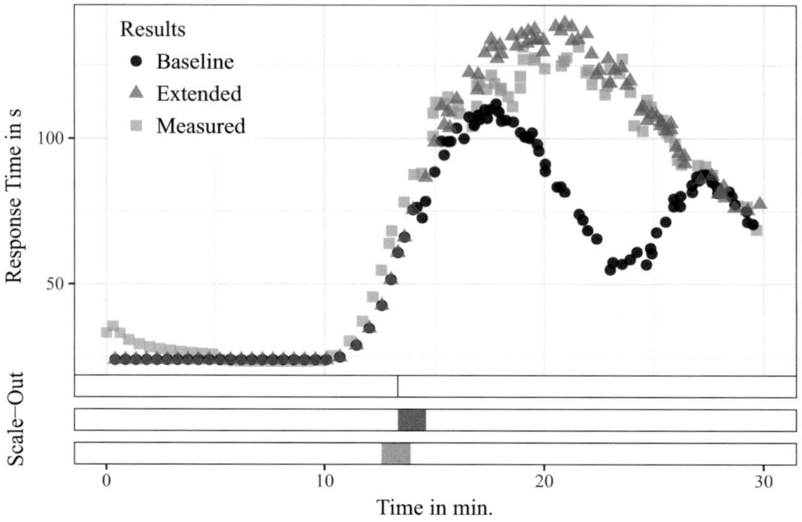

Figure 7.25.: Average response time and scale-out actions over time for Scenario 1. Each dot represents a moving window average at the given time calculated over the last five minutes. The three bars at the bottom show the scale-out durations as colored bars that span the interval between the scale-out start and completion.

and baseline simulation to the missing consideration of the scale-out execution time. In the baseline simulation, the additional *Reencoder* instance was available immediately once the system issued the scale-out action. Consequently, the second *Reencoder* instance could immediately process incoming re-encoding requests. The simulation extended with our approach followed the measured response time curve more closely. Response times from the extended simulation surpassed the measurements with a maximum response time of 139.7 seconds. The response time started to recover around the 21 minutes mark.

In the simulated median run the scale-out took 76 seconds, compared to the measured 78 seconds. Even after the additional instance had become available, the response time did not immediately recover in the measured and extended simulation runs. We attribute this prolonged rise in response time to contention. The user load was almost doubled at ten minutes. Due to the execution time of scale-out, additional resources to process further requests only became available after the scale-out had finished. During the wait time, incoming requests filled up the single *Reencoder* instance. The tail of high response times was much longer in reality than in the baseline simulation, since the scale-out execution time prolonged the build-up of contention.

We conclude from the results that the consideration of transient effects increases the accuracy of performance predictions for the single server scale-out scenario of Media Store (Question 4.1).

7.4.4.2. Scenario 2: Scale-Out with Multiple Reencoder Instances

In the second scenario, we investigated the effect of our approach on prediction accuracy for the horizontally scaling Media Store with a higher peak workload and number of *Reencoder* instances. We evaluated whether the system would be able to meet the response time requirement that Section 7.4.1 introduced. The requirement stated that the average response time of the re-encoding component should not surpass 120 seconds.

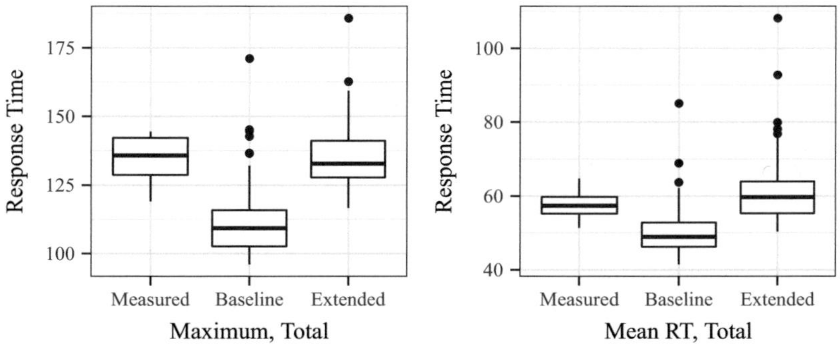

Figure 7.26.: Aggregated response times from measurements and simulation for experiment B.

Accuracy Evaluation Figure 7.26 shows aggregate metrics of the response time distribution of the second scenario runs. Comparing maximum and mean response times from measurements, extended, and the baseline simulation, we see that the aggregate response time metrics of the extended simulation matched the measurements much more closely. The median of the maximum response times of the baseline simulation was 109.2 seconds. The median of the extended simulation and measured runs was 132.8 and 135.8, respectively.

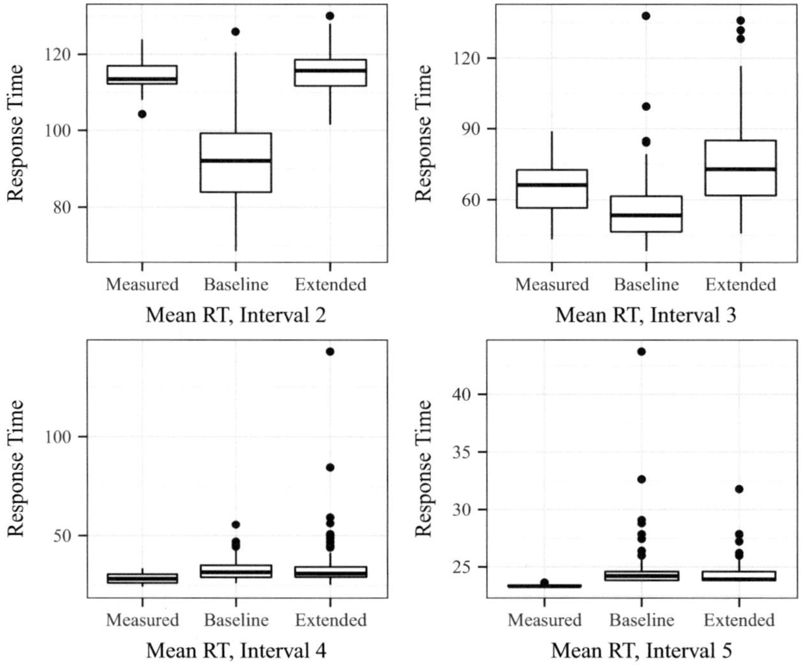

Figure 7.27.: Comparison of response times from measurements and simulation for experiment B in intervals 2 to 5 from consecutive intervals of 10 minutes.

The average response time distributions per interval depicted in Figure 7.27 show a consistent improvement in prediction accuracy in intervals 2 and 3. The response time distribution of baseline and extended was identical in interval 1, as the first scale-out occurred after ten minutes in all simulation runs. In intervals 4 and 5 we could only observe a marginal difference in distribution between measurement and simulation runs.

Table 7.16.: Response time prediction error per interval for experiment B. Error for the Baseline (Base) and our Extended (Ext) SimuLizar implementations. The error rate was calculated by comparing 10 measurement runs and 100 simulation runs.

Interval	Median Error		Mean Error		Estd. Std. Dev.	
	Base	Ext	Base	Ext	Base	Ext
1	1.5%	1.5%	1.5%	1.5%	0.1%	0.1%
2	19.1%	4.6%	20.1%	5.6%	10.4%	4.3%
3	23.0%	23.1%	25.2%	32.5%	18.8%	31.1%
4	13.8%	13.1%	19.6%	25.4%	18.6%	47.5%
5	3.6%	2.4%	5.8%	4.7%	9.8%	5.0%
Total	14.0%	9.8%	14.6%	13.1%	7.9%	15.3%

Table 7.16 lists the aggregate error statistics per interval of the second experiment. Our extended approach managed to reduce the median error from 14.0% to 9.8% from the simulation baseline. In the second interval, the prediction error went from 19.1% down to 4.9%. In intervals 3 and 4 the mean prediction error of the extended simulation was higher than the error of the extended simulation. We traced the higher error to a number of response time outliers in the mean response times of the extended simulation. Figure 7.27 depicts the outliers as points. All other error metrics values, including the median error in intervals 3 and 4, were lower for the extended simulation. Small deviations in intervals 3 and 4 finally had a greater impact on the prediction error due to the low response time values in these intervals.

Figure 7.28 shows the running average response time runs of the response times medians for the second scenario. The bars in the lower half display scale-out start and and finish times as a bar. The baseline simulation had predicted three scale-outs to be executed, as can be seen by the three bars. In the measurement run, the rules led to four scale-outs. The extended run matched the four scale-outs. Over one hundred simulation runs, the baseline had predicted 3.46 scale-outs per run on average. Using our extended approach, 3.79 scale-outs were executed per simulation run. The average over the ten measurement runs was 3.9. We thus concluded that the consideration of transient effects enabled us to predict the number of *Reencoder*

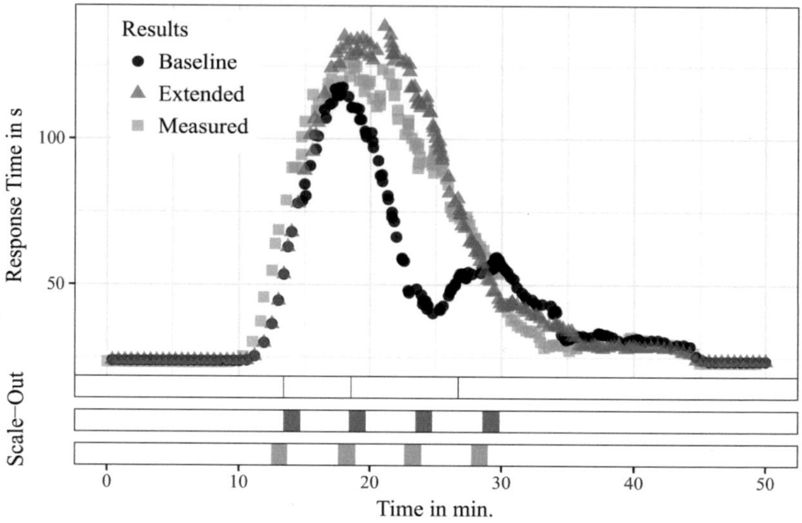

Figure 7.28.: Average response times from measurements and simulation for scenario 2. Each dot represents a moving window average at the given time calculated over the last five minutes. The three bars at the bottom show the scale-out durations as colored bars that span the interval between the scale-out start and completion.

instances with greater accuracy. The maximum number of instances used is an important factor in determining the resources that are required to run the system.

In summary, our approach improved the response time prediction accuracy in the second scenario. Our approach additionally enabled us to predict the maximum number of *Reencoder* instances more accurately. The results thus positively Question 4.1.

Identification of Design Deficiencies We recall the requirement stated in Section 7.4.1. The requirement postulated that the running average response time over five minutes of the re-encoding service shall not surpass 120 seconds. The measurements for scenarios 1 and 2 showed that the horizontal scaling rules we had defined did not manage to meet this requirement. The maximum running average response time reached response times of over 125 seconds in more than 75% of the measurement runs. However, the baseline simulation had predicted that the system would manage to meet the requirement in over 75% of the runs. Using our extended approach that considered the scale-out execution times, we were able to correctly predict the requirement violation. More than 75% of the maximum response times over all simulation runs were higher than 125 seconds. Figure 7.26 illustrates this.

Regarding Question 4.2, we conclude that the increased accuracy allowed us to detect a design deficiency that would have otherwise remained undetected.

Resolution of Identified Design Deficiencies Our approach for considering transient effects in software performance analyses showed that the scale-out rules presented in Section 7.4.1 did not manage to uphold the required maximum response time of 120 seconds. This was confirmed by the measurements we performed for the Media Store implementation.

In order to improve the scaling rules to maintain the response time requirement, we applied SimuLizar extended by our approach. We iteratively refined the scale-out rules via simulations. This led to the following modified scale-out rules. Changes to the rules are highlighted. The design rationale of the changes was to scale the number of instances more proactively.

1. The average response time of the re-encoding service over the last *three* minutes is at least *30 seconds*.
2. At least *three* minutes have passed since the last scale-out action has been started.
3. All previous scale-outs have been completed.
4. There are less than *n* active *Reencoding* instances.

The simulation results indicated that the modified scale-out rules would likely manage to meet the response time requirement. Figure 7.29 illustrates this. Over 75% of simulation runs reached maximum response times that were lower than 120 seconds.

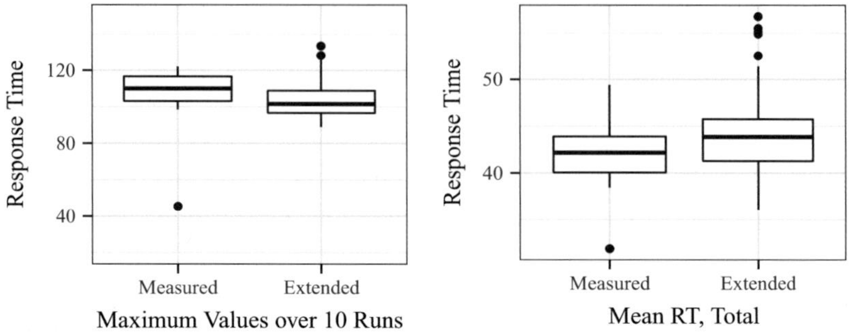

Figure 7.29.: Aggregated response times from measurements and simulation for the refined scale-out rule.

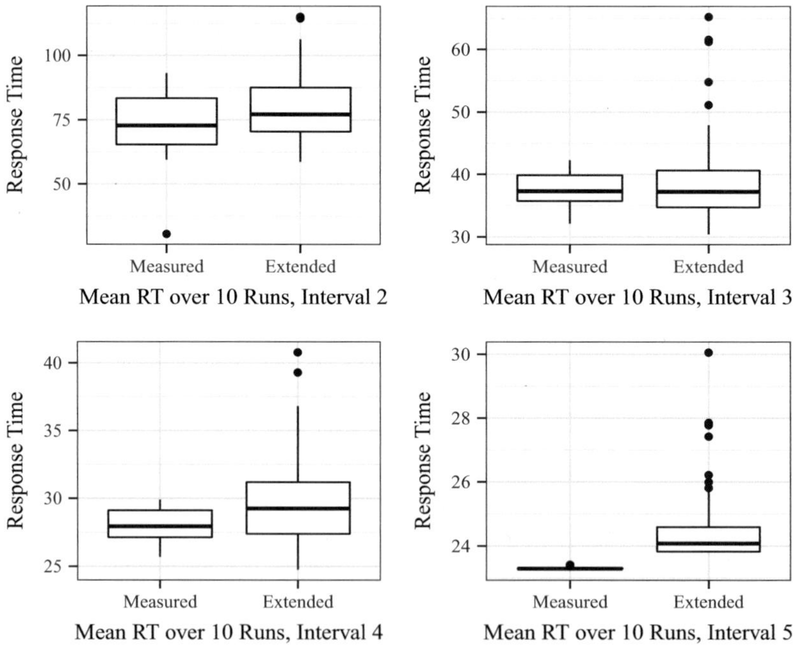

Figure 7.30.: Comparison of response times from measurements and simulation for the refined scale-out rule.

Due to the lower threshold response time defined in rule 1, and the smaller aggregation interval of rules 1 and 2, the system reacted more quickly to response time increases. The earlier scale-out start times significantly reduced the response time in transient phases. Due to the early scale-out, contention did not build up as quickly as in the previous system iteration. The median of the average response times in interval 2 in simulation was lowered from just below 120 to less than 80 seconds. as Figures 7.27 and 7.30 illustrate. The prediction results indicated that our system would be able to maintain a maximum moving average response time of 120.

We validated our findings from the simulation-based analysis against measurements. For this, we applied the changes to the rules to the implementation of our scale-out rules. Figure 7.30 displays box plots of the predictions and measurements. We compared ten measurement runs of the implementations with one hundred simulation runs. The measurements closely matched the predictions. Over 75% of measurement runs reached maximum running average response times that were lower than 120 seconds. The predicted mean of the running average response time was 4.2% higher than the measured value.

The consideration of transient effects using our approach enabled us to resolve deficiencies in the design of the scale-out rules. Overall, the results answer Question 4.3 positively.

7.5. Discussion of Results

This chapter presented the validation of architecture-level modeling and analysis approach for predicting the energy efficiency of static and self-adaptive systems. The case studies show that our modeling language provides suitable input for accurate architecture-level energy efficiency predictions. We demonstrated that our power model extraction method produced power models with a high accuracy for a large set of Big Data and enterprise workloads. Furthermore, a study illustrated the benefit and showed the accuracy of our modeling approach for considering transient effects in design time simulations. The following summarizes the findings related to the identified validation questions.

7.5.1. Goal Fulfillment

This section summarizes to which extent the validation case studies addressed the goals stated in our GQM plan.

Goal 1. Our power consumption prediction accurately predicted the power consumption of two component-based software systems, and a set of IaaS data center resource management scenarios. Throughout all case studies, the absolute power consumption prediction error remained below 7.08%. The prediction accuracy was high enough to evaluate the impact of architectural design decisions on energy efficiency, as shown in Section 7.2.1.5. The accuracy of our predictions was higher than the state of the art approach by Brunnert et al. [35], or matched it if the same linear power model type was used.

Goal 2. The appropriateness of the modeling abstraction concerns all of the intended use cases of our Power Consumption model. Consequently, all case studies that involve our model contributed towards this validation goal. The case studies presented in Section 7.2 showed that the modeling abstraction is detailed enough to produce accurate power consumption predictions. Section 7.2.3 illustrated that our model supports the modeling of model data center environments with a suitable degree of abstraction. The Power Consumption model integrates power models to capture the consumption characteristics of computing resources in relation to their activity.

Our Power Consumption metamodel offers higher expressiveness compared to state of the art architecture-level prediction [35] and eco-cost estimation [182] approaches. State of the art models assume a linear relationship between system utilization and power consumption. Our model enables the modeling of complex non-linear relationships between system metrics and power consumption. A novel feature supported by our language is the flexible modeling of conversion losses incurred by the power distribution infrastructure.

The increased expressiveness compared to state of the art poses no additional restrictions or requirements for the application of our model. The use of sophisticated non-linear power models is optional. It is possible to use a subset of the model features to construct purely linear power models as done by Brunnert et al. [35]. Section 3.2 used linear power models as a running example to discuss central concepts of the Power Consumption metamodel.

The power model extraction method presented in this thesis supports the automated learning of power models. This eases the identification and application of non-linear power models. The high degree of automation in the construction of model instances makes the use of power models with higher accuracy feasible for use at design time.

Goal 3. We were able to show that our power model extraction method produces accurate power models. The extracted power models accurately predicted the power consumption of a set of Big Data and enterprise applications. The model with the highest AIC score had a maximum energy consumption prediction error of 5.2%. The PetClinic case study illustrated the end to end applicability of our model extraction, and our energy efficiency prediction approach. The model with the highest AIC ranking produced power consumption predictions with an error of less than 3%. Power consumption predictions performed using the recommended model were accurate for all aforementioned applications and workloads. This demonstrated that our method enabled us to accurately predict the power consumption of a wide range of server workloads without prior knowledge of the target workload.

We applied the power model extraction method to evaluate the accuracy of resulting models for scenarios involving VM migrations. The resulting models accurately predicted the energy consumed during VM migration, except for high load levels. Further work is needed to construct accurate performance and power models of systems that use proprietary DVFS techniques.

Goal 4. We applied our modeling and analysis approach for considering transient effects in design time analyses to a horizontally scaling Media Store case study system. The results indicated that the consideration of transient effects improves the prediction accuracy of software performance analyses. Our approach allowed us to resolve a design deficiency for the system under investigation that would have otherwise remained unnoticed.

The CACTOS project used the presented Adaptation Action metamodel to model self-adaptation actions in a self-adaptive IaaS data center. Our SimuLizar transient effects analysis extension supported the analysis of all adaptation actions covered by the CACTOS framework [43, 115]. The case study discussed in Section 7.2.3 leveraged this implementation. The energy consumption prediction error was below 7.08% for all scenarios of the data center resource management case study. The application in the CACTOS project and its tooling illustrates that the metamodel enables the modeling of realistic, complex adaptation actions.

7.5.2. Future Work

An area of future work is a further validation of interactions between power consumption and reconfigurations. With regards to server-based systems, preliminary studies we conducted indicated that the most significant portion of additional power consumption caused by VM migrations can be derived from their transient effects on performance. The only exceptions we had identified are the startup and shutdown of servers. Servers consume power while booting, or shutting down. Performance metrics can not be measured while the respective operating system API is not yet available. Our model supports the modeling of performance independent power consumption via power state transitions, outlined in Section 3.2.2. Krach [114] showed the need for state-based power consumption modeling for mobile devices. The author used a previous iteration of the models presented in Chapter 3. Our work addressed the requirements identified by Krach [114] with an explicit modeling of power states and transitions. The state-based modeling in this thesis could be re-applied to mobile systems. This would evaluate by which degree the introduced model extensions improve the prediction accuracy for mobile systems.

An intrinsic limitation of our approach is its dependence on the accuracy of the input performance metric predictions, which performance analyses provide. Throughout all case studies, we were able to accurately predict the power consumption of the systems under investigation. Even when the performance models of the system were coarse grained (Section 7.2.3), or derived from an average case resource demand estimation (Section 7.2.2), our approach produced power consumption predictions that were sufficiently accurate for architecture-level decision making. The VM migration case study showcased the need for accurate performance and power models of multi-core systems which use proprietary DVFS techniques. We did not explicitly model the proprietary DVFS features of the server under investigation. While our power models accurately predicted energy consumption at all other load levels, their accuracy was low for high load on a small number of cores.

The validation did not empirically validate the usability of our approach with a user study. The presented case studies illustrate the applicability of our approach to evaluate the energy efficiency of software systems, and the impact of reconfigurations on performance. The core parts of the Power Consumption models construction, and the energy efficiency analysis are automated. Due to the high degree of automation, we deemed that a user study would provide little additional insights on the applicability of our approach. For the Adaptation Action metamodel, an empirical user study could answer to what extent a coupled specification of adaptation effect on system state and behavior reduces the effort for modeling self-adaptive software systems.

8. Related Work

This section describes work related to the contributions of this thesis. It contrasts our work with approaches from different research areas. We identified five areas that are closely related to our work. Each of the following sections discusses approaches from one of the areas. Section 8.1 outlines power consumption modeling and estimation approaches. They are closely related to our Power Consumption metamodel and PCA prediction approaches. Section 8.2 focuses on approaches for power model extraction. The wider field of Green Software Engineering research is investigated in Section 8.3. In Section 8.4, we survey the area of energy efficiency benchmarks and classification. We distinguish between power model extraction and benchmarking, as extraction is concerned with the creation of predictive models, while the other approaches classify and compare the energy efficiency of servers. Cloud simulator research is a field related to both our power consumption prediction approach and the modeling and analysis of transient effects. Section 8.5 contrasts our work with modeling and prediction methods from Cloud simulation. Section 8.6 investigates related work in the area of self-adaptive systems modeling and analysis. Section 8.7 contrasts our Adaptation Action metamodel from other performance model completion approaches.

8.1. Power Consumption Modeling and Estimation

This section assesses differences and commonalities of our power modeling approach and consumption analysis PCA with related work. Section 8.1.1 contrasts our design time prediction approach with runtime methods. Section 8.1.2 compares our work with other energy consumption approaches aimed at the design time power or energy consumption estimation. Section 8.1.3 discusses methods that support the implementation of energy efficient software systems. They either guide software developers through a code level power consumption estimation, or offer reusable programming constructs that improve energy efficiency.

8.1.1. Runtime Power Estimation

Runtime power estimation aims at the estimation of power consumption in an operational software system. Runtime estimation methods support reasoning on power consumption of servers that are not, or not permanently, equipped with power measurement equipment. They use measurable system metrics such as CPU utilization as input variables of a consumption estimation model.

In data center environments, runtime power estimation techniques enable data center operators to evaluate power consumption on a per-server basis. Automated optimization frameworks may use power estimates as the basis of adaptation decisions, which aim to increase energy efficiency. Runtime power estimation techniques can leverage all low level performance counters that can be measured in a system [28, 58]. If the availability of power estimations is time critical, e.g., as part of a power capping mechanism, the computational complexity of the estimation technique may be restricted.

Noureddine et al. [149] present a framework for runtime power estimation. The authors' approach leverages system level metrics to estimate the power consumption of software systems. Their framework estimates the power consumption per software component. It derives the estimate from the fraction of work that each software component causes on a hardware component. The framework estimates the power consumption of the hardware based on the equation that correlates power consumption with the frequency and voltage of a processor [160]. While the consideration of frequency and voltage in the power models allows estimating the effects of DVFS, it disregards the effect of utilization on power consumption when voltage and frequency are constant.

Seo et al. [185] outline a framework for runtime energy consumption estimation of Java applications. Their framework relies on a bookkeeping energy model as introduced in Definition 2.1 of Section 2.1. The authors assign each bytecode operation with an energy consumption, which results from its execution. Their approach derives the energy consumption of a Java program over time as the sum of all calls performed in the time frame. Seo et al. accumulate the program consumption with consumption estimates for communication overhead and static server consumption.

As part of the EU project Fit4Green Basmadjian et al. [16] developed a runtime power consumption prediction approach for data center environments. Basmadjian et al. propose to predict the power consumption of each server in a data center as a sum of the power consumption of CPUs, memory, Hard Disk Drives (HDDs), network, and a constant factor. The authors use linear power models to predict the power consumption of CPU, memory and HDD resources. Basmadjian et al. use utilization measurements gathered on the actual infrastructure to parametrize these power models. This produces consumption estimates on the level of individual resources, servers, and the full data center. Basmadjian et al. only evaluated the precision of their runtime power models for a single server running a synthetic workload. The authors managed to maintain error rates below 10% in their experiments. However, it is not clear how precise the models are for varying workload intensities since the synthetic workload applies a constant load to the system. In addition, it remains uncertain whether the proposed distinction between individual resources improves the accuracy over a linear power that is purely based on the CPU utilization. The authors only vary CPU load and memory usage in their experiments. Since the memory usage is scaled up with the CPU load, the benefit of having separate power models for CPU and memory is uncertain.

8.1.2. Design Time Power Estimation

The goal of design time power estimation techniques is the support of a systematic consideration of power consumption as part of software design.

Brunnert et al. [35] present an approach based on Palladio that targets capacity planning in data centers for enterprise applications. In order to evaluate the energy consumption of servers, the authors couple a linear power model with the PCM. Brunnert et al. [35] intrusively extend the Resource Environment of PCM with linear power consumption factors per processing resource. Their modeling approach does not support different power model types. It neglects power distribution characteristics. The authors uses the linearity of their power model to reason on the total energy consumption of the software system under evaluation. Brunnert et al. [35] estimate the energy consumption as the result of the linear power model parametrized with the average CPU and HDD utilization, multiplied with the total time. Their approach hence relies on an average case analysis. The prediction method lacks support for the evaluation of power consumption at individual points in time. It is impossible to use the approach to evaluate power consumption over time. Consequently, reasoning on peak power consumption, and consumption in a specific time interval is not supported. Brunnert et al. focuses on static software systems. In contrast to our work, the authors do not address power consumption prediction for self-adaptive software systems. Their approach also lacks support for the evaluation of power consumption under usage trends, i.e., changes in the number and behavior of users over time.

Seo et al. [184] analyze the impact of architectural communication styles on power consumption. Considered styles are, e.g., client-server and publish-subscribe. An energy bookkeeping model forms the foundation of their analysis. Seo et al. assume each remote call to consume a specific amount of energy. Seo et al. do not investigate how internal component behavior affects energy consumption. The authors assume the energy consumption of components to be mostly unaffected by the communication style. In order to predict the energy consumption of components, Seo et al. rely on their bytecode-based estimation discussed in Section 8.1.1.

Another architectural energy consumption estimation approach that uses bookkeeping energy models is outlined by Meedeniya et al. [136]. The intended area of application of their work is embedded systems. The authors do not distinguish between hardware and software components. Rather, Meedeniya et al. consider *system components* that integrate software and hardware. In contrast to Seo et al. [184], Meedeniya et al. do not differentiate between energy consumption of individual calls. The authors assume that any call to the same component consumes the same amount of energy. Their model uses an average estimate to model energy consumption caused by communication. Meedeniya et al. [136] model static energy consumption on a per-component basis.

PowerPerfCenter [5] is an application performance simulator that supports the consideration of power management mechanisms. The authors rely on a probabilistic workload and system description language. Compared to PCM, the language models the system on a lower level. The introduction of programming constructs like *for* statements moves the models closer to a performance prototyping language. Users can simulate the effect of frequency scaling mechanisms as implemented by the Linux frequency scaling governors. PowerPerfCenter predicts the power consumption using a piecewise defined linear power model. It predicts the power consumption at each frequency level f as a fraction u of the power consumption at f under full load $u = 1$. Other power model types are not explored.

Bunse and Höpfner [39] discuss a model-based power estimation approach for embedded systems. The approach builds upon the *MARMOT* [38] method. MARMOT extends the KobrA method [11] to the embedded software systems domain. MARMOT and KobrA structure the development of component-based software systems. They employ three orthogonal viewpoints to specify different aspects of a software system. The viewpoints are the structural, functional and behavioral viewpoint. Different UML diagram types realize each viewpoint.

MARMOT leverages PSMs to describe the power consumption of embedded systems. Each PSM models the power consumption of an embedded component. The PSM is specific to the combination of hardware and the software components that are deployed on it [39]. Additionally, all services provided by the components are annotated with energy consumption estimates which are not included in the PSM model. MARMOT estimates the consumption of methods by evaluating UML timing diagrams. For this, it accumulates the energy consumption from state transitions, service calls and the consumption in the states during a modeled interaction.

It remains unclear under which conditions the energy consumption caused by a service is included in the PSM, and when it should be described with service consumption annotations. This lacking separation of application and power consumption modeling makes it difficult to reuse the power models to compare different architectural design decisions. For example, it is challenging to estimate how the choice of a different component implementation would affect the energy consumption of a software system: Both the PSM and the annotation model may include parts of the consumption that results from calls to the initially chosen component.

8.1.3. Implementation Time Methods

Zimmermann [232] presents an approach for an emulation-based evaluation and optimization of embedded systems energy efficiency. The author uses PSMs, in combination with a bookkeeping power model to model the power consumption of embedded hardware resources. The bookkeeping model specifies the consumption of individual hardware instructions. Zimmermann emulates the implemented software to estimate its energy consumption. The emulation serves as the foundation of a configuration optimization that varies the parameters of dynamic power management mechanisms. In comparison to our work, Zimmermann focuses on single, embedded systems. The emulation requires the full application implementation as input for the emulation-based analysis. Potentially, changes have to be applied to the implementation to make it compatible to the interfaces of the emulator. The approach thus can only be applied to optimize existing embedded applications on the implementation level. The prediction method by the author requires a highly accurate power state simulation and modeling to produce accurate results.

Wilke [223] estimates the energy consumption of specific application usage scenarios using bookkeeping energy models. The author annotates user activities with their estimated contribution to energy consumption. His bookkeeping model characterizes the energy consumption of activities dependent on the system state in which they are performed. The thesis [223] provides example bookkeeping energy models but does not investigate their accuracy for the given systems. Wilke infers the energy consumption of user activities. His model assumes that the energy consumed by a call does not depend on the level of system activity. This is inaccurate for most modern server systems since they showcase a non-linear relation between energy consumption and utilization level [58, 172].

Li et al. [128] outline a measurement-based approach for estimating the contribution of individual source code lines to the total power consumption. Their approach targets the consumption estimation for mobile applications. The authors use heuristics based on bookkeeping power models to break down the total device consumption to individual source code lines. The heuristics aim to consider parallel program execution and tail states in the per-line source code consumption estimates. The validation applies the method to a set of Android applications. Their heuristics could be transferred for use with our architecture-level design time analysis. The heuristics could be used to contribute the energy consumption to individual services or actions in an RDSEFF. The power measurements and application level monitoring of a runtime system would be substituted with power consumption and performance analysis results from Palladio and our PCA.

8.2. Power Model Extraction

Composable Highly Accurate OS-based power models (CHAOS) by Davis et al. [58] is a method for the automated extraction of power models based on system level performance counters. CHAOS passively monitors a set of workload runs. This contrasts the profiling approach from our power model extraction method, which actively steers the load to reach specific load levels. CHAOS selects a set of relevant hardware performance counters using a feature reduction algorithm. The feature reduction algorithm runs during the profiling. CHAOS relies on the availability of a large number of low level performance counters. This makes their profiling approach difficult to to apply to the extraction of power models for use in design time analyses. In order to validate their approach, Davis et al. [58] evaluate the accuracy of a set of power models. The power models include linear power models, piecewise linear power models, quadratic power models and a model which the authors refer to as a *switching power model.* The latter model defines power models per p-state of the system. Davis et al. train the models on the features selected by CHAOS. The authors conclude that the consideration of storage metrics significantly improves prediction accuracy compared to power models that only consider CPU utilization and fixed consumption factors. Our experiments did not confirm this observation for our profiling approach.

Mantis [65] is a power consumption profiling framework. Mantis runs individual synthetic workloads [141] at different load levels. Mantis uses a specific workload per system component. Example components are CPU, storage, and network. Unlike our profiling approach, Mantis lacks support for hybrid workloads, i.e., workloads that stress multiple resources at the same time.

GreenOracle [52] extracts energy models for Android applications using systematic experiments. The energy models use system call traces and CPU utilization as independent input variables for a predictive runtime power model. GreenOracle trains the power model on measurement data collected from device profiling. It executes a set of test cases on multiple versions of different applications. Finally, it trains the energy models on the collected measurements. The proposed approach does not systematically vary load. Thus, the produced profile may not provide represent the full measurement range of independent variables.

Kansal et al. [104] outline a model for VM metering that estimates the contribution of individual VMs to the total power consumption of a server. Instead of training a server wide power model, Kansal et al. train power models that estimate the per-VM consumption. The constructed model is a helpful foundation of VM pricing models. It is questionable how accurate the model is compared to full-system power models. The authors note that the total server power consumption of their evaluation server follows a non-linear trend. Their composed per-VM power model, however, assumes that each VM linearly contributes to the total consumption. This in turn results in a composed linear power model for the full server. The limitations of VM power model construction by Kansal et al. [104] make VM power models difficult to apply at design time. The authors train each VM power model after the VM has been instantiated. The per-VM power model parameters strongly depend on the server and the components deployed in the VM. This makes the VM power models difficult to apply to new VM configurations, i.e., due to the redeployment of components on another VM.

8.3. Green Software Engineering

Green Software Engineering subsumes all methods that aim to quantify or improve the ecological footprint of software. Most common, energy consumption is used to quantify the ecological footprint.

There are different sub-fields of Green Software Engineering. The subsequent sections outline related approaches in each of the sub-fields. Section 8.3.1 discusses approaches that quantify the impact of design decisions made during software evolution on energy efficiency. Section 8.3.2 presents methods that aim to detect and resolve design deficiencies which negatively affect energy efficiency. In Section 8.1.2, we introduced different design time power estimation approaches. These approaches can also be categorized as Green Software Engineering methods. Section 8.3.3 complements the prior section with a discussion of Software Eco-Cost Model (SECoMo). SECoMo supports the modeling of the ecological footprint with metrics otherr than energy consumption, e.g., greenhouse gas emissions.

8.3.1. Repository Mining and Comparison of Energy Consumption across Software Releases

Software repository mining approaches aim to identify trends and patterns throughout software evolution from the commit history of a source code Version Control System (VCS). They have been applied to identify changes that influence the energy efficiency of software systems. Hindle [87] proposes a method to compare the energy consumption of different software versions. The approach aims at the identification of changes in power consumption due to source code changes. Hindle et al. [89] apply the method to compare the power consumption characteristics across different versions of Android projects hosted on GitHub. Their *GreenMiner* approach uses an automated testbed to measure the energy consumption of different user interactions across mobile application software releases.

Hasan et al. [81] apply GreenMiner to compare the power consumption of different Java collection libraries for Android. In a first step, the authors evaluate the power consumed while performing a set of collections-based microbenchmarks. Second, they investigate the effect the replacement of collections libraries had on a set of small-scale case study systems. Their experimental investigation on one Android-based device provides an interesting state-of-the-art insight into the efficiency of different collections implementations. It is unclear to what extent the results can be generalized to other execution environments, e.g., enterprise servers. Furthermore, future implementation changes in the libraries require a re-evaluation.

Moura et al. [144] perform a thorough analysis of commits on GitHub that targeted an energy consumption reduction. Some of the commits also consider tradeoffs with other quality dimensions, such as performance. Moura et al. do not experimentally evaluate whether the commits actually effectively reduced energy consumption.

Jagroep et al. [100] propose a method to compare energy consumption across different releases of a software product. Their approach aims to promote awareness for the effect of design decisions on energy consumption during soware evolution. The authors collect and compare measurements of the same usage scenarios for different versions of the software system. Compared to our predictive approach, the approach by Jagroep et al. can not be used at design time as it relies on the availability of the full implementation of the software system under analysis. In their consecutive work, Jagroep et al. [101] outline a question catalog which supports software architects in the identification of potential energy efficiency improvements. These improvements target both architectural and implementation decisions. Jagroep et al. apply their profiling method [100] to evaluate the effect of decisions on energy consumption.

8.3.2. Detection and Resolution of Design Deficiencies

Procaccianti et al. [165] compile a set of design decision categories that aim to increase energy efficiency. The categories are energy monitoring, self-adaptation, and Cloud federation. Energy monitoring design decisions intend to inform software architects of the effects of her decisions on energy efficiency. Self-adaptation and cloud federation design decisions integrate self-adaptation mechanisms with a software system. They enable the adaptation and exchange of services on the basis of specified quality goals, e.g., energy efficiency. Procaccianti et al. do not provide a model for, or experimental evidence of the effect of the presented design decisions on energy efficiency. In later work, Procaccianti et al. [164] experimentally evaluate the effect of two best practices on energy efficiency.

Reimann and Aßmann [169] propose a generic method for the identification and resolution of model smells to improve connected functional and non-functional qualities. The authors apply their approach to remove a Java code smell which affects energy consumption. Reimann and Aßmann employ quality analyses to assess the effect of refactorings on QoS attributes. The refactoring approach treats each quality analysis as a black box. It would be possible to couple our energy consumption analysis with the refactoring approach to assess the effect of software architecture refactorings on energy efficiency.

Gottschalk et al. [74] present an approach for the detection and resolution of energy code smells in Android apps. The approach relies on a measurement-based evaluation of refactorings. Thus, it can not be applied in early design stages. The authors provide no details on the degree of automation supported by their approach. A combination of their work with an automated measurement approach, e.g., GreenMiner [89], is conceivable.

The *SEEDS* framework [131] optimizes the configuration of an implemented software system in order to decrease its energy consumption. As input, the framework uses the implementation, a definition of potential variation points, and a description of the deployment environment. The framework aims to identify an optimal configuration by estimating the consumption of each configuration. Manotas et al. [131] note that the consumption estimation of each configuration could be derived from measurements on the deployment environment, hardware and software co-simulation, or higher level energy consumption estimation models. An example of an estimation model referenced by the authors is the model by Noureddine et al. [149], which we discussed in Section 8.1.1. The prototypical implementation of the SEEDS framework varies the used Java collections, and measures the effect on energy consumption by profiling the resulting implementation variant. The meta-heuristics based energy optimization approach of SEEDS could be applied at design time by combining our energy consumption model and analysis with the existing architecture optimization framework PerOpteryx [111]. This would enable an automated selection of optimal architectures at design time with respect to energy consumption and further QoS characteristics.

8.3.3. SECoMo Estimation Model

This section discusses an estimation model that enables the estimation of the ecological footprint of an application. Section 8.1.2, presented different design time power estimation approaches. The discussed approaches also employ estimation models. In contrast to SECoMo, they focus on the estimation of energy consumption as the only eco-cost metric.

The Software Eco-Cost Model (SECoMo) by Schulze [182] enables users, software architects, and operators to estimate the eco-cost of a software system. Schulze defines ecological cost as "any factor influencing the ecological footprint arising in an attempt to reach a certain goal". The cost may expressed in terms of energy consumption, greenhouse gas emission, or a monetary value. SECoMo assigns eco-costs to different types of interactions with the software system. Users and architects of a system can estimate the effect of different types of interactions on eco-costs using metrics. Example interactions are the use of a service or access to stored data. SECoMo considers the usage, deployment context, and provided functionality as factors that impact eco-costs of a system. It uses the KobrA method [11] to capture these factors in UML models.

The descriptive approach by Schulze complements the prescriptive *GreenSLAs* [10]. GreenSLAs define the acceptable eco-costs of service calls. GreenSLAs can be used as a basis of service matching, or selection. Additionally, SECoMo effectively complements energy consumption prediction approaches, as the one presented in this thesis. Its metrics can be applied to energy consumption estimations. This empowers software software architects to reason on the ecological footprint, e.g., of a specific user group. Section 9.4.2 discusses the combined use of our approach and SECoMo.

8.4. Energy Efficiency Benchmarks and Classification

This section differentiates our work on power model extraction and energy efficiency analysis from related work in the benchmarking and classification domain. Benchmarking frameworks evaluate the energy efficiency of deployment environments for predefined workload sets or types. Classification frameworks monitor and rate the efficiency of a software system. Unlike benchmarking, classification evaluates operational systems and user load.

8.4.1. Benchmarks

JouleSort [173] is a benchmark that evaluates energy efficiency (EE) of software systems. It quantifies EE as the energy consumption that a software system consumes to sort a data set of a specified input size. Algorithm engineers and system architects use JouleSort as a tool to compare the practical efficiency of sorting algorithms in specific execution environments. TPC-Energy [209] complements existing TPC benchmarks, like TPC-W, with a measurement method and metric for EE. Its EE metric is a ratio of total energy consumed over all considered performance measurement intervals, and the number of completed transactions. SPECpower_ssj [119] is an energy efficiency benchmark for enterprise servers. The SPECpower_ssj workload simulates user interactions with a warehouse management system. User requests may arrive at the system at varying rates. The benchmark determines energy efficiency as the ratio of user request throughput and power consumption. SPECpower_ssj measures EE at different throughput levels, which it derives from the maximum measured throughput on a server.

Unlike our estimation approach, benchmarks require the full implementation of the software system under analysis to quantify EE. The benchmarks do not evaluate energy consumption at different load levels. Thus, power consumption and system metric measurements collected during the benchmarks may fail to cover a representative set of measurements. This makes the standalone benchmarks unsuitable for server profiling.

SERT [29, 187, 188] is a framework for classifying server energy efficiency across a range of workload types. SERT defines energy efficiency as an aggregated metric over the energy efficiency of multiple worklets run at different load levels. A load level is defined as a factor $u \in [0, 1]$. For each load level, SERT defines energy efficiency (EE) as follows:

Definition 8.1 (Energy Efficiency per SERT Load Level). *The energy efficiency at a load level $tp_u = u \cdot tp_{max}$, and $u \in [0, 1]$ is*

$$EE_{tp_u} = \frac{\textit{Normalized Performance}}{\textit{Power Consumption}}, \textit{ where}$$

tp_{max} is the maximum throughput that is reached for the worklet on the server under investigation. EE_{tp_u} is the efficiency when the workload is executed with the share tp_u is a share of maximum throughput.

SERT aggregates the EE at different load levels into a metric for a specific application type. It performs this aggregation using the geometric mean. SERT refers to the types of applications as *worklets*. From the worklet scores, SERT calculates a total server EE metric. The metric weights workloads depending on the type of workload it issues. The weighting stresses the scores of CPU intensive worklets over memory intensive, and storage intensive worklets. An example worklet is SSJ, which simulates a web shop. SPECpower_ssj [119] also uses this workload. SERT quantifies EE as a ratio of throughput and energy consumption. It does not consider other performance metrics, e.g., the response time distribution at different throughput levels.

SERT rates the EE of a server in relation to the EE of a baseline server for a specific set of workloads. Out of scope of SERT are the prediction or estimation of power consumption for workloads outside this set. Additionally, SERT does not target the extraction of power models. We employed the technical foundation of SERT to implement our systematic power model extraction approach, as Section 5.4.1 discussed. This enabled us to reuse the existing SERT workload definitions to create representative enterprise server workloads.

8.4.2. Profiling of Existing Applications

Energy efficiency benchmarks evaluate the energy efficiency of an execution environment using a set of workloads. The execution environment may be, e.g., an enterprise server. Benchmarks enable the comparison of energy efficiency across different environments on the basis of the executed workloads. The interpretation of benchmark results for specific real scenarios is challenging. Profiling approaches avoid this challenging interpretation. They evaluate the power consumption of full-stack software system configurations instead of benchmarking workloads. Profiling approaches provide software engineers and operators with the exact power consumption characteristics of a running software system, including actual user load. Profiling frameworks thus can only be applied if:

- the software implementation and deployment environment are available, and

- the environment can be instrumented with dedicated measurement equipment.

PowerPack [72] characterizes the power consumption of distributed applications. It supports reasoning on the influence of application phases on power consumption of individual hardware components. PowerPack passively monitors existing applications to gain insights on their power consumption over time. This differs from our profiling approach, which aims to produce a representative server consumption profile for a variety of workloads.

Alonso et al. [3] present a profiling framework for parallel High Performance Computing (HPC) applications. The framework offers interfaces to commercial and custom power monitoring equipment. It supports the recording of software and system level metrics. The authors apply the framework to validate a power model for task-parallel applications. The work by Alonso et al. could be combined with our profiling framework to support a broader range of power meters. Particularly, their implementation could be leveraged to integrate power meters that monitor the individual consumption of server components.

JouleUnit [224] is a power consumption profiling framework. Like PowerPack [72], it supports distributed measurement and workload execution. JouleUnit specifically has been designed to support the profiling of a variety of systems, including cyber-physical systems. Wilke et al. [224] illustrate the applicability of their approach for Android applications and a robotics platform.

Performance counter Event Trigger (PET) [180] is a framework that supports the emulation of complex distributed workloads using a recorded performance counter profile. PET aims to replicate the observed profile by running a combined set of small workloads that trigger the observed counters. As PET assumes transactional workloads, its emulation method could be integrated with our profiling approach. This would enable the power consumption profiling of workloads that emulate large distributed applications.

8.5. Cloud Simulators

Cloud Computing offers "on-demand [...] access to a shared pool of configurable computing resources [...] that can be rapidly provisioned and released with minimal management effort" [137]. Cloud simulators have been developed to support large scale experiments for Cloud scenarios without the costly provisioning of actual servers. The central goal metrics of Cloud simulator evaluations relate to the operational data center efficiency. Hence, the simulators cover metrics relevant to Cloud operators, e.g., resource utilization and energy efficiency. Unlike architectural analyses, the application models of Cloud simulators offer no abstraction compared to the application implementation [150], or model applications purely in terms of the load issued over time [45, 118].

DCworms by Kurowski et al. [118] is a framework for simulating the performance and energy consumption of distributed computing infrastructures. It builds upon *GSSIM* by Bąk et al. [12]. The performance model of both *DCworms* and *GSSIM* is limited to non-interactive HPC tasks. Each modeled HPC task issues a set of sequentially processed resource demands on CPU, storage devices, and network. While this abstraction is suitable for modeling the performance of sequentially processed HPC applications, it does not fit user-facing distributed enterprise applications. DCworms and GSSIM provide predictions for the energy consumption of applications. They perform their predictions using power models derived from system metrics (c.f. Section 2.1). Kurowski et al. [118] evaluate the accuracy of static and linear power models, as well as an application-specific non-linear power model for a set of HPC benchmarks. The authors state that their framework supports the addition of further power models as simulation plugins.

CloudSim by Calheiros et al. [45] is a performance and energy consumption simulator for Cloud environments. CloudSim simulates the dynamic deployment and migration of VMs. Calheiros et al. employ linear power models to predict the energy consumption of cloud-based systems. Later versions of CloudSim extend the range of supported power models, e.g., by piecewise defined linear power models [24]. The main simulation entity of CloudSim are VMs. Unlike DCworms [118] and GSSIM [12], CloudSim does not perform its predictions for a set of VMs that are executed in isolation. In CloudSim, collocated VMs mutually impact their performance.

The behavior of applications simulated by CloudSim can be defined in Java code. The implementation-centric performance approach chosen by Calheiros et al. [45] theoretically allows to model application behavior of arbitrary complexity. However, it also lacks the abstractness and generality of component-based architectural performance models such as Palladio [22]. In CloudSim, applications and services are not modeled as a sequence of actions and service calls to different components. Applications running in each virtual machine do not communicate with the services running in other VMs. Another drawback of CloudSim is its lack of an explicit usage or workload model. Fluctuations in the user demands need to be manually mapped to changing resource demands of a VM. Piraghaj et al. [157] extend CloudSim to support the modeling and simulation of containers. Piraghaj et al. treat containers as another virtualization layer. Behavior and power consumption modeling are unaffected by the added layer.

CloudSim approximates the transient effect of VM migrations as a fixed, linear overhead on CPU utilization [24]. The migration duration is estimated as the memory size of the VM divided by the available network bandwidth. This is inaccurate for pre-copy live migrations, where the migration duration depends its memory page dirty rate.

The Cloud simulator *iCanCloud* [150] requires users to implement Cloud simulations against a low level programming API. Instead of performing actual operating system or cloud platform calls, application developers may issue calls to the simulator API. Due to this high level of detail, iCanCloud is not suited for the evaluation of large scenarios, and scenarios where information on executed workloads is limited. Castañé et al. [48] extend iCanCloud with an energy consumption model. Castañé et al. distinguish operational states of hardware components, e.g., CPU and memory. The authors propose a specific energy model per device. Each power model predicts the energy consumption using system metrics and device states. In its current state, iCanCloud does not support VM migrations or other reconfigurations.

Vondra and Šedivý [218] present a queueing network-based Cloud simulator. The authors specifically constructed the simulator for the analysis of auto-scaling algorithms. The simulator only analyzes steady states that are reached after scale outs or scale ins have been executed. Unlike our work, the simulator lacks support for the analysis of transient phases. The authors focus on performance metrics, e.g., utilization and request latency. Energy efficiency is out of scope of their work.

8.6. Modeling and Analysis of Self-Adaptive Software Systems

In this section, we contrast our approaches for the modeling and analysis of energy-conscious self-adaptive software systems, and modeling and analysis of transient effects with related work. Section 8.6.1 discusses runtime models and analyses that enable an efficient operation of software systems. Section 8.6.2 outlines analyses that predict the quality of self-adaptive software systems at design time. In Section 8.6.3 we delineate related work that models the performance and energy consumption of VM migrations.

8.6.1. Runtime Models and Analyses

SOFA 2.0 by Bures et al. [41] explicitly models adaptation points. The authors argue that runtime adaptations should be reflected in the architectural design to prevent "an uncontrolled modification of the architecture" [41]. SOFA 2.0 reflects adaptation points as services offered by *Controller* components. The Controller components are woven into all components, to which the adaptation points of a Controller apply. Adaptations that do not directly affect an existing component, e.g., the launch of a new component instance, cannot be described using this modeling approach.

Stitch [51] is a Domain Specific Language (DSL) for the specification of reconfiguration mechanisms based on the S/T/A approach. Section 2.4.2 introduced the S/T/A approach. Stitch assigns each tactic with its expected adaptation cost. It defines a fixed delay after which the intended effect of a strategy or tactic should have been observed. Cámara et al. [46] and Moreno et al. [142] extend Stitch to proactively adapt the system to changes in the system environment, e.g., increasing user demand. Their approach assumes a fixed execution time for adaptation rules. The delay-based model [46, 51, 142] is inadequate as input for performance predictions when the execution time of adaptations depends on transient effects.

Rosa et al. [174] enrich component specifications with an adaptation point model. The authors define adaptation costs in multiple dimensions per component. They acknowledge that adaptations may result in different transient effects depending on resource utilization. The adaptation cost are a constant overhead added to, or a factor times the current utilization. The adaptation point model only supports the specification of upper bound adaptation delays.

Descartes [93] is a proactive adaptation approach. Descartes represents the current system state as an instance of DML. DML encompasses an adaptation point model, and a monitoring data model. It uses architecture-level performance predictions to identify future performance bottlenecks at runtime. Descartes triggers adaptation mechanisms once it has identified one or multiple performance bottlenecks. These mechanisms may derive an adaptation plan, which aims to resolve the bottlenecks. Descartes evaluates the result of the plan using architectural performance analysis. The analysis disregards the transient phase. Instead, it evaluates the expected system performance after the plan has been executed. DML does not model reconfiguration cost.

Götz [75] proposes a model-based runtime adaptation framework for single-user software systems [75, p. 168]. Its aim is to find optimal system configurations based on predefined QoS requirements. The optimization method uses the runtime models to reason on QoS characteristics of a software system. Götz presents a behavior model for a state-based description of hardware. The author illustrates how this model can be applied to create PSMs. Their runtime optimization framework uses predefined PSMs as input to a DES-based analysis. The simulator estimates the energy consumption for an expected user request.

The expressiveness of the energy model and the accuracy of the simulator-based predictions by Götz [75] is lower than our approach. In addition to PSM models, our Power Consumption metamodel supports the modeling of power distribution infrastructure characteristics and system metric-based power models. Our approach thereby can differentiate the dynamic power consumption in each state. An advantage of the simplified modeling and simulation over our approach is that it is easier and faster to determine QoS predictions of different system configurations. This is important in the scope of the work by Götz [75], since their framework continuously analyzes a system for potential runtime optimizations. The work [75] lacks a quantitative evaluation of the presented approach.

Bunse and Höpfner [39] propose to integrate an *energy management component* with a software system. The energy management component aims to increase the energy efficiency of the system by adapting its configuration to changes in user behavior or different execution environments. The authors [40] apply this principle to enable an application to dynamically select the most energy efficient sorting algorithm from a set of available algorithms. The energy management component determines an optimal configuration based on a set of power models that estimate the energy consumption dependent on application and system metrics. These power models are specific to each potential application configuration and deployment environment. The authors manually construct the power models by profiling the sorting algorithm implementations on a specific deployment environment. The models presented in [40] only consider the size of the sorted collection as an input factor.

8.6.2. Architecture-Level Design Time Analyses

Architecture-level design time analyses of self-adaptive software systems evaluate the quality of these systems at design time. They enable software architects in the selection, configuration and design of runtime adaptation mechanisms.

D-KLAPER by Grassi et al. [77] is an approach for model-based design time analysis of self-adaptive software systems. Unlike SimuLizar, D-KLAPER only considers adaptations that affect the composition and deployment of components. A further difference is that D-KLAPER does not support the analysis of reconfigurations, which trigger as a result of variations in monitored QoS characteristics. Instead, reconfigurations execute randomly according to specified stochastic models. All possible configuration states must be proactively known and specified by the architect. This is infeasible for adaptation mechanisms that only implicitly state the results of adaptations. D-KLAPER supports the specification of resource demands that are caused by reconfigurations. Each reconfiguration defines a transition between two specific states. This contrasts our transient effect model, which supports the modeling of transient effects independent of specific state transitions.

SLAstic.SIM [133] enables simulation-based design time analyses of self-adaptive software systems. It analyzes self adaptation mechanisms specified using the *SLAstic* self-adaptation framework. PCM serves as the architecture model used to describe the system under analysis. The simulator SLAstic.SIM does not consider transient effects. Reconfigurations immediately transition the system from the initial to the target state.

8.6.3. Performance and Energy Models of VM Migrations

VM migrations are an important type of adaptation action in virtualized data center environments. The performance and energy consumption modeling of VM migrations has been extensively investigated in the Cloud and SPE research community.

Alansari and Bordbar [2] outline an approach for modeling the performance impact of VM migrations. Colored Petri Nets serve as the foundation of their modeling. Their performance model does not consider migration time or performance impact of VM migrations. The authors estimate migration times in a subsequent simulation results analysis. Thus, their approach does not allow for a consideration of transient effects which affect VM migrations, or result from them.

Akoush et al. [1] investigate factors that impact performance of live migrations. The authors propose two simulative models that estimate the remaining migration time of a VM using runtime performance measurements. Strunk [206] extends the model by Akoush et al. with an energy model. Their model uses a linear power model to estimate the energy consumption based on network bandwidth and VM size.

Maio et al. [129] estimate the energy consumption of VM migrations. The presented model estimates the energy consumption proportional to the performance overhead of the migration. The model calculates the full system power consumption using a linear power model.

8.7. Performance Model Completions

Performance completions [228] enrich software models with performance specifications. Performance completions may also enhance existing performance models with detailed performance information, e.g., platform specific resource demands. This closes "the gap between available high-level models and required low level details" [80].

Happe et al. [80] apply the concept of performance completions to PCM. The authors introduce parameters to the completions. This allows the consideration of different platforms in a single completion. Platform specific characteristics are mapped to parameters. The authors apply their approach to support a lightweight, reusable specification of communication middleware overhead.

Lehrig et al. [126] integrate the completion concept with an approach which enables architects to reuse architectural knowledge. Examples for architectural knowledge are a reusable specification of architectural tactics, e.g., vertical scaling. Lehrig et al. annotate PCM with these specifications. The annotation-based approach reduces the analysis effort for architects, and enables a lightweight exploration of alternative tactics and application frameworks.

Our approach for the consideration of transient effects in design time analyses employs parametric model completions, which describe the performance effect of reconfigurations. The previously discusses approaches by Happe et al. [80] and Lehrig et al. [126] enhance PCM architecture models prior to an analysis. This requires knowledge in which parts of the system the completions should be applied. In contrast, we employ the completions concept to enhance architecture models during an analysis. This allows us to apply performance completions to parts of the system which are not part of the initial system configuration.

9. Integration with Existing Software Engineering Processes

This chapter discusses how our contributions can be used as part of existing software engineering methods and processes.

9.1. Using Energy Efficiency Modeling and Analysis with Palladio

Section 2.5.4 introduced the workflow for the quality analysis with Palladio. Our approach extends this workflow with modeling and analysis of power and energy consumption characteristics. The Power Consumption metamodel represents these characteristics. PCA uses instances of the model to reason on power and energy consumption.

Figure 9.1 depicts the extended Palladio quality analysis workflow. In addition to her existing duties, the system deployer is responsible for providing a description of the power consumption characteristics of the deployment environment. For this, the deployer describes the power distribution infrastructure and connected servers using the Infrastructure viewpoint of our Power Consumption metamodel. The deployer can either use power model catalogs, or derive the power models from systematic experiments or historical measurements. Section 3.3 and Chapter 5 discussed the construction or retrieval of power models. Infrastructure distribution losses can be modeled based on vendor specification, or estimates from literature, e.g., as presented in [13].

The deployer may provide different Resource Environment and Allocation models. She thereby enables reasoning on the effect of alternative alloca-

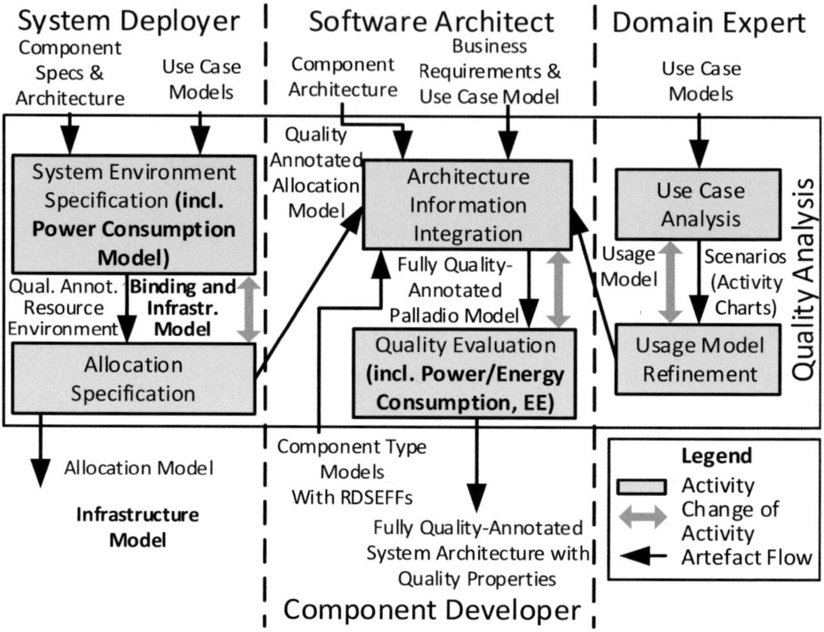

Figure 9.1.: Palladio quality analysis workflow extended with modeling activities and artifacts of our power consumption modeling and analysis approach. Figure based on [170, p. 213]. New parts are highlighted in bold.

tion strategies and hardware selection on energy efficiency and other QoS characteristics. The deployer has to provide an Infrastructure model for each alternative Resource Environment model. The Infrastructure model annotates the environment with its consumption characteristics. If no power models are available for the target deployment environment, the deployer can apply our power model extraction method to obtain the power models.

Multiple alternative Infrastructure models can be provided for the same Resource Environment model. This supports the exploration of alternative distribution infrastructures, and infrastructure sizing decisions.

It is possible to split off the tasks related to power consumption modeling from the system deployer role. In this case, a system operator can take on these tasks.

The software architect integrates the additional models in the *Architecture Information Integration*. The architect can leverage the Power Consumption metamodel and Power Consumption Analyzer (PCA) consumption analysis if the business requirements

- include power consumption, energy consumption and efficiency goals, or
- aim at a reduction of operational costs while maintaining other QoS requirements.

The architect can use substitute power models of similar deployment environments if no power models are available for the environment under investigation.

In *Quality Analysis*, the software architect can evaluate power consumption over time, the aggregate energy consumption, and energy efficiency using our PCA. Depending on the type of system, the architect may choose different performance analysis methods to derive the prediction input for PCA. Section 4.3 discussed the alternative simulation-based methods.

9.2. Engineering Energy-Conscious Self-Adaptive Systems with SimuLizar

SimuLizar extends the role of the software architect to cover the selection and design of self-adaptation mechanisms. Becker [17] refers to the architect as the *self-adaptive system architect* due to the added range of design responsibilities. We discussed these responsibilities in Section 2.5.2. We extended SimuLizar to support the specification of energy-conscious adaptation mechanisms. These mechanisms adapt the system to meet quality goals related to energy consumption.

The self-adaptive system architect has to perform the following additional tasks evaluate the efficiency and effectiveness of energy-conscious self-adaptation mechanisms:

- **Specify power and energy consumption Monitors.** Adaptation mechanisms specified in SimuLizar rely upon system measurements to determine if adaptations should be performed. The architect or system deployer have to specify points in the Infrastructure model where power and consumption measurements should be collected. They define measuring points, measurement frequency and interval in the Monitor model.

- **Integrate or implement energy-conscious adaptation mechanisms.** The self-adaptive software systems architect implements energy-conscious adaptation mechanisms as in-place model transformations on PCM. The transformations derive adaptation decisions based on the measurements which are collected as specified in the Monitors.
- **Specify transient effects of adaptations.** If the execution of adaptations induces a significant overhead, the architect can apply our Adaptation Action metamodel to consider the resulting transient effects.
- **Evaluate effect of adaptation mechanisms on QoS.** The architect has to validate that the self-adaptive system under investigation meets the quality demands derived from the business requirements. This includes constraints on peak power and aggregate energy consumption. The constraints can stem from business concerns like the price of power, or availability of renewable energy sources. Additionally, the architect can validate if the power distribution infrastructure meets the peak power consumption of the software system.

The architect has to adjust the design or renegotiate the business requirements if the energy-conscious self-adaptive system under investigation violates any of the QoS requirements. This matches the respective activity in the baseline Palladio quality analysis workflow, which we presented in Section 2.5.4.

9.3. Integration with Software Development Approaches

Our approach extends the Palladio approach for the quality-aware development of component-based software systems. Palladio is not a proprietary modeling process. Rather, it complements existing development approaches with systematic, light-weight quality analyses based on the PCM architecture modeling language. Software architects can apply Palladio to avoid costly re-implementations due to unsatisfactory QoS of the developed system. Reussner et al. [170, pp. 217-223] discuss how Palladio can be integrated with different development processes. The authors outline the compatibility of Palladio with the most common development processes. These processes include:

- Iterative, incremental, and evolutionary processes,
- sequential process models ("waterfall-like"),
- iterative process models,
- agile development approaches.

Our modeling approach extends Palladio to consider power consumption, energy consumption, and energy efficiency. The modeling workflow of Palladio remains unchanged, barring the extensions we introduced in Section 2.5.4. Hence, we consider our approach to be compatible with these development processes and approaches.

In iterative or agile development, the Power Consumption metamodel instance of the system under development can be refined based on the identified resource requirements. The resource requirements depend on the QoS goals which the software architect derives from business requirements. Additional information on the deployment environment from later iterations informs the modeling of the power distribution characteristics. The architect can incorporate more accurate power models based on the information. This results in a higher accuracy of energy consumption and energy efficiency predictions in later iterations.

The consideration of energy-related quality metrics in early design phases reduces the risk of QoS violations in sequential development processes. Initial models and estimates tend to be inaccurate in forward engineering. It thus makes sense to update the Power Consumption metamodel specification in later development phases. This can help inform decisions made in later phases, e.g., the choice of runtime management policies to reduce the energy consumption of idle servers.

9.4. Combination with Green Software Engineering Approaches

This section discusses how our modeling and analysis approach can be integrated with existing Green Software Engineering approaches. It describes how the approaches complement each other in increasing the energy efficiency of software systems and promoting energy-awareness among developers, operators, and management.

9.4.1. GREENSOFT Model

The *GREENSOFT Model* is a well-known reference model that captures and guides "software developers, administrators, and software users in creating, maintaining and using software in a more sustainable way" [146]. The GREENSOFT Model encompasses the whole life-cycle of a software system. This includes development, usage, and end of life. In these stages, the model distinguishes first-, second- and third-order effects of software on sustainability. A first-order impact results from the construction and use software systems. It includes the energy consumed by servers, or environmental waste from server production. Second- and third-order impacts are short and long term effects like the prioritization of sustainability as a goal of a software development organization.

The GREENSOFT Model identifies the lack of a software tool "that allows the estimation of energy consumption in [...] early design stages" [146]. The authors hence recommend the use of utilization metrics from software performance prediction approaches as an energy efficiency indicator.

Our design time prediction approach closes the gap identified by Naumann et al. It enables reasoning on the first-order impacts throughout the development and usage phase of design decisions on infrastructure sizing, energy consumption, and energy efficiency. In turn, second- and third-order effects may be induced due to a heightened awareness of interactions between software design and energy efficiency.

9.4.2. Software Eco-Cost Model (SECoMo)

SECoMo by Schulze [182] is an approach for modeling the eco-cost of a software system. We differentiated our contributions from SECoMo in Section 8.3.3. Our approach and SECoMo both aim to enable a systematic engineering of energy efficient software systems. The approaches, however, focus on different roles and associated activities in the software development process. The following discusses how both approaches can be integrated and used complementary to each other.

SECoMo as prescriptive model for design and implementation. SECoMo covers descriptive and prescriptive aspects associated with eco-costs. An implementation of a system can be checked against SECoMo estimates from early design estimates. Large differences between early estimates and implementation indicate a poor estimation accuracy or a lackluster implementation. Large differences hence can be used as a trigger to review the implementation architecture. As SECoMo associates each service call with its effect on energy consumption, it is possible to trace the mismatch between implementation and prediction down to individual calls.

SECoMo as a heuristic for hotspot and blame analyses. SECoMo estimates total energy consumption based on the estimated contribution of individual calls to the total consumption. SECoMo thus supports the evaluation of individual contributions for user groups, components, etc., to the overall energy consumption. When applied on the predictions from PCA, SECoMo can be leveraged to perform an architectural energy consumption hotspot analysis similar to Brüseke et al. [36]. Instead of UML entities, the consumption contributions could be mapped to PCM. This would enable the software architect to identify potential areas of improvement in the architectural design. A continuous evaluation of energy consumption throughout development using SECoMo enables software architects to validate if their design decisions had the intended effect on energy efficiency. The development feedback from SECoMo can inform future decisions of the architect during software evolution and agile development.

Use of Power Consumption metamodel and PCA to calibrate SECoMo. SECoMo relies on measurements or expert knowledge to obtain the eco-cost estimations. Schulze [182] discuss software and hardware power meters as alternative sources of energy measurements for the calibration of the eco-cost models. These measurement-based calibration approaches rely on the availability of a (prototype) implementation. This makes the SECoMo calibration difficult to apply in early design phases if no "previously developed software from the same domain is already available" [182, p. 271]. Our PCA analysis approach supports the analysis of energy consumption in early design stages. It produces predictions based on an architecture model and an instance of our Power Consumption metamodel.

It is possible to estimate the contribution of individual service calls to the total energy consumption by applying the per-call energy estimation technique of JouleUnit method [224] to our predictions. JouleUnit estimates the contribution of individual service calls to the total energy consumption of a system. Our approach thereby could be used to calibrate the SECoMo models from an architectural description of the software system.

SECoMo as the basis of a pricing model. SECoMo accumulates the estimated total consumption from the estimated energy consumption of individual calls. The consumption caused by individual users can be derived from this. Using SECoMo, it is possible to construct pricing models which bill users of a system proportional to their contribution to the energy consumption. Business model experts and management can consider the per-user consumption predictions in business model design. When applied the predictions from PCA, the cost estimates from SECoMo can ease coordination of software architects, business model experts and management in early design stages.

9.5. Consideration of Transient Effects in Self-Adaptive Systems Design with SimuLizar

This thesis contributes the Adaptation Action metamodel that supports the systematic consideration of transient effects in design time quality analyses. Section 6.2.6 described a process for the definition of Adaptation Action model instances. This section discusses how this process integrates with the engineering processes of Palladio and SimuLizar.

The self-adaptive systems architect collaborates with developers of reconfiguration middleware components to define instances of the metamodel. The component developers provide a specification of reconfiguration middleware components as an instance of PCM components. The components describe the performance effect of the adaptation action execution. The middleware component developers also provide a specification of adaptation action parameters, and action effects on the system configuration. The component developers, together with the software architect, describe the adaptation behavior as an instance of our Adaptation Action metamodel.

A self-adaptive systems architect can consider transient effects of reconfigurations by integrating the modeled adaptation actions into her adaptation mechanism specifications. For this, the architect inserts the adaptation actions into their mechanism specifications as Section 6.4.2 outlined.

We designed the Adaptation Action metamodel to support the reusable, composable specification of adaptations. The performance models contain performance effect specifications as RDSEFFs. The resource demand estimates in the RDSEFFs can, however, be specific to a set of execution platforms. In this case, the component developer or system deployer can adapt the specification with platform specific resource demand estimates.

10. Conclusion

This chapter concludes the thesis. It consists of the following sections: Section 10.1 summarizes the presented contributions. Section 10.2 discusses benefits of our approach. Section 10.3 gives an overview of assumptions and limitations. Section 10.4 outlines potential directions for future work.

10.1. Summary

Our thesis presented an adaptation-aware approach for the systematic consideration of energy efficiency for software systems at design time. It provided four central contributions. In combination with their validation, they address the Research Questions (RQs) that we discussed in Section 1.4. The central contributions are:

C1: Design of a modeling language for the description of power consumption characteristics of software systems. Our Power Consumption metamodel enables the modeling of the power consumption characteristics of software systems. Instances of the metamodel hierarchically structure the consumption characteristics of servers and power distribution infrastructure. We found this structuring to be a good abstraction for modeling the consumption characteristics of servers and power distribution infrastructure (RQ 1). The designed metamodel enables accurate consumption predictions (RQ 2), as we demonstrated in a set of case studies.

Our metamodel has a higher expressiveness than state of the art modeling languages. The use of its extended modeling capabilities is optional. The Power Consumption metamodel still supports simple power consumption characterizations when a feature subset is used. A strict layered structuring of the metamodel eases the reuse of consumption specifications for different deployment environments.

C2: Development of an approach for energy efficiency analysis at design time. The developed approach predicts the power consumption using an architecture-level description of the software system. The analysis uses an instance of an architecture modeling language, e.g., PCM, in combination with a Power Consumption metamodel instance as input models. Our analysis leverages existing performance analysis methods to evaluate the effect of design decisions on energy efficiency. Even though the power consumption modeling abstracts from application specific details, the prediction results are sufficiently accurate to evaluate the effect of architectural design decisions on energy efficiency (RQ 4). The analysis supports the evaluation of energy efficiency for static and self-adaptive software systems. For self-adaptive systems, the analysis considers the effects of power management policies and adaptation mechanisms that indirectly affect energy efficiency. Examples of this are the use of alternative VM migration policies.

C3: A method for the extraction of power models for use in design time predictions. A central part of the extraction method is an automated server profiling approach. The approach performs representative power consumption and performance measurements on a server. The automated server profiling significantly reduces the effort required for the manual profiling of server power consumption (RQ 5). The profiling employs different workload types to stress the server. It measures power consumption at different load levels. A representative server profile consisting of power and system metrics results from the profiling. We train a set of power models on this profile.

An AIC-based ranking orders the trained model according to their expected power consumption prediction accuracy. Our validation confirmed that we were able to reason on the effect of system metrics on prediction accuracy using this ranking (RQ 7). The user of our method can select a power model based on its expected accuracy and the required input metrics of the power model. Thereby, the user can rule out input metrics which fail to improve the prediction accuracy.

We found the use of system-level CPU utilization to be sufficient as input to architecture level power consumption predictions for server environments. The consideration of other metrics, e.g., HDD read and write throughput, only marginally increased the prediction accuracy (RQ 6).

C4: Development of a systematic modeling and analysis approach for considering transient effects in software quality analyses. We introduced the Adaptation Action metamodel for the coupled specification of adaptation actions and their transient effect. The metamodel enables the modeling of inter-dependencies between adaptation actions, performance and power consumption (RQ 9). Instances of the metamodel capture the performance and adaptation effect depending on a set of input parameters. Self-adaptive software system architects can reuse adaptation action specifications across different architectural models.

We developed an analysis that supports the consideration of transient effects that uses instances of the Adaptation Action metamodel as input. The analysis builds upon a formalization of adaptation action execution semantics, which we introduced in this thesis. The formalization of execution semantics and their implementation address Research Question 10. We coupled the analysis with the existing SimuLizar analysis for self-adaptive software systems. We illustrated the application of adaptation action specifications by an architect in the specification of adaptation mechanisms, and outlined a process for the modeling of new adaptation actions.

We validated our contributions in a set of case studies. We structured the validation according to the GQM method. The validation showed that our architecture-level modeling and prediction approach produces accurate power and energy consumption predictions (RQ 3). The absolute prediction error was less than 5.5% for the two investigated enterprise applications across a variety of usage scenarios. The validation accuracy was high enough to qualitatively and quantitatively assess the effect of a design decision on energy efficiency (RQ 4). Four data center management scenarios illustrated the benefits of our power consumption modeling and prediction approach for self-adaptive software systems. Our approach predicted the total energy consumption with an error no higher than 7.08%, despite a set of limitations regarding the quality of input data.

We demonstrated the appropriateness of our Power Consumption metamodel in a comparison with state of the art modeling languages. Our metamodel offers a higher expressiveness and accuracy than state of the art architecture level energy consumption models. The Power Consumption metamodel supports a more flexible and lightweight specification of power models compared to the power modeling abstraction of Cloud simulators.

Three case studies showed a significant increase in prediction accuracy over the only existing state of the art architecture-level energy consumption modeling and prediction approach [35]. The use of modeling constructs with a higher expressiveness is optional. Software architects and system deployers can use a subset of the metamodel features, e.g., when simple linear power models are sufficiently accurate. The strict layering of the Power Consumption metamodel eases an iterative refinement of its instances. In later development stages, initial models based on expert estimates can be replaced with a description of the actual target deployment environment.

The validation applied our power model extraction method to a variety of Big Data and enterprise applications. Its model training produced power models with a high prediction accuracy. The power models were at least as accurate as state of the art for power models built solely using CPU utilization. Our approach produced significantly more accurate power models than state of the art when multiple system metrics were considered, e.g., CPU utilization, HDD read and write throughput. The AIC-based power model ranking was consistent with the ranking based on measured accuracy.

We validated our approach for considering transient effects using a horizontally scaling media hosting application. Our measurements demonstrated that the transient effects of the scale-out adaptation action had a large impact on user response times (RQ 8). The validation showed that the use of our approach for considering transient effects in design time quality analyses significantly improved the prediction accuracy for the investigated self-adaptive software system. The increased accuracy enabled us to identify a design deficiency that would have remained undetected. This confirmed Research Question 11 for the system under investigation.

Our Adaptation Action metamodel was employed in the CACTOS project to model the diverse set of adaptation actions supported by its autonomic data center resource management framework [115, 196]. This illustrated the applicability and appropriateness of the Adaptation Action metamodel to describe complex adaptation logic.

10.2. Benefits

The contributions of this thesis enable software architects to systematically consider energy efficiency in the design of static and self-adaptive software systems. The benefits of our approach are as follows.

Using our prediction approach, software architects can evaluate the impact of design decisions on energy efficiency from early design phases. The specification of power consumption characteristics with our approach only concerns the deployment environment. Component developers do not need to model the effect of service calls on energy consumption. Our approach avoids redundant behavior specifications by using an architecture level performance model as input to our prediction approach. This simplifies the adoption of energy efficiency as a quality concern in architectural design and analysis workflows.

We extended Simulizar to support the design and selection of energy-conscious adaptation mechanisms. Energy-conscious adaptation mechanisms dynamically adjust the state and amount of available servers to improve energy efficiency, while maintaining other quality goals. The simulation-based evaluation of adaptation mechanisms helps to avoid costly and time consuming experimentation in a real data center testbed.

The advantages of our approach extend beyond design time into system planning and operation. System operators and architects are able to evaluate the effect of adaptation mechanism selection and configuration on energy consumption, and trade-offs with other quality dimensions.

System deployers and operators can use our approach for infrastructure sizing decisions. This helps avoid the costly acquisition and operation of inefficient or oversized server and power distribution infrastructure. Deployment environment resource planning thereby can be founded on the requirements of the target system architecture and the expected workload mix. This goes beyond the state of the art, where resource planning relies on operator experience and rough estimates to plan the power distribution infrastructure.

Software architects and system deployers benefit from the high degree of automation of our power model extraction method. They can choose from a set of workload definitions and relevant system metrics to conduct server profiling. The server profiling is decoupled from power model learning. This enables the refinement of the power model used to describe the server consumption characteristics. System deployers can choose from a set of standard model learning techniques to construct power models for use in design time predictions, e.g., non-linear regression or Multivariate Adaptive Regression Splines (MARS). The proposed AIC-based model selection method relieves the users from a trial-and-error selection of a power model from a set of candidates.

Self-adaptive systems architects and engineers profit from the increased prediction accuracy, which results from our transient effects modeling and prediction approach. The consideration of transient effects enables architects to identify situations where the execution of superfluous adaptations reduces energy efficiency or performance, instead of increasing it. The design of our Adaptation Action metamodel promotes reuse of adaptation action specifications. Once an adaptation action has been specified, it can be reused in different self-adaptation mechanisms. The actions are composable by design. Software architects can integrate them into the adaptation execution logic of adaptation frameworks, e.g., S/T/A-based frameworks like Descartes. This eases the evaluation of adaptation frameworks and mechanisms at design time.

10.3. Assumptions and Limitations

This thesis discussed assumptions and limitations of the contributions in the respective sections. Section 3.3 outlined assumptions and limitations of our Power Consumption metamodel. Section 4.5 presented assumptions and limitations of our design time power consumption analysis approach. In Section 5.5 we discussed these concerns for the power model extraction method. Section 6.5 described assumptions and limitations of our modeling language and analysis for considering transient effects in design time quality analyses. This section summarizes the central assumptions and substantiates why we deem them reasonable.

Availability of architecture performance model. Our architecture-level power and energy consumption analysis relies on architecture performance models in combination with instances of the Power Consumption metamodel as input to its predictions. The consumption analysis leverages existing performance analyses to predict system level performance metrics, e.g., CPU utilization or HDD throughput. It derives its consumption predictions from these system metric predictions. The description of formal architecture performance models like PCM requires a higher modeling effort than informal architecture models, which purely document existing or planned components and their interfaces. According to Reussner et al. [170, p. 197], the effort for performance model construction is justified if there are high risks connected to the quality of the developed software system. This is the case if the uncertainty regarding the effect of design decisions on system quality is large, or if the system needs to meet SLAs.

While it would be possible to predict energy consumption in isolation of performance theoretically, we consider both qualities to be closely connected. The energy consumption of a software system usually can be minimized by using a minimal number of servers. Software architects interested in increasing energy efficiency have to ensure that the software architecture still satisfies performance requirements. We thus consider the availability of an architecture performance model not only to be a prerequisite for the application of our approach but also for meaningful architectural trade-offs between energy efficiency and performance.

Availability of server power consumption characteristics description or access to measurement infrastructure. Instances of our Power Consumption metamodel describe the consumption characteristics of software systems. Information on the consumption characteristics of the servers in a deployment environment need to be available in order to construct the instances. Our power model extraction method can be applied to construct server power models if the target deployment environment and power measurement infrastructure are available. The final deployment environment may not be available or fully known in early design phases. In this case, substitute power models from similar hardware can be used. It is possible to derive power models from the publicly available SPEC SERT results [68] if no power models of comparable servers are available [181]. The SERT results quantify server energy efficiency at different load levels. The substitute models can be refined as additional information on the deployment environment becomes available. We consider this assumption to have a weak effect on the applicability of our approach due to the variety of alternative methods by which the server consumption characteristics can be obtained.

Limited influence of hidden device states. The power consumption modeling and analysis approach presented in this thesis builds on the assumption that the power consumption of software systems correlates with a set of measurable system metrics. Example system metrics are CPU utilization or HDD throughput. The measurable system metrics can be insufficient to accurately predict the power consumption based on them. A common source of this shortcoming is the presence of hidden device states [135]. Hidden device states are power saving states which are not explicitly documented, and can not be monitored. An example of such hidden states is the proprietary DVFS mechanism Intel Turbo Boost [135]. Our modeling and analysis can be leveraged to model the behavior of DVFS mechanisms and other power management policies. We assume the central conditions of power management to be known.

The missing knowledge of proprietary power management mechanism behavior is a limitation that is not specific to our approach. We identified the reconstruction of power management behavior models as an area for future work. Section 10.4 discusses this in greater detail. Once a behavior model is available, it can be integrated into the system model using our PSM-based power models and the model-based analysis interfaces for energy-conscious adaptation mechanisms.

Transient effect model semantics based on DES. The model semantics of our Adaptation Action metamodel for describing the transient effects of adaptation actions are specific to DES-based software simulators. All existing architecture level quality analyses and Cloud simulators that support the analysis of transient phases, which we identified in our survey of related work, are based on DES. Section 8.6 provided an overview of the state of the art in this area. As our transient effect analysis approach is compatible with all existing analysis methods, we consider this a weak limitation.

10.4. Future Work

We have identified a number of areas and topics for future work in the scope of the work which led to this thesis.

Automated extraction of Adaptation Performance Models. Our Adaptation Action metamodel enables architects to consider transient effects in software quality analyses. This thesis presents a manual process for the modeling of adaptation actions. The software architect or adaptation middleware component developer has to provide a coupled description of the adaptation outcome and the performance effect of the adaptation execution. The adaptation outcome is described as a sequence of *AdaptationSteps* and embedded in-place model transformations. Its modeling is a straightforward task for the adaptation middleware developer. Conversely, the adaptation performance modeling requires in-depth knowledge of the interdependencies between adaptation action execution, system performance and current load. We manually constructed the Adaptation Performance Model for horizontal scaling in an IaaS Cloud, which we presented in the validation. Existing methods for automated load testing and performance model extraction could be applied to automate the Adaptation Performance Model construction and training for adaptation middleware components.

Predictive models for proprietary performance and power management mechanisms. Modern multi-core CPUs use integrated power and performance management mechanisms to offer different power-performance trade-offs. Intel Turbo Boost is a widespread example of this. It supports the temporary increase in performance of a subset of cores in exchange for higher power consumption. Our experimental evaluation of energy consumption during VM migration indicated that Turbo Boost has a significant impact on power consumption for workloads that heavily utilize a subset of cores. There is a gap in performance and power modeling techniques for multi-core CPUs that reflect proprietary power and performance mechanisms. The construction of descriptive models for these mechanisms is an interesting direction for future work. The use of unsupervised machine learning techniques, such as rule-based machine learning, could be a potential starting point. These techniques could be applied to construct an approximate model of proprietary performance and power management mechanisms.

Reduced power profiling measurement time. The server profiling method presented in this thesis supports the flexible definition of target system metric levels. By default, we used the combined domain of all considered system metrics to derive the profiling levels. The profiling effort increases exponentially with the number of profiled system metrics when this simple definition strategy is used. The profiling collects measurement data over a fixed measurement interval at each load level, even when the measurement values are stable. Adaptive measurement strategies could be developed to reduce the number of profiling runs and measurement time.

Evaluation of concepts for different domains. This thesis introduced a systematic approach for the energy efficiency evaluation of static and self-adaptive software systems. We focused on the energy efficiency of enterprise systems and data center environments. While we consider our modeling abstraction to be domain independent, its applicability to other domains has to be investigated in future work. Krach [114] applied an earlier version of our approach in the context of mobile computing. In the scope of the work by Krach we identified a set of necessary extensions to support accurate predictions in the mobile computing domain. These extensions include state-based power models and the consideration of power management mechanisms. A re-evaluation of the extended approach to the mobile computing domain is worthwhile. The evaluation of Cloud offloading decisions on the energy efficiency of the full system consisting of mobile device and Cloud backend would be an interesting extension to the evaluation scenario investigated by Krach.

Power consumption prediction of General-Purpose computing on Graphics Processing Units (GPGPU) is becoming increasingly relevant with the emerging adoption of blockchain and machine learning techniques in enterprise systems. Performance and energy efficiency of these techniques benefits massively from the use of GPGPU. Architecture-level performance modeling techniques are yet to incorporate GPGPUs with sufficient abstraction and accuracy [226]. Our power consumption modeling and analysis approach could be evaluated for systems involving GPGPU, once the challenges associated with GPGPU performance modeling have been tackled. The survey by Bridges et al. [32] can serve as a reference point for GPU power modeling techniques that could be incorporated into our approach.

Validation for large case study systems. Additional validation of our approach for large case study systems is desirable. The application to further systems could help identify potential areas for improvements of our approach, and aid in the identification of future research. As part of the work, the model extraction tooling could be refined, e.g., to support the automated extraction of PSM transition states that capture the power consumed during server boot-ups and shutdowns.

Integration with runtime prediction methods. Self-adaptive software systems adapt their structure and deployment, as well as functionality to meet quality requirements under changing environmental conditions. Approaches, e.g., Descartes [93], leverage architectural performance models to evaluate alternative adaptation tactics during runtime. Our modeling and power consumption prediction method could be integrated with a runtime adaptation approach. The integration would enable the approach to proactively evaluate the effect of adaptation tactics on energy efficiency. Aside from a potential cost reduction, the runtime prediction could be used as part of *data center demand response* [222]. Data center demand response enables a flexible management of data center load based on available total or renewable energy. Our approach could be used to predict the expected data center energy consumption for an expected load.

Acronyms

AC Alternating Current.

ACPI Advanced Configuration and Power Interface.

ADL Architecture Description Language.

AIC Akaike's Information Criterion.

ATL ATL Transformation Language.

CHAOS Composable Highly Accurate OS-based power models.

DC Direct Current.

DES Discrete Event Simulation.

DLIM Descartes Load Intensity Model.

DML Descartes Modeling Language.

DSL Domain Specific Language.

DVFS Dynamic Voltage and Frequency Scaling.

eco-cost ecological cost.

EDP2 Experiment Data Persistency & Presentation.

EE energy efficiency.

EMF Eclipse Modeling Framework.

EMOF Essential Meta-Object Facility.

ERP Enterprise Resource Planning.

EWMA exponentially moving weighted average.

FCFS first come, first served.

FSM Finite State Machine.

GPGPU General-Purpose computing on Graphics Processing Units.

GQM Goal Question Metric.

HDD Hard Disk Drive.

HPC High Performance Computing.

HRM Hardware Resource Modeling.

IaaS Infrastructure as a Service.

IPMI Intelligent Platform Management Interface.

IQR interquartile range.

KDE Kernel Density Estimation.

MAE Mean Absolute Error.

MAPE-K Monitor, Analyze, Plan, Execute, Knowledge.

MARS Multivariate Adaptive Regression Splines.

MVC Model-View-Controller.

PCA Power Consumption Analyzer.

PCM Palladio Component Model.

PDU Power Distribution Unit.

PET Performance counter Event Trigger.

PMX Performance Model eXtractor.

PRM Palladio Runtime Measurement Model.

PSM Power State Machine.

PSU Power Supply Unit.

PUE Power Usage Effectiveness.

QoS Quality of Service.

QuAL Quality Analysis Lab.

QVTo Operational QVT.

QVTr QVT Relations.

RDSEFF Resource-Demanding Service Effect Specification.

REST Representational State Transfer.

RQ Research Question.

RT response time.

S/T/A Strategies, Tactics, Action.

SAS Serial Attached SCSI.

SD Story Diagram.

SECoMo Software Eco-Cost Model.

SEFF Service Effect Specification.

SERT Server Efficiency Rating Tool.

SLA Service Level Agreement.

SMM Structured Metric Metamodel.

SPE Software Performance Engineering.

SPUE Server Power Usage Effectiveness.

StoEx Stochastic Expressions.

TCO Total Cost of Ownership.

UML Unified Modeling Language.

UPS Uninterruptible Power Systems.

UUID Universally Unique Identifier.

VCS Version Control System.

VM Virtual Machine.

Wh Watt hour.

A. Prediction Error per Power Model for Combined Profiling

Table A.1.: Prediction error per power model and workload type, errors in percent. Power models 1 and 2 trained on combined profiling measurements. Microbenchmarks, web search and clustering workloads.

Power Model	Params.	Metrics	Workload Type							
			Microbenchmarks					Web Search		Clustering
			Sort	Word Count	TeraSort	DFSIOe	Sleep	Page Rank	Nutch Indexing	K-means
1		u_{cpu}	13.6	10.8	9.8	10.0	24.4	9.8	8.4	10.7
		$u_{cpu}, u_{read}, u_{write}$	12.1	9.4	9.6	8.6	22.5	8.4	7.1	9.3
2		u_{cpu}	4.7	5.2	5.6	4.9	10.9	5.3	1.7	7.2
	$l = 3$	u_{cpu}, u_{read}	3.6	4.2	5.3	3.9	9.5	4.3	0.5	6.6
		u_{cpu}, u_{write}	3.3	3.7	5.0	3.5	8.8	3.9	0.5	5.5
		$u_{cpu}, u_{read}, u_{write}$	3.2	3.7	5.0	3.5	8.7	3.8	0.3	5.6
		u_{cpu}	5.5	5.6	5.8	5.4	12.4	5.5	2.3	7.3
	$l = 2$	u_{cpu}, u_{read}	4.8	4.9	5.7	4.7	11.5	4.8	1.5	6.8
		u_{cpu}, u_{write}	4.5	4.5	5.4	4.4	11.0	4.4	1.4	6.0
		$u_{cpu}, u_{read}, u_{write}$	4.4	4.4	5.5	4.3	10.9	4.3	1.3	6.0

Table A.2.: Prediction error per power model and workload type, errors in percent. Power models 1 and 2 trained on combined profiling measurements. Analytical and server workloads.

Power Model	Params.	Metrics	Workload Type: Analytical Queries: Join	Workload Type: Analytical Queries: Aggre-gation	Workload Type: Analytical Queries: Scan	Workload Type: Server: SPECjbb-2015
1		u_{cpu}	13.1	13.5	13.4	11.5
		$u_{cpu}, u_{read}, u_{write}$	11.5	12.0	11.9	10.1
2	$l = 3$	u_{cpu}	4.3	4.6	4.0	9.3
		u_{cpu}, u_{read}	3.2	3.6	2.9	8.5
		u_{cpu}, u_{write}	2.8	3.0	2.5	8.1
		$u_{cpu}, u_{read}, u_{write}$	2.7	3.0	2.4	8.0
	$l = 2$	u_{cpu}	4.9	5.4	4.9	9.1
		u_{cpu}, u_{read}	4.1	4.7	4.1	8.5
		u_{cpu}, u_{write}	3.7	4.3	3.8	8.0
		$u_{cpu}, u_{read}, u_{write}$	3.7	4.2	3.7	7.9

Table A.3.: Prediction error per power model and workload type, errors in percent. Power models 3–6 trained on combined profiling measurements. Microbenchmarks, web search and clustering (Clust.) workloads.

Power Model	Params.	Metrics	Workload Type							
			Microbenchmarks					Web Search		Clust.
			Sort	Word Count	TeraSort	DFSIOe	Sleep	Page Rank	Nutch Indexing	K-means
		u_{cpu}	4.8	5.2	5.6	4.9	11.0	5.3	1.7	7.2
	$l = 3$	u_{cpu}, u_{read}	3.6	4.2	5.3	3.9	9.6	4.3	0.5	6.6
		u_{cpu}, u_{write}	4.7	5.2	5.6	4.9	11.0	5.3	1.7	7.2
		$u_{cpu}, u_{read}, u_{write}$	3.6	4.2	5.3	3.9	9.5	4.3	0.5	6.6
		u_{cpu}	5.3	5.5	5.8	5.3	12.0	5.5	2.1	7.3
3	$l = 2$	u_{cpu}, u_{read}	4.5	4.8	5.6	4.6	11.1	4.7	1.3	6.8
		u_{cpu}, u_{write}	5.3	5.6	5.8	5.3	12.0	5.5	2.1	7.3
		$u_{cpu}, u_{read}, u_{write}$	4.5	4.8	5.7	4.5	11.1	4.7	1.3	6.8
		u_{cpu}	16.5	12.8	11.4	11.7	28.6	11.5	10.6	12.1
	$l = 1$	u_{cpu}, u_{read}	15.9	12.3	11.4	11.2	27.9	11.0	10.0	11.8
		u_{cpu}, u_{write}	16.5	12.8	11.4	11.7	28.6	11.5	10.6	12.1
		$u_{cpu}, u_{read}, u_{write}$	15.9	12.3	11.4	11.2	27.9	11.0	10.0	11.8
4		u_{cpu}	7.5	6.7	6.5	6.6	15.8	6.2	3.8	7.9
5		u_{cpu}	1.9	4.3	5.6	3.3	2.2	5.5	0.3	7.5
6		u_{cpu}	2.5	5.0	6.3	3.9	0.6	6.4	1.3	8.2

Table A.4.: Prediction error per power model and workload type, errors in percent. Power models 3–6 trained on combined profiling measurements. Analytical and server workloads.

Power Model	Params.	Metrics	Workload Type			
			Analytical Queries			Server
			Join	Aggregation	Scan	SPECjbb-2015
3	$l = 3$	u_{cpu}	4.3	4.6	4.1	9.3
		u_{cpu}, u_{read}	3.2	3.6	2.9	8.5
		u_{cpu}, u_{write}	4.3	4.6	4.0	9.4
		$u_{cpu}, u_{read}, u_{write}$	3.2	3.6	2.8	8.6
	$l = 2$	u_{cpu}	4.7	5.3	4.7	9.2
		u_{cpu}, u_{read}	4.0	4.5	3.9	8.6
		u_{cpu}, u_{write}	4.7	5.3	4.7	9.2
		$u_{cpu}, u_{read}, u_{write}$	4.0	4.5	3.9	8.6
	$l = 1$	u_{cpu}	16.0	16.4	16.5	12.2
		u_{cpu}, u_{read}	15.4	15.8	15.9	11.7
		u_{cpu}, u_{write}	16.0	16.4	16.5	12.3
		$u_{cpu}, u_{read}, u_{write}$	15.4	15.8	15.9	11.7
4		u_{cpu}	6.5	7.4	7.0	8.8
5		u_{cpu}	1.9	1.7	0.9	9.7
6		u_{cpu}	2.6	2.3	1.5	10.1

B. Bibliography

[1] S. Akoush, R. Sohan, A Rice, AW. Moore, and A Hopper. "Predicting the Performance of Virtual Machine Migration". In: *Modeling, Analysis Simulation of Computer and Telecommunication Systems (MASCOTS), 2010 IEEE International Symposium on.* Aug. 2010, pp. 37–46. DOI: 10.1109/MASCOTS.2010.13.

[2] M.M. Alansari and B. Bordbar. "Modelling and Analysis of Migration Policies for Autonomic Management of Energy Consumption in Cloud via Petri-Nets". In: *Cloud and Autonomic Computing (ICCAC), 2014 International Conference on.* Sept. 2014, pp. 121–130. DOI: 10.1109/ICCAC.2014.7.

[3] P. Alonso, R. M. Badia, J. Labarta, M. Barreda, M. F. Dolz, R. Mayo, E. S. Quintana-Ortí, and R. Reyes. "Tools for Power-Energy Modelling and Analysis of Parallel Scientific Applications". In: *2012 41st International Conference on Parallel Processing.* Sept. 2012, pp. 420–429. DOI: 10.1109/ICPP.2012.57.

[4] *Apache HBase.* Last retrieved 2017-08-11. The Apache Software Foundation. URL: https://hbase.apache.org/.

[5] Varsha Apte and Bhavin Doshi. "PowerPerfCenter: A Power and Performance Prediction Tool for Multi-tier Applications". In: *Proceedings of the 5th ACM/SPEC International Conference on Performance Engineering.* ICPE '14. Dublin, Ireland: ACM, 2014, pp. 281–284. ISBN: 978-1-4503-2733-6. DOI: 10.1145/2568088.2576758. URL: http://doi.acm.org/10.1145/2568088.2576758.

[6] Thorsten Arendt, Enrico Biermann, Stefan Jurack, Christian Krause, and Gabriele Taentzer. "Henshin: Advanced Concepts and Tools for In-Place EMF Model Transformations". In: *Model Driven Engineering Languages and Systems: 13th International Conference, MODELS 2010, Oslo, Norway, October 3-8, 2010, Proceedings, Part I.* Ed. by Dorina C. Petriu, Nicolas Rouquette, and Øystein Haugen. Berlin, Heidelberg: Springer Berlin Heidelberg, 2010, pp. 121–135. ISBN: 978-3-642-16145-2. DOI: 10.1007/978-3-642-16145-2_9. URL: http://dx.doi.org/10.1007/978-3-642-16145-2_9.

[7] Sylvain Arlot and Alain Celisse. "A survey of cross-validation procedures for model selection". In: *Statist. Surv.* 4 (2010), pp. 40–79. DOI: 10.1214/09-SS054. URL: http://dx.doi.org/10.1214/09-SS054.

[8] Patricia Arroba, José L. Risco-Martín, Marina Zapater, José M. Moya, and José L. Ayala. "Enhancing Regression Models for Complex Systems Using Evolutionary Techniques for Feature Engineering". In: *Journal of Grid Computing* 13.3 (2015), pp. 409–423. ISSN: 1572-9184. DOI: 10.1007/s10723-014-9313-8. URL: http://dx.doi.org/10.1007/s10723-014-9313-8.

[9] C. Atkinson and T. Kuhne. "Model-driven development: a metamodeling foundation". In: *IEEE Software* 20.5 (Sept. 2003), pp. 36–41. ISSN: 0740-7459. DOI: 10.1109/MS.2003.1231149.

[10] C. Atkinson and T. Schulze. "Towards application-specific impact specifications and GreenSLAs". In: *2013 2nd International Workshop on Green and Sustainable Software (GREENS).* May 2013, pp. 54–61. DOI: 10.1109/GREENS.2013.6606422.

[11] Colin Atkinson, Joachim Bayer, and Dirk Muthig. "Component-Based Product Line Development: The KobrA Approach". In: *Software Product Lines: Experience and Research Directions.* Ed. by Patrick Donohoe. Boston, MA: Springer US, 2000, pp. 289–309. ISBN: 978-1-4615-4339-8. DOI: 10.1007/978-1-4615-4339-8_16. URL: https://doi.org/10.1007/978-1-4615-4339-8_16.

[12] Sławomir Bąk, Marcin Krystek, Krzysztof Kurowski, Ariel Oleksiak, Wojciech Piątek, and Jan Węglarz. "GSSIM – A Tool for Distributed Computing Experiments". In: *Sci. Program.* 19.4 (Oct. 2011), pp. 231–251. ISSN: 1058-9244. URL: http://dl.acm.org/citation.cfm?id=2590384.2590388.

[13] Luiz André Barroso, Jimmy Clidaras, and Urs Hölzle. *The Datacenter as a Computer: An Introduction to the Design of Warehouse-Scale Machines, Second Edition.* Synthesis Lectures on Computer Architecture. Morgan & Claypool Publishers, 2013, pp. 1–154. ISBN: 9781627050104.

[14] Luiz Andre Barroso and Urs Holzle. "The Case for Energy-Proportional Computing". In: *Computer* 40.12 (2007), pp. 33–37. ISSN: 0018-9162. DOI: http://doi.ieeecomputersociety.org/10.1109/MC.2007.443.

[15] Victor R. Basili, Gianluigi Caldiera, and H. Dieter Rombach. "The Goal Question Metric Approach". In: *Encyclopedia of Software Engineering.* Wiley, 1994.

[16] Robert Basmadjian, Nasir Ali, Florian Niedermeier, Hermann de Meer, and Giovanni Giuliani. "A Methodology to Predict the Power Consumption of Servers in Data Centres". In: *Proceedings of the 2Nd International Conference on Energy-Efficient Computing and Networking.* e-Energy '11. New York, New York: ACM, 2011, pp. 1–10. ISBN: 978-1-4503-1313-1. DOI: 10.1145/2318716.2318718. URL: http://doi.acm.org/10.1145/2318716.2318718.

[17] Matthias Wilhelm Becker. "Engineering Self-adaptive Systems with Simulation-Based Performance Prediction". PhD thesis. Paderborn: Universität Paderborn, 2017.

[18] Matthias Becker, Steffen Becker, and Joachim Meyer. "SimuLizar: Design-Time Modelling and Performance Analysis of Self-Adaptive Systems". In: *Proceedings of Software Engineering 2013.* SE2013. Aachen, Feb. 2013.

[19] Matthias Becker, Sebastian Lehrig, and Steffen Becker. "Systematically Deriving Quality Metrics for Cloud Computing Systems". In: *Proceedings of the 6th ACM/SPEC International Conference on Performance Engineering (ICPE 2015).* Accepted for publication. ACM, 2015.

[20] Matthias Becker, Markus Luckey, and Steffen Becker. "Performance Analysis of Self-Adaptive Systems for Requirements Validation at Design-Time". In: *Proceedings of the 9th ACM SigSoft International Conference on Quality of Software Architectures (QoSA'13).* ACM, June 2013.

[21] Steffen Becker. "Coupled Model Transformations for QoS Enabled Component-Based Software Design". PhD thesis. University of Oldenburg, Germany, 2008.

[22] Steffen Becker, Heiko Koziolek, and Ralf Reussner. "The Palladio component model for model-driven performance prediction". In: *Journal of Systems and Software* 82.1 (2009). Special Issue: Software Performance - Modeling and Analysis, pp. 3–22. ISSN: 0164-1212. DOI: http://dx.doi.org/10.1016/j.jss.2008.03.066. URL: http://www.sciencedirect.com/science/article/pii/S0164121208001015.

[23] Frank Bellosa. "The Benefits of Event-Driven Energy Accounting in Power-Sensitive Systems". In: *Proceedings of the 9th Workshop on ACM SIGOPS European Workshop: Beyond the PC: New Challenges for the Operating System.* EW 9. Kolding, Denmark: ACM, 2000, pp. 37–42. DOI: 10.1145/566726.566736. URL: http://doi.acm.org/10.1145/566726.566736.

[24] Anton Beloglazov. "Energy-Efficient Management of Virtual Machines in Data Centers for Cloud Computing". PhD thesis. The University of Melbourne, 2013.

[25] Anton Beloglazov, Rajkumar Buyya, Young Choon Lee, and Albert Y. Zomaya. "A Taxonomy and Survey of Energy-Efficient Data Centers and Cloud Computing Systems". In: *Advances in Computers* 82 (2011), pp. 47–111.

[26] Luca Benini, Robin Hodgson, and Polly Siegel. "System-level Power Estimation and Optimization". In: *Proceedings of the 1998 International Symposium on Low Power Electronics and Design.* ISLPED '98. Monterey, California, USA: ACM, 1998, pp. 173–178. ISBN: 1-58113-059-7. DOI: 10.1145/280756.280881. URL: http://doi.acm.org/10.1145/280756.280881.

[27] Luca Benini and Giovanni de Micheli. "System-level Power Optimization: Techniques and Tools". In: *ACM Trans. Des. Autom. Electron. Syst.* 5.2 (Apr. 2000), pp. 115–192. ISSN: 1084-4309. DOI: 10.1145/335043.335044. URL: http://doi.acm.org/10.1145/335043.335044.

[28] W.L. Bircher and L.K. John. "Complete System Power Estimation Using Processor Performance Events". In: *Computers, IEEE Transactions on* 61.4 (Apr. 2012), pp. 563–577. ISSN: 0018-9340. DOI: 10.1109/TC.2011.47.

[29] Hansfried Block, Jeremy A. Arnold, John Beckett, Sanjay Sharma, Mike G. Tricker, and Kyle M. Rogers. "Server Efficiency Rating Tool (SERT) 1.0.2: An Overview". In: *Proceedings of the 5th ACM/SPEC International Conference on Performance Engineering*. ICPE '14. Dublin, Ireland: ACM, 2014, pp. 229–230.

[30] Rainer Böhme and Ralf Reussner. "Validation of Predictions with Measurements". In: *Dependability Metrics: Advanced Lectures*. Ed. by Irene Eusgeld, Felix C. Freiling, and Ralf Reussner. Berlin, Heidelberg: Springer Berlin Heidelberg, 2008, pp. 14–18. ISBN: 978-3-540-68947-8. DOI: 10.1007/978-3-540-68947-8_3. URL: http://dx.doi.org/10.1007/978-3-540-68947-8_3.

[31] G. Brataas, E. Stav, and S. Lehrig. "Analysing Evolution of Work and Load". In: *2016 12th International ACM SIGSOFT Conference on Quality of Software Architectures (QoSA)*. Apr. 2016, pp. 90–95. DOI: 10.1109/QoSA.2016.18.

[32] Robert A. Bridges, Neena Imam, and Tiffany M. Mintz. "Understanding GPU Power: A Survey of Profiling, Modeling, and Simulation Methods". In: *ACM Comput. Surv.* 49.3 (Sept. 2016), 41:1–41:27. ISSN: 0360-0300. DOI: 10.1145/2962131. URL: http://doi.acm.org/10.1145/2962131.

[33] Franz Brosch, Barbora Buhnova, Heiko Koziolek, and Ralf Reussner. "Reliability Prediction for Fault-tolerant Software Architectures". In: *Proceedings of the Joint ACM SIGSOFT Conference – QoSA and ACM SIGSOFT Symposium – ISARCS on Quality of Software Architectures – QoSA and Architecting Critical Systems – ISARCS*. QoSA-ISARCS '11. Boulder, Colorado, USA: ACM, 2011, pp. 75–84. ISBN: 978-1-4503-0724-6. DOI: 10.1145/2000259.2000274. URL: http://doi.acm.org/10.1145/2000259.2000274.

[34] Fabian Brosig, Philipp Meier, Steffen Becker, Anne Koziolek, Heiko Koziolek, and Samuel Kounev. "Quantitative Evaluation of Model-Driven Performance Analysis and Simulation of Component-based Architectures". In: *Software Engineering, IEEE Transactions on* 41.2 (Feb. 2015), pp. 157–175. ISSN: 0098-5589. DOI: 10.1109/TSE.2014.2362755.

[35] Andreas Brunnert, Kilian Wischer, and Helmut Krcmar. "Using Architecture-level Performance Models As Resource Profiles for Enterprise Applications". In: *Proceedings of the 10th International ACM Sigsoft Conference on Quality of Software Architectures.* QoSA '14. Marcq-en-Bareul, France: ACM, 2014, pp. 53–62. ISBN: 978-1-4503-2576-9. DOI: 10.1145/2602576.2602587. URL: http://doi.acm.org/10.1145/2602576.2602587.

[36] Frank Brüseke, Henning Wachsmuth, Gregor Engels, and Steffen Becker. "PBlaman: Performance Blame Analysis Based on Palladio Contracts". In: *Concurr. Comput. : Pract. Exper.* 26.12 (Aug. 2014), pp. 1975–2004. ISSN: 1532-0626. DOI: 10.1002/cpe.3226. URL: http://dx.doi.org/10.1002/cpe.3226.

[37] Barrett R Bryant, Jeff Gray, Marjan Mernik, Peter J Clarke, Robert B France, and Gabor Karsai. "Challenges and directions in formalizing the semantics of modeling languages". In: *Computer Science and Information Systems* 8.2 (2011), pp. 225–253.

[38] Christian Bunse and Hans-Gerhard Gross. "Unifying Hardware and Software Components for Embedded System Development". In: *Architecting Systems with Trustworthy Components.* Ed. by Ralf H. Reussner, Judith A. Stafford, and Clemens A. Szyperski. Berlin, Heidelberg: Springer Berlin Heidelberg, 2006, pp. 120–136. ISBN: 978-3-540-35833-6.

[39] Christian Bunse and Hagen Höpfner. "RESOURCE SUBSTITUTION WITH COMPONENTS - Optimizing Energy Consumption". In: *Proceedings of the Third International Conference on Software and Data Technologies - Volume 2: ICSOFT,* INSTICC. SciTePress, 2008, pp. 28–35. ISBN: 978-989-8111-52-4. DOI: 10.5220/0001879000280035.

[40] Christian Bunse, Hagen Höpfner, Suman Roychoudhury, and Essam Mansour. "CHOOSING THE "BEST" SORTING ALGORITHM FOR OPTIMAL ENERGY CONSUMPTION". In: *Proceedings of the 4th International Conference on Software and Data Technologies - Volume 2: ICSOFT,* INSTICC. SciTePress, 2009, pp. 199–206. ISBN: 978-989-674-010-8. DOI: 10.5220/0002245401990206.

[41] T. Bures, P. Hnetynka, and F. Plasil. "SOFA 2.0: Balancing Advanced Features in a Hierarchical Component Model". In: *Software Engineer-*

ing Research, Management and Applications, 2006. Fourth International Conference on. Aug. 2006, pp. 40–48. DOI: 10.1109/SERA.2006.62.

[42] K. P. Burnham and D. R. Anderson. *Model Selection and Multimodel Inference: A Practical Information-Theoretic Approach.* 2nd ed. New York: Springer-Verlag, 2002.

[43] James Byrne, Sergej Svorobej, Gabriel González Castañé, Christian Stier, Sebastian Krach, Ahmed Ali-Eldin, Jakub Krzywda, and Peter J. Byrne. *Final results from optimisation models validation and experimentation: project deliverable D6.5.* Tech. rep. 2017. DOI: 10.18725/oparu-4312. URL: https://oparu.uni-ulm.de/xmlui/handle/123456789/4351.

[44] CACTOS Consortium. *CACTOS Infrastructure Models.* GitHub Repository. 2017. URL: https://github.com/cactos/Cactos-Basics/tree/master/Infrastructure-Models (visited on 08/11/2017).

[45] Rodrigo N. Calheiros, Rajiv Ranjan, Anton Beloglazov, César A. F. De Rose, and Rajkumar Buyya. "CloudSim: A Toolkit for Modeling and Simulation of Cloud Computing Environments and Evaluation of Resource Provisioning Algorithms". In: *Softw. Pract. Exper.* 41.1 (Jan. 2011), pp. 23–50. ISSN: 0038-0644. DOI: 10.1002/spe.995. URL: http://dx.doi.org/10.1002/spe.995.

[46] Javier Cámara, Gabriel A. Moreno, David Garlan, and Bradley Schmerl. "Analyzing Latency-aware Self-adaptation using Stochastic Games and Simulations". In: *ACM Transactions on Autonomous and Adaptive Systems* (2015). To Appear.

[47] Eugenio Capra, Chiara Francalanci, and Sandra A. Slaughter. "Is software "green"? Application development environments and energy efficiency in open source applications". In: *Information and Software Technology* 54.1 (2012), pp. 60–71. ISSN: 0950-5849. DOI: http://dx.doi.org/10.1016/j.infsof.2011.07.005. URL: http://www.sciencedirect.com/science/article/pii/S0950584911001777.

[48] Gabriel G. Castañé, Alberto Núñez, Pablo Llopis, and Jesús Carretero. "E-mc2: A formal framework for energy modelling in cloud computing". In: *Simulation Modelling Practice and Theory* 39.Supplement C (2013). Special Issue on Energy efficiency in grids and clouds, pp. 56–75. ISSN: 1569-190X. DOI: https://doi.org/10.1016/j.simpat.2013.

05.002. URL: http://www.sciencedirect.com/science/article/pii/S1569190X13000816.

[49] Hao Chen, Can Hankendi, Michael C. Caramanis, and Ayse K. Coskun. "Dynamic Server Power Capping for Enabling Data Center Participation in Power Markets". In: *Proceedings of the International Conference on Computer-Aided Design*. ICCAD '13. San Jose, California: IEEE Press, 2013, pp. 122–129. ISBN: 978-1-4799-1069-4. URL: http://dl.acm.org/citation.cfm?id=2561828.2561853.

[50] Tse-Hsun Chen, Weiyi Shang, Zhen Ming Jiang, Ahmed E. Hassan, Mohamed Nasser, and Parminder Flora. "Detecting Performance Anti-patterns for Applications Developed Using Object-relational Mapping". In: *Proceedings of the 36th International Conference on Software Engineering*. ICSE 2014. Hyderabad, India: ACM, 2014, pp. 1001–1012. ISBN: 978-1-4503-2756-5. DOI: 10.1145/2568225.2568259. URL: http://doi.acm.org/10.1145/2568225.2568259.

[51] Shang-Wen Cheng and David Garlan. "Stitch: A language for architecture-based self-adaptation". In: *Journal of Systems and Software* 12 (2012). Self-Adaptive Systems, pp. 2860–2875. ISSN: 0164-1212. DOI: http://dx.doi.org/10.1016/j.jss.2012.02.060. URL: http://www.sciencedirect.com/science/article/pii/S0164121212000714.

[52] Shaiful Alam Chowdhury and Abram Hindle. "GreenOracle: Estimating Software Energy Consumption with Energy Measurement Corpora". In: *Proceedings of the 13th International Conference on Mining Software Repositories*. MSR '16. Austin, Texas: ACM, 2016, pp. 49–60. ISBN: 978-1-4503-4186-8. DOI: 10.1145/2901739.2901763. URL: http://doi.acm.org/10.1145/2901739.2901763.

[53] Eric Clayberg and Dan Rubel. *Eclipse Plug-ins*. Third Edition. Pearson Education, 2008. ISBN: 0-321-55346-2.

[54] Paul Clements and Linda Northrop. *Software Architecture: An Executive Overview*. Tech. rep. CMU/SEI-96-TR-003. Pittsburgh, PA: Software Engineering Institute, Carnegie Mellon University, 1996. URL: http://resources.sei.cmu.edu/library/asset-view.cfm?AssetID=12509.

[55] Gregory W. Corder and Dale I. Foreman. *Nonparametric Statistics for Non-Statisticians*. John Wiley & Sons, Inc., May 2009. DOI: 10.1002/9781118165881. URL: https://doi.org/10.1002/9781118165881.

[56] *Data Center Tradeoff Tools.* Last retrieved 2017-11-03. Schneider Electric. URL: https://www.schneider-electric.com/b2b/en/solutions/system/s2/data-centers-networks-trade-off-tools.jsp.

[57] John D. Davis, Suzanne Rivoire, and Moises Goldszmidt. "Star-Cap: Cluster Power Management Using Software-Only Models". In: *2014 43rd International Conference on Parallel Processing Workshops.* Sept. 2014, pp. 114–120. DOI: 10.1109/ICPPW.2014.27.

[58] John D. Davis, Suzanne Rivoire, Moises Goldszmidt, and Ehsan K. Ardestani. "CHAOS: Composable Highly Accurate OS-based Power Models". In: *Proceedings of the 2012 IEEE International Symposium on Workload Characterization (IISWC).* IISWC '12. Washington, DC, USA: IEEE Computer Society, 2012, pp. 153–163. ISBN: 978-1-4673-4531-6. DOI: 10.1109/IISWC.2012.6402920. URL: http://dx.doi.org/10.1109/IISWC.2012.6402920.

[59] M. Dayarathna, Y. Wen, and R. Fan. "Data Center Energy Consumption Modeling: A Survey". In: *IEEE Communications Surveys Tutorials* 18.1 (2016), pp. 732–794. ISSN: 1553-877X. DOI: 10.1109/COMST.2015.2481183.

[60] Markus von Detten, Christian Heinzemann, Marie Christin Platenius, Jan Rieke, Dietrich Travkin, and Stephan Hildebrandt. *Story Diagrams - Syntax and Semantics.* Tech. rep. tr-ri-12-324. Version 0.2. Software Engineering Group, Heinz Nixdorf Institute, University of Paderborn, July 2012.

[61] Gaurav Dhiman, Giacomo Marchetti, and Tajana Rosing. "vGreen: A System for Energy-Efficient Management of Virtual Machines". In: *ACM Trans. Des. Autom. Electron. Syst.* 16.1 (Nov. 2010), 6:1–6:27. ISSN: 1084-4309. DOI: 10.1145/1870109.1870115. URL: http://doi.acm.org/10.1145/1870109.1870115.

[62] J. Doweck, W. F. Kao, A. K. y. Lu, J. Mandelblat, A. Rahatekar, L. Rappoport, E. Rotem, A. Yasin, and A. Yoaz. "Inside 6th-Generation Intel Core: New Microarchitecture Code-Named Skylake". In: *IEEE Micro* 37.2 (Mar. 2017), pp. 52–62. ISSN: 0272-1732. DOI: 10.1109/MM.2017.38.

[63] Corentin Dupont, Thomas Schulze, Giovanni Giuliani, Andrey Somov, and Fabien Hermenier. "An Energy Aware Framework for Virtual Machine Placement in Cloud Federated Data Centres". In: *Proceedings of the 3rd International Conference on Future Energy Systems: Where Energy, Computing and Communication Meet.* e-Energy '12. Madrid, Spain: ACM, 2012, 4:1–4:10. ISBN: 978-1-4503-1055-0. DOI: 10.1145/2208828.2208832. URL: http://doi.acm.org/10.1145/2208828.2208832.

[64] Zoya Durdik. "Architectural design decision documentation through reuse of design patterns". PhD thesis. Karlsruhe: Karlsruher Institut für Technologie, 2016. ISBN: 978-3-7315-0292-0. URL: http://dx.doi.org/10.5445/KSP/1000043807.

[65] Dimitris Economou, Suzanne Rivoire, Christos Kozyrakis, and Partha Ranganathan. "Full-System Power Analysis and Modeling for Server Environments". In: *Workshop on Modeling Benchmarking and Simulation (MOBS).* 2006.

[66] P. Efros, E. Buchmann, and K. Böhm. "FRESCO: A Framework to Estimate the Energy Consumption of Computers". In: *2014 IEEE 16th Conference on Business Informatics.* Vol. 1. July 2014, pp. 199–206. DOI: 10.1109/CBI.2014.28.

[67] Timur V. Elzhov, Katharine M. Mullen, Andrej-Nikolai Spiess, and Ben Bolker. *minpack.lm: R Interface to the Levenberg-Marquardt Nonlinear Least-Squares Algorithm Found in MINPACK, Plus Support for Bounds.* R package version 0.4-1. 2016. URL: https://cran.r-project.org/package=minpack.lm.

[68] ENERGY STAR. *ENERGY STAR Certified Enterprise Servers - CSV Datasheet.* Feb. 2017. URL: https://www.energystar.gov/productfinder/download/certified-enterprise-servers/ (visited on 02/02/2017).

[69] Xiaobo Fan, Wolf-Dietrich Weber, and Luiz Andre Barroso. "Power Provisioning for a Warehouse-sized Computer". In: *SIGARCH Computer Architecture News* 35.2 (June 2007), pp. 13–23. ISSN: 0163-5964. DOI: 10.1145/1273440.1250665. URL: http://doi.acm.org/10.1145/1273440.1250665.

[70] Oliver Flasch, Olaf Mersmann, Thomas Bartz-Beielstein, Joerg Stork, and Martin Zaefferer. *rgp: R genetic programming framework.* R package version 0.4-1. 2014. URL: https://cran.r-project.org/package=rgp.

[71] Jerome H. Friedman. "Multivariate Adaptive Regression Splines". In: *Ann. Statist.* 19.1 (Mar. 1991), pp. 1–67. DOI: 10.1214/aos/1176347963. URL: http://dx.doi.org/10.1214/aos/1176347963.

[72] R. Ge, X. Feng, S. Song, H. C. Chang, D. Li, and K. W. Cameron. "PowerPack: Energy Profiling and Analysis of High-Performance Systems and Applications". In: *IEEE Transactions on Parallel and Distributed Systems* 21.5 (May 2010), pp. 658–671. ISSN: 1045-9219. DOI: 10.1109/TPDS.2009.76.

[73] Michel Goraczko, Jie Liu, Dimitrios Lymberopoulos, Slobodan Matic, Bodhi Priyantha, and Feng Zhao. "Energy-optimal Software Partitioning in Heterogeneous Multiprocessor Embedded Systems". In: *Proceedings of the 45th Annual Design Automation Conference.* DAC '08. Anaheim, California: ACM, 2008, pp. 191–196. ISBN: 978-1-60558-115-6. DOI: 10.1145/1391469.1391518. URL: http://doi.acm.org/10.1145/1391469.1391518.

[74] Marion Gottschalk, Jan Jelschen, and Andreas Winter. "Refactorings for Energy-Efficiency". In: *Advances and New Trends in Environmental and Energy Informatics: Selected and Extended Contributions from the 28th International Conference on Informatics for Environmental Protection.* Ed. by Jorge Marx Gomez, Michael Sonnenschein, Ute Vogel, Andreas Winter, Barbara Rapp, and Nils Giesen. Cham: Springer International Publishing, 2016, pp. 77–96. ISBN: 978-3-319-23455-7. DOI: 10.1007/978-3-319-23455-7_5. URL: https://doi.org/10.1007/978-3-319-23455-7_5.

[75] Sebastian Götz. "Multi-Quality Auto-Tuning by Contract Negotiation". PhD thesis. Dresden, Germany: Technische Universität Dresden, Feb. 2013.

[76] Sriram Govindan, Di Wang, Anand Sivasubramaniam, and Bhuvan Urgaonkar. "Leveraging Stored Energy for Handling Power Emergencies in Aggressively Provisioned Datacenters". In: *SIGPLAN Not.* 47.4 (Mar. 2012), pp. 75–86. ISSN: 0362-1340. DOI: 10.1145/2248487.2150985. URL: http://doi.acm.org/10.1145/2248487.2150985.

[77] Vincenzo Grassi, Raffaela Mirandola, and Antonino Sabetta. "A Model-driven Approach to Performability Analysis of Dynamically Reconfigurable Component-based Systems". In: *Proceedings of the 6th International Workshop on Software and Performance*. WOSP '07. Buenes Aires, Argentina: ACM, 2007, pp. 103–114. ISBN: 1-59593-297-6. DOI: 10.1145/1216993.1217011.

[78] Vincenzo Grassi, Raffaela Mirandola, and Antonino Sabetta. "From Design to Analysis Models: A Kernel Language for Performance and Reliability Analysis of Component-based Systems". In: *Proceedings of the 5th International Workshop on Software and Performance*. WOSP '05. Palma, Illes Balears, Spain: ACM, 2005, pp. 25–36. ISBN: 1-59593-087-6. DOI: 10.1145/1071021.1071024. URL: http://doi.acm.org/10.1145/1071021.1071024.

[79] Henning Groenda, Christian Stier, Jakub Krzywda, James Byrne, Sergej Svorobej, Zafeirios Papazachos, Craig Sheridan, Darren Whigham, and Per-Olov Östberg. *Model integration method and supporting tooling: project deliverable D5.1*. Tech. rep. Universität Ulm, 2017. DOI: 10.18725/oparu-4317. URL: https://oparu.uni-ulm.de/xmlui/handle/123456789/4356.

[80] Jens Happe, Steffen Becker, Christoph Rathfelder, Holger Friedrich, and Ralf H. Reussner. "Parametric performance completions for model-driven performance prediction". In: *Performance Evaluation* 67.8 (2010). Special Issue on Software and Performance, pp. 694–716. ISSN: 0166-5316. DOI: http://dx.doi.org/10.1016/j.peva.2009.07.006. URL: http://www.sciencedirect.com/science/article/pii/S0166531609000996.

[81] S. Hasan, Z. King, M. Hafiz, M. Sayagh, B. Adams, and A. Hindle. "Energy Profiles of Java Collections Classes". In: *2016 IEEE/ACM 38th International Conference on Software Engineering (ICSE)*. May 2016, pp. 225–236. DOI: 10.1145/2884781.2884869.

[82] Taliver Heath, Bruno Diniz, Enrique V. Carrera, Wagner Meira Jr., and Ricardo Bianchini. "Energy Conservation in Heterogeneous Server Clusters". In: *Proceedings of the Tenth ACM SIGPLAN Symposium on Principles and Practice of Parallel Programming*. PPoPP '05. Chicago, IL, USA: ACM, 2005, pp. 186–195. ISBN: 1-59593-080-9.

[83] Christoph Heger. “An Approach for Guiding Developers to Performance and Scalability Solutions”. PhD thesis. Karlsruher Institut für Technologie, 2015. URL: http://digbib.ubka.uni-karlsruhe.de/volltexte/1000048535.

[84] Nikolas Roman Herbst, Samuel Kounev, and Ralf Reussner. “Elasticity in Cloud Computing: What It Is, and What It Is Not”. In: *Proceedings of the 10th International Conference on Autonomic Computing (ICAC 13).* San Jose, CA: USENIX, 2013, pp. 23–27. ISBN: 978-1-931971-02-7. URL: https://www.usenix.org/conference/icac13/technical-sessions/presentation/herbst.

[85] Hewlett Packard Enterprise. *UEFI System Utilities User Guide for HPE ProLiant Gen9 and Synergy Servers.* Jan. 2017. URL: http://h20564.www2.hpe.com/hpsc/doc/public/display?docId=c04398276 (visited on 02/01/2017).

[86] Hewlett-Packard Corporation, Intel Corporation, Microsoft Corporation, Phoenix Technologies Ltd., Toshiba Corporation. *Advanced Configuration and Power Interface Specification.* 2013. URL: http://acpi.info/spec.htm.

[87] A. Hindle. “Green mining: A methodology of relating software change to power consumption”. In: *Mining Software Repositories (MSR), 2012 9th IEEE Working Conference on.* June 2012, pp. 78–87. DOI: 10.1109/MSR.2012.6224303.

[88] A. Hindle. “Green Software Engineering: The Curse of Methodology”. In: *2016 IEEE 23rd International Conference on Software Analysis, Evolution, and Reengineering (SANER).* Vol. 5. Mar. 2016, pp. 46–55. DOI: 10.1109/SANER.2016.60.

[89] Abram Hindle, Alex Wilson, Kent Rasmussen, E. Jed Barlow, Joshua Charles Campbell, and Stephen Romansky. “GreenMiner: A Hardware Based Mining Software Repositories Software Energy Consumption Framework”. In: *Proceedings of the 11th Working Conference on Mining Software Repositories.* MSR 2014. Hyderabad, India: ACM, 2014, pp. 12–21. ISBN: 978-1-4503-2863-0. DOI: 10.1145/2597073.2597097. URL: http://doi.acm.org/10.1145/2597073.2597097.

[90] André van Hoorn, Jan Waller, and Wilhelm Hasselbring. "Kieker: A Framework for Application Performance Monitoring and Dynamic Software Analysis". In: *Proceedings of the 3rd ACM/SPEC International Conference on Performance Engineering*. ICPE '12. Boston, Massachusetts, USA: ACM, 2012, pp. 247–248. ISBN: 978-1-4503-1202-8. DOI: 10.1145/2188286.2188326. URL: http://doi.acm.org/10.1145/2188286.2188326.

[91] S. Huang, J. Huang, J. Dai, T. Xie, and B. Huang. "The HiBench benchmark suite: Characterization of the MapReduce-based data analysis". In: *2010 IEEE 26th International Conference on Data Engineering Workshops (ICDEW)*. Mar. 2010, pp. 41–51.

[92] N. Huber, S. Becker, C. Rathfelder, J. Schweflinghaus, and R. H. Reussner. "Performance modeling in industry: a case study on storage virtualization". In: *2010 ACM/IEEE 32nd International Conference on Software Engineering*. Vol. 2. May 2010, pp. 1–10. DOI: 10.1145/1810295.1810297.

[93] N. Huber, F. Brosig, S. Spinner, S. Kounev, and M. Bahr. "Model-Based Self-Aware Performance and Resource Management Using the Descartes Modeling Language". In: *IEEE Transactions on Software Engineering* PP.99 (2016), pp. 1–1. ISSN: 0098-5589. DOI: 10.1109/TSE.2016.2613863.

[94] Nikolaus Huber. "Autonomic Performance-Aware Resource Management in Dynamic IT Service Infrastructures". PhD thesis. Karlsruhe Institute of Technology (KIT), Karlsruhe, Germany, 2014.

[95] Nikolaus Huber, Fabian Brosig, and Samuel Kounev. "Modeling Dynamic Virtualized Resource Landscapes". In: *Proceedings of the 8th International ACM SIGSOFT Conference on Quality of Software Architectures*. QoSA '12. Bertinoro, Italy: ACM, 2012, pp. 81–90. ISBN: 978-1-4503-1346-9. DOI: 10.1145/2304696.2304711. URL: http://doi.acm.org/10.1145/2304696.2304711.

[96] Nikolaus Huber, André van Hoorn, Anne Koziolek, Fabian Brosig, and Samuel Kounev. "Modeling run-time adaptation at the system architecture level in dynamic service-oriented environments". English. In: *Service Oriented Computing and Applications* 8.1 (2014), pp. 73–89. ISSN: 1863-2386. DOI: 10.1007/s11761-013-0144-4. URL: http://dx.doi.org/10.1007/s11761-013-0144-4.

[97] Markus C. Huebscher and Julie A. McCann. "A Survey of Autonomic Computing —Degrees, Models, and Applications". In: *ACM Comput. Surv.* 40.3 (Aug. 2008), 7:1–7:28. ISSN: 0360-0300. DOI: 10.1145/1380584.1380585. URL: http://doi.acm.org/10.1145/1380584.1380585.

[98] IBM. *System x Energy Efficiency.* 2014. URL: http://www.lenovo.com/images/products/system-x/pdfs/white-papers/XSW03162USEN.PDF.

[99] Intel and Hewlett-Packard and NEC and DELL. *Intelligent Platform Management Interface Specification v2.0 rev. 1.1.* Oct. 2013.

[100] Erik A. Jagroep, Jan Martijn van der Werf, Sjaak Brinkkemper, Giuseppe Procaccianti, Patricia Lago, Leen Blom, and Rob van Vliet. "Software Energy Profiling: Comparing Releases of a Software Product". In: *Proceedings of the 38th International Conference on Software Engineering Companion.* ICSE '16. Austin, Texas: ACM, 2016, pp. 523–532. ISBN: 978-1-4503-4205-6. DOI: 10.1145/2889160.2889216. URL: http://doi.acm.org/10.1145/2889160.2889216.

[101] Erik Jagroep, Jan Martijn van der Werf, Sjaak Brinkkemper, Leen Blom, and Rob van Vliet. "Extending software architecture views with an energy consumption perspective". In: *Computing* 99.6 (June 2017), pp. 553–573. ISSN: 1436-5057. DOI: 10.1007/s00607-016-0502-0. URL: https://doi.org/10.1007/s00607-016-0502-0.

[102] A. Jansen and J. Bosch. "Software Architecture as a Set of Architectural Design Decisions". In: *5th Working IEEE/IFIP Conference on Software Architecture (WICSA'05).* 2005, pp. 109–120. DOI: 10.1109/WICSA.2005.61.

[103] Gueyoung Jung, M.A Hiltunen, K.R. Joshi, R.D. Schlichting, and C. Pu. "Mistral: Dynamically Managing Power, Performance, and Adaptation Cost in Cloud Infrastructures". In: *Distributed Computing Systems (ICDCS), 2010 IEEE 30th International Conference on.* June 2010, pp. 62–73. DOI: 10.1109/ICDCS.2010.88.

[104] Aman Kansal, Feng Zhao, Jie Liu, Nupur Kothari, and Arka A. Bhattacharya. "Virtual Machine Power Metering and Provisioning". In: *Proceedings of the 1st ACM Symposium on Cloud Computing.* SoCC '10. Indianapolis, Indiana, USA: ACM, 2010, pp. 39–50. ISBN: 978-1-

4503-0036-0. DOI: 10.1145/1807128.1807136. URL: http://doi.acm.org/10.1145/1807128.1807136.

[105] J.O. Kephart and D.M. Chess. "The Vision of Autonomic Computing". In: *IEEE Computer* 36.1 (Jan. 2003), pp. 41–50. ISSN: 0018-9162. DOI: 10.1109/MC.2003.1160055.

[106] Jóakim Von Kistowski, Nikolas Herbst, Samuel Kounev, Henning Groenda, Christian Stier, and Sebastian Lehrig. "Modeling and Extracting Load Intensity Profiles". In: *ACM Trans. Auton. Adapt. Syst.* 11.4 (Jan. 2017), 23:1–23:28. ISSN: 1556-4665. DOI: 10.1145/3019596. URL: http://doi.acm.org/10.1145/3019596.

[107] Jóakim von Kistowski, Hansfried Block, John Beckett, Klaus-Dieter Lange, Jeremy A. Arnold, and Samuel Kounev. "Analysis of the Influences on Server Power Consumption and Energy Efficiency for CPU-Intensive Workloads". In: *Proceedings of the 6th ACM/SPEC International Conference on Performance Engineering (ICPE 2015).* ICPE '15. Austin, TX, USA: ACM, Feb. 2015. DOI: http://dx.doi.org/10.1145/2668930.2688057.

[108] Jóakim von Kistowski, Hansfried Block, John Beckett, Cloyce Spradling, Klaus-Dieter Lange, and Samuel Kounev. "Variations in CPU Power Consumption". In: *Proceedings of the 7th ACM/SPEC on International Conference on Performance Engineering.* ICPE '16. Delft, The Netherlands: ACM, 2016, pp. 147–158. ISBN: 978-1-4503-4080-9. DOI: 10.1145/2851553.2851567. URL: http://doi.acm.org/10.1145/2851553.2851567.

[109] Cristian Klein, Martina Maggio, Karl-Erik Årzén, and Francisco Hernández-Rodriguez. "Brownout: Building More Robust Cloud Applications". In: *Proceedings of the 36th International Conference on Software Engineering.* ICSE 2014. Hyderabad, India: ACM, 2014, pp. 700–711. ISBN: 978-1-4503-2756-5. DOI: 10.1145/2568225.2568227. URL: http://doi.acm.org/10.1145/2568225.2568227.

[110] Jonathan Koomey. *Growth in data center electricity use 2005 to 2010.* Analytics Press. Completed at the Request fo the New York Times. 2011.

[111] Anne Koziolek, Danilo Ardagna, and Raffaela Mirandola. "Hybrid Multi-Attribute QoS Optimization in Component Based Software Systems". In: *Journal of Systems and Software* 86.10 (2013). Special Issue on Quality Optimization of Software Architecture and Design Specifications, pp. 2542–2558. ISSN: 0164-1212. DOI: 10.1016/j.jss.2013.03.081. URL: http://www.sciencedirect.com/science/article/pii/S0164121213000800.

[112] Heiko Koziolek. *Parameter Dependencies for Reusable Performance Specifications of Software Components.* Vol. 2. The Karlsruhe Series on Software Design and Quality. Universitätsverlag Karlsruhe, 2008. ISBN: 978-3-86644-272-6.

[113] Heiko Koziolek and Ralf Reussner. "A Model Transformation from the Palladio Component Model to Layered Queueing Networks". In: *Performance Evaluation: Metrics, Models and Benchmarks, SIPEW 2008.* Vol. 5119. Lecture Notes in Computer Science. Springer-Verlag Berlin Heidelberg, 2008, pp. 58–78. ISBN: 978-3-540-69813-5. URL: http://www.springerlink.com/content/w14m0g520u675x10/fulltext.pdf.

[114] Sebastian Krach. *Energy-conscious deployment optimization for component-based cyber-foraging systems.* Am Fasanengarten 5, 76131 Karlsruhe, Germany: Karlsruhe Institute of Technology (KIT), 2015.

[115] Sebastian Krach, Christian Stier, and Athanasios Tsitsipas. "Modeling IaaS Usage Patterns for the Analysis of Cloud Optimization Policies". In: *Proceedings of the Symposium on Software Performance (SSP) 2016.* Softwaretechnik-Trends. Nov. 2016.

[116] Klaus Krogmann. *Reconstruction of Software Component Architectures and Behaviour Models using Static and Dynamic Analysis.* Vol. 4. The Karlsruhe Series on Software Design and Quality. KIT Scientific Publishing, 2012. DOI: 10.5445/KSP/1000025617. URL: http://digbib.ubka.uni-karlsruhe.de/volltexte/1000025617.

[117] Jakub Krzywda, Ali Rezaie, Zafeirios Papazachos, Ryan Hamilton-Bryce, Per-Olov Östberg, Ahmed Ali-Eldin, Barry McCollum, and Jörg Domaschka. *Extended optimization model: project deliverable D3.3.* Tech. rep. Universität Ulm, 2017. DOI: 10.18725/oparu-4307. URL: http://dx.doi.org/10.18725/OPARU-4307.

[118] K. Kurowski, A. Oleksiak, W. Piątek, T. Piontek, A. Przybyszewski, and J. Węglarz. "{DCworms} – A tool for simulation of energy efficiency in distributed computing infrastructures". In: *Simulation Modelling Practice and Theory* 39 (2013). S.I. Energy efficiency in grids and clouds, pp. 135–151. ISSN: 1569-190X. DOI: http://dx.doi.org/10.1016/j.simpat.2013.08.007. URL: http://www.sciencedirect.com/science/article/pii/S1569190X1300124X.

[119] K. D. Lange. "Identifying Shades of Green: The SPECpower Benchmarks". In: *Computer* 42.3 (Mar. 2009), pp. 95–97. ISSN: 0018-9162. DOI: 10.1109/MC.2009.84.

[120] Philip Langer, Konrad Wieland, Manuel Wimmer, and Jordi Cabot. "EMF Profiles: A Lightweight Extension Approach for EMF Models". In: *Journal of Object Technology* 11.1 (Apr. 2012), 8:1–29. ISSN: 1660-1769. DOI: 10.5381/jot.2012.11.1.a8. URL: http://www.jot.fm/contents/issue_2012_04/article8.html.

[121] Charles Lefurgy, Xiaorui Wang, and Malcolm Ware. "Power capping: a prelude to power shifting". In: *Cluster Computing* 11.2 (2008), pp. 183–195. ISSN: 1573-7543. DOI: 10.1007/s10586-007-0045-4. URL: http://dx.doi.org/10.1007/s10586-007-0045-4.

[122] M. M. Lehman, J. F. Ramil, P. D. Wernick, D. E. Perry, and W. M. Turski. "Metrics and laws of software evolution-the nineties view". In: *Proceedings Fourth International Software Metrics Symposium.* Nov. 1997, pp. 20–32. DOI: 10.1109/METRIC.1997.637156.

[123] Sebastian Lehrig. *Quality Analysis Lab (QuAL): Software Design Description and Developer Guide Version 1.0.* Tech. rep. Universität Paderborn, Faculty of Electrical Engineering - Computer Science - Mathematics, Apr. 2016. URL: http://www.cloudscale-project.eu/media/filer_public/2016/05/11/qualityanalysislab.pdf.

[124] Sebastian Lehrig and Matthias Becker. *Approaching the Cloud: Using Palladio for Scalability, Elasticity, and Efficiency Analyses.* Tech. rep. University of Stuttgart, Faculty of Computer Science, Electrical Engineering, and Information Technology, 2014.

[125] Sebastian Lehrig and Steffen Becker. "Using Performance Models for Planning the Redeployment to Infrastructure-as-a-Service Environments: A Case Study". In: *2016 12th International ACM SIGSOFT*

Conference on Quality of Software Architectures (QoSA). Apr. 2016, pp. 11–20. DOI: 10.1109/QoSA.2016.17.

[126] Sebastian Lehrig, Marcus Hilbrich, and Steffen Becker. "The architectural template method: templating architectural knowledge to efficiently conduct quality-of-service analyses". In: *Software: Practice and Experience* (). spe.2517, n/a–n/a. ISSN: 1097-024X. DOI: 10.1002/spe.2517. URL: http://dx.doi.org/10.1002/spe.2517.

[127] Adam Lewis, Jim Simon, and Nian-Feng Tzeng. "Chaotic Attractor Prediction for Server Run-time Energy Consumption". In: *Proceedings of the 2010 International Conference on Power Aware Computing and Systems*. HotPower'10. Vancouver, BC, Canada: USENIX Association, 2010, pp. 1–16. URL: http://dl.acm.org/citation.cfm?id=1924920.1924929.

[128] Ding Li, Shuai Hao, William G. J. Halfond, and Ramesh Govindan. "Calculating Source Line Level Energy Information for Android Applications". In: *Proceedings of the 2013 International Symposium on Software Testing and Analysis*. ISSTA 2013. Lugano, Switzerland: ACM, 2013, pp. 78–89. ISBN: 978-1-4503-2159-4. DOI: 10.1145/2483760.2483780. URL: http://doi.acm.org/10.1145/2483760.2483780.

[129] V. De Maio, G. Kecskemeti, and R. Prodan. "A Workload-Aware Energy Model for Virtual Machine Migration". In: *2015 IEEE International Conference on Cluster Computing*. Sept. 2015, pp. 274–283. DOI: 10.1109/CLUSTER.2015.47.

[130] I. Manotas, C. Bird, R. Zhang, D. Shepherd, C. Jaspan, C. Sadowski, L. Pollock, and J. Clause. "An Empirical Study of Practitioners' Perspectives on Green Software Engineering". In: *2016 IEEE/ACM 38th International Conference on Software Engineering (ICSE)*. May 2016, pp. 237–248. DOI: 10.1145/2884781.2884810.

[131] Irene Manotas, Lori Pollock, and James Clause. "SEEDS: A Software Engineer's Energy-optimization Decision Support Framework". In: *International Conference on Software Engineering (ICSE)*. ACM/IEEE, June 2014.

[132] Anne Martens, Heiko Koziolek, Lutz Prechelt, and Ralf Reussner. "From monolithic to component-based performance evaluation of software architectures". In: *Empirical Software Engineering* 16.5 (2011), pp. 587–622. ISSN: 1382-3256. DOI: 10.1007/s10664-010-9142-8. URL: http://dx.doi.org/10.1007/s10664-010-9142-8.

[133] Robert von Massow, André van Hoorn, and Wilhelm Hasselbring. "Performance Simulation of Runtime Reconfigurable Component-Based Software Architectures". English. In: *Software Architecture*. Ed. by Ivica Crnkovic, Volker Gruhn, and Matthias Book. Vol. 6903. Lecture Notes in Computer Science. Springer Berlin Heidelberg, 2011, pp. 43–58. ISBN: 978-3-642-23797-3. DOI: 10.1007/978-3-642-23798-0_5. URL: http://dx.doi.org/10.1007/978-3-642-23798-0_5.

[134] Tanja Mayerhofer, Philip Langer, Manuel Wimmer, and Gerti Kappel. "xMOF: Executable DSMLs based on fUML". In: *International Conference on Software Language Engineering*. Springer. 2013, pp. 56–75.

[135] John McCullough, Yuvraj Agarwal, Jaideep Chandrashekhar, Sathyanarayan Kuppuswamy, Alex C. Snoeren, and Rajesh Gupta. "Evaluating the Effectiveness of Model-Based Power Characterization". In: *Proceedings of the USENIX Annual Technical Conference*. Portland, OR, June 2011.

[136] Indika Meedeniya, Barbora Buhnova, Aldeida Aleti, and Lars Grunske. "Architecture-Driven Reliability and Energy Optimization for Complex Embedded Systems". English. In: *Research into Practice - Reality and Gaps*. Ed. by George T. Heineman, Jan Kofron, and Frantisek Plasil. Vol. 6093. Lecture Notes in Computer Science. Springer Berlin Heidelberg, 2010, pp. 52–67. ISBN: 978-3-642-13820-1. DOI: 10.1007/978-3-642-13821-8_6. URL: http://dx.doi.org/10.1007/978-3-642-13821-8_6.

[137] Peter M. Mell and Timothy Grance. *SP 800-145. The NIST Definition of Cloud Computing*. Tech. rep. Gaithersburg, MD, United States: National Institute of Standards and Technology, 2011.

[138] Philipp Merkle and Jörg Henss. "EventSim – An Event-driven Palladio Software Architecture Simulator". In: *Palladio Days 2011 Proceedings (appeared as technical report)*. Ed. by Steffen Becker, Jens Happe, and Ralf Reussner. Karlsruhe Reports in Informatics ; 2011,32.

Karlsruhe: KIT, Fakultät für Informatik, 2011, pp. 15–22. URL: http://digbib.ubka.uni-karlsruhe.de/volltexte/1000025188.

[139] *Metrics.* Last retrieved 2016-08-18. Coda Hale, Yammer Inc. URL: metrics.dropwizard.io.

[140] Stephen Milborrow. *earth: Multivariate Adaptive Regression Splines.* R package version 4.5.1. 2017. URL: https://cran.r-project.org/package=earth.

[141] J Moore. *Gamut-Generic Application eMUlaTion.* URL: http://www.cs.duke.edu/nicl/cod/.

[142] Gabriel A. Moreno, Javier Cámara, David Garlan, and Bradley Schmerl. "Proactive Self-adaptation Under Uncertainty: A Probabilistic Model Checking Approach". In: *Proceedings of the 2015 10th Joint Meeting on Foundations of Software Engineering.* ESEC/FSE 2015. Bergamo, Italy: ACM, 2015, pp. 1–12. ISBN: 978-1-4503-3675-8. DOI: 10.1145/2786805.2786853. URL: http://doi.acm.org/10.1145/2786805.2786853.

[143] Ryan Morgan. *SIGAR - System Information Gatherer And Reporter.* Last retrieved 2016-08-18. URL: sigar.hyperic.com.

[144] I. Moura, G. Pinto, F. Ebert, and F. Castor. "Mining Energy-Aware Commits". In: *2015 IEEE/ACM 12th Working Conference on Mining Software Repositories.* May 2015, pp. 56–67. DOI: 10.1109/MSR.2015.13.

[145] Ripal Nathuji. "VirtualPower: Coordinated Power Management in Virtualized Enterprise Systems". In: *In Proceedings of International Symposium on Operating System Principles (SOSP.* 2007.

[146] Stefan Naumann, Markus Dick, Eva Kern, and Timo Johann. "The GREENSOFT Model: A reference model for green and sustainable software and its engineering". In: *Sustainable Computing: Informatics and Systems* 1.4 (2011), pp. 294–304. ISSN: 2210-5379. DOI: https://doi.org/10.1016/j.suscom.2011.06.004. URL: http://www.sciencedirect.com/science/article/pii/S2210537911000473.

[147] Qais Noorshams, Roland Reeb, Andreas Rentschler, Samuel Kounev, and Ralf Reussner. "Enriching Software Architecture Models with Statistical Models for Performance Prediction in Modern Storage Environments". In: *Proceedings of the 17th International ACM Sigsoft Symposium on Component-based Software Engineering.* CBSE '14. Accep-

tance Rate (Full Paper): 14/62 = 23%. Marcq-en-Bareul, France: ACM, 2014, pp. 45–54. ISBN: 978-1-4503-2577-6. DOI: 10.1145/2602458.2602475. URL: http://doi.acm.org/10.1145/2602458.2602475.

[148] Qais Noorshams, Roland Reeb, Andreas Rentschler, Samuel Kounev, and Ralf Reussner. "Enriching Software Architecture Models with Statistical Models for Performance Prediction in Modern Storage Environments". In: *Proceedings of the 17th International ACM Sigsoft Symposium on Component-based Software Engineering*. CBSE '14. Marcq-en-Bareul, France: ACM, 2014, pp. 45–54. ISBN: 978-1-4503-2577-6. DOI: 10.1145/2602458.2602475. URL: http://doi.acm.org/10.1145/2602458.2602475.

[149] A. Noureddine, A. Bourdon, R. Rouvoy, and L. Seinturier. "Runtime Monitoring of Software Energy Hotspots". In: *Automated Software Engineering (ASE), 2012 Proceedings of the 27th IEEE/ACM International Conference on*. Sept. 2012, pp. 160–169. DOI: 10.1145/2351676.2351699.

[150] Alberto Núñez, Jose L. Vázquez-Poletti, Agustin C. Caminero, Gabriel G. Castañé, Jesus Carretero, and Ignacio M. Llorente. "iCanCloud: A Flexible and Scalable Cloud Infrastructure Simulator". In: *Journal of Grid Computing* 10.1 (Mar. 2012), pp. 185–209. ISSN: 1572-9184. DOI: 10.1007/s10723-012-9208-5. URL: https://doi.org/10.1007/s10723-012-9208-5.

[151] *OpenStack*. Last retrieved 2017-10-26. The OpenStack Foundation. URL: https://www.openstack.org/.

[152] P-O Östberg, Henning Groenda, Stefan Wesner, James Byrne, Dimitrios S. Nikolopoulos, Craig Sheridan, Jakub Krzywda, Ahmed Ali-Eldin, Johan Tordsson, Erik Elmroth, Christian Stier, Klaus Krogmann, Jörg Domaschka, Christopher Hauser, PJ Byrne, Sergej Svorobej, Barry McCollum, Zafeirios Papazachos, Loke Johannessen, Stephan Rüth, and Dragana Paurevic. "The CACTOS Vision of Context-Aware Cloud Topology Optimization and Simulation". In: *Proceedings of the Sixth IEEE International Conference on Cloud Computing Technology and Science (CloudCom)*. Singapore: IEEE Computer Society, 2014, pp. 26–31. DOI: 10.1109/CloudCom.2014.62.

[153] Abhinav Pathak, Y. Charlie Hu, Ming Zhang, Paramvir Bahl, and Yi-Min Wang. “Fine-grained Power Modeling for Smartphones Using System Call Tracing”. In: *Proceedings of the Sixth Conference on Computer Systems.* EuroSys ’11. Salzburg, Austria: ACM, 2011, pp. 153–168. ISBN: 978-1-4503-0634-8. DOI: 10.1145/1966445.1966460. URL: http://doi.acm.org/10.1145/1966445.1966460.

[154] D. Pavlović and S. Abramsky. “Specifying interaction categories”. In: *Category Theory and Computer Science: 7th International Conference, CTCS ’97 Santa Margherita Ligure Italy, September 4–6, 1997 Proceedings.* Ed. by Eugenio Moggi and Giuseppe Rosolini. Berlin, Heidelberg: Springer Berlin Heidelberg, 1997, pp. 147–158. ISBN: 978-3-540-69552-3. DOI: 10.1007/BFb0026986. URL: http://dx.doi.org/10.1007/BFb0026986.

[155] Ashkan Paya and Dan C. Marinescu. “Energy-Aware Load Balancing and Application Scaling for the Cloud Ecosystem”. In: *IEEE Transactions on Cloud Computing* 5.1 (2017), pp. 15–27. ISSN: 2168-7161. DOI: doi.ieeecomputersociety.org/10.1109/TCC.2015.2396059.

[156] J. F. Pérez and G. Casale. “Assessing SLA Compliance from Palladio Component Models”. In: *2013 15th International Symposium on Symbolic and Numeric Algorithms for Scientific Computing.* Sept. 2013, pp. 409–416. DOI: 10.1109/SYNASC.2013.60.

[157] Sareh Fotuhi Piraghaj, Amir Vahid Dastjerdi, Rodrigo N. Calheiros, and Rajkumar Buyya. “ContainerCloudSim: An environment for modeling and simulation of containers in cloud data centers”. In: *Software: Practice and Experience* 47.4 (2017). spe.2422, pp. 505–521. ISSN: 1097-024X. DOI: 10.1002/spe.2422. URL: http://dx.doi.org/10.1002/spe.2422.

[158] Pivotal Software, Inc. *Distributed version of Spring Petclinic built with Spring Cloud.* GitHub Repository. 2017. URL: https://github.com/spring-petclinic/spring-petclinic-microservices (visited on 12/05/2016).

[159] Pivotal Software, Inc. *Spring PetClinic Sample Application.* GitHub Repository. 2017. URL: https://github.com/spring-projects/spring-petclinic (visited on 05/03/2017).

[160] Johan Pouwelse, Koen Langendoen, and Henk Sips. "Dynamic Voltage Scaling on a Low-power Microprocessor". In: *Proceedings of the 7th Annual International Conference on Mobile Computing and Networking*. MobiCom '01. Rome, Italy: ACM, 2001, pp. 251–259. ISBN: 1-58113-422-3. DOI: 10.1145/381677.381701. URL: http://doi.acm.org/10.1145/381677.381701.

[161] *Power Consumption Analyzer*. Last retrieved 19.02.2017. URL: https://sdqweb.ipd.kit.edu/wiki/Power_Consumption_Analyzer.

[162] *Power Consumption Profiler*. Last retrieved 02.08.2017. URL: https://sdqweb.ipd.kit.edu/wiki/Power_Consumption_Profiler.

[163] *PowerEdge R815 Technical Guide*. 5.0. Dell Technologies, Inc. Dec. 2012. URL: http://i.dell.com/sites/doccontent/business/solutions/engineering-docs/en/Documents/r815-tech-guide.pdf.

[164] Giuseppe Procaccianti, Héctor Fernández, and Patricia Lago. "Empirical evaluation of two best practices for energy-efficient software development". In: *Journal of Systems and Software* 117.Supplement C (2016), pp. 185–198. ISSN: 0164-1212. DOI: https://doi.org/10.1016/j.jss.2016.02.035. URL: http://www.sciencedirect.com/science/article/pii/S0164121216000777.

[165] Giuseppe Procaccianti, Patricia Lago, and Grace A. Lewis. "Green Architectural Tactics for the Cloud". In: *Software Architecture (WICSA), 2014 IEEE/IFIP Conference on*. Apr. 2014, pp. 41–44. DOI: 10.1109/WICSA.2014.30.

[166] Asfandyar Qureshi, Rick Weber, Hari Balakrishnan, John Guttag, and Bruce Maggs. "Cutting the Electric Bill for Internet-scale Systems". In: *Proceedings of the ACM SIGCOMM 2009 Conference on Data Communication*. SIGCOMM '09. Barcelona, Spain: ACM, 2009, pp. 123–134. ISBN: 978-1-60558-594-9. DOI: 10.1145/1592568.1592584. URL: http://doi.acm.org/10.1145/1592568.1592584.

[167] Ramya Raghavendra, Parthasarathy Ranganathan, Vanish Talwar, Zhikui Wang, and Xiaoyun Zhu. "No "Power" Struggles: Coordinated Multi-level Power Management for the Data Center". In: *SIGARCH Computer Architecture News* 36.1 (Mar. 2008), pp. 48–59. ISSN: 0163-5964. DOI: 10.1145/1353534.1346289. URL: http://doi.acm.org/10.1145/1353534.1346289.

[168] Neil Rasmussen. *Electrical Efficiency Modeling for Data Centers.* Tech. rep. Version 2. American Power Conversion (APC), 2011. URL: http://www.apc.com/salestools/NRAN-66CK3D/NRAN-66CK3D_R2_EN.pdf.

[169] Jan Reimann and Uwe Aßmann. "Quality-Aware Refactoring for Early Detection and Resolution of Energy Deficiencies". In: *Proceedings of the 2013 IEEE/ACM 6th International Conference on Utility and Cloud Computing.* UCC '13. Washington, DC, USA: IEEE Computer Society, 2013, pp. 321–326. ISBN: 978-0-7695-5152-4. DOI: 10.1109/UCC.2013.70. URL: http://dx.doi.org/10.1109/UCC.2013.70.

[170] Ralf H. Reussner, Steffen Becker, Jens Happe, Robert Heinrich, Anne Koziolek, Heiko Koziolek, Max Kramer, and Klaus Krogmann. *Modeling and Simulating Software Architectures – The Palladio Approach.* Cambridge, MA: MIT Press, Oct. 2016. 408 pp. ISBN: 9780262034760. URL: http://mitpress.mit.edu/books/modeling-and-simulating-software-architectures.

[171] Ralf Reussner, Steffen Becker, Erik Burger, Jens Happe, Michael Hauck, Anne Koziolek, Heiko Koziolek, Klaus Krogmann, and Michael Kuperberg. *The Palladio Component Model.* Tech. rep. Karlsruhe: KIT, Fakultät für Informatik, 2011. URL: http://digbib.ubka.uni-karlsruhe.de/volltexte/1000022503.

[172] Suzanne Rivoire, Parthasarathy Ranganathan, and Christos Kozyrakis. "A Comparison of High-level Full-system Power Models". In: *Proceedings of the 2008 Conference on Power Aware Computing and Systems.* HotPower'08. San Diego, California: USENIX Association, 2008, pp. 3–3. URL: http://dl.acm.org/citation.cfm?id=1855610.1855613.

[173] Suzanne Rivoire, Mehul A. Shah, Parthasarathy Ranganathan, and Christos Kozyrakis. "JouleSort: A Balanced Energy-efficiency Benchmark". In: *Proceedings of the 2007 ACM SIGMOD International Conference on Management of Data.* SIGMOD '07. Beijing, China: ACM, 2007, pp. 365–376. ISBN: 978-1-59593-686-8. DOI: 10.1145/1247480.1247522. URL: http://doi.acm.org/10.1145/1247480.1247522.

[174] L. Rosa, L. Rodrigues, A. Lopes, M. Hiltunen, and R. Schlichting. "Self-Management of Adaptable Component-Based Applications". In:

Software Engineering, IEEE Transactions on 39.3 (Mar. 2013), pp. 403–421. ISSN: 0098-5589. DOI: 10.1109/TSE.2012.29.

[175] S.M. Ross. *Introductory Statistics.* 3rd ed. Elsevier Science, 2010. ISBN: 9780080922102.

[176] Kiana Rostami, Johannes Stammel, Robert Heinrich, and Ralf Reussner. "Architecture-based Assessment and Planning of Change Requests". In: *Proceedings of the 11th International ACM SIGSOFT Conference on Quality of Software Architectures.* QoSA '15. Montreal, QC, Canada: ACM, 2015, pp. 21–30. ISBN: 978-1-4503-3470-9. URL: http://dl.acm.org/citation.cfm?id=2737198.

[177] Peter Rousseeuw, Christophe Croux, Valentin Todorov, Andreas Ruckstuhl, Matias Salibian-Barrera, Tobias Verbeke, Manuel Koller, and Martin Maechler. *robustbase: Basic Robust Statistics.* R package version 0.92-6. 2016. URL: CRAN.R-project.org/package=robustbase.

[178] Conor Ryan, J.J. Collins, Jj Collins, and Michael O'Neill. "Grammatical Evolution: Evolving Programs for an Arbitrary Language". In: *Lecture Notes in Computer Science 1391, Proceedings of the First European Workshop on Genetic Programming.* Springer-Verlag, 1998, pp. 83–95.

[179] Kateryna Rybina, Abhinandan Patni, and Alexander Schill. "Analysing the Migration Time of Live Migration of Multiple Virtual Machines." In: *4th International Conference on Cloud Computing and Services Science (CLOSER 2014), April 3-5, Barcelona, Spain.* 2014.

[180] Norbert Schmitt, Jóakim von Kistowski, and Samuel Kounev. "Emulating the Power Consumption Behavior of Server Workloads using CPU Performance Counters". In: *Proceedings of the 25th IEEE International Symposium on the Modelling, Analysis, and Simulation of Computer and Telecommunication Systems.* MASCOTS '17. Banff, Canada, Sept. 2017.

[181] Norbert Schmitt, Jóakim von Kistowski, and Samuel Kounev. "Predicting Power Consumption of High-Memory-Bandwidth Workloads". In: *Proceedings of the 8th ACM/SPEC on International Conference on Performance Engineering.* ICPE '17. L'Aquila, Italy: ACM, 2017, pp. 353–356. ISBN: 978-1-4503-4404-3. DOI: 10.1145/3030207.3030241. URL: http://doi.acm.org/10.1145/3030207.3030241.

[182] Thomas Schulze. "A cost model for expressing and estimating ecological costs of software-driven systems". PhD thesis. University of Mannheim, Germany, 2016. URL: http://d-nb.info/1132590388.

[183] Chiyoung Seo. "Prediction of Energy Consumption Behavior in Component-based Distributed Systems". AAI3324944. PhD thesis. Los Angeles, CA, USA: University of Southern California, 2008. ISBN: 978-0-549-78221-6.

[184] Chiyoung Seo, G. Edwards, S. Malek, and N. Medvidovic. "A Framework for Estimating the Impact of a Distributed Software System's Architectural Style on its Energy Consumption". In: *Software Architecture, 2008. WICSA 2008. Seventh Working IEEE/IFIP Conference on.* Feb. 2008, pp. 277–280. DOI: 10.1109/WICSA.2008.28.

[185] Chiyoung Seo, Sam Malek, and Nenad Medvidovic. "An Energy Consumption Framework for Distributed Java-based Systems". In: *Proceedings of the Twenty-second IEEE/ACM International Conference on Automated Software Engineering.* ASE '07. Atlanta, Georgia, USA: ACM, 2007, pp. 421–424. ISBN: 978-1-59593-882-4. DOI: 10.1145/1321631.1321699. URL: http://doi.acm.org/10.1145/1321631.1321699.

[186] Chiyoung Seo, Sam Malek, and Nenad Medvidovic. "Component-Level Energy Consumption Estimation for Distributed Java-Based Software Systems". In: *Component-Based Software Engineering.* Ed. by MichelR.V. Chaudron, Clemens Szyperski, and Ralf Reussner. Vol. 5282. Lecture Notes in Computer Science. Springer Berlin Heidelberg, 2008, pp. 97–113. ISBN: 978-3-540-87890-2. DOI: 10.1007/978-3-540-87891-9_7. URL: http://dx.doi.org/10.1007/978-3-540-87891-9_7.

[187] *Server Efficiency Rating Tool (SERT) Design Document 1.1.1.* Tech. rep. Gainesville, VA, USA: Standard Performance Evaluation Corporation (SPEC), Jan. 2016. URL: https://www.spec.org/sert/docs/SERT-Design_Document.pdf.

[188] *Server Efficiency Rating Tool (SERT) Design Document 2.0.0.* Tech. rep. Gainesville, VA, USA: Standard Performance Evaluation Corporation (SPEC), Feb. 2017. URL: https://www.spec.org/sert2/SERT-design document.pdf.

[189] V. S. Sharma and S. Anwer. "Performance Antipatterns: Detection and Evaluation of Their Effects in the Cloud". In: *2014 IEEE International Conference on Services Computing*. June 2014, pp. 758–765. DOI: 10.1109/SCC.2014.103.

[190] Arman Shehabi, Sarah Josephine Smith, Dale A. Sartor, Richard E. Brown, Magnus Herrlin, Jonathan G. Koomey, Eric R. Masanet, Nathaniel Horner, Inês Lima Azevedo, and William Lintner. "United States Data Center Energy Usage Report". In: (June 2016).

[191] Ravjot Singh, Cor-Paul Bezemer, Weiyi Shang, and Ahmed E. Hassan. "Optimizing the Performance-Related Configurations of Object-Relational Mapping Frameworks Using a Multi-Objective Genetic Algorithm". In: *Proceedings of the 7th ACM/SPEC on International Conference on Performance Engineering*. ICPE '16. Delft, The Netherlands: ACM, 2016, pp. 309–320. ISBN: 978-1-4503-4080-9. DOI: 10.1145/2851553.2851576. URL: http://doi.acm.org/10.1145/2851553.2851576.

[192] *SPEC PTDaemon Design Document*. Tech. rep. Gainesville, VA, USA: Standard Performance Evaluation Corporation (SPEC), Oct. 2012.

[193] *SPECjbb2015 Benchmark Design Document*. Tech. rep. Gainesville, VA, USA: Standard Performance Evaluation Corporation (SPEC), May 2015. URL: www.spec.org/jbb2015/docs/designdocument.pdf.

[194] Shekhar Srikantaiah, Aman Kansal, and Feng Zhao. "Energy Aware Consolidation for Cloud Computing". In: *Proceedings of the 2008 Conference on Power Aware Computing and Systems*. HotPower'08. San Diego, California: USENIX Association, 2008, pp. 10–10. URL: http://dl.acm.org/citation.cfm?id=1855610.1855620.

[195] Dave Steinberg, ed. *EMF - Eclipse Modeling Framework*. 2. ed., revised and updated. The eclipse series. Boston, Mass.: Addison-Wesley, 2009. ISBN: 978-0-321-33188-5.

[196] Christian Stier, Jörg Domaschka, Anne Koziolek, Sebastian Krach, Jakub Krzywda, and Ralf Reussner. "Rapid Testing of IaaS Resource Management Algorithms via Cloud Middleware Simulation". In: *Proceedings of the 2018 ACM/SPEC International Conference on Performance Engineering*. ICPE '18. Berlin, Germany: ACM, 2018, pp. 184–191. ISBN: 978-1-4503-5095-2. DOI: 10.1145/3184407.3184428. URL: http://doi.acm.org/10.1145/3184407.3184428.

[197] Christian Stier and Henning Groenda. “Ensuring Model Continuity when Simulating Self-Adaptive Software Systems”. In: *Proceedings of the Modeling and Simulation of Complexity in Intelligent, Adaptive and Autonomous Systems 2016 (MSCIAAS 2016) and Space Simulation for Planetary Space Exploration (SPACE 2016)*. MSCIAAS. Pasadena, CA, USA: Society for Computer Simulation International, 2016, 2:1–2:8. ISBN: 978-1-5108-2319-8. URL: `http://dl.acm.org/citation.cfm?id=2962664.2962666`.

[198] Christian Stier, Henning Groenda, and Anne Koziolek. *Towards Modeling and Analysis of Power Consumption of Self-Adaptive Software Systems in Palladio.* Tech. rep. Stuttgart, Germany: University of Stuttgart, Faculty of Computer Science, Electrical Engineering, and Information Technology, Nov. 2014, p. 18.

[199] Christian Stier and Anne Koziolek. “Considering Transient Effects of Self-Adaptations in Model-Driven Performance Analyses”. In: *Proceedings of the 12th International ACM SIGSOFT Conference on the Quality of Software Architectures.* QoSA’16. Venice, Italy: ACM, 2016.

[200] Christian Stier, Anne Koziolek, Henning Groenda, and Ralf Reussner. “Model-Based Energy Efficiency Analysis of Software Architectures”. In: *Proceedings of the 9th European Conference on Software Architecture (ECSA ’15).* Lecture Notes in Computer Science. Dubrovnik/Cavtat, Croatia: Springer, 2015. DOI: `10.1007/978-3-319-23727-5_18`. URL: `http://dx.doi.org/10.1007/978-3-319-23727-5_18`.

[201] Christian Stier, Dominik Werle, and Anne Koziolek. “Deriving Power Models for Architecture-Level Energy Efficiency Analyses”. In: *Computer Performance Engineering.* Ed. by Philipp Reinecke and Antinisca Di Marco. Cham: Springer International Publishing, 2017, pp. 214–229. ISBN: 978-3-319-66583-2.

[202] M. Stone. “An asymptotic equivalence of choice of model by cross-validation and Akaike’s criterion”. In: *Journal of the Royal Statistical Society, Series B* 39 (1977), pp. 44–47.

[203] Misha Strittmatter and Robert Heinrich. “Challenges in the Evolution of Metamodels”. In: *3rd Collaborative Workshop on Evolution and Maintenance of Long-Living Software Systems.* Vol. 36(1). Softwaretechnik-Trends. 2016, pp. 12–15.

[204] *Structured Metrics Metamodel (SMM).* Tech. rep. Version 1.0. Object Management Group, Inc. (OMG), 2012.

[205] A. Strunk. "Costs of Virtual Machine Live Migration: A Survey". In: *Services (SERVICES), 2012 IEEE Eighth World Congress on.* June 2012, pp. 323–329. DOI: 10.1109/SERVICES.2012.23.

[206] A.1 Strunk. "A Lightweight Model for Estimating Energy Cost of Live Migration of Virtual Machines". In: *Cloud Computing (CLOUD), 2013 IEEE Sixth International Conference on.* June 2013, pp. 510–517. DOI: 10.1109/CLOUD.2013.17.

[207] T.K. Tan, A. Raghunathan, G. Lakshminarayana, and N.K. Jha. "High-level software energy macro-modeling". In: *Design Automation Conference, 2001. Proceedings.* 2001, pp. 605–610. DOI: 10.1109/DAC.2001.156211.

[208] Wolfgang Theilmann, Ramin Yahyapour, and Joe Butler. "Multi-level SLA Management for Service-Oriented Infrastructures". English. In: *Towards a Service-Based Internet.* Ed. by Petri Mähönen, Klaus Pohl, and Thierry Priol. Vol. 5377. Lecture Notes in Computer Science. Springer Berlin Heidelberg, 2008, pp. 324–335. ISBN: 978-3-540-89896-2. DOI: 10.1007/978-3-540-89897-9_28. URL: http://dx.doi.org/10.1007/978-3-540-89897-9_28.

[209] *TPC-Energy Specification.* Tech. rep. Transaction Processing Performance Council, 2012. URL: http://www.tpc.org/tpc%5C_documents%5C_current%5C_versions/pdf/tpc-energy%5C_v1.5.0.pdf.

[210] Dimitris Tsirogiannis, Stavros Harizopoulos, and Mehul A. Shah. "Analyzing the Energy Efficiency of a Database Server". In: *Proceedings of the 2010 ACM SIGMOD International Conference on Management of Data.* SIGMOD '10. Indianapolis, Indiana, USA: ACM, 2010, pp. 231–242. ISBN: 978-1-4503-0032-2. DOI: 10.1145/1807167.1807194. URL: http://doi.acm.org/10.1145/1807167.1807194.

[211] *UML Profile for MARTE: Modeling and Analysis of Real-Time Embedded Systems, Version 1.1.* Tech. rep. Object Management Group, Inc., 2011.

[212] *Unified Modeling Language (UML) – Version 2.5 (Formal/2015-03-01).* Tech. rep. Object Management Group (OMG), 2015. URL: http://www.omg.org/spec/UML/2.5.

[213] Simon Urbanek. *Rserve: Binary R server.* R package version 1.7-3. 2013. URL: https://cran.r-project.org/package=Rserve.

[214] VedantaTree. *ExpressionOasis.* GitHub Repository. 2015. URL: https://github.com/mohitkgupta/expressionoasis (visited on 01/17/2017).

[215] Akshat Verma, Puneet Ahuja, and Anindya Neogi. "pMapper: Power and Migration Cost Aware Application Placement in Virtualized Systems". In: *Middleware 2008.* Ed. by ValÃ©rie Issarny and Richard Schantz. Vol. 5346. Lecture Notes in Computer Science. Springer Berlin Heidelberg, 2008, pp. 243–264. ISBN: 978-3-540-89855-9. DOI: 10.1007/978-3-540-89856-6_13. URL: http://dx.doi.org/10.1007/978-3-540-89856-6%5C_13.

[216] L. Vogel and M. Milinkovich. *Eclipse Rich Client Platform.* vogella series. Lars Vogel, 2015. ISBN: 9783943747140. URL: https://books.google.de/books?id=AC4%5C_CQAAQBAJ.

[217] Thomas Vogel and Holger Giese. "Model-Driven Engineering of Self-Adaptive Software with EUREMA". In: *ACM Trans. Auton. Adapt. Syst.* 8.4 (Jan. 2014), 18:1–18:33. ISSN: 1556-4665. DOI: 10.1145/2555612. URL: http://doi.acm.org/10.1145/2555612.

[218] T. Vondra and J. Šedivý. "Cloud autoscaling simulation based on queueing network model". In: *Simulation Modelling Practice and Theory* 70.Supplement C (2017), pp. 83–100. ISSN: 1569-190X. DOI: https://doi.org/10.1016/j.simpat.2016.10.005. URL: http://www.sciencedirect.com/science/article/pii/S1569190X16302398.

[219] William Voorsluys, James Broberg, Srikumar Venugopal, and Rajkumar Buyya. "Cost of Virtual Machine Live Migration in Clouds: A Performance Evaluation". English. In: *Cloud Computing.* Ed. by MartinGilje Jaatun, Gansen Zhao, and Chunming Rong. Vol. 5931. Lecture Notes in Computer Science. Springer Berlin Heidelberg, 2009, pp. 254–265. ISBN: 978-3-642-10664-4. DOI: 10.1007/978-3-642-10665-1_23. URL: http://dx.doi.org/10.1007/978-3-642-10665-1_23.

[220] Jürgen Walter, Christian Stier, Heiko Koziolek, and Samuel Kounev. "An Expandable Extraction Framework for Architectural Performance Models". In: *Proceedings of the 8th ACM/SPEC on International Conference on Performance Engineering Companion.* ICPE '17

Companion. L'Aquila, Italy: ACM, 2017, pp. 165–170. ISBN: 978-1-4503-4899-7. DOI: 10.1145/3053600.3053634. URL: http://doi.acm.org/10.1145/3053600.3053634.

[221] Hans-Joachim Werner, Peter J. Knowles, Gerald Knizia, Frederick R. Manby, and Martin Schütz. "Molpro: a general-purpose quantum chemistry program package". In: *Wiley Interdisciplinary Reviews: Computational Molecular Science* 2.2 (2012), pp. 242–253. ISSN: 1759-0884. DOI: 10.1002/wcms.82.

[222] A. Wierman, Z. Liu, I. Liu, and H. Mohsenian-Rad. "Opportunities and challenges for data center demand response". In: *International Green Computing Conference.* Nov. 2014, pp. 1–10. DOI: 10.1109/IGCC.2014.7039172.

[223] Claas Wilke. "Energy-Aware Development and Labeling for Mobile Applications". PhD thesis. Technische Universität Dresden, Fakultät Informatik, Mar. 2014. URL: http://nbn-resolving.de/urn:nbn:de:bsz:14-qucosa-139391.

[224] Claas Wilke, Sebastian Götz, and Sebastian Richly. "JouleUnit: A Generic Framework for Software Energy Profiling and Testing". In: *Proceedings of the 2013 Workshop on Green in/by Software Engineering.* GIBSE '13. Fukuoka, Japan: ACM, 2013, pp. 9–14. ISBN: 978-1-4503-1866-2. DOI: 10.1145/2451605.2451610. URL: http://doi.acm.org/10.1145/2451605.2451610.

[225] Felix Willnecker, Markus Dlugi, Andreas Brunnert, Simon Spinner, Samuel Kounev, Wolfgang Gottesheim, and Helmut Krcmar. "Comparing the Accuracy of Resource Demand Measurement and Estimation Techniques". In: *Computer Performance Engineering: 12th European Workshop, EPEW 2015, Madrid, Spain, August 31 - September 1, 2015, Proceedings.* Ed. by Marta Beltrán, William Knottenbelt, and Jeremy Bradley. Cham: Springer International Publishing, 2015, pp. 115–129. ISBN: 978-3-319-23267-6. DOI: 10.1007/978-3-319-23267-6_8. URL: http://dx.doi.org/10.1007/978-3-319-23267-6_8.

[226] Felix Willnecker and Helmut Krcmar. "Towards Predicting Performance of GPU-dependent Applications on the Example of Machine Learning in Enterprise Applications". In: *Proceedings of the Sympo-*

sium on Software Performance (SSP) 2017. Softwaretechnik-Trends. to appear. Nov. 2017.

[227] Ian H. Witten. *Data mining : practical machine learning tools and techniques*. Ed. by Eibe Frank, Mark A. Hall, and Christopher J. Pal. Fourth edition. Amsterdam: Elsevier, MK, Morgan Kaufmann, 2017. ISBN: 978-0-12-804357-8. URL: http://lib.myilibrary.com?id=958352.

[228] M. Woodside, D. Petriu, and K. Siddiqui. "Performance-related completions for software specifications". In: *Proceedings of the 24th International Conference on Software Engineering. ICSE 2002*. May 2002, pp. 22–32. DOI: 10.1145/581344.581346.

[229] M. Xu, A. V. Dastjerdi, and R. Buyya. "Energy Efficient Scheduling of Cloud Application Components with Brownout". In: *IEEE Transactions on Sustainable Computing* 1.2 (July 2016), pp. 40–53. ISSN: 2377-3782. DOI: 10.1109/TSUSC.2017.2661339.

[230] Chanmin Yoon, Dongwon Kim, Wonwoo Jung, Chulkoo Kang, and Hojung Cha. "AppScope: Application Energy Metering Framework for Android Smartphone Using Kernel Activity Monitoring". In: *Presented as part of the 2012 USENIX Annual Technical Conference (USENIX ATC 12)*. Boston, MA: USENIX, 2012, pp. 387–400. URL: https://www.usenix.org/conference/atc12/technical-sessions/presentation/yoon.

[231] X. Zhang, J. Lu, and X. Qin. "BFEPM: Best Fit Energy Prediction Modeling Based on CPU Utilization". In: *Networking, Architecture and Storage (NAS), 2013 IEEE Eighth International Conference on*. July 2013, pp. 41–49. DOI: 10.1109/NAS.2013.12.

[232] Jochen Zimmermann. "Applikationsspezifische Analyse und Optimierung der Energieeffizienz eingebetteter Hardware/Software-Systeme". PhD thesis. Eberhard Karls Universität Tübingen, 2013.

The Karlsruhe Series on Software Design and Quality

Edited by Prof. Dr. Ralf Reussner // ISSN 1867-0067

Band 1 **Steffen Becker**
Coupled Model Transformations for QoS Enabled Component-Based Software Design.
ISBN 978-3-86644-271-9

Band 2 **Heiko Koziolek**
Parameter Dependencies for Reusable Performance Specifications of Software Components.
ISBN 978-3-86644-272-6

Band 3 **Jens Happe**
Predicting Software Performance in Symmetric Multi-core and Multiprocessor Environments.
ISBN 978-3-86644-381-5

Band 4 **Klaus Krogmann**
Reconstruction of Software Component Architectures and Behaviour Models using Static and Dynamic Analysis.
ISBN 978-3-86644-804-9

Band 5 **Michael Kuperberg**
Quantifying and Predicting the Influence of Execution Platform on Software Component Performance.
ISBN 978-3-86644-741-7

Band 6 **Thomas Goldschmidt**
View-Based Textual Modelling.
ISBN 978-3-86644-642-7

Band 7 **Anne Koziolek**
Automated Improvement of Software Architecture Models for Performance and Other Quality Attributes.
ISBN 978-3-86644-973-2

Die Bände sind unter www.ksp.kit.edu als PDF frei verfügbar oder als Druckausgabe bestellbar.

Band 8 **Lucia Happe**
Configurable Software Performance Completions through Higher-Order Model Transformations.
ISBN 978-3-86644-990-9

Band 9 **Franz Brosch**
Integrated Software Architecture-Based Reliability Prediction for IT Systems.
ISBN 978-3-86644-859-9

Band 10 **Christoph Rathfelder**
Modelling Event-Based Interactions in Component-Based Architectures for Quantitative System Evaluation.
ISBN 978-3-86644-969-5

Band 11 **Henning Groenda**
Certifying Software Component Performance Specifications.
ISBN 978-3-7315-0080-3

Band 12 **Dennis Westermann**
Deriving Goal-oriented Performance Models by Systematic Experimentation.
ISBN 978-3-7315-0165-7

Band 13 **Michael Hauck**
Automated Experiments for Deriving Performance-relevant Properties of Software Execution Environments.
ISBN 978-3-7315-0138-1

Band 14 **Zoya Durdik**
Architectural Design Decision Documentation through Reuse of Design Patterns.
ISBN 978-3-7315-0292-0

Band 15 **Erik Burger**
Flexible Views for View-based Model-driven Development.
ISBN 978-3-7315-0276-0

Band 16 **Benjamin Klatt**
Consolidation of Customized Product Copies into Software Product Lines.
ISBN 978-3-7315-0368-2

Band 17 **Andreas Rentschler**
Model Transformation Languages with Modular Information Hiding.
ISBN 978-3-7315-0346-0

Band 18 **Omar-Qais Noorshams**
Modeling and Prediction of I/O Performance in Virtualized Environments.
ISBN 978-3-7315-0359-0

Band 19 **Johannes Josef Stammel**
Architekturbasierte Bewertung und Planung von Änderungsanfragen.
ISBN 978-3-7315-0524-2

Band 20 **Alexander Wert**
Performance Problem Diagnostics by Systematic Experimentation.
ISBN 978-3-7315-0677-5

Band 21 **Christoph Heger**
An Approach for Guiding Developers to Performance and Scalability Solutions.
ISBN 978-3-7315-0698-0

Band 22 **Fouad ben Nasr Omri**
Weighted Statistical Testing based on Active Learning and Formal Verification Techniques for Software Reliability Assessment.
ISBN 978-3-7315-0472-6

Band 23 **Michael Langhammer**
Automated Coevolution of Source Code and Software Architecture Models.
ISBN 978-3-7315-0783-3

Band 24 **Max Emanuel Kramer**
Specification Languages for Preserving Consistency between Models of Different Languages.
ISBN 978-3-7315-0784-0

Band 25 **Sebastian Michael Lehrig**
Efficiently Conducting Quality-of-Service Analyses by Templating Architectural Knowledge.
ISBN 978-3-7315-0756-7

Band 26 **Georg Hinkel**
Implicit Incremental Model Analyses and Transformations.
ISBN 978-3-7315-0763-5

Band 27 **Christian Stier**
Adaptation-Aware Architecture Modeling and Analysis of Energy Efficiency for Software Systems.
ISBN 978-3-7315-0851-9